Wide-
Open
Desert

Wide-Open Desert

A Queer History
of New Mexico

JORDAN BIRO WALTERS

University of Washington Press
Seattle

Wide-Open Desert was made possible in part by a grant
from the Samuel and Althea Stroum Endowed Book Fund.

UNIVERSITY OF WASHINGTON PRESS   *uwapress.uw.edu*

LIBRARY OF CONGRESS CATALOGING-IN-PUBLICATION DATA

Names: Biro Walters, Jordan, author.

Title: Wide-open desert : a queer history of New Mexico / Jordan Biro Walters.

Description: Seattle : University of Washington Press, [2023] |
Includes bibliographical references and index.

Identifiers: LCCN 2022038378 | ISBN 9780295751016 (hardcover) |
ISBN 9780295751023 (paperback) | ISBN 9780295751030 (ebook)

Subjects: LCSH: Sexual minorities—New Mexico—History—20th century. |

Sexual minorities—Identity. | New Mexico—History—20th century.

Classification: LCC HQ73.3.U6 B58 2023 | DDC 306.760978909/04—dc23
LC record available at https://lccn.loc.gov/2022038378

♾ This paper meets the requirements of ANSI/NISO Z39.48-1992
(Permanence of Paper).

FOR MARTIN

CONTENTS

Acknowledgments ix

ACKNOWLEDGMENTS

In January 2019 I embarked on my first academic leave to finish researching and writing this book. After six weeks of writing, I headed to the Gay, Lesbian, Bisexual, Transgender Historical Society in San Francisco to revisit an archival collection and finalize selecting illustrations for the manuscript. I made it one day in the archive before the city of San Francisco shut down. I never imaged that during my leave, I would face a challenging moment of public health crises. The COVID-19 pandemic, coupled with ongoing structural and racist violence in the United States and worsening income inequality, made it difficult to finish this project. I battled an existential crisis—does my book even matter? I sought solace in reading other people's writings, particularly when they wrote during times of distress. Virginia Woolf, a year into World War II, penned the phrase "Thinking is my fighting" in her essay "Thoughts on Peace in an Air Raid." A thinker and a fighter, Woolf advocated for women to wage a mental war to ensure peace and equality. Her words resonated, spurring me onward. I finished this book because I had people counting on me to tell their stories and to fight for sexual and gender equality. I owe a debt of gratitude to all of the oral history participants from whom I've learned. Their narratives have given clarity of purpose to this project and have been my most critical teachers. The participants I interviewed and who consented to sharing their stories include Ginger Chapman, Vangie Chavez, Therese Councilor, Ronald Donaghe, Jean Effron, Zonnie Gorman, Bennett Hammer, Barbara Korbal, Havens Levitt, Ann Nihlen, Margaret Randall, Linda Siegle, Tanya Struble, Martha Trolin, Nancy Tucker, Helene Vann, and Rich Williams.

I received financial and academic support for my oral histories from the Southwest Oral History Association, University of Nevada, Las Vegas, and the Hammer Educational LGBT Archives Project. The Archives Project offered both resources to help me conduct oral histories and a repository space to preserve the interviews now housed at the Center for Southwest Research, University of New Mexico, Albuquerque. I owe a special thanks to Barbara Korbal and Bennett Hammer, who took me under their wing and introduced me to New Mexico's LGBTQ+ community.

This project began a decade ago in the History Department at the University of New Mexico. It would not exist without the support of Virginia Scharff, Cathleen Cahill, A. K. Sandoval-Strausz, and Peter Boag. I especially appreciate Virginia's encouragement about the significance of the book and most importantly invaluable lessons on writing clearly and creatively. I was also fortunate to be academically nurtured at UNM by many talented scholars. Numerous times I turned to Melissa Bokovoy and Michael Ryan for their sage advice on best practices for excellence in professionalism, research, and teaching. Durwood Ball and Sam Truett both guided me in comprehending the complexities of New Mexico history. Durwood read and commented on the first chapter of this book and pushed me to grapple with the geographical and cultural borderlands of the American Southwest. I am thankful for support from Elizabeth Hutchison, Judy Bieber, Tiffany Florvil, David Prior, Luis Campos, and Shannon Withycombe.

I am tremendously grateful to the archivists, staff, and volunteers at the GLBT Historical Society in San Francisco; the Lesbian Herstory Archives in Brooklyn; the New York and San Francisco Public Libraries; the ONE National Gay and Lesbian Archives in Los Angeles; the Center for Southwest Research, University of New Mexico, Albuquerque; New Mexico State Records and Archives in Santa Fe; and the Fray Angélico Chávez History Library, part of the Palace of the Governors in Santa Fe. At the Center for Southwest Research, special thanks go to former director Mike Kelly, who first directed me to sources on queer New Mexico, and archivist Beth Silbergleit, my dear friend and colleague; archivist Samuel Sisneros and university archivist Portia Vescio helped me gather the final pieces of research needed to bring this project to fruition.

I recognize various institutions for the financial resources that made this research possible: the Feminist Research Institute at UNM for a research grant; the Dean's Dissertation Scholarship at UNM; the Office of the New Mexico State Historian for the support of the New Mexico History Scholarship; the UNM Department of History for the one-year Dorothy Woodward Memorial Fellowship; the Juliana Wilson Thompson Lectureship from the College of Wooster; and the Harry Ransom Center Research Fellowship in the Humanities at the University of Texas at Austin. My fellowship summer in Austin was pivotal to the research in chapter 2. As I shared my findings with the summer cohort, I received interest and excitement about delving deeper into issues of censorship. There, too, I met Jo Winning. After intellectual conversations about our research we ventured out of the archives, and one hot and humid Austin night we visited Bass Performance Hall to listen to k.d. lang, Neko Case, and Laura Veirs. This moment fueled my creativity for months. Young scholars, leave the archives to channel your creativity and meet interesting people.

A network of scholars has inspired, supported, and challenged me. Amy Scott offered sound guidance on chapter 5 and encouraged me to think broadly about how my work advances historians' understanding of the interconnected nature of post-sixties social movement politics. Jon Hunner and Rebecca Ullrich helped with locating sources to tell the narrative of the rise of the national security apparatus in New Mexico. Sylvia Rodríguez offered her insights into exploring queer history across classes and ethnic groups in Santa Fe and Taos. Conversations with Flannery Burke on sexuality in 1920s New Mexico influenced the structure and framing of chapter 1. Most importantly, Patrick Ettinger has been a kind, generous, and thoughtful mentor since my undergraduate days. He has served as a role model for me as a teacher, advisor, and scholar. I owe him a debt of gratitude I feel I can never repay.

I feel thankful to have found a highly engaged intellectual community at the College of Wooster. My colleagues Shannon King and Jeff Roche read and commented on my book proposal and introduction, which became much stronger for their insights and input. Shannon listened to my woes about finding time to write and offered advice on balancing teaching and writing. Michelle Leiby and Angie Bos organized faculty bootcamps, providing a space to get serious work done. Without my writing group, none of this would have been possible. Each month I relied on Wee-Siang Margaret Ng's, Christina Welsch's, Julia Bernier's, and Lucy Barnhouse's generous critiques that made this book stronger. They read every part of the manuscript, often more than once. I am so very appreciative of their help but even more appreciative of our camaraderie. This book and I are better off because of their friendship.

I am grateful to have worked with the University of Washington Press. Larin McLaughlin saw promise in this project at an early stage. Larin and Caroline Hall made themselves available for all of my many queries. Sarah C. Smith offered thoughtful and thorough copyediting.

The press's two outside reviewers provided careful suggestions and enthusiastic support, which propelled me to keep revising.

As a non-Native writing a project that is inclusive of Indigenous people, I relied on the expertise of American Indian historians to ensure that I did not participate in perpetuating a colonial discourse that has erased the specificity of Native cultures. I consulted with Martha Austin-Garrison (Diné/Navajo), a Navajo language professor at Diné College, for translations. Also at Diné College, Brian King provided a close reading of the first section of chapter 1. Zonnie Gorman (Diné/Navajo) was an incredibly thoughtful reader as well. At the Western History Association conference, I benefited from the advice of Kent Blansett (Cherokee, Creek, Choctaw, Shawnee, and Potawatomi) on how to approach queer Indigenous histories.

I must especially acknowledge the generosity and support of fellow LGBT scholars. I would like to thank Gayle Rubin for her kind and repeated offers to assist me with my project; Jerry Lee Kramer, who guided me with framing a non-urban LGBT project; Daniel Hurewitz, who commented on my first conference paper as a graduate student all the way to my last one on this project, has provided many valuable insights. Jonathan Ned Katz opened his home to LGBT scholars during the 2015 American Historical Association Annual meeting. He threw a rocking party where early scholars of LGBT history mixed with a new generation of LGBT historians. Nowhere else in the academic world have I felt so welcomed and supported.

This project reignited my own connection to art. My dad, an artist, taught me to appreciate art. Our family often ventured to art museums. At each gallery, my father asked me and my brother to pick our favorite painting, but he also asked us to explain why. We learned to describe the elements of the work, its technical qualities, and to ponder the subject matter and artist of the piece. "What had the artist hope to convey?" my dad would ask. We learned to articulate how the piece made us feel and why it spoke to us. Without these sojourns and informal art critiques as a child, I would have missed the meaning behind many of the works explored in this book.

I am lucky to have a supportive family and amazing friends. I am eternally thankful for my mom, who stood by my decision to embark on the path to become a professor of history and offered countless hours of moral support. My other constant supporters have been my grandparents, Alex and Ethel Biro. My brothers, Martin Biro and Nick LaSpina, housed and fed me on my many research trips to New York City. They also provided lots of love and care. Martin, this book is for you. I will always be your ally. Lastly, I would be lost without my dearest friends, Jennifer McPherson and Denée Hernandez, who buoy my spirits. Your kind patience and great fun have kept me sane in the wild world of academics and beyond. I look forward to always making good trouble together.

My greatest thanks goes to my husband, David Walters. He never tired of hearing about my research and asked thought-provoking questions. He also made sure that not working was just as an important part of life. He filled nonwork hours with antics, laughter, adventures, movies, and long hikes with our beloved dog, Cordelia. Your love, intellectual curiosity, and humor sustain me.

Wide-Open Desert

Land of Enchantment

An aspiring artist and free-spirited white lesbian, Agnes "Agi" Sims grew up in the small town of Devon, Pennsylvania. She left her hometown of wealthy country residences to attend the Philadelphia School of Design for Women and in search of other lesbians. While she met some like-minded women in East Coast literary circles, it was not until her vacation to Santa Fe in 1938 that she would find her niche. The city's characteristics of cultural pluralism, rebellion against the status quo, gender transgression, and sexual freedom within vibrant art circles enchanted Sims. The story goes that Sims immediately returned to Philadelphia to pack up all of her belongings and move permanently to Santa Fe.[1] She settled in the Canyon Road neighborhood, which in the late 1930s retained much of its rural character of original Nuevomexicano farms and adobe homes while existing alongside a new avant-garde culture of fine artists, writers, and musicians. She purchased a home for herself and long-time partner, Mary Louise Aswell, where they mentored and entertained other lesbian and gay artists. Sims devoted her artistic career to painting, sculpting, and preserving Puebloan petroglyphs in the Galisteo Basin.[2] In the wide-open desert of New Mexico, Sims cultivated her own style of living and indulged her twin passions of art and women.

One year after Sims's arrival, on October 24, 1939, Elias Lee Francis and Ethel Haines Francis (Laguna Pueblo/Métis) welcomed their daughter Paula Marie Francis into the world. In retelling the story of her upbringing, Francis called it "a multicultural event."[3] She grew up in Cubero, a tiny land grant village from the Mexican era nestled near the Pueblo of Laguna, two hours southwest of Santa Fe. Cubero housed a population of fewer than one hundred families, including Latinos, Pueblos, Navajos, and Anglos. Growing up in Cubero and her own mixed ancestry taught Francis how to bridge perspectives across cultures, a worldview she would later apply to her writing—for which she became known as Paula Gunn Allen. Additionally, she asserted that the Laguna women who raised her instilled a "woman-centered" standpoint that has been "important to my work."[4]

While New Mexico fostered Allen's ethnoracial and gender identities, she waited until her thirties, when she lived in the Castro, a gay neighborhood in San Francisco, California, to "finally" come out. In New Mexico Allen had witnessed homophobia of surprising vehemence among nongay Indians.[5] Damage caused by settler colonialism led to the dissolution of cultural support systems for gender- and sexuality-variant Native people on tribal lands. Urban relocation and migration in the 1970s, however, created a space for American Indians to come out as gay and later to define themselves as two-spirit as well.[6] Allen publicly revealed her own lesbian identity and championed the restoration of two-spirit identity in Native nations when she published her groundbreaking essay "Beloved Women: Lesbians in American Indian Cultures" (1981) in *Conditions*, a lesbian feminist literary periodical. She penned some of the earliest and most notable pieces of Native American two-spirit literature, and much of her writing attracted a significant lesbian readership.[7]

In contrast to Allen, self-identified Chicana and Nuevomexicana native Nadine Armijo remained grounded in her Catholic, Spanish- and English-speaking household in the village of Corrales, outside Albuquerque. When Armijo started exploring her lesbian identity, she moved only as far as the house across the street from her parents to live with her partner, Rosa Montoya.[8] The homebound lesbian couple negotiated their sexual identity within family and church structures rather than in a city. Armijo attended Catholic Mass every morning and family dinners with Rosa, her "friend," on Sunday nights. In the close-knit village community, the couple felt compelled to monitor their public sexual expression. They never engaged in physical or emotional affection with each other in front of other people, even in their own home.[9] Armijo explains, "It's been kind of hard here in Corrales for me. . . . The folks you know. I never told them" because they believe "that it is really bad to be gay."[10]

Frustrated with sublimating their erotic desires, Armijo and Montoya eventually decided to publicly announce their lesbian relationship. They both agreed to appear in the widely circulated and highly acclaimed *Word Is Out: Stories of Some of Our Lives* (1977).[11] In the 1970s, filmmaker Peter Adair and the Mariposa Film Group conducted interviews across the United States with two hundred gay men and lesbians for the first feature-length documentary about lesbian and gay identity made by gay filmmakers.[12] Importantly, the filmmakers' approach prioritized representing a plurality of voices, including African American, Asian American, and Latinx interviewees, who were encouraged to tell their own stories in their own way. The pioneering film reached audiences nationwide in movie theaters and on television, debuting during a time when homosexuality was rarely a topic of documentaries.[13] Armijo and Montoya opened their rustic adobe home to the film crew. The couple sat side by side on their bed, a set of rosary beads hanging from their headboard, and answered questions about their lesbian relationship.[14] Armijo and Montoya embraced the film as a safe arena to discuss lesbianism, a topic they felt was off-limits within their Nuevomexicano community.

Agnes Sims's, Paula Gunn Allen's, Nadine Armijo's, and Rosa Montoya's stories represent forays into New Mexico's twentieth-century queer past. This book begins with their voices because the narratives of queer women have long been overshadowed by those about men. Specifically, a great deal of the inquiry into queer western history "has anchored itself in the excavation and analysis of same-sex desire between men."[15] But the history recounted here is not queer women's alone. This book centers on experiences of Pueblo, Navajo, Nuevomexicanx, and white queer people who possessed a wide range of desires, sexual subjectivities, and gender variance. It tells the stories of native New Mexicans, transplants, migrants, and temporary residents of the state whose creative and academic works have documented what it meant to be queer beginning in the 1920s through the 1980s. Queer New Mexicans responded to their marginalization and underrepresentation by partaking in mobility and art, cultural practices well embedded in the region's history. I argue that geographic mobility and the discourse and diffusion of queer creative productions are the foremost elements that shaped queer cultures and politics in the state. The ability of an individual to move for queer association is a right and often a necessary step in embracing a queer self, and Sims, Allen, Armijo, and Montoya all utilized that mobility.[16] After securing a place to embrace same-gender desire, they then engaged in queer cultural production. Sims nurtured a network of queer creatives; Allen brought conversations about queer sexuality into the realm of Native literature; Armijo and Montoya showcased a positive representation of Chicana lesbianism to national audiences. Building on the identity formation process, queer creatives established networks that cultivated knowledge about queerness. Sexual discourse, which stemmed from a variety of sources including creative endeavors, served as the center of the emerging sexual revolution and remained an organizing principle during the modern gay liberation movement.

Uncovering the lives of sexual and gender nonnormative New Mexicans was a challenging task because of the paucity of written sources on queer history in the state. My project began with a series of thirty oral histories. Since the 1970s, oral history projects with queer people have been a critical resource for excavating the queer past.[17] I collected oral histories in cooperation with the LGBT Educational Archives Project, devoted to preserving LGBTQ+ voices, particularly in the Southwest. Many of the interviews have been preserved and are available at the Center for Southwest Research, University of New Mexico Libraries, as part of the Bennett Hammer LGBT Collection.[18] By design, these interviews are constructed to yield diversity in terms of gender, class, race, ethnicity, and region.[19] To rectify gaps in my oral histories, I also draw on interviews conducted by others.[20] Taken together, I examine the lives of well-known queer people such as homophile activist Harry Hay and queer author Paula Gunn Allen as well as the experiences of ordinary queer folks, such as the Chicana lesbian couple Nadine Armijo and Rosa Montoya. My initial conversations with participants began with a simple question: What was it like to identify as queer and live in New Mexico? I used "queer" in my initial question to encapsulate the wide spectrum of sexual and gender identities, but participants self-identified their sexual orientation and gender identity, and I employ their own terminology here. I teased out this large question with three overlapping themes: living conditions, social life, and forms of organization against discrimination. As I listened to their intimate life histories, I realized that interviewees narrated their lives through movement and pathways. Most had a mobility narrative, but their tales of movement were different from the typical rural-to-urban migration stories embedded in LGBT literature.[21] Their stories also illustrated an unruliness of racial, class, and gender dynamics that transgressed an easy understanding of New Mexican queer lives. I needed to be committed to making race and gender as central as sexuality.

The oral histories that unfolded made me focus less on spatialized settings and more on the circulation of sexual subjects and knowledge. I puzzled over how to reimagine traditional ways of uncovering queer lives—using cities themselves as a documentary source for interpreting queer pasts, police records and jury trials to uncover same-sex acts, and vice culture, particularly bars, for revealing publicly visible queer cultures and as agents for resistance. I consulted a growing body of interdisciplinary scholarship on the "rural turn" in gay and lesbian history that elucidates how queer sexualities and subjectivities manifest in rural locations.[22] I structured my own project without the geographic dualisms of urban and rural, opting for a state-based approach that views the varied landscapes of New Mexico as interconnected—though, admittedly, much of the queer past I have documented takes place in the northern part of the state. I also take geographical detours to Arizona, Nevada, California, and elsewhere. When people or ideas moved, I followed them.

As I searched for evidence that might reveal flows, practices, and dimensions of an alternative mapping of sexual geographies that linked disparate locations, this line of inquiry led me to art and literature. Personal narratives and visual and textual queer evidence, some public but most private and unpublished, represent a site wherein queer people conceptualized their place within a homophobic nation and found a means for spreading sexual subjectivities.[23] For most of the twentieth century, LGBTQ+ Americans lived in a homophobic climate where disclosing their sexual identity in mainstream society brought fear of persecution, an environment that prevented the development of an art movement centered on overt homoerotic content until the 1970s with the birth of the modern gay liberation movement. Queer artists and writers, through various forms of creative expression, indirectly conveyed sexual difference and gender variance. As queer art historian Jonathan D. Katz argues, portraiture alone is a rich "untapped" archive. Katz explains, "we have literally thousands of images—paintings, sculptures, watercolors, prints, films, and photographs—that eloquently attest to forms of sexual desire and association long before the advent

This photograph is an excellent example of the "yet still untapped" archive of queer portraiture. Lesbian photographer Laura Gilpin took the photograph of lesbian artist Agnes Sims in her Santa Fe studio in 1946. Sims nurtured a network of queer creatives, including Gilpin. Agnes Sims, 1946, gelatin silver print, 9 ½ × 7 ³/₁₆ in., Amon Carter Museum of American Art, Fort Worth, Texas, gift of the artist P1978.92.35, © 1979 Amon Carter Museum of American Art.

of our modern lesbian and gay identity." Many artistic works have queer themes, but such themes often pass undetected.[24] I scrutinized poetry, fiction, little magazines, documentaries, and queer male erotic photography as expressions of self-love, points of connectivity to find other queer people, and spaces to imagine belonging. My use of art and literature as evidence provides a useful corrective to dominant narratives of twentieth-century American LGBT history—white, urban, and male—and recovers the experiences of lesbians, queer people of color, and, to a lesser extent, bisexuals, asexuals, and nonbinary people.[25]

Oral histories and queer creative evidence consulted for this project offered only a partial history of New Mexico's queer past. Not until I paired such materials with archival collections, government documents, university records, and newspaper articles was I able to uncover how queer cultural development overlapped with and inspired the beginning of sexual politics in the American Southwest and, to an extent, the rest of the United States. Studying LGBTQ+ lives in New Mexico reveals different processes—art and mobility—that have shaped equality movements. An array of Pueblo, Navajo, Nuevomexicanx, and white queer people conducted acts of everyday resistance against sexual and gender oppression through their practices of cultural production and physical movement to places they made or viewed as queer—plazas, fiestas, tribal land, writing groups, and art exhibitions. Santa Fe was a particularly vibrant site of the artistic expression essential in the construction of a southwestern queer identity politics. In contrast, other desert states, such as Nevada and Arizona, took first steps toward establishing queer community in the postwar era through their bars, nightclubs, and, beginning in 1976, through gay rodeo circuits that offered a space for rural LGBTQ+ people.[26] The political histories of queer New Mexicans began much earlier and reveal an alternative way to understand the creation of a different type of identity politics focused on cultural activism—blending creative activities with activism to advocate for sociopolitical change in society.[27] When cultural activism is knit together with other forms of conventional political activism, New Mexico emerges as a critical site of the national fight for gay and lesbian civil rights.

Wide-Open Desert first traces the movement of queer bodies. Sims embarked on an urban-to-urban sexual migration when she moved from the large city of Philadelphia, where she had access to lesbian literary circles, to the smaller city of Santa Fe, where she forged a world of queer artistic networks. Outside large metropolises, art colonies proved to be additional spaces that forged sexual cultures, and by the time Sims moved, Santa Fe had begun to acquire a queer reputation. Allen moved many times in adulthood, but it was not until she made the "quintessential" sexual migration, abandoning her rural community of origin to settle in a gay mecca, that she was able to grapple with her homoerotic feelings. She also followed a well-worn path of Native Americans to San Francisco: a path that fostered the birth of the first gay Native American organization in the United States when Barbara Cameron (Hunkpapa Lakota) and Randy Burns (Northern Paiute/Pyramid Lake Indian Tribe) cofounded Gay American Indians in July of 1975, an organization Allen had consistent contact with.[28] The migration patterns of Allen and Sims illustrate the significance of geographic mobility for developing one's queer identity and forming queer affiliations.

While two prominent forms of methodology in LGBT history—community studies and political histories—both acknowledge the vital role sexual migrations played in relation to building a sexual equality movement, scholars have given little attention to how people and sexual knowledge have moved across internal boundaries in the United States.[29] Most studies gloss over these migrations, instead showing how urban migrants built a collective gay identity and fought homosexual oppression in America through political organization.[30] The relatively new research area of queer mobilities, alongside feminist and postcolonial studies of migration, offers avenues for further analysis and empirical development.[31] Mobility studies takes a qualitative turn toward narratives of mobility by examining social phenomena—relationships between bodies, objects, and ideas—that form motivations for relocation. For many members of the LGBTQ+ community, practices and understandings of love and sexuality inform their experiences of mobility. Movement could improve life circumstances, particularly when queer people acquired significant new social ties, even by moving within the boundaries of their birth state, like Armijo and Montoya did. Latina lesbians, who were often pressured to stay close to home, still moved within hometowns or short distances away. I employ the term *queer mobility*, one's ability (or inability) to move influenced by their queer inclinations, to discuss these practices.[32] Narratives of fleeing, settling, itinerant paths, small movements, going home, or sometimes the refusal to settle are complexities of grappling with a queer identity. Additionally, the variable scales of queer mobility—urban to urban, rural to urban, and urban to rural—show how queer people built and utilized an expansive sexual landscape that may or may not be predicated on urbanity.

Equally important is the way an array of queer lives materialize when scholars study places outside urban centers and vice culture.[33] Many gay spaces emerged out of the sexual topography of cities, as historian George Chauncey argues: "The making of the gay world can only be understood in the context of the evolution of city life and the broader contest over the urban moral order." Historians have validated that "urban environments remain the sites where gay identity coalesced first and most profoundly."[34] However, gay urban studies, foundational to the formation of a white, gay male identity, sometimes leave out rural folks, working-class queers, lesbians, and queers of color who often could not make sexual migrations to cities or embarked on smaller-scale versions.[35] Queer movement, which has been imagined as urban, exists in other contexts, especially for those who might not possess equal access to privacy, property, and mobility.[36] *Wide-Open Desert* thus reassesses the power of urbanism within contemporary notions of queer identities and politics. Mobility mattered more in forming queer cultures than did settlement in an urban space. I underscore how New Mexico's rural desert landscape, land communes, freewheeling art circles, and university classrooms engendered queer cultural construction and gay civil rights activism, not as a product of an urban existence, but through the use of movement and aesthetics.

Creative centers, like large cities, inspired queer people to move and place-make.[37] By the 1920s, Taos's and Santa Fe's reputations as art colonies influenced the migration of primarily white gay and lesbian artists and writers. Whereas gay men and lesbians in the urban centers of New York, San Francisco, and Los Angeles carved out gay neighborhoods for socialization within certain districts of the city, Santa Fe and Taos lesbians and gay men were sewn into the landscape's fabric. Instead of activities associated with urban vice—bars, nightclubs, and bathhouses—Santa Fe and Taos queer bohemians crafted small-town activities: creating homes with partners, participating in Santa Fe Fiesta, and meeting at writing groups and art exhibitions.

New Mexico possesses a rich artistic history that dates back to its earliest inhabitants, who created images based on their religious connections to natural surroundings. By the twentieth century, New Mexico attracted and inspired a range of artistic aesthetics from Catholic iconography to romanticized images of Indigenous people.[38] In particular, depictions of southwestern culture spurred the establishment of a tourist-centered art industry and led to the blossoming of art colonies, solidifying the Southwest's reputation as an artistic mecca. Simultaneously, American Indian and Latinx artists continued to assert their own culture through provocative artworks. Art proved to be an expression of cultural struggles for New Mexico's diverse peoples. All of these artistic endeavors have made Santa Fe the third-largest art market in the United States.[39]

At the same time, American society at large suppressed homosexuality as an artistic and literary theme. This is particularly evident during the Cold War, when the security state effectively shut down sexual politics in New Mexico and stifled queer aesthetics. World War II ushered in a different kind of mobility, as millions of Americans moved toward the centers of an advancing nuclear industry centered in the American West, including New Mexico. Newcomers to the state prioritized an appreciation for high-technology enterprises over artistic sensibilities and embraced heteronormative conceptions of settlement—homeownership, men as the primary breadwinners, and the nuclear family ideal. Nationwide, queer people came under attack, and the perception of "homosexuals" as security risks transformed queer openness in the art world. Pervasive homophobia and concerns about gay people in the arts eroded visible networks of support for queer artists.

Nonetheless, LGBTQ+ artists' and writers' creation of works despite a national climate of homophobic censorship is a significant and overlooked aspect of the burgeoning sexual equality movement. Queer New Mexicans produced a body of work on queer expression. The stark and beautiful landscape of the state has long inspired the region's peoples to make art and literature that evinced their sense of sociocultural distinctiveness. Two-Spirit Pueblo potters and Navajo weavers created the earliest pieces of queer art.[40] By the 1920s white gay and lesbian artists and writers who migrated to northern New Mexico produced queer art and literature that tackled themes of their emotional lives. Latinx queers added their representations beginning in the late 1970s, when the first wave of Chicana lesbian writers, as they called themselves, wrote their formerly silenced histories. Over several decades, both subtle and explicit queer cultural production opened sexual discourse, which served as a foundation for the later triumphs of the modern gay liberation movement.[41]

Excluded from formal channels of citizenship and public life, queer people in New Mexico resorted to creative means and media to form their communities and engage with others. I use the term *queer cultural production* to refer to the dialogue between queer subjects' art, literature, and culture that produce a site of sexual meaning.[42] It is a germinal space to construct, contest, and respond to alternative sexualities. I cast a wide net in interpreting the links between art, literature, and queer culture: evidence in this book ranges from fine art works to Nuevomexicano folksongs, community commemoration, male homoerotic photography, and queer artistic networks, such as the one Sims fostered. Sims, whose artistic notoriety has largely been forgotten but whose lesbianism has recently surfaced, generated queer creative production even though her artwork never focused on homoerotic themes.[43] Instead, she participated in building a strong lesbian coterie to such a degree that her efforts helped to garner the city of Santa Fe's reputation as the "dyke capital of the country."[44]

Creative queers advocated for a space to produce deep, private interior subjectivities of gender and sexual nonconformity. By connecting creativity and queerness, they established a domain "which offered possibilities for minoritarian forms of sexual being otherwise denied within the majoritarian spaces of heterosexual culture." When they built art colonies and developed queer artistic networks, "it was through such networks of confidential discursive exchange that queer artists were able to share unofficial knowledge about art and homosexuality, while at the same time building some rudimentary form of sexual identity and community otherwise denied to them by a culture intent on seeing homosexuality as an isolating 'affliction,'" observes historian Gavin Butt.[45] The affiliation of art and homosexuality meant that artists contributed substantially to conceptions of nonnormative sexuality, often in ways that subverted mainstream society's ideas. Scholars have articulated how cities played a role in loosening sexual morals, which helped to connect urbanization and homosexuality, yet the association of art and homosexuality was equally strong and is less explored in the literature of LGBT history.[46]

This work centers on how creative expression became a battleground for sexual politics and thus expands historians' understanding of where LGBTQ+ activism takes form. Scholars have argued that the gay movement succeeded at subnational levels through a three-pronged method—passing protective legislation for lesbians and gays, countering antigay acts, and repealing state sodomy laws.[47] Studying the movement in New Mexico adds another, somewhat overlooked method—cultural activism. In a state that had far fewer incidents of police brutality, bar raids, entrapment, and street harassment, queer New Mexicans spent less time countering antigay acts and instead asserted their queer lives through cultural production and defending their right to make and share such works at both the local and federal levels.

There has yet to be a full-length consideration of New Mexican art colonies as a vital site of analysis in LGBT history. Scholars of LGBT history have barely touched on gay and lesbian sexuality in the American Southwest.[48] Likewise, seldom have academics investigated New Mexico's history by centering queer mobility and sexual freedom.[49] This is surprising since the US West as a site of migration, settlement, and displacement has spawned contests over who can and cannot have full citizenship rights, and sex has often been a deciding factor. Conceptions of sexual propriety often meant social and legal equality, while those of sexual impropriety resulted in social and legal inequality.[50] Interest in sexuality, specifically LGBT history in the American West, is recent.[51] Historians have uncovered that beginning in the nineteenth century, the North American West served as a generative context where queer people forged alternative ways of living. Men built homosocial worlds in Gold Rush mining camps. The region made space for cross-dressing men and women, some of whom might be understood today as transgender, to transgress sexual and gender boundaries.[52] As the West transformed to modern industrial states, communities cracked down on gender nonconformity and queer spaces narrowed. Nonetheless, the region still offered an alternative sexual imaginary. Fruitful discussions appear in the interdisciplinary scholarship of Western American literature, where the pervasiveness of male homosocial friendships is made visible. Mainstream audiences could recognize queerness at the very heart of American West narratives through Ang Lee's 2005 Academy Award–winning film *Brokeback Mountain*. Such endeavors illustrate that the particularity of western places such as New Mexico has shaped understandings of queerness.

Since the latter nineteenth century, New Mexico's population has been racially and ethnically diverse, with different groups each claiming their own connection to its land. New Mexico contains twenty-three federally recognized tribes as well as long-standing Spanish and Mexican settlements.[53] In the early twentieth century, white Americans migrated to the state because they envisioned it as a place free from modern ills. Later, they came as a result of the development of modern nuclear weapons, which spurred new job opportunities. A tiny number of Asian immigrants, Asian Americans, and African Americans came for economic reasons, their numbers slightly increasing after World War II.[54] The encounters of these groups have involved conditions of cooperation, coercion, inequality, and conflict and generated a complex system of racial identification. In this project, I broadly use *Anglo* or *white* to refer to people of European American descent. I use the terms *American Indian*, *Native American*, and *Indigenous* interchangeably, along with specific tribal names, to describe the region's first inhabitants. Recently, some Pueblo nations have rejected descriptive names given to them by Spanish colonists and have resumed using their own tribal names.[55] I use *Latino* and *Latina* to describe those who identify themselves as of Latin American descent, and I embrace the ungendered noun *Latinx* to convey a wider array of gender identities and expressions.[56] These nomenclatures defy the variegated subjectivities of the state's overall cultural prism and emergent relations and serve as a starting point for comprehending the state's peoples and regionalized cultures. To add precision, the terms *Nuevomexicano* and *Nuevomexicana* are employed to describe the descendants of Spaniards, Pueblos, or Mexicans.[57] I also use *Chicana* and *Chicano* following people's self-identifications. Whenever possible, I prioritize identifying people as they understood themselves.

Likewise, *queer* encapsulates a spectrum of identities, genders, desires, sexualities, and transgressive erotic life, as well as its intersection with issues of race, ability, class, and gender. *Queer* also comprises nonbinary gender identity and erotic life as understood by some nonwhite communities. In New Mexico, the Indigenous populations of the Navajo Nation, the Mescalero Apache Tribe, and nine Pueblo Nations—Acoma, Isleta, Laguna, Santa Ana, Kewa, San Felipe, Ohkay Owingeh, Tesuque, and Zuni—possess, to some extent, a documented history of a flexible sex/ gender system, now often referred to as two-spirit.[58] I use the term *two-spirit* to interlink references to historical foundations of gender and sexual diversity in American Indian societies with contemporary LGBTQ+ identities and politics. However, I avoid using *two-spirit* as a universal category and, where possible, instead employ tribally specific formations of gender and sexuality such as the Navajo's nádleehí, a genderfluid identity that roughly translates in English to "one who constantly transforms."[59] I also use contemporary LGBTQ+ terminology since "the term 'Two-Spirits' is not universally accepted as a term of identification for Navajo LGBTQI."[60] In doing so, I underscore the variety of queer lives throughout the American Southwest. The messiness of terminology in this book reflects the limited sexual and gender schema and the highly fluid and changeable nature of desires and identities. I alternate between *homosexual, gay, lesbian, bisexual, two-spirit, LGBTQ+,* and *queer,* first honoring individuals' self-identification and second to broaden notions of sexuality and gender identity. For some nonbinary people, I use they/them pronouns to better align with how they identified. For two-spirit people who in their lifetime were constrained by Western binary gender and sexual roles, I adopt the pronouns they used to describe themselves. No terminology works perfectly; variable categories of gender and desire are part of this story.

Wide-Open Desert is divided into six chapters that move chronologically and thematically. Chapters, 1, 3, and 5 explore incoming and outgoing waves of migration, while chapters 2, 4, and 6 focus on the cultural and political manifestations of queer mobility. I begin this study at the end of World War I, following the lead of historian Daniel Hurewitz, who argues that queer identity politics, typically linked to the sixties and seventies, is rooted in the post–World War I artistic and leftist milieu of Los Angeles.[61] Chapter 1 charts cultural constructions of queer ideology and identity in New Mexican art circles when incipient queer cultures formed in conjunction with the growth of Santa Fe and Taos as art colonies in the 1920s. I also address how, in constructing an emergent queer community, migrants, along with influxes of government officials, missionaries and anthropologists, disrupted existing cultures of nonbinary gender and flexible sexual norms in the surrounding Native nations, pueblos, and, to a lesser extent, Nuevomexicano communities. To elucidate how the Indigenous inhabitants of the region formed and enacted queer identities within their own communities, this chapter examines the life and work of nádleehí Hastíín Klah (Diné/Navajo).

Once settled in the colonies, queer artists and writers defended the dissemination of sexual materials and created a framing of sexual privacy rights for advancing the cause of sexual civil liberties in the coming decades, as I discuss in chapter 2. Queer cultural production and political activism collided during fights against censoring obscenity—a policy issue of the long sexual revolution. Politically, New Mexicans began their long sexual revolution in 1929, when white queer residents fought against a national censorship force—the Smoot-Hawley Tariff Act—that upheld prohibitions on literature with sexual themes from entering the United States. The debate over the Tariff Act invoked privacy rights to advance the cause of sexual civil liberties. I also examine other ways queer people evaded censorship. Mixed-race Cherokee playwright Rollie Lynn Riggs, who found it too risky to openly write about indigeneity and his same-gender attractions, wrote coded queer Indigenous presences into his poetry and plays.

Chapter 3 focuses on how the security state during and after World War II in New Mexico unsettled the state's formative queer cultures, displacing and outnumbering artists and writers by a new population of military personnel and scientists. By 1945 New Mexico was home to military training and weapons research at Kirtland Air Force Base and Sandia National Laboratory in Albuquerque and Los Alamos National Laboratory near Santa Fe, which during the war served as one of the Manhattan Project's key scientific laboratories. The military-industrial complex produced consequences for lesbians and gay men including a shift from sexual privacy rights toward imposed concealment of sexual identity and rising levels of homophobia. In response, queer New Mexicans passed as straight, migrated to cities, and constructed an underground queer culture that consisted of bars, primarily in Albuquerque, and the circulation of male homoerotic photographs and stories through a clandestine pornographic market. Chapter 4 focuses on the severest consequence of the deployment of the security state—the imposition of heteronormative citizenship—as evidenced by a failed attempt to decriminalize sodomy in the state. It also discusses how queer cultural producers witnessed and endured the pervasive silencing of same-sex desire and gender variance. They ensconced themselves in the protective isolation of the desert and harnessed the "open secret" strategy.

By 1970 the gay population of New Mexico grew again with a new wave of sexual migrants that included radical gay liberationists, LGBTQ+ students, lesbian feminists, Radical Faeries, back-to-the-landers, and queer artists and writers. Chapter 5 investigates how this wave of migration dispersed the state's queer population geographically and traces the connections and exchanges between rural and urban lives, particularly through lesbian feminist do-it-yourself periodicals, which to some extent reached and included Latina lesbians. By examining migrants who chose not to settle in cities but instead made a migration to a rural setting, this chapter uncovers a lesser-understood aspect of sexual migrations: urban to rural.

Chapter 6 returns to a defense of sexual politics in 1969 during an event known as the "Love-Lust" controversy—when an erotic poem spurred a statewide debate over the boundaries of public sexuality. Debate tactics shifted to public disclosures of sexuality (coming out), and some activists drew attention to the entanglements of race and gender. I trace diversified visibility of queer people through a discussion of the documentary film *Word Is Out: Stories from Some of Our Lives*, which provided a platform for intersecting identities. The book ends in the 1980s, with a discussion of white lesbian feminist artists and activists of color who worked to upend sexual and racial norms.

In covering more than seventy years of New Mexican history, this book brings together the narratives of queer mobility and cultural productions to consider their relevance to the politicization of sexuality. New Mexico offers a multifaceted and complex story of building sexual networks and politics using creative production and mobility, as well as a lens to examine who is included and who is excluded. Understanding the narrative of New Mexico's queer past as a shared experience of community activism is an oversimplification. The construction of queer creative networks introduced boundaries between emergent and existing communities. When white artists inserted themselves into the Southwest, they falsely imagined that they lived in harmony with the state's colonized peoples. In their quest for queer expression, they often overlooked or misunderstood centuries of colonialism that continued to manifest as material inequality, racialized relations, and disruption of cultural practices, including nonbinary gender roles and flexible sexual norms. Even as queer spaces for white artists and writers grew, avenues of expression for nonconforming gender and homoeroticism among Navajos, Pueblos, and Nuevomexicanxs weakened. Nonetheless, Native and Latinx residents formed and enacted queer identities within their own communities. This book charts these transformations. Although unevenly distributed, queer New Mexicans nurtured environments to produce radical visions of sexual and gender equality that strove to be inclusive of racially and ethnically diverse participants. Queer activists and cultural makers pushed for progressive (and often competing) visions of queer identity and gay liberation. New Mexico affords scholars an opportunity to better understand the flourishing of racially diverse queer representations as well as the roles of mobility, creative expression, and cultural activism in fostering a national movement for sexual equality.

ONE

"Going Santa Fe"

The Making and Unmaking
of Queer Cultures

In the 1920s and 1930s a small group of gay and lesbian writers shunned large cities looking instead to foster queer identities in the high desert. An inspirational southwestern landscape had already attracted Anglo-American artists who settled in the area and founded the Taos Society of Artists in 1915. Early art colonists advertised the intercultural history of the region, particularly Indigenous cultures, by exhibiting their art throughout the United States. Concurrently, the state promoted economic development through cultural tourism. Both efforts sparked a second wave of sculptors, musicians, playwrights, poets, and writers. These bohemian migrants ushered in a period of flowering and diversification of Taos's and Santa Fe's aesthetic communities, including a niche for gay men and women.

Queer sojourners came for similar reasons—relative isolation, a low cost of living, and a climate that celebrated artistic experimentation—but distinguished themselves by their rebellion against mainstream sexual norms, gender transgression, and converging sexual and creative identities. Open and semi-open queers edged into art and literary societies, circles that could also provide cover for their nonnormative sexual proclivities. According to Santa Fe native Ford Ruthling, gay men and lesbians became so ubiquitous that the local saying "going Santa Fe" was a coded way of identifying them.[1] Scholars have crafted a vast literature about the bohemian migration to the Southwest. Still, few have imagined the art enclaves, writing groups, museums, fiestas, and other gatherings of creative intellectuals as a significant contribution from queer people to the growth of northern New Mexico's art colonies or considered their larger role in the development of queer identities in America. An aim of this chapter is to bridge existing scholarship and queer biographical literatures to unveil the making of a white, queer creative culture and the disintegration of Indigenous cultural networks, within the context of ongoing settler colonialism, that supported two-spirit people.[2]

When a small cohort of queer authors, particularly Harold Witter "Hal" Bynner and Walter Willard "Spud" Johnson, decided to settle in northern New Mexico, they encouraged friends and acquaintances loosely affiliated with creative centers in major cities to come to the Southwest. Rollie Lynn Riggs (Cherokee Nation), Marian Winnek, Myron Brinig, Cady Wells, Agnes Sims, and others followed. Together, they spearheaded initial contact zones for exploring sexual subjectivities. An organization called The Rabble afforded authors an opportunity to write poetry about homoerotic love. Queer themes also emerged in the abstract paintings by Marsden Hartley and the literature of Marian Winnek and Myron Brinig. Collectively, creators emphasized the emotional aspect of homosexuality, love, and the subsequent loneliness they endured in a world that stigmatized and punished same-sex attraction. Such works, which often circulated nationally, challenged Americans to reconceptualize their views of homosexuality by placing a desire for love at the heart of understanding queer relationships. Emboldened by their integration into the cultural fabric of New Mexico, queer migrants widened their presence. They built an array of public spaces in and around Santa Fe's Plaza—La Fonda (The Inn), Villagrá Book Shop, Santa Fe Fiesta, and various cruising sites.[3] These spaces facilitated the construction of a primarily white queer culture.

White queer people's ability to blend into the landscapes of New Mexico, particularly its artistic arenas, opens up more complicated questions about intersections of racial, gender, and sexual identity: especially how New Mexicans, as a broader community, negotiated conflicting and competing cultural understandings of erotic intimacy. Pueblo dances, a centerpiece of cultural tourism, provided an initial site for whites to dialogue about sexuality. Gay men sexualized and eroticized Pueblo religious ceremonies to diverge from restrictive normative American sexual ideals. At the same time, white missionaries and reformers condemned Pueblo dances, imagining them as sites of unrestrained sexual license and hindrance to assimilation. Pueblo men, in response, distanced their ceremonies from the imposed sexual discourse by refusing to engage in sexual discussion.[4] They also began to embrace stricter sexual standards for their communities as a protective mechanism. Nuevomexicanos, as they called themselves, defined as the descendants of Spaniards, Pueblos, or Mexicans, had already begun to adapt similar practices after New Mexico achieved statehood in 1912. Nuevomexicanos turned toward embracing Anglo sexual norms as a way to restore and expand their cultural and political power.[5] Even as queer spaces for white artists and writers widened, sensibilities of nonbinary gender and homoeroticism for Navajos, Pueblos, and Nuevomexicanos narrowed.

This is not to say that Indigenous two-spirit roles disappeared. In contrast to the white queer bohemians who used migration out of their hometowns to explore their sexual identity, Hastíín Klah (Diné/Navajo) returned home to foster their status as nádleehí, a fluid gender role.[6] In their life span (1867–1937), Klah witnessed both a revival and disruption of their tribe's gender-cultural categories. Hastíín Klah navigated shifting cultural practices, under the threat of assimilation, by articulating their nádleehí status through their art production as a weaver, at the time considered the domain of women, combined with their religious practices as a hataałii (Diné healer), a male profession.[7] By bringing art and ceremony together, Klah produced a new art form—sandpainting textiles—and an act of resistance. They became recognized as the first Navajo to translate religious images from sandpaintings into permanent woven form, a direct expression of being nádleehí.

Going Home

The forced removal of Diné from their ancestral lands began in 1863. After a failed series of treaties, the US Army devised a scorched-earth campaign against the Navajos in today's western New Mexico and Arizona, destroying their crops, slaughtering sheep and cattle, invading Navajo lands, and murdering those who resisted. In response, Navajos took livestock, attacked the army's horses, and refused to surrender. Destitution and starvation eventually pushed some Navajos to admit defeat. Under orders from James

H. Carleton, Christopher "Kit" Carson then forcibly marched more than ten thousand Navajos from their home and imprisoned them at Hwéeldi (Bosque Redondo) in east-central New Mexico from 1863 to 1866. Approximately two hundred Navajo people died of exposure to the elements and starvation during the near four-hundred-mile Long Walk. The US government then kept surviving members of the Navajo Nation in captivity for close to four years; more died from inhumane conditions.[8]

Ultimately, the military's internment of the Navajo people failed. Navajo leaders secured the Navajo Treaty of 1868 to relocate back to some of their traditional lands.[9] Even before the treaty had been signed, many Navajos and Mescalero Apaches had abandoned Bosque Redondo. Among them were a newly married couple, Ahson Tsosie and Hoskay Nolyae, who were expecting their first child. They asked the fort commandant for permission to leave, and, low on provisions and frustrated with high desertion rates, he granted their request.[10] Two months into their journey home, in December of 1867, Tsosie and Nolyae welcomed the birth of their first child, who grew up to be Hastíín Klah.[11] Klah, born in an era of peace, still felt the trauma of removal during their upbringing near the Tunicha Mountains; family members told of incarceration and genocide.[12] But the Navajo people also sought to balance the trauma of Hwéeldi with a recommitment to the Diné philosophy of Hózhó, a way of living and a belief system that encompasses harmony, beauty, and "everything that is positive."[13] They celebrated their path toward self-determination. The coerced displacement of a colonized population ended with a reverse migration, a return home and a treaty that testified to the sovereignty of the Navajo Nation.[14]

Given the context of their early years, it is perhaps not surprising that Klah felt drawn to learning healing ceremonies around the age of ten.[15] Klah's uncle, Dinnae Nez, trained Klah in the art of becoming a hataałii. In Diné culture, singers are medicine people who perform sacred practices of blessing and healing rites intended to restore an individual's physical, spiritual, and mental health.[16] The religious practices that Klah learned included "the origin histories of the Navajo people, the specific chants and prayers which accompany the particular ceremony, the sand paintings, the herbs, the contents of the medicine bundle and the procedures for ritual participation." Klah's aunt taught them which healing herbs and pollens to gather for each ritual.[17] Klah possessed an aptitude for memorizing the prayers, myths, and, in particular, producing sandpaintings for ceremonies, using crushed dried plants and stones to depict Diné worldviews.

As a young adult, Klah also felt called to weave. During their lifetime, women weavers produced most hand-woven textiles. Even though nádleehí and men practiced this tradition under the guidance of maternal kin, "their work has been rarely acknowledged." Knowledge of religion, in contrast, was primarily the domain of men.[18] Because Klah pursued skills associated with both genders, their community in Newcomb (Bis Deez'áhí) identified them as a nádleehí. Within tribal customs, nádleehí both possess an affinity for religious pursuits and engage in feminine work such as sheepherding, basketry, pottery, farming, or weaving. Navajo people recognize four genders—asdzáán (feminine woman), hastiín (masculine man), nádleehí (feminine man), and dilbaá (masculine woman).[19] According to ethnographer Carolyn Epple, "a male nádleehí may (to varying degrees) wear women's clothing; participate in activities associated with women, such as cooking and washing; and have sexual relations with other men." Epple describes Navajo gender traits as fluid: "Many Navajos know of masculine and feminine as a dynamic cycling of male into female, with its valuation dependent on the setting."[20] "The reasons the Navajo called him [Klah] 'one-who-has-been-changed' [nádleehí] were chiefly that he wove blankets and was not interested in women," recorded Gladys Reichard, an anthropologist who studied the Navajo people between 1930 and 1960.[21] Klah left almost no firsthand history concerning their gender identity, sexuality, or intimate relationships.[22] They did, however, leave extensive documentation of their art and religious knowledge that are deeply connected to their nádleehí expression and desire to preserve Navajo ceremonial customs.[23]

Klah's parents' move back to the Navajo Nation gave Klah the freedom to live their life as a nádleehí. Despite the federal government's persistent assimilation efforts, Klah had a tribal education at home, studying medicinal plants, Navajo stories in ceremonial hogans, and ancestral songs.[24] They trained as both a healer and weaver, an acknowledgment of their nádleehí status. During Klah's lifetime, elders on the Navajo reservation continued to revere nádleehí, as this elder conveys: "You must respect a nadle. They are, somehow, sacred and holy."[25] Klah grew up to become a well-known and highly respected one.

Even non-Navajos who knew Klah were aware of their nádleehí standing.

Frances "Franc" Johnson Newcomb and her husband, Arthur, operated a trading post on the Navajo Nation, a few miles from where Klah and their relatives lived. Klah frequently visited the store, and Newcomb claims that she developed a personal relationship with the family. "Klah always invit[ed] us to any special occasion," remembers Newcomb. Certainly, Klah and the Newcombs were present for many of the significant events in each other's lives. They traveled together, cared for each other in illness, celebrated births, and mourned deaths. Newcomb understood Klah's status among the Navajos: "they believed him to be honored by the gods and to possess unusual mental capacity combining both male and female attributes." Reichard, who worked with Klah as a community consultant, recorded that Klah "was a transvestite" noted for their skill as a healer and "beloved" among Navajos for their generosity.[26] One of the most prolific chroniclers of Klah's life, anthropologist Will Roscoe, argues that two-spirit people challenged how white newcomers to New Mexico thought about gender and sexuality: "Klah as a *nádleehé* was a frequent subject of discussion among the avantgarde artists, writers, and intellectuals in Santa Fe, who met him on occasions when he accompanied Mary Wheelwright."[27]

Additionally, Klah's occasional wearing of cross-gender attire marked them as nádleehí. Nádleehí traits are bounded by Navajo cultural ideals of interconnecting masculinity and femininity. Nádleehí are comfortable with their gender presentation shifting, particularly within specific contexts. Klah likely wore the apparel of another gender for ceremonial purposes as a hataɫii and embodied the nádleehí characteristic of a "male in women's attire doing women's work" when they wove.[28] The historical record indicates that Klah might have cross-dressed, as it has been described, outside the reservation when they demonstrated weaving at the World's Columbian Exposition in Chicago.[29] At the age of twenty-six, Klah had earned a reputation as an expert weaver, resulting in a commissioner for the World's Fair recruiting them to demonstrate weaving at the 1893 fair. According to St. Sukie de la Croix, at the fair, "a Navajo woman sat before a backdrop of blankets weaving rugs and applying sacred designs of the Navajo sandpaints. The woman was most likely Hastiin Klah."[30] Klah is widely recognized as the first Navajo to incorporate sacred designs of the sandpaintings on textiles.[31] Additionally, ethnologist Frank Hamilton Cushing, who helped to design the exhibits for the 1893 exposition, wrote that the Bureau of Ethnology's exhibition room "included a portrait of one of the most celebrated blanket-makers in the Navajo tribe." Cushing added, "While costumed as a *woman*, this figure really represents a man belonging to a peculiar class of 'women-men.'"[32] Although neither references Klah by name, Klah did participate in the World's Fair as an expert Navajo weaver, and it is quite possible that they wore women's attire at the fair as they would have done on the Navajo Nation.

A closer look at Klah's social expression of nádleehí through cross-gender attire reveals how their gender variance became constrained by settler colonialism. Some evidence suggests that Klah cross-dressed as a young adult but wore only masculine attire later in life, after facing harassment from a new generation of Navajos educated through government schools. Anthropologist Willard W. Hill identified six nádleehí on the Navajo reservation, including Klah, whom Hill portrayed as "having a voice like a woman and doing woman's work but dressing sometimes as a woman and sometimes as a man."[33] A younger generation of Navajos, heavily pressured to assimilate and to convert to Christianity or Mormonism, questioned and mocked the outward expression of gender fluidity.[34] Roscoe states that by the 1930s, "white ridicule and changing Navajo attitudes had created significant pressures on nádleehí not to cross-dress."[35] In boarding school environments, two-spirit behaviors were suppressed, and students who persisted were expelled. Cultural anthropologist Elsie Clews Parsons recorded in 1931 that authorities at Santa Fe's boarding school forced a young Laguna two-spirit student to wear male clothing and socialize with other boys after discovering the student's sex assigned at birth.[36] These punishments spread negative attitudes toward two-spirit people, reversing earlier positive interpretations that youths would have learned through tribal education. Instead of being offered a secure place in the Navajo Nation, future generations of nádleehí and dilbaá would find their social positions challenged.[37]

Klah resisted settler colonialism by claiming their nádleehí status through their occupations—combining male ceremonial knowledge with the female practice of weaving. Klah initially learned how to weave from their mother, an accomplished weaver, and sister, in the style of their region called Two Grey Hills. Over time, Klah's own artistic style blossomed to combine "only background of tan undyed wool from the bellies of brown sheep" with "dyes

Nádleehí Hastíín Klah (Diné/Navajo) mediated between the masculine and feminine by combining the skills of healing and weaving. Photograph courtesy of Palace of the Governors Photo Archives (NMHM/DCA), 047924.

carefully prepared from local plants and indigo and cochineal."[38] The addition of the ceremonial sandpaintings as designs on their textiles completed their artistic aesthetic.

Many Navajos objected to depicting ceremonial art on textiles, arguing that weaving sandpaintings violated tribal customs. Like many Native people, Navajos consider certain ceremonial knowledge sacred and powerful.[39] Such information is only to be shared within specialized religious societies that rightfully possess it. Sandpaintings, in the context of Navajo ceremonies, are intended to be ephemeral. Healing ceremonies involve drawing intricate designs of mythological scenes, on the floor of the ceremonial hut, to serve as temporary altars for ritual action.[40] They invoke healing energy and summon the order of the Holy People. Once a ceremony is complete, a hataałii sweeps away the image and participants return the materials to the earth.[41] To be sure, weaving sandpaintings is a cultural anomaly and at odds with their intended purpose. Klah wrestled for quite some time over the decision to make sandpaintings permanent. They concluded that weaving a textile of a sandpainting was not a direct part of a healing ceremony and therefore presented no spiritual danger to themself or other Navajos.[42] Additionally, their status as both a hataałii and a nádleehí protected them. Klah was trained to handle forces in nature and innately understood how to balance energies.[43] According to Elayne Zorn, some viewers have suggested that textiles made by Klah have deliberate errors as a way to mitigate cultural tensions and still provide consumers with a product they desired.[44] Klah may have been economically incentivized to make a living weaving sandpaintings. Selling textiles served as an essential source of income for many Navajo families, and the "exceptionally large rugs" Klah wove would have garnered higher prices.[45] Despite their controversial decision, their prestige as both a hataałii and weaver continued to rise on the Navajo reservation.

In their lifetime, Klah made more than twenty weavings with sandpainting patterns, a large body of work by a known nádleehí. Such a contribution marked Klah as a queer participant of northern New Mexico's art colonies. They were an integral part of making the state an art mecca known for its cultural mosaic of artistic expressions. Archaeologist Sarah Nelson notes the significance of Klah's art: "Although there are ethnographic references to works of art conducted by persons of nonbinary gender, there are few instances when the design elements have been directly influenced by a nonbinary person's identity."[46] Klah remains the most well-known non-female weaver. In 2004 the Navajo Nation Museum presented an exhibition intended to demystify the well-embedded idea that weaving is only a women's art, prominently featuring Klah: "The legacy left by this revered hataalii (chanter) [Hastíín Klah] is vast. For the weavers of the exhibit *Men Who Weave* it is the knowledge that there was one before them—one who was respected and honored because of his weaving gifts."[47] Activist, master weaver, and president of a local weaving guild on the Navajo Nation, Roy Kady, who exhibited his weavings in the show, cited Klah as his personal inspiration.[48] Then and now, Klah earned respect for their weavings from both members of their tribe and art collectors.

In the early 1920s, Klah's weavings caught the eye of collectors for their exceptional quality and creativity. A wealthy white patron, Mary Cabot Wheelwright, purchased one.[49] In her own way, Wheelwright led a queer life. Remembered as an eccentric and difficult "New England spinster," she spent her life unpartnered and used her substantial inheritance to embrace a nomadic existence, periodically leaving the East Coast to take guided treks through the deserts and mountains of western New Mexico and eastern Arizona. By 1923 Wheelwright had purchased a home in Alcalde, north of Ohkay Owingeh Pueblo, that she called Los Luceros. Her residence served as a social hub for queer New Mexicans, including renowned artist Georgia O'Keeffe; photographer Laura Gilpin and her partner of fifty years, Elizabeth W. Forster; printmaker and artist Dorothy Stewart and her then-intimate partner, writer Maria Chabot.[50] Wheelwright never identified as a lesbian but wrote openly about New Mexico's freedom from gender conventions; it was a place where one could "be a good sport and also drink tea."[51] Her peripatetic lifestyle enabled her to divide her time between three homes, engage in travel, and rejective heteronormative confines of settling down. Coming back from one of her excursions, she met Klah through the Newcombs, a meeting that would inspire her life's work to establish a museum dedicated to the cultural preservation of Navajo religious customs.[52] Klah and Wheelwright were both cultural revivalists who contributed to the growth of New Mexico's artistic reputation. Cultural revivalists fit into a distinct period of the evolving art colonies in the Santa Fe–Taos movement.[53] Many revivalist programs and institutions are still active a century later, including the one Klah and Wheelwright formed together—a Museum of Navajo Religion, later renamed the Wheelwright Museum of the American Indian.

The museum began with the preservation of Navajo religious knowledge. According to Wheelwright, Klah themself proposed that she record their ceremonial expertise: "Klah said that he had begun to realize that while it was all right for Navajo boys to go to school, that, after they had been there, they could not memorize the long myths; consequently he was beginning to feel that he would like to have this old knowledge recorded, and he asked me to record his songs." Klah worried about the effects of assimilation.[54] By 1921, when Klah decided to collaborate with two white women, they had witnessed decades of relentless efforts by the US government and by missionaries to suppress Navajo lifeways. Ceremonial knowledge weakened, and the Navajo language eroded. The loss of language made it difficult for students to practice, converse, and learn from their elders, who were often the source of information on religion and ceremonial practices.[55] Typically, a hataałii took on several apprentices. Klah had only one apprentice, his nephew Beaal Begay, who never completed his training.[56] Klah's collaboration with Newcomb and Wheelwright, as well as anthropologists Gladys Reichard and Harry Hoijer, was another controversial decision, but one they felt compelled to make in light of the destructive consequences of settler colonialism. Other Navajos made similar decisions. Klah's mentors, Hataałii Natloi (Laughing Singer) and Hataałii Nez (Tall Chanter), both worked with Washington Matthews, a US Army surgeon who studied Navajo language and lifeways.[57]

Klah recorded the first of several ceremonial songs, in 1927, at San Gabriel Ranch.[58] Klah dictated; Clyde Beall (Diné/Navajo) translated; Wheelwright recorded; and Newcomb recreated sandpaintings on paper. Over time, the foursome established a repository of sound recordings, manuscripts, paintings, and sandpainting tapestries of the Navajo creation story and other Navajo religious narratives. Subsequently, the recordings took place in various locations—Wheelwright's homes, El Navajo Hotel in Gallup, and in Phoenix and Tucson, Arizona—tellingly, all outside the Navajo Nation.[59] Roscoe posits that Klah "felt more comfortable doing this off the reservation, where it was less likely to attract the attention of other Navajos." Certainly, many Navajos restricted the passing of knowledge to white researchers. In an era of assimilation when divulging traditional knowledge could generate negative consequences, Native communities often questioned the motives of outsiders.[60]

Although she felt compelled to preserve Navajo religion, Wheelwright made no effort to learn Diné Bizaad. Unlike Newcomb, who was conversant in the Navajo language, Wheelwright hired a translator. She also requested that Klah provide her with narrative forms of ceremonies, such as a full rendering of the Nightway (Tł'ééjí) ceremony. Klah recounted the Nightway outside of the boundaries of the ritual itself, as a narrative reconstruction divorced from the ceremonial's actual context of a healing practice.[61] To meet Wheelwright's demand for a complete text, Klah imposed order, linking events to craft a story for a non-Navajo audience, but Wheelwright vastly shortened the account when she published it.[62] In so doing, Wheelwright claimed authority over Indigenous knowledge that was not hers to claim. Many hataałii held that compositional elements of ceremonies should not be freely shared, replicated, or divorced from their contexts. Disregarding these concerns, by the 1930s and 1940s, Wheelwright, with cooperation from Klah and others, published sacred Navajo ceremonial knowledge, including fully illustrated sandpaintings. Klah assisted Wheelwright with making Navajo religion open to outsiders and part of a permanent record, a maneuver that some hataałii condemned and fought to reverse in the coming decades.[63]

In the interest of preserving Navajo culture, Klah collaborated with Wheelwright to establish a formal space for preserving Navajo art and ceremonial knowledge. After the American Association of Museums and a group of archaeologists voted to develop a new anthropological laboratory and public museum in Santa Fe, Wheelwright pitched them her idea to add a freestanding repository to house Navajo collections. In consultation with Wheelwright on the design, Klah suggested that a museum of Navajo religion must conform to Navajo traditions of being contained within a hogan, a traditional eight-sided one-room house that may serve as a place of spiritual importance. In particular, Klah contributed design elements for the area "opposite the front door and at the east end of the exhibitions hall on the ground level."[64] When the formal committee rejected the idea of a hogan, Wheelwright broke ties with them and found another way to bring to fruition Klah's vision of the museum. Wheelwright received a land donation near the Laboratory of Anthropology from her friend Amelia Elizabeth White and sold one of her homes to fund the venture.

In November 1937 Wheelwright presided over the opening of her collaborative museum devoted to the preservation of Navajo religion, art, and culture.[65] Absent from the inaugural proceedings was Klah, who had passed away from pneumonia a few months prior.[66] Nevertheless, the majority in attendance were Navajos and Klah's relatives. Hataałii Big Man performed a traditional Navajo house blessing over the site—a testament to Klah's stewardship in the establishment of the museum. Unlike many museum endeavors of the early twentieth century, which sought to justify colonialism and uphold the superiority of whites, Klah's partnership with Wheelwright enabled their knowledge to guide the process of designing a museum space in the traditional Navajo dwelling, the hogan. Wheelwright admitted that "without Klah neither Mrs. Newcomb nor I could have begun nor carried on our work."[67]

"A Place to Be"

An influx of gay men and women, particularly writers, to the art colonies in the 1920s ushered in a new queer culture in northern New Mexico. Anglo artists and writers sought out the area as a space for alternative gender and sexual possibilities. One of the earliest gay male artists to migrate to northern New Mexico was Marsden Hartley, a well-known modernist in the New York arts community, who moved to Taos in June 1918. Hartley migrated frequently throughout his life, moving almost every year, on a quest for artistic inspiration and queer belonging. His constant mobility was in part a response to a world that marginalized him as a semi-open gay man.[68] In a letter to his friend and mentor Alfred Stieglitz, Hartley confided, "I want so earnestly a 'place to be.'"[69] No single place shaped Hartley. He merged queer and artistic elements from drag balls in Paris, sexology in Berlin, and Pueblo dances in New Mexico to form his queer identity and artistic representations. Even though his stint in New Mexico was only eighteen months, the landscape and its people had a profound impact on his art. Ultimately, New Mexico failed to be Hartley's queer salvation. He arrived too early to benefit from the burgeoning queer subculture that would transpire in the middle of the writer's era (1916–41).[70] Still, his narrative illustrates the

Artist Marsden Hartley searching for "a place to be." This was "his first trip abroad" in 1912. Unknown photographer. Yale Collection of American Literature, Beinecke Rare Book and Manuscript Library.

embodied and affective dimensions of queer geographic mobility and how he searched for a place conducive to homoerotic love and art.

Looking to gain greater exposure to modern art and locate spaces of homosexual expression, Hartley first turned to Europe. Going to Paris in the spring of 1912, Hartley socialized at the Quartres Arts Ball, Gertrude Stein's salons, and in the bohemian cafes of Montparnasse, where he met Karl von Freyburg, an officer in the German army, a man he grew to love.[71] He followed von Freyburg to Berlin in early 1913, although the extent to which von Freyburg returned Hartley's feelings is unknown. Shortly after Hartley arrived, impending war darkened Berlin's bohemian environment and sent von Freyburg away to serve in the fourth regiment of the Kaiser

Guards. In a letter dated October 23, 1914, Hartley informed his art dealer and confidant, Alfred Stieglitz, of von Freyburg's death in battle, admitting "the acute pain of this experience" because of their "intense" friendship.[72] Although Hartley confessed his agony to Stieglitz, he was unable to fully mourn the loss of von Freyburg, which was complicated by homoerotic feelings and American anti-German sentiment. To process his grief, he painted a memorial to his love. Art historians and scholars have suggested that *Portrait of a German Officer* indirectly referenced Hartley's affection for von Freyburg.[73]

Hartley, who along with hundreds of American artists fled Europe during World War I, found his reacclimation to the East Coast difficult. After the war, a coterie of artists reassessed their relationship to modernity and to New York City in particular. They turned instead to the natural world for personal and artistic inspiration. Seeking an antidote to the malaise of modern life, some found solace in the rural countryside of the eastern United States, including the seaside art colony of Provincetown, Massachusetts, and the farming community of Croton-on-Hudson, New York. Hartley lived in both places as well as in Bermuda between 1915 and 1918.[74] But each sojourn left him depressed and disenchanted. Hartley lamented, "There is something deadly in the east, there is something sapping the vitality of one in all this lethargy of the soul that settles down on one here."[75]

Still searching for queer belonging and a private space to grieve von Freyburg, his friend Mabel Dodge, a writer and patron of the arts, suggested he try Taos, New Mexico. Hartley knew Dodge from having frequented her weekly salon in Greenwich Village, New York, where between 1913 and 1916 some, including Dodge herself, challenged sexual conformity and experimented with erotic same-sex relationships.[76] Like Hartley, Dodge and some of her salon participants looked to replicate bohemianism and contemplate sexual possibilities in natural settings. At the pastoral enclave of Croton-on-Hudson, Dodge met her third husband, a sculptor named Maurice Sterne, who eventually led her to Taos. By June 1918, she determined to transform the small mountain town, which already possessed an art colony, into a bohemian art destination. She settled in and purchased twelve acres of land that adjoined Pueblo territory.[77] Dodge cultivated a richly creative community of famous artists and writers who made pilgrimages to visit her. Hartley was one of the first among them.

Arriving before a queer culture cohered, Hartley found a space to contemplate sexuality through Pueblo dances. By the early twentieth century, an elite group of Anglo boosters capitalized on the commercial potential of promoting Indigenous dances as part of the state's tourism economy. Such ceremonies became a centerpiece of New Mexico tourism.[78] At the same time, missionaries and government agents condemned the "horribly immoral" dances, arguing they impeded assimilation efforts. Missionaries organized a campaign to eradicate the alleged immoralities in the dances of the Hopi Tribe in Arizona and among members of the Pueblos in New Mexico.[79] A cohort of new art colonists seized the opportunity to defy Victorian sexual ethics and defend the "natural" sexual expression in Pueblo ceremonies. The Pueblo dance controversy, as it came to be known, was an arena of sexual contestation for white residents of the state.

While the reasons for performing dances vary among the nineteen Pueblos of New Mexico, collectively dances represent a necessary religious component of community life. As specified by anthropologist Alfonso Ortiz (Ohkay Owingeh Pueblo), Pueblo ceremonies "mobilize a community's moods and motivations and reflect their collective identity" of adaptability and cultural tenacity.[80] Pueblo Indians, like Navajos, lived in their homeland and retained their ancient ways but encountered threats of assimilation from a network of paternalistic government agents and missionaries. After New Mexico achieved statehood in 1912, reformers ushered in a period of increased government control over the land, water, and lives of the Pueblo people.[81]

Hartley attended a number of Pueblo dances in July 1918. He then painted a series and authored several essays on Pueblo ceremonial dance, both of which were widely circulated and warmly received.[82] His works primarily emphasized an appreciation of Pueblo dance as a form of artistry. However, some of Hartley's descriptions of dances centered on a visual spectacle of sensuality. In a 1922 article he wrote, "All primitive peoples believe in and indulge the sensuous aspects of their religions. They provide for the delight of their bodies in the imagined needs of the soul." Hartley then contrasts Pueblo Indians' embrace of "sensuous frankness" with "Christian prudery." In a poem about the so-called Corn Dance at the Pueblo of Kewa, which he explained as celebrating fertility and the growth of corn, Hartley continued to link bodies and pleasure: "The young red blood is dripping from the flanks of laughing red bodies aching with the sensuousness of the passing pagan hour."[83] Hartley admired Indigenous male bodies, "naked but for the breech-cloth," via sexually charged language—"dripping," "aching," and "sensuous." Poet and art colony member Spud Johnson similarly fetishized dancers' bodies in his private journal: "watched a feather dance at the Pueblo. . . . One particularly, whose legs & chest & back & arms was painted yellow-green caught my attention. He was of that short, stocky build which is so attractive to me. I watched him & watched him. The green-yellow loin-cloth clinging and flapping as he danced, almost revealing his buttocks—promising even to blow up or be bounced by his dance-steps to reveal his very penis!"[84] Gay men imagined Pueblo dances as a realm for fantasizing about cross-racial sexual liaisons and reformulating constructs of sexuality. Scholars have pointed out sexualized depictions by white women, but gay men participated as well.[85]

Stirrings of concern over Pueblo dances surfaced in 1915 and culminated in an organized campaign to curtail their practice by the 1920s. Both Mabel Dodge and writer Mary Austin contested the proposed restrictions and argued that Pueblo dances should be interpreted unencumbered by "our [white] particular taboos." Neither classified the ceremonies as promiscuous. Likewise, Alice Corbin Henderson interpreted the Kewa Pueblo Corn Dance as "a beautifully archaic, conventionalized symbol of fertility," and feminist anthropologist Elsie Clews Parsons referenced the sexual intimacy of Pueblo dances.[86] Historian Margaret Jacobs has argued that white women took a significant interest in the controversy and advanced a "sexually relativist" position. Collectively, white feminists called for the appreciation of Pueblo Indians' different sexual standards, including greater frequency of premarital sex, adultery, and divorce; open discussions of sexuality; fluid gender categories; and Pueblo women's sexual agency.[87] White Americans tended to associate sexual divergence from Victorian sexual norms with populations of color. They cast Native peoples as a counterpoint through which to make visible the appearance of sexual variation, which made it problematic for Indigenous peoples with sexual and gender variation to enact and embody such differences. White women and gay men's sexual objectification of Native men likely impeded variant sexual and gender expression for nonwhite LGBTQ+ and two-spirit people.

There is no easy categorization of the Pueblo perspective on the dance controversy. Pueblo women were absent from the discussion because, typ-ically, Pueblo men were initiated and trained to perform their religious ceremonies, while women and children had access to ceremonial knowledge as participants.[88] Pueblo men split over the issue. Some, such as Joe Lujan (Taos Pueblo), who was educated in government schools, sided with moral reformers. Lujan argued that the dances "interfere with the progress of the children," although he informed moral reformers that he did not "know of any immorality connected with them."[89] Others, most notably members of the pan-Pueblo political group the All Indian Pueblo Council, defended dancing as part of religious freedom, denouncing the prohibition of their dances as "religious persecution."[90] They rejected the sexually relativist view that their culture had a healthy and natural sexual standard. Instead, as Martin Vigil (Tesuque Pueblo) articulated, "our dances are not wicked." No matter which side they took, all Pueblo men involved in the debate decoupled dances from Pueblo sexual norms. In contrast, white feminists equated Pueblo sexual norms with their religious ceremonies.[91]

Pueblo society did have different sexual standards, but they had become unstable after decades of settler colonialism. A mere two years after the dance controversy, social scientist Sophie D. Aberle ventured to Ohkay Owingeh Pueblo to study sexuality and reproductive health among the In-digenous inhabitants.[92] She observed no stigma against premarital sex, but when she inquired about the intimate lives of the Pueblo Indians and asked them questions about "sexual techniques," "perverse behavior," and "guilt feelings associated with masturbation," members of the Pueblo responded with utter silence, avoidance, and resistance. Aberle concluded that Pueblo Indians did not wish to talk about sex.[93] Pueblo Indians learned to keep sexual matters private and outside the purview of whites.[94] Additionally, some began to adopt strict Christianized sexual norms.

For white bohemians, Pueblo dances provided an avenue for public dis-course on sexuality in the state. Even though the sexual discourse faded by 1927, the controversy demonstrates how whites publicly adopted a specific racial logic that intertwined race and sexuality, simultaneously pathologiz-ing and celebrating Native sexuality. As art colonists perpetuated notions of Pueblo sexuality to empower their own sexual inclinations without con-sideration of the consequences for Pueblo Indians, Pueblos retreated to a culture of silence, refusing to speak to outsiders about sexual customs.

"Going Santa Fe"

Word spread that within the art circles of New Mexico queerness and creativity fit together. Gay men and women recounted tales of finding a place to be themselves, writing about a variety of emotional, affective, and sexual attachments and linking them with creative expectations that stemmed from being in high desert outposts. The writers' era of the art colonies established its initial queer outlets in private groups and events, such as the writing club The Rabble, then shifted to an array of public spaces centered in and around the Santa Fe Plaza. New Mexican writers have left a trail of their perceptions of homoerotic desire through poetic, fictionalized, and often autobiographical descriptions that contributed to the development of queer identities in twentieth-century America. Nationwide, a new generation of modernists challenged normative sexual values through music, theater, literature, film, visual arts, and other cultural venues that began to reshape sexual standards.[95]

In 1922 Harold Witter "Hal" Bynner and Walter Willard "Spud" Johnson arrived in Santa Fe as partners. Bynner, a professor of poetry, and Johnson, a student of poetry, had met at the University of California at Berkeley a few years earlier. Bynner took an interest in the aspiring young writer and introduced Johnson to the larger world of bohemianism beyond campus. The two men eventually became "lovers and friends, but also father and son, teacher and student."[96] In January 1922 Bynner, who traveled and lectured around the country and abroad on poetry and the rights of women and minorities, began a lecture tour that took him through the Southwest. Bynner's biographer describes his incessant travel as seeming "as if these trips had become a search for a place he could remain."[97] When he arrived in Santa Fe on February 22, Bynner canceled the rest of his speaking engagements due to a respiratory infection and physical exhaustion. At the invitation of his friend Alice Corbin Henderson, who had migrated to Santa Fe from Chicago in 1916, he stayed in Santa Fe to recuperate.[98] After a few weeks, Bynner decided to move from San Francisco to Santa Fe. Johnson followed him. Although the couple separated by 1926, both remained in New Mexico for the rest of their lives. The permanent settlement of openly queer households inculcated the area's standing as a queer refuge and creative center.

Another queer migrant was playwright and poet Rollie Lynn Riggs. Born in Indian Country in 1899, he was an enrolled member of the Cherokee Nation. Riggs suffered a breakdown at the University of Oklahoma after he privately admitted his homosexual nature.[99] Where might a queer, mixed-race Cherokee go to recover? Bynner, who knew Riggs through his visiting lectureship at the University of Oklahoma, assured him he would be safe in Santa Fe. Riggs moved there in the fall of 1923 and wrote Bynner on December 3: "Feeling much better, thanks to you. Only it will take several decades to overcome wrong habits of thought, won't it? . . . Hal, you saved my life, you know."[100] The restorative experience as well as being in the company of literary residents and celebrated visiting writers such as Willa Cather and D. H. Lawrence inspired Riggs to devote his life to writing plays, the literary genre that brought him national acclaim (Riggs is best known for writing *Green Grow the Lilacs*, which became the musical *Oklahoma!*). The Southwest also offered Riggs a safe space to delve into his homosexual feelings.

In the early 1920s Marian Winnek, a graduate of Radcliffe College, followed the advice of her friend Connie to write her first novel in Santa Fe. Winnek recalled that she "went there [Santa Fe] intending to stay a year and stayed thirteen." Stimulated by a network of creative lesbians, she purchased an adobe home on Canyon Road. She envisioned crafting an autobiographical trilogy of novels beginning with her first, *Juniper Hill*.[101] The first book focused on her childhood summers spent at Coldspring Farm in Westford, Massachusetts. The sequel, never published, continued the narrative of Marguerite (Marian) into young adulthood, as she works in a theater and falls in love with her drama professor, a woman. The lovers "decide to sacrifice a future together for the sake of those who would be hurt" by their relationship. Winnek, nurtured by a cohort of lesbians, felt emboldened to write her truth, describing her novels as "art as subliminal sex."[102]

Jewish American writer Myron Brinig shared a similar experience when he visited New Mexico in 1922 and permanently settled in Taos in 1939. Brinig began a love affair with modernist painter Cady Wells. During this time, he drafted his only two published works, out of twenty-one novels, that include homosexual characters.[103] Farrar and Rinehart published *Singermann* in 1929, and Brinig continued this narrative in *This Man Is My Brother*, published a decade later. Both follow the story of Moses Singermann, his wife, Rebecca, and their six children, including an openly gay brother named Harry. Brinig created one of the earliest positive representations of a homosexual character in Harry Singermann. Although Singermann accidentally drowns while trying to express homoerotic feelings for another man, his final thoughts focused on love—what is wrong at revealing one's love for a person of the same sex?[104] In writing these words, Brinig placed a desire for love at the center of a gay man's life.

Queer mobility to the art colonies forged sexual creative endeavors. Writers, then, looked to establish additional avenues to delve deeper into expressing erotic identities. The strongest example is The Rabble, a group of poets including Alice Henderson Corbin, Witter Bynner, Haniel Long, Spud Johnson, and Lynn Riggs, that met weekly at Corbin's home in the early 1920s. Johnson described the workshop "as a stimulus to make us write when we might otherwise have fallen into the good old *mañana* spirit."[105] Group members inspired and critiqued each other's poetry, socialized together at dinner, read poetry aloud, and even played a sonnet-writing game. Member Haniel Long recalled that the group "shared more than the artistic life" when they gathered. The Rabble fostered individuality, offering an arena "where people are valued for what they are." Riggs credited the group as a forum for him to discover who he was.[106] Riggs, Bynner, Long, and Johnson all identified as gay men, and while it is difficult to ascertain how often the group wrestled with questions of desire during Rabble workshops, the cohort offered a space in which to be openly gay.

Material Johnson workshopped indicates that club members engaged with issues of queer identity. He introduced drafts of personal poetry with queer themes that he eventually published in a volume entitled *Horizontal Yellow* in 1935. The collection of fifty-six poems includes a final section called "Adobe House," which are among his most personal pieces of writing. In the last poem, "When I Am Left," Johnson tackles the theme of loneliness:

When I am left standing in an empty house,
All the forgotten days of my life
That have been stark with loneliness
Come and pass over me.[107]

Member of The Rabble, Rollie Lynn Riggs (Cherokee
Nation). Unknown photographer. Photograph courtesy
of the Claremore Museum of History.

Johnson's split with Bynner and a series of fleeting sexual encounters
often left him feeling isolated. He found some sexual gratification, but locating a relationship more substantial proved elusive. In his private journal,
Johnson repeatedly expressed a desire for both frequent sexual partners
and long-term and permanent relationships.[108] He voiced these sentiments
publicly by publishing subtle queer poetry. Johnson's homoerotic themes
likely passed undetected by straight audiences.

His poems still show the power of such musings in reaching other queer
people well beyond New Mexico. The Writers' Edition, a cooperative publishing venture, printed four hundred copies of *Horizontal Yellow*. Johnson
kept a list of names and places of those who purchased his volume. According to his records, *Horizontal Yellow* reached people in three countries,

twenty-three states, and the District of Columbia.[109] After publication, Johnson received a letter from Harold W. Hawk, whom he did not know and who does not appear in his records: "I've just read *Horizontal Yellow*. It's one of the too few things in words to come out of Taos which speak to my heart in accents of simple and unaffected beauty, and I thought I should tell you so. Why, I don't know—except in the secret fantasies of my own soul I, too, have known the loneliness you evoke with such tender grace in your verse."[110] Johnson's gay sensibility was camouflaged, but a man with presumably similar sentiments recognized himself in Johnson's work. Such poetry generated a hidden forum for sharing queer thoughts, fears, and hopes. It also put Taos on the map as a space conducive for authoring such works, if not for alleviating loneliness.

Both Johnson and his ex-partner, Bynner, in reaction to the isolation they felt, fought against locking away their sexual essence. They attempted to speak about it, and their queer cultural productions played an active role in building queer solidarity among a larger cohort of queer creatives. Bynner, a major figure in the modern American poetry movement, published his only poetic musing about same-sex love in 1931.[111] In *Eden Tree*, inspired by his most recent ex-lover, Clifford "Don" McCarthy, and dedicated to a budding new romance with Robert Nicholas Montague Hunt, Bynner publicly declared his homosexuality, a rare and brave act. Most queer writers in the 1920s and 1930s avoided direct public declaration of their sexuality.[112] Despite the promise of a new love in Bynner's life, the poem is bittersweet. It discloses homoerotic love and describes its consequence—alienation and isolation. His biographer, James Kraft, argues, "Bynner's deep sense of being separate from others and unable to relate to people is at the center of the poem's vision, and being homosexual reinforces this isolation." Most gay literature of the early twentieth century was negative in depicting homosexuality, and Bynner's work is reflective of this larger trend. *Eden Tree* ends with the fate of men who love men: "It is the seal / Of double solitude."[113]

When overt homoerotic writings left the bubble of queer circles, reaching critics and national audiences, writers often faced condemnation for sexual themes. Bynner's openly homosexual poem met with harsh criticism, leading to his own self-censorship in the national literary community. Before *Eden Tree*, Bynner's work had been widely reviewed and well received, but after his relocation to New Mexico, the positive reception of his poetry declined.[114] Tellingly, his reputation within the national literary community receded after his publication of *Eden Tree*. He had marked himself as a homosexual poet. Take, for example, Louis Untermeyer's review of the poem. Untermeyer compared Bynner's *Eden Tree* to Bynner's older autobiographical poetry entitled *The New World*. In the latter, Untermeyer argued, Bynner's "approach was direct; the tone ingratiating if reminiscent; the method simple and straightforward," but in "'Eden Tree' all is changed. The approach is by way of fantasy running, at times to phantasmagoria; the tone troubled with self-contradictions; the method is confused and confusing." Untermeyer concluded, "The semi-realistic narrative is personal rather than universal. It is not, in the words of the jacket, 'a philosophy of life at fifty,' but a confession."[115] Reviews like this one, and an otherwise decided lack of reviews, suggest that many editors were uncomfortable with Bynner's homosexual admission. Afterward, some critics chose to ignore Bynner's work.

However, in the city of Santa Fe, Bynner was a fixture in literary circles, civic and cultural life, and queer society. He was active in Santa Fe's first community theater.[116] He formed the Spanish-Indian Trading Company, whose collection of American Indian jewelry composed "the nucleus of exhibits at the Museum of New Mexico." For many years, he led the Santa Fe Fiesta parade. He embraced the cultural scene of the city. As an out gay man, with a "commanding stature, splendid good looks, and infectious energy," he refined his own sense of style, which he often wore around town.[117] He sometimes dressed in a dark blue, Navajo blouse, cut by a large turquoise-and-silver belt worn with undulating, white wide-leg pants. Johnson claimed that Bynner popularized the Navajo blouse trend (a cultural appropriation from Navajo culture) in the 1920s for "both sexes" but particularly for men. Other times, he preferred flowing embroidered Chinese robes accompanied by "a cloud of plum-blossom incense," and a cigarette smoked from a long holder.[118] Bynner, who took his first trip to China in 1917, collected Chinese art and artifacts and incorporated his admiration of Chinese aesthetics into his own personal style. By appearing in public in stunning attire, he helped to normalize alternative gender sensibilities in the city.[119]

Bynner was most known for his legendary and unruly parties. Bynner and his partner, Robert Hunt, offered a space for convivial gay socialization in their queer household. Bynner purchased a modest three-room adobe home located on the southwest corner of East Buena Vista Street and Old Santa Fe Trail in June of 1922. He enhanced his space through the purchase of two additional adjacent properties. With the assistance of Hunt, the son of a famous architect, they designed, over several decades, a rambling two-story structure with more than thirty rooms. Here, Bynner entertained his guests with bawdy piano songs and furnished lavish food and beverage spreads. Mary Austin recalled that some of Bynner's events "were more respectable," while others contained an "assortment" of individuals and "drinking." Historian Lois Rudnick interprets this distinction as Bynner throwing some mixed parties—straights and gays—while others were just for queer people. The private gay politician Bronson Cutting only attended Bynner's respectable parties. And yet, at one such party, Cutting stole Bynner's boyfriend, Clifford McCarthy.[120] Bynner soon after met Robert Hunt, who was visiting Santa Fe from California and, like Riggs, was recuperating from a mental breakdown. Hunt stayed in Santa Fe with Bynner the rest of his life.

While at times gay men and lesbians socialized separately from heterosexuals, over time their socialization became integrated. Lesbians and gay men became part of the cultural fabric of New Mexico; in Santa Fe, gays and straights, locals and tourists used the Santa Fe Plaza, a commercial, social, and political center of the city, much like plazas common throughout traditional Spanish American towns.[121] Lesbians and gay men dined and drank at La Fonda, browsed for books, socialized at Villagrá Book Shop, and cut loose in gender-bending costumes during Fiesta.

La Fonda (The Inn), owned by the Santa Fe Railway and developed as a Fred Harvey tourist hotel, became a popular gathering place and exhibition space for artists in the 1920s and 1930s, but it equally acted as a social spot for non-artists and in these decades served tourists and locals alike. Built on the southeast corner of Santa Fe's Plaza in 1922, the five-story adobe hotel looked down San Francisco Street toward St. Francis Cathedral and featured a heavily patronized bar and restaurant. La Fonda was built to both increase tourism and serve as a social hub for the community.[122] "The New Mexican Room at La Fonda was where everybody lunched," Santa Fe resident Calla Hay recalled. Amalia Sena Sanchez concurred: "We went there all the time, because that was the center of activities, where everybody

Lifelong partners Witter Bynner and Robert Hunt lived openly together as a married couple in Santa Fe. Photograph courtesy of Palace of the Governors Photo Archives (NMHM/DCA), 099906.

would meet. There was no other place to meet but La Fonda." Chuck Barrows remembered the La Fonda lobby as "the center of town."[123] Gay men and lesbians frequented La Fonda just as often. Hay recollected, "Through the years, the men who were homosexual in no way flaunted it or made a public show. But there was a large group of lesbians who seemed to want everybody to look at them. They just went around together. Some of them were very nice. They lunched at La Fonda, the same table every day. In mannish clothes and the big hats." Marian Winnek rode horseback each day to lunch at La Fonda with her circle of big-hatted lesbian friends. Many Santa Fe lesbians favored masculine attire, including "dungarees, chaps, flannel shirts, bandanas, dusters, and Tom Mix-style cowboy hats," as a means of attracting other lesbians and revealing their lesbianism.[124] Locals noticed.

As Hay's comment reveals, Nuevomexicanos rejected open displays of same-sex desires. Nuevomexicanos operated under what I call a "culture of privacy," similar to what Pueblo Indians developed after the dance controversy. Reticence provided a cover for exploring sexual activity outside the bounds of normative sex. The culture of silence entailed an arranged system of privacy toward sexual identity and behavior as long as individuals maintained discretion in public places. Amalia Sena Sanchez affirms that Nuevomexicanos kept sexual matters private. Sanchez, born in 1892 in Santa Fe, recalled, "If a girl got pregnant before she was married, they [her family] were so very, very secretive." Similarly, Nancy Campbell, who grew up in rural areas of northern New Mexico, recollected of the 1930s that sex "was hardly talked about." Andreita Padilla from Los Padillas remembers reticence on sexual topics and strict monitoring of her sexual behavior. Another oral history from Carol Lee Sanchez, the older sister of Paula Gunn Allen, cautions that open lesbianism or same-sex expression would have been heavily censured by her community.[125] Locals generally supported the art colonists but drew the line at queer public expression. Even gender-ambiguous attire raised eyebrows at La Fonda. While La Fonda, as a shared communal space, indicates that straights and gays interacted and often crossed paths in their daily lives, displays of same-sex desires had boundaries.

However, white lesbians in Santa Fe sported masculine outfits.[126] Two different groups of lesbians, who mingled with each other, and straight women who preferred to build women-centered lives distinguished themselves with their clothing. A longtime lesbian resident recalled that the wealthier group "were early ranch-style ladies." They wore "ranch-type clothes," which drew little attention.[127] Santa Fe artist Dorothy "Betty" Stewart, who grew up on a cattle ranch near Logan, New Mexico, frequently wore a cowboy hat and tie. Gay and straight women, in their everyday style and on special occasions, defied gender fashion conventions by cutting their hair short and wearing masculine attire. The bohemian group was more daring in dress. At costume parties, Agnes Sims was known for sexually exciting women when she donned her Abraham Lincoln outfit, including a beard and stovepipe hat. Lesbians exhibited a queer sensibility through gender-ambiguous and cross-gender apparel.[128]

More complicated questions about cross-gender dress and intersections of racial attitudes arise through the exploration of Santa Fe Fiesta. Fiesta, an annual public event in the plaza that commemorates the Spanish conquest of the city from Pueblo control in 1692, began in 1919.[129] Edgar L. Hewett, director of the School of American Research, and his staff crafted a romanticized portrayal of the state's cultural heritage and history for commercial gain.[130] As the Fiesta evolved, the artists and writers who had recently arrived in the city added their own ideas to Fiesta celebrations. For instance, Bynner and Dolly Sloan, wife of Santa Fe artist John Sloan, organized a program of free Fiesta events called Pasatiempo in 1924. Bynner's and Sloan's Pasatiempo is remembered as "a revolutionary protest fiesta" including concerts, singing, dancing, and a children's animal show—all free events. In response to Hewett's decision to charge attendees a fee for certain aspects of Fiesta, Sloan and Bynner challenged the commercialization of the "traditional" Fiesta because it excluded the participation of many Santa Fe residents. Art historian Joseph Traugott explains, "Charging for events gave the impression that the Fiesta was being organized for tourists, not locals, and contradicted the egalitarian spirit of inclusion that had attracted modernists artists to Santa Fe."[131]

When art colonists gained control of Fiesta in 1927, they contributed many of its enduring features. One of the most popular of the free events was a parody of the Santa Fe Fiesta called the Hysterical Pageant. This carnivalesque parade encouraged everyone to don costumes and mock cultural conventions. Here, we see the merging of Fiesta with queer sensibilities. Bohemians, who flouted norms, created an additional event that encouraged a reprieve from social judgment and cultivated an anything-goes attitude in a public arena. For years, Bynner and Sloan, because of their popular contributions to the celebration, led the Pasatiempo parade.[132]

Unlike the gay drag balls that flourished in the 1920s and 1930s in places such as New York City and Harlem, where gay men appropriated masquerade balls and created their own separate event, via Santa Fe's Fiesta gay people incorporated themselves into an existing celebration, transforming it into their own. Gay men and lesbians, as part of Santa Fe's community, added to the Fiesta events their own queer twist—irreverent humor and style—that encouraged cross-gender and cross-racial costuming.[133] Bynner dressed up as a "Chinese savant" and took advantage of an opportunity to wear feminine Chinese robes, an aesthetic staple of gay camp. But in becoming part of the community, white gay men and lesbians also embraced entrenched racial hierarchies. Many individuals actively engaged in notions of the racial other by wearing costumes across racial and ethnic lines. Cross-racial costuming, intended to subvert racial stereotypes, more often reproduced hierarchies of power. Fiesta is illuminating, then, for what it reveals about power. Queers held greater power during the Fiesta. They could embrace outlandish cross-gender personas in public without social disapprobation. But in wearing cross-racial costuming, they asserted white domination over racial others.

For many Nuevomexicanos, the Santa Fe Fiesta serves as a display of Nuevomexicano unity and of the "preservation of Hispanic culture."[134] The Fiesta, after all, privileges "Spanish" ancestry, and here Nuevomexicanos uphold a racial hierarchy over Indigenous people. The De Vargas Pageant (also known as the Entrada) is a case in point. The historical pageant enacts Spanish conquistadors' reclaiming Santa Fe from the Pueblo Indians. When the pageant portion of the Fiesta was revived, Pueblo Indians hesitated to participate in a play that emphasized the Spanish conquest over them, so organizers recruited whites to play the part of Pueblos engaging in battle and surrendering to the Spanish by kneeling in front of a cross, symbolizing their conversion to Catholicism.[135] Fiesta offered a time of year to celebrate alternative visions to American identity. Nuevomexicanos took pride in their distinctive elements of Spanish culture, as did art colonists, who showcased their way of life. During the Fiesta, queer bohemians claimed authority over their own identities in their new hometown. But in privileging bohemian visions and Nuevomexicano history, the Fiesta minimized Native cultures. In making Santa Fe queer, Anglo gay men and lesbians felt little need to hide their sexual orientations, but the city's queer history developed differently for other groups.

———

Queer narratives in this chapter are a succession of stories about making and unmaking spaces of queer belonging. Queer identities in the Southwest were negotiated again and again across multiple terrains—the Navajo Nation, Pueblo Nations, and the city of Santa Fe—and informed by experiences of mobility, (re)settlement, intercultural encounters, emotional ties, creative production, gender norms, sexualization, and racialization. In particular, I have highlighted the role geographic mobility played in queer cultural formation. Yet, importantly, not all queer people leave their birthplace or familial home to embrace a queer self. The vast majority of queer migration narratives fail to include Indigenous people, whose experiences draw attention to the ways a migration framing of following a queer subject from a community of origin to a city of sexual freedom privileges certain types of queer experiences. A return to their ancestral homeland validated Klah's group identity—Navajo—and their communal identity—nádleehí. Once home, Klah was socialized into a cultural upbringing that nurtured their nádleehí role. However, while Navajo peoples' return home initially helped to revitalize community and cultural traditions, that continuity was offset by persistent federal policies aimed at destroying traditional gender roles and sexuality, especially among children removed to boarding schools. By the mid-twentieth century within tribal communities in New Mexico, many members began to internalize and embrace binary-gender ideologies, which exacerbated issues of homophobia and misogyny on some reservations.[136] After Klah's generation, invisibility often enveloped those who possessed two-spirit traits. As a consequence, two-spirit individuals had no contemporary role models. Some worked to recover the long history of two-spirit people, who "lived, loved, and created art since time immemorial."[137] Klah's life and artwork serves as an early example of two-spirit creative resistance.

For queer, white newcomers who place-made in New Mexico, home was a destination. Socialized into heteropatriarchal families, they implemented movement away from birth homes to find desired sites of love, comfort, and belonging. They embraced the cultural distinctiveness of New Mexico, including the region's Indigenous inhabitants and the isolation of the locale, in building lives that flouted conventional gender and sexual sensibilities. Pueblo dances provided an initial site for cogitating on unrestrained sexual license. Queer writers generated a distinct southwestern queer culture through cultivating gender nonconformity and queer creative aspirations. As inheritors of settler colonialism, they used tribal land bases and customs as liberating forces and adapted Latino traditions of public plazas and community fiesta celebrations. Scholars, in understanding the history of southwestern art colonies, have debated whether Anglo artists were culpable in the exploitation and objectification of Native and Latino peoples and their cultures or if they worked to cultivate a national appreciation of American Indian and Nuevomexicano cultures in an effort to halt assimilationist policies. What is missing from these conversations is a consideration of queerness. Who has the ability to claim and practice cultural gender and sexual identities and express them within the context of their own worldview? In early twentieth-century New Mexico, those who could best voice gender and sexual alternatives were white gay men and women. The mobility of their queer bodies simultaneously engendered new sexual boundaries while undoing others.

———

TWO

Decency Debate

The Smoot-Hawley
Tariff Act, 1930

Throughout his literary career, Walter Willard "Spud" Johnson authored, edited, published, and collected a body of work on southwestern queer expression that began with the little magazine *Laughing Horse*. Johnson, along with James T. Van Rensselaer Jr. and Roy E. Chanslor, founded *Laughing Horse* in 1922, after meeting in an English class at the University of California, Berkeley. Johnson had recently picked up in a used bookshop a "charming little magazine called 'The Lark,' which a group of gay San Francisco Bohemians had published. . . . The spirit of this predecessor was our inspiration." A coterie of San Francisco Renaissance participants—Gelett Burgess, Ernest Peixotto, Bruce Porter, and Willis Polk—had cofounded *The Lark*, one of the earliest little magazines, in spring of 1895. Grounded in the ideals of "art, youth, and freedom," they filled the short-lived publication with nonsense verse, essays on esthetics, witty observations about social conventions, and a large number of illustrations.[1] Its youthful, lighthearted tone and critiques of the strictures attached to the practices of art and literature functioned as a model for the early issues of *Laughing Horse*.

Johnson, Rensselaer, and Chanslor created *Laughing Horse* as a "cheap, lewd, boorish, sensational" university publication that launched a bohemian assault on literature.[2] Because of their subversive content, the founders initially wrote under pen names—Jane Cavendish, Noel Jason, and Bill Murphy, respectively—but in their fourth issue revealed their true identi-

ties. *Laughing Horse*, as did other little magazines, battled against censorship forces.[3] The fledging publication gained notoriety for publishing an
"obscene" review of Ben Hecht's privately printed novel *Fantazius Mallare:
A Mysterious Oath* (1922). The novella itself was deemed obscene for its
exploration of madness, horror, and sexual ecstasy. Hecht, his publishers, Pascal Covici and W. F. McGee, and his illustrator, Wallace Smith,
were arrested, convicted, and fined one thousand dollars for its distribution.[4] Johnson, who had dropped out of college to live in New Mexico, had
solicited a review of *Fantazius Mallare* from the well-known author D. H.
Lawrence. The two men developed a friendship during Lawrence's stay in
the state from 1922 to 1923.[5]

Lawrence wrote a blistering review, in the form of a letter, peppering
it with explicit sexual language. The *Laughing Horse* editors, aware of the
consequences of publishing Lawrence's offending words, replaced them
with long dashes and explained: "We were advised at the last moment to
leave out words in this letter which might be considered objectionable. We
hope that this censorship will in no way destroy the sense of the text."[6]
The cheeky censored version had little effect on toning down Lawrence's
wording: "The word *penis* or *testicle* or *vagina* doesn't shock me. Why should
it? Surely, I am enough of a man to think of my own *organs* with calm, even
with indifference."[7] Despite *Fantazius Mallare*'s provocative content, Lawrence communicated that the novella "didn't thrill" him; he found it "crass"
and "strained." Because the publication was distributed on campus, the
University of California administration perceived the review as a violation
of state obscenity law, which harmed "the University" and "the ideals which
it represents."[8] They charged *Laughing Horse* with printing obscene material,
took the publication to court, and pursued administrative measures against
the editors. The court dismissed the obscenity charge, but the Undergraduate Student Affairs Committee found Roy Chanslor, the only editor still
registered at the university, guilty and recommended expulsion. President
David P. Barrows carried out the expulsion in December of 1922.[9]

The scandal elevated *Laughing Horse*'s appeal, but after the incident, the
three former students drifted apart. Johnson pondered continuing the endeavor alone.[10] He corresponded with his friend and author Mary Austin,
who encouraged him to keep going: "I do think there is a chance for a
[little] magazine in the Southwest."[11] He agreed, relocating its publishing

headquarters to Santa Fe and adding a regional focus. Johnson, now the sole editor, endured a second attack from censorship authorities, one that would spark a national debate on the censorship clause of the Tariff Act of 1930, dubbed "the decency debate" by *Time Magazine*.[12]

In 1929, while traveling, Johnson purchased several copies of salacious literature authored by D. H. Lawrence, which US Customs confiscated in Saint Louis, Missouri, charging Johnson with obscenity. When he returned home, Johnson wrote to his friend Bronson Cutting, a New Mexico senator, to ask for assistance with fighting his personal obscenity charges and changing the importation law. The two knew each other from fraternizing in the same circles, particularly at private parties held by Witter Bynner that offered a space for gay socialization. Cutting remained private about his gay identity his entire life, but his homosexuality is evidenced in his fight against censorship and personal correspondence, which includes tender and loving letters to two long-term male partners.[13] Although involved in politics and news media—Cutting owned and ran a daily newspaper the *Santa Fe New Mexican*—he preferred to spend his free time with artists and writers or alone in his private library reading and writing. His personal library contained close to a thousand volumes, including a robust collection of classic literature and erotica purchased abroad and brought through the Customs Bureau.[14] At Johnson's urging, and due to his own private gay identity, Cutting initiated a campaign against the long-established censorship powers of the US Customs Bureau by opposing section 305 of the Tariff Act of 1930, commonly known as the Smoot-Hawley Tariff Act. At the US federal level, two apparatuses regulated obscenity: the US Customs Service Bureau under the Tariff Act of 1842 and the post office under the Comstock Act of 1873. The primary motivation for the new tariff bill was economic, but like previous ones, it included a section devoted to restrictions on the importation of obscene materials. The federal government spent eighteen months debating the Smoot-Hawley Tariff Act, marking, according to historian Margaret A. Blanchard, the "first time that either house of Congress had ever discussed the ramifications of censorship at length."[15]

Johnson, who generated interest in federal censorship regulations through a special issue of *Laughing Horse*, and Senator Cutting, who worked at the congressional level, both prompted a larger national debate on expanding the right to import and access various erotic literatures. They argued that the right to privacy should extend to intimate personal decisions, in this case the freedom to access and consume obscenity. In so doing, they validated notions of sexual privacy.[16] These early arguments later developed into a sexual civil liberties agenda and bridged the so-called first sexual revolution of the 1910s and 1920s to the second in the 1960s and 1970s, a period that altogether might be better understood as a long sexual revolution.[17] Johnson, Cutting, and other gay people who rallied behind them had a personal stake in accessing banned books, and their defense of obscene literature enhanced the circulation of works that validated queer and gender-variant people's existence.

For queer people like Johnson and Cutting, the cultural capital of literacy and the means to obtain sexological texts, pictorial erotica, and classic homoerotic literature offered a path to self-identify, foster solidarity, and experience a degree of sexual liberation.[18] Seldom in these bodies of work were queer people of color depicted. Obscene literature disproportionally reflected and influenced the experience of white, middle-class, and well-educated gay men and lesbians. Defending the dissemination of obscene literature that depicted and reflected its audience had a negligible impact on helping queers of color form community.[19]

Through the cultural censorship of queer people of color's gender and sexual expressions and the legal censorship of primarily Eurocentric sexual obscenity texts, this chapter documents the historical attempt to suppress and silence homoeroticism and in turn, the insistence of queer people to prevail over censorship. Cultural censorship further limited queer representation. In authoring creative works, queer people often self-censored keeping same-gender sexual themes hidden. This was especially true for queer people of color, who encountered several informal mechanisms of cultural censorship. Queer writers of color felt pressure to shape writings for a white readership and shouldered the burden of correcting notions of racial inferiority, which took precedence over exploring other identity aspects. Therefore, discussions of homoerotic sexuality seem largely absent from queer authors of color in the 1920s and 1930s literature. For example, while African American writers during the Harlem Renaissance produced some sexually candid works, most of this writing focused on a heterosexual perspective, with a few notable exceptions.[20]

Richard Bruce Nugent published "Smoke, Lilies and Jade," a forthright, uncoded homoerotic short story in the little magazine *Fire!* in 1926.[21] A group of younger African American artists conceived of *Fire!* earlier that year as a manifesto of revolt against the censorship of controversial material for the sake of racial uplift. The first and only issue was not well received by Harlem Renaissance luminaries, who held to the notion that "one did not proclaim one's homoerotic sentiments in print." Nugent refused to conceal his sexual interest in men. He found sexual partners by moving within smaller circles "where same-sex erotic interest was pervasive but rarely acknowledged publicly."[22] Many of the major Harlem Renaissance figures—Wallace Thurman, Countee Cullen, Claude McKay, Alain Locke, and Langston Hughes among them—were behaviorally bisexual.[23] Though not a queer community per se, Harlem possessed a visible and historically documented queer presence, most notably through various music clubs and drag balls attended by interracial audiences.[24] Queer white men from the New Mexico art colonies and elsewhere, sought sexual stimulation in Harlem, aroused by the prospect of sexual contact with nonwhite bodies. Carl Van Vechten, a white patron of the Harlem Renaissance, often took white visitors to New York City on tours of Harlem. In 1924 Van Vechten escorted Witter Bynner and his then-lover, Spud Johnson, to Small's, one of Harlem's hotspots. Van Vechten shared Bynner and Johnson's erotic interest in other men.[25] Johnson returned to New York in 1934, staying with the writer Jean Toomer. Through him, Johnson met Harlem Renaissance participant Countee Cullen. Johnson recorded in his journal that he "made love" with Cullen.[26] Johnson's journal frequently mentions his desire for the bodies of nonwhite men, although, he seldom recorded sexual experiences with queer men of color. Harlem afforded Johnson the opportunity to do so; he made the city his sexual playground.

Harlem Renaissance participants themselves (with the notable exception of Nugent) found greater possibilities for sexual exploration in music and the public landscape of Harlem but felt constrained by cultural censorship in the literary scene.[27] Likewise, in the context of New Mexico's artistic and literary milieu, Nuevomexicano and Indigenous writers also encountered cultural censorship barriers. Nuevomexicano writers who published in the robust Spanish-language newspapers focused on fostering positive self-representations in hopes of bringing about their economic, social, and cultural betterment.[28] Literary themes of ethnic and racial identity and community belonging dominate. Occasionally, fictional characters transgress gender and sexual boundaries, but the narratives serve as cautionary tales to stay within proscribed social parameters of heteropatriarchy.[29] Moreover, gay and mixed-race Cherokee playwright Rollie Lynn Riggs found it too risky to openly write about indigeneity and his same-gender attractions during a period of extensive white-Indigenous cultural relations and continued erasure of two-spirit roles. However, a coded queer Indigenous presence exists in his play *The Cherokee Night* (1932), written during the decency debate, and his even earlier poem "The Arid Land," published in *Laughing Horse*.[30]

Johnson's Censorship Battle

Johnson joined an emerging transnational anticensorship coalition of writers and editors who opposed literary censorship. The rise of transnational anticensorship networks partially stemmed from tightened control over circulating obscene and seditious writing across national borders imposed both by Europe and the United States before and during World War I. In the United States, prewar modifications to the Tariff Act of 1842 added lewd books and pamphlets to the list of obscene materials banned from importation. Wartime legislation such as the Espionage Act of 1917 and Sedition Act of 1918 further suppressed radical and pacifist speech and publications.[31] In response, free speech groups such as PEN (Poets, Essayists, Novelists) International, formed in 1923, incited writers to protest stricter legal restrictions on the distribution of books and journals that had been suppressed for obscenity. An anticensorship coalition took shape—a small transnational contingent of Europeans and Americans who advocated broadly for their authorial rights and specifically to lift restrictions on sexual speech.[32]

"Little magazines" became an important platform for publishing censorable material and decrying censorious culture. The early 1910s witnessed a critical mass of little magazines. These largely noncommercial periodicals were known for their "little" (small) readership, experimental nature, radical cultural revaluation, and artistic innovation.[33] They helped to proliferate bohemian culture and modernism in different regions of the world. Many concentrated on debates about cultural politics. Some, such as *The Seven Arts*, addressed censorship as a theme, while the *Little Review* incorporated content that embraced a growing sexual discourse.[34]

Lesbian writer Margaret Anderson founded one of the most well-known little magazines, the *Little Review* (1914–29), in Chicago. For a time, Anderson coedited the *Little Review* with her romantic partner, Jane Heap. She also published her own sex-positive works, including a defense of homosexuality, and featured other lesbian writers as contributors to the *Little Review*.[35] The sexually vocal periodical faced censorship on more than one occasion. When the *Little Review* serialized the publication of James Joyce's *Ulysses*, the US Post Office seized and burned multiple issues before charging Anderson and Heap with violating obscenity laws. In 1921 Anderson and Heap were convicted and fined. Undaunted, they continued to publish sexual content and spoke out against censorship.[36] Collectively, queer participants of little magazines and anticensorship agitators mounted a defense of sexual materials in the 1920s that helped frame fights for the cause of sexual civil liberties in the coming decades.

The rise of little magazines also coincided with an emerging sexual discourse in American society. Postwar sexual permissiveness in magazines, scientific studies, music, theater, and books pushed the erotic into the public realm. Lesbian and bisexual blues singers and musicians Bessie Smith, Gertrude "Ma" Rainey, Lucille Bogan, and Gladys Bentley referenced queer sexual practices and gender identities that were embraced by working-class African American communities in Harlem.[37] Sexological literature about "inversion" furnished information on nonnormative gender identities and sexual behaviors. A few authors vocalized same-gender relationships and attractions in poetry and fiction.[38] Censorship forces targeted the growing public discourse on sexuality by working to prohibit the flow of sexual information. But within the context of a new sexual era, some Americans rejected the ideal of sexual reticence. Such shifts encouraged anticensorship coalitions to embrace sexual speech as part of their defense of literary freedom.[39]

Laughing Horse joined the print culture of little magazines, and its seventeenth issue was a call to action against censorship. What started as a collegiate, satirical magazine evolved into a literary journal that characterized New Mexico as a site for creative experimentation. *Laughing Horse* helped to popularize the idea of New Mexico as an alternative environment through its critique of restrictive social conventions. It also served as a vehicle of expression for gay male authors and its editor. When Johnson's and Bynner's romantic relationship ended in 1923, Johnson refocused his attention to establishing a literary career. In addition to editing and publishing *Laughing Horse*, Johnson authored poetry, wrote articles for local papers, and worked as a freelancer for the *New Yorker* until 1927.[40] As a lesser-known writer with limited financial resources, he occasionally performed secretarial tasks for famous authors D. H. Lawrence, Mabel Dodge, and Mary Austin. He further supplemented his income by buying and selling books sometimes from a pushcart, other times from his home.[41]

Using his literary connections, Johnson developed a transnational audience for *Laughing Horse*. He claimed that it circulated within modernist networks in "Copenhagen, Guadalajara, Chicago, San Francisco, New York, Hollywood, Kansas City, Dallas, Boston and Alamogordo, to mention but a few of the cities where it is popular." This claim is validated by a log he kept of close to three hundred subscribers in the United States, Denmark, Mexico, and England.[42] The periodical had a fairly wide geographic reach within the States, with most subscribers hailing from California and New Mexico.

Laughing Horse's transnational bent extended to the magazine's content. It addressed the Southwest's Indigenous and Mexican heritages, even grappling with its variable geographic boundaries through its inclusion of Mexico as part of the Southwest. Issue 8 contained poetry about Mexico, an essay authored by Mexican president Álvaro Obregón (1920–24), a recipe for tepache (a fermented beverage made from the peel and rind of pineapples and sold by street vendors), and visual art contributions from New Mexico artists.[43] There are limits to the little magazine's recognition of diverse cultures, however. Despite the region's English-Spanish bilingualism, Johnson never learned Spanish, which limited his ability to fully engage with southwestern culture. Nuevomexicano and Indigenous voices rarely speak in the magazine. Instead, Anglo writers speak for them. Latino writers looked to Nuevomexicano-controlled, Spanish-language newspapers as the venue for their cultural and creative expression. Only a few Nuevomexicano writers, such as Isidoro Armijo, crossed over from the Spanish-language press to *Laughing Horse*.[44]

Laughing Horse is notable for its inclusion of queer male authors such as Witter Bynner, Haniel Long, Lynn Riggs, and Spud Johnson himself. Collectively, they emphasized the creativity of the Southwest and found in it the promise of modernist aesthetics, political radicalism, and erotic and social pleasures. Johnson's queer identity directly affected his editorial decisions and is particularly evident in the *Laughing Horse*'s political issue on national censorship, spurred by his obscenity charge. In 1929 Johnson purchased three copies of D. H. Lawrence's controversial novel *Lady Chatterley's Lover* for ten dollars from Florence, Italy; he likely intended to sell them.[45] Johnson had not yet read *Lady Chatterley's Lover* but was aware that it was known for sexually explicit passages, language, and an extramarital relationship between a man and a woman of different social classes. In *Lady Chatterley's Lover*, Lawrence devoted more pages to the act of sex, with greater detail and graphic language, than most books sold. Lawrence, a writer obsessed with the primacy of bodies and sex, had long been on the radar of censors in Britain and the United States. He chafed against Victorian notions of sexual morality and wrote in defense of *Lady Chatterley's Lover*: "I want men and women to be able to think sex, fully, completely, honestly and cleanly."[46]

Johnson had to get the copies of *Lady Chatterley's Lover* through the US Customs Service, which reviewed material entering the United States for obscenity drawing on a standard set by the 1868 English case *Regina V. Hicklin*.[47] Most censors, using the so-called Hicklin test, based their decisions on isolated passages in books that might "deprave and corrupt those whose minds are open to such immoral influences."[48] Customs inspectors thus held wide discretionary power in their determinations. They made conflicting decisions; a book banned at one point of entry might pass through at another. Inconsistences prompted authorities in Washington, DC, to call for efforts to regularize the customs process in tandem with the post office procedures, which operated under the Comstock Act. When customs agents seized and confiscated Johnson's books, the procedures had recently been standardized. In August of 1928, lawyers from both agencies had compiled a shared list of more than seven hundred books that would be prohibited from mailing *and* importation.[49] While the blocklist was kept secret, D. H. Lawrence's *Lady Chatterley's Lover* had clearly made

New Mexico Senator Bronson Cutting initiated a campaign
against the long-established censorship powers of the US Customs
Bureau. He succeeded in liberalizing American obscenity standards,
including expanding the right to import and access various erotic
literatures. Photograph courtesy of Palace of the Governors
Photo Archives (NMHM/DCA), HP.1992.21.030.

the list. Furious, Johnson vowed to fight the confiscation and destruction of his three copies of *Lady Chatterley's Lover*.

Back in New Mexico, Johnson reached out to Bronson Cutting for advice. Unlike Johnson, Cutting had no previous involvement with censorship issues. A progressive Republican drawn to the liberal wing of the party, Cutting fought the suspension of sexual literature, propelled by his personal sexual identity and public interactions with bohemian art colonies. He began by writing a letter to the acting commissioner of the Customs Bureau. Cutting argued that the copies of *Lady Chatterley's Lover* were "works of art." He asked that the books not be destroyed but instead returned to Johnson. The commissioner responded that the books are "grossly obscene" and would not be released back to Johnson but that Johnson had the right to contest the decision in the US Customs Court under section 514 of the Tariff Act.[50] Cutting then connected Johnson with a lawyer named Henry Somers Janon, who agreed to take on the case pro bono.

After an inspector's decision, citizens could appeal directly to the secretary of the treasury.[51] Thus, Cutting also corresponded with Secretary Andrew W. Mellon informally on Johnson's behalf. He disclosed the situation and asked if anything could be done. More broadly, Cutting sought Mellon's personal opinion on the matter of "the average Bureau reviewer" having discretionary power "over determining obscenity." Mellon wrote back regarding the bureau's seizure and destruction of the book: "The laws make no exception in favor of the so called classics or of the work of leading writers of the day, and such are not admitted to entry without regard to their character." Mellon, like the acting commissioner of US Customs, advised that Johnson could protest the obscenity decision in Customs Court.[52]

Johnson contemplated fighting the charges through the court system, but he faced a slim chance of winning. The majority of prior cases upheld the decision of the local customs inspector. A decision could be appealed to the federal courts, but this was rarely done. Ultimately, Johnson decided that going to trial might be too costly. "You are most generous to offer your legal services, but I fear that would not be the only expense," wrote Johnson to attorney Janon. Johnson worried about being able to pay a large fine if he lost the trial, which was the likely outcome.[53] Limited financial means shaped Johnson's decision to forgo a trial, but he did not give up the fight.

Cutting's Censorship Battle

Cutting had intervened in a critical moment when the national fight against censorship was gaining traction. By the late 1920s, new voices joined censorship resisters, people like Johnson directly involved in conflicts over texts and others in response to the Clean Books crusade (1923–25). A variety of religious and social groups formed the Clean Books League, aimed at revising the New York obscenity law to strengthen the conviction and punishment of publishers who produced "dirty books."[54] The Clean Books campaign, which historian Paul Boyer has called "the most far-reaching challenge to American literary freedom in the 1920s, if not this century," threatened the publishing industry and set in motion its organized opposition to the Clean Books League.[55] Additionally, it propelled the American Civil Liberties Union (ACLU) to publicly fight censorship by violating the law and inviting a trial in April 1929.[56]

Johnson's censorship incident happened to coincide with a new tariff bill in US Congress introduced in 1929 by Republican senator Reed Smoot of Utah and Republican representative Willis Hawley of Oregon. The Smoot-Hawley Tariff Act proposed to raise tariffs on imported goods in an effort to protect farmers and manufactures from foreign economic competition. The highly criticized Tariff Act of 1930, its divisive passage, and the triggering of international retaliation against US exports have overshadowed scholarly discussions about the act's restrictions on the importation of obscene materials.[57] Section 305 perpetuated the Customs Bureau's ban on allegedly obscene literature. Cutting seized the opportunity to use the Smoot-Hawley Tariff Act as a platform to oppose federal censorship regulations.

Cutting prepared for a congressional fight. He began by contacting Mercer G. Johnston of the People's Legislative Service, a Washington, DC, fact-finding agency linked to progressive members of Congress, to help supply him with more details on section 305. Cutting knew that a defense of D. H. Lawrence's work would be too risky. While there was a small growing contingent of Americans who defended public sexual expression, particularly in sexually explicit books and magazines, most Americans had operated for decades by maintaining sexual boundaries between public and private and supported bans on public sexual expression. Even literary agencies had long resisted taking a pro-stance on sexual texts. Cutting needed a nonsexual example of obscenity. At Johnston's suggestion, Cutting focused on the unexpurgated British edition of Erich Maria Remarque's *All Quiet on the Western Front*, a story of a company of volunteer German soldiers stationed behind the front lines in the last weeks of World War I that was controversial for its realistic depictions of the horrors of war. It was also an international best-seller that spoke to a generation coping with the trauma of war.[58] Cutting drafted a press statement on July 28, 1929, to raise awareness about section 305 of the Tariff Act, calling it "irrational, unsound, and un-American." He warned of the "danger" of permitting unqualified Customs officers "to dictate what the American people may or may not read" and pointed to *All Quiet on the Western Front* as an example of an "outstanding masterpiece" denied to the reading public.[59] Cutting's attention to Smoot-Hawley Tariff Act's censorship clause spurred a national conversation on the US Customs Bureau's regulation of obscenity.

Previously, anticensorship issues had received minimal publicity. The tide shifted with the rise of anticensorship attorney Morris Ernst. Ernst, who served as ACLU general counsel from 1929 to 1955, orchestrated a publicity campaign on his April 1929 case on the lesbian novel *The Well of Loneliness*. Ernst had risen to prominence as an anticensorship ally after co-authoring *To the Pure: A Study of Obscenity and the Censor* (1928), which received critical praise for outlining strategies to dismantle censorship law. Ernst argued that each work deserved to be considered "as a whole, even though some paragraphs standing by themselves might be objectionable."[60] Ernst also contradicted the existing interpretation of obscenity law that prioritized the public good and a common sense of decency over an individual's freedom in private. He applied to intimate matters the legal definition of privacy, "that one had the right to be left alone." Due to Ernst's growing reputation, Cutting sought his advice. Cutting adopted Ernst's "whole book" approach and "personal freedom" argumentation.[61] While Ernst worked through the courts, Cutting brought the same ideas to Congress. In a few decades, the right to privacy would move from an idea used by a small number of liberal lawyers and politicians to a mainstream discourse about sex and the law.

On October 10, 1929, the Senate debated the Tariff Act (HR 2667), including section 305, its obscenity clause. Cutting proffered his amendment to strike the provision that banned the importation of literature for obscenity or sedition. While he urged eradicating both clauses, his entire discussion on the first day focused on obscenity. Cutting argued, "in the case of a work of literature, it is very difficult to judge any work by sentences or paragraphs or pages. . . . It is hardly a fair way of judging the literature which the American people ought to be entitled to read." Instead, he proposed that each state should be permitted to determine for itself what books its residents might read.[62] Conveniently, New Mexico was the only state that lacked an obscenity law, a fact Cutting did not mention.[63]

Cutting identified a variety of literary examples, including the English poet and intellectual John Milton and Italian poet Dante Alighieri, but his references to sexual content in literature were noteworthy. First, Cutting carefully avoided directly naming the controversial novel *Lady Chatterley's Lover* so "as not to injure the morals of any American citizen." Nonetheless, he condemned the decision to ban it. "When a work of one of the leading writers of the day, sent to one of my constituents in New Mexico, was barred at the port I appealed to Mr. Mellon as an individual," recounted Cutting. He also mentioned the lesbian novel *The Well of Loneliness* but again distanced himself from it, calling it "a book, which I have not read and about which I do not care to express an opinion." Cutting defended two notable sexological texts that were often used by gay men and lesbians to self-identify, conveying "that many important, serious, solemn discussions of medical questions, such as the works of Havelock Ellis and Krafft-Ebing are barred by the Bureau of Customs. . . . The customs clerk is required by law under the severest penalty, to keep them out." Cutting employed the common tactic of circumventing explicit homosexual signifiers while still enabling a defense of sexual themes in literature.[64] He grasped that an open dialogue about sexual content would have instantaneously killed his amendment. And yet, he made sure to include, as part of the congressional record, references to sexual literature. The debate resumed the next day, and the Senate approved Cutting's amendment by a slim margin of 38–36.[65]

The news media substantially covered Cutting's amendment and, in the process, educated the general public about censorship issues. The *New York Times*, for example, reported on the history of banning obscene literature through American tariff laws. *Time Magazine*, in a series of articles on "the decency debate," highlighted how Cutting contested the efficacy of Customs Bureau agents to "decide what the U. S. public might read." *Publisher's Weekly* called October 11, 1929, a "day of new hope." Cutting's Washington assistant wrote him on January 1930, "There is more interest in the censorship fight here [Washington, DC] now than ever before." He added, "It is all favorable from the newspaper point of view."[66] The news coverage persuaded various groups to rally behind Cutting. The National Book Association "wrote to every U.S. Senator" in support of Cutting's amendment. PEN International invited Cutting to speak at their National Arts Club in New York to honor his efforts.[67] Ezra Pound, a major literary figure and vocal anticensorship advocate, thanked Cutting for taking aim at the Customs Bureau. Nonetheless, Pound critiqued Cutting for only going after the tariff bill: "In the account of Senator Cutting's speech that has reached me I see no mention of our post office. . . . This appears to me to be a serious omission in Senator Cutting's program." He pressed Cutting to push his censorship crusade further but acknowledged that "Cutting has put New Mexico on the map." John Dewey, professor of philosophy at Columbia University, also recognized the significant role of New Mexico in the censorship cause: "It is a reflection upon the eastern states that boasts of superior culture that the leadership in this fight should come from New Mexico."[68] The press designated New Mexico as an anticensorship state.

Privately, Cutting gave Spud Johnson credit for the whole affair. After the amendment victory, Cutting wrote to Johnson, cautioning that the bill was still in the early stages, there would be "more work to do," and "yet I believe we won at least nine tenths of the fight."[69] In his letter, he attached a copy of the Congressional Record with a note: "Dedicated to Spud Johnson, without whose inspiration this issue of the Congressional Record might have read otherwise. B.C." Johnson responded by sharing how he intended to rally New Mexicans to the cause. In the *Santa Fe New Mexican*, Johnson had announced his plans for a hurried symposium on censorship in the *Laughing Horse*: "The censorship issue . . . is being rushed for immediate publication because of the timely element involved—the censorship clause in the tariff bill being a vital controversy in the Unites States senate which will probably come up for a deciding vote within the next few weeks. This issue of the Horse is of course a New Mexico gesture in support of Senator Cutting who has been responsible for the revival of the question in congress and who is making such a laudable fight for a sensible revision of the

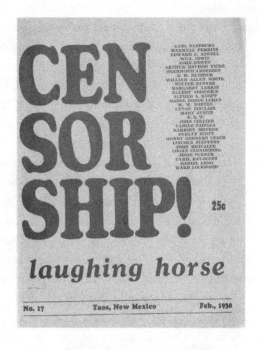

Spud Johnson gathered the voices of anticensorship agitators from across the nation for a special censorship issue of the *Laughing Horse*. Center for Southwest Research, University of New Mexico, Albuquerque, AP2.L394 1967.

present law." After the announcement, Johnson solicited comments from literati, editors, academics, and critics nationwide for the special issue.[70] By the end of the month, he had assembled a compendium of anticensorship arguments from twenty-nine prominent publishers and American authors.

Johnson recalled that the special censorship issue "printed the most impressive list of famous contributors," whose names were displayed on the cover.[71] Despite living in New Mexico, Johnson maintained his ties to literary communities in large cities such as New York and Chicago. Two members of the Chicago literary renaissance—Carl Sandburg and Sherwood Anderson—contributed. "Until censorship shows more intelligence, we should have less of it," reasoned poet Carl Sandburg.[72] Novelist Sherwood Anderson, whose *Winesburg, Ohio* was considered scandalous due to its sympathetic portrayal of homosexuality and frank sexual discussions, offered his stance: "You may be dead sure that I am in sympathy with the intelligent fight being made against a senseless censorship by Senator Cutting and with your [Johnson's] effort to back him up."[73] *Laughing Horse* cultivated a forum for the growing anticensorship coalition of writers, intellectuals, and publishers to vocally critique federal censorship laws. Interestingly, no members of the Harlem Renaissance contributed. A few queer white women, such as Harriet Monroe, gave their opinions. Impressed by the special censorship issue of the *Laughing Horse*, Cutting applauded Johnson for his editorial work: "I want to thank you again for the fine assistance you have given me in this fight." Cutting encouraged Johnson to print copies of the *Laughing Horse* and send it to senators before the vote on the floor.[74] Johnson obliged.

At Senator Smoot's request, the Senate undertook a reconsideration of section 305 on March 17, 1930.[75] Smoot, sitting poised behind piles of obscene literature, awaited his moment to read aloud sexually provocative paragraphs to strengthen his argument to retain censorship strictures. Senator Cutting, described by the press as "sophisticated," "soft-spoken" with a "faint lisp," and "broadminded," was equally prepared to counter.[76] He came armed with letters from around the nation in support of his position. Cutting appeared as the measured anticensorship advocate, while Smoot became the outspoken ideological foe. The censorship issue captivated the American public. Scores of spectators crowded into the Senate gallery to hear the ongoing decency debate.

Smoot began with a burst of rage. He shouted: "This question is one that strikes at the morals of every young boy and girl in the United States. Mr. President, I have here books the reading of which would so disgust Senators of the United States that they would never dream of agreeing to the amendment proposed by the Senator from New Mexico. I did not believe there were such books printed in the world—books that the Senator from New Mexico referred to and said out to be in the libraries of the people of the United States. They are lower than the beasts!"[77] Smoot relied on a long-standing argument among supporters of government regulation of morality—the potential of sexually oriented material to corrupt the minds of the young and impressionable—an argument that continues to hold weight with the American public.[78] Smoot singled out two books, *Lady Chatterley's Lover* and *My Life and Love*, that he claimed Senator Cutting wanted "to be in the libraries of the people of the United States." Cutting immediately disaffirmed Smoot's assertation: "I deny absolutely that I ever referred to *Lady Chatterley's Lover*." Prepared, Smoot confronted Cutting about his letter to Secretary Mellon that defended "the vilest book." The "disgusting, dirty and vile book," exclaimed Smoot, "is most damnable! It is written by a man with a diseased mind and a soul so black that he would obscure even the darkness of hell!" Smoot insisted Cutting submit a copy of the letter for the Senate to read.[79] Cutting refused, claiming the letter was not relevant.

Smoot pressed on by shaming the Senate for its previous vote: "I have been distressed that in the Senate of the United States, so few voices were raised in debate against a proposal to abolish the prohibition of the importation of obscene books." He condemned sexological literature as a class of books disguised as science. He pointed to an incident where "a sailor was recently caught on the docks smuggling in from his ship a number of books especially designed to encourage sexual vices in boys. . . . This is the so-called literature which my good friend, the Senator from New Mexico, desires to have admitted to the shores of our country." The overt focus on sexual content weakened Cutting's position, putting him on the defensive. Smoot concentrated on the impetus for Cutting's involvement—*Lady Chatterley's Lover*—and took advantage of circulating rumors about Senator Cutting's sexuality.[80]

Smoot's core focus on erotica proved effective. South Carolina's senator Coleman Livingston Blease agreed, "I'd rather see the democratic and republican form of government forever destroyed if necessary to protect the virtue of the womanhood of America."[81] Senator Blease's deep-rooted gendered sexual conventions conveyed an urgent necessity to protect young women from indecent literature. Senator James Thomas Heflin from Alabama concurred, "I do not think that a book that offends the moral sense of the average person ought to be allowed to come into the United States."[82] Midway through the debate, Senator Hugo Black proposed a new amendment to restore the ban on obscene books.

On the second day of debate, Cutting took the floor. "The debate last night," Cutting began, "took us, I think rather far from the fundamental features of the question at issue: What is censorship?" To help define censorship, he introduced the work of William Allan Neilson of Smith College, whom he described as a "Presbyterian, almost a Victorian in his general attitude toward the arts." Cutting quoted Neilson's position on censorship: "The saving of a man's soul, which one must presume is the object of censorship, is, after all, a man's own affair, and is not to be achieved by external compulsion or guardianship. . . . If he wants to pander to the lower side of his nature, no censor will prevent him." Cutting then argued that "the reading of a book is a matter for the individual himself to consider. . . . What right have we to interfere with the adult citizen at all as to what he is going to read?" He advanced a framing for sexual privacy rights—an individual's right to read what they pleased in the privacy of their own home. He further pivoted to a line of argumentation that advocated for adults' determining obscenity for themselves rather than its effect upon juveniles. Cutting countered Smoot by referencing broad principles of rights to privacy and freedom of speech.[83]

Because Smoot concentrated on explicit sexual content, he convinced the Senate to rescind their support of the Cutting amendment and accept Senator Hugo Black's proposed amendment that restored the banning of obscene books. However, Black's amendment contained three caveats that heeded Cutting's points. First, the proposed amendment agreed with Cutting that "any book" had to be "taken as a whole." The dominant theme of the book would determine its obscenity rather than isolated passages. Second, Smoot yielded to pressure for a judicial provision. Customs agents would seize obscenity, but district and federal courts would determine if the material was obscene. Third, the amendment "provided further, that the Secretary of the Treasury may, in his discretion, admit the so-called classics or books of recognized and established literary or scientific merit."[84] A 54–28 procedural vote reinstated the censorship amendment to the tariff bill with these modifications. The final enactment of the Smoot-Hawley Tariff Act came on June 17, 1930. Both Smoot and Cutting claimed to be satisfied with the final result.

Prior to the Smoot-Hawley Tariff debate, advocates of free speech in America worked primarily at the local and state levels, using courtrooms and coalition building to protest censorship restrictions.[85] Cutting and Johnson, along with other anticensorship agitators, galvanized a defense of sexual materials at the federal level, formulating privacy rights as a way to advance sexual civil liberties. Historian Marc Stein has argued that of the five major policy arenas toward LGBT progress, "liberalization arguably occurred first in obscenity law."[86] The Smoot-Hawley Tariff Act's section 305 kicked off a process of liberalizing American sexual standards. During and after the decency debate, the Customs Bureau pursued a less restrictive obscenity enforcement policy. For example, in July 1929, the Customs Courts reversed its ban on Radcliffe Hall's *The Well of Loneliness*.[87]

Both Cutting and Johnson continued this work after the new amendment was enacted. Cutting pressed for the right to disseminate obscenity, turning his attention toward postal censorship. "I am just as much opposed to Article 211 of the Penal Code as I was to the corresponding section of the tariff law," wrote Cutting to new anticensorship ally Ezra Pound.[88] Pound had been outspoken about the repeal of article 211, which allowed postal authorities to confiscate obscene materials and initiate criminal prosecutions, since his time as foreign editor of the *Little Review* (1917–19).[89] After Cutting acquired a reputation for his campaign against federal censorship, Pound initiated a correspondence with him. Pound and Cutting exchanged dozens of letters from 1930 to 1935, many of them on the issue of postal censorship.[90] Pound also looked to a new little magazine in New Mexico, *Morada* (Johnson had taken a hiatus from publishing the *Laughing Horse* due to the Great Depression) to help bring down Article 211 of the Criminal Code.[91] Pound's significant article on "Small Magazines," published in November 1930, praised *Morada* "as the best bet successor to the *Little Review*."[92] Norman Macleod, an undergraduate at the University of New Mexico–Albuquerque, had founded *Morada* with faculty support in fall 1929. Pound wrote a short piece called "Kick" for the inaugural issue and argued that New Mexico would lead the fight in bringing down article 211.[93]

In 1931 and 1932 Cutting worked to amend article 211 with support from the ACLU's newly formed National Council on Freedom from Censorship. *Publishers Weekly* reported that Cutting's amendment to article 211 sought to administer "the same procedure of trial by jury as is now used for printed matter coming from abroad."[94] Similar to section 305, Cutting's article 211 amendment enabled district and federal courts, rather than postal inspectors, to adjudicate alleged obscenity. Unfortunately, his two attempts failed, primarily because of the growing economic depression, which diverted the government's attention to passing social welfare legislation. Cutting maintained his support of the arts by speaking in favor of federally funded relief programs.[95] New Mexico, one of the poorest states, received federal support for reviving arts and literary production and bolstering agriculture and stock raising. Cutting remained a prominent spokesperson for artists, writers, editors, and educators until his tragic death in May 1935 in a plane crash at the age of forty-six.[96]

One year after Cutting's death, Johnson persisted with making available works deemed obscene. He became the manager of Santa Fe's Villagrá Bookshop and started his own circulating library, which included a collection of obscene books and pictures. Villagrá Bookshop owner, Roberta Robey, who opened the store in 1921 and expanded it six years later, credited the writers of Santa Fe for its success: "I cannot begin to express the invaluable aid which they gave." In 1936 Robey sold the shop to Clifford McCarthy, Bronson Cutting's intimate partner before his death, and for a time it was then owned and managed by gay men.[97] Villagrá served as an integral extension of Santa Fe's queer literati. While not solely a gay and lesbian bookstore in terms of stock, it functioned as a center for the queer community.[98]

Johnson operated the bookstore for a short time, but he left the managerial position disgruntled, claiming that he rarely received compensation for his work. Instead, Johnson purchased books for a second small circulating library that he started in the mid-1930s. Johnson embarked on a decades-long search for books documenting romantic and erotic relationships. In his journal, he sometimes noted the titles of books he purchased while traveling and visiting secondhand bookstores or others given to him by friends. He collected works by Edna St. Vincent Millay, a celebrated poet known for her frank portrayal of women's sexuality. The circulating library included works by French novelist George Sand, who adopted a man's pen name, often dressed in men's clothing, and wrote about androgyny, feminist politics, and sexual complexities. On October 17, 1934, Johnson wrote in his journal that he "went to bed with a couple of books. One was Havelock Ellis on Sexual Inversion!"[99] Johnson felt emboldened to purchase and sell sexological literature and classic fiction featuring same-gender relationships in the years after the Smoot-Hawley Tariff's amendment.

Access to such materials shaped queer art colonists of northern New Mexico. Many books deemed obscene referenced same-gender romantic and erotic relationships. The ability to read such works enabled individuals to self-identify and create social networks that constituted alternative cultures. Queer literary and scientific representations strengthened northern New Mexico's queer circle. They consumed queer literature, shared it, dis-

Spud Johnson sold a variety of books from his pushcart. Mixed in with his collection was sexological, autobiographical, and fictional literature that validated queer and gender-variant people's identity. Photograph courtesy of the Harry Ransom Center, University of Texas, Austin.

cussed it, and created it. However, it is necessary to give serious weight to the limited reach of these materials. Only some queer people identified with representations within LGBT literature, classified by scholar Eve Sedgwick as "durable and broadly based Anglo-American" definitions of sexuality.[100]

Riggs's Censorship Battle

Despite the Customs Court legalizing of some works previously banned, such as *The Well of Loneliness*, support for censorship of homoerotic themes remained strong. In 1933 queer writers Charles Henri Ford and Parker Tyler authored *The Young and the Evil*, a stream of consciousness presentation of New York City's gay subcultures—Harlem drag balls, Greenwich Village's gay bar scene, and vivid descriptions of cruising sites—published in Paris by Obelisk. American customs agents refused to allow copies into the United States.[101] Censorship of books with clear homoerotic content persisted, and that legal threat combined with the pressure of cultural censorship preempted candid queer discussions. Nevertheless, there were notable successes in challenging cultural censorship forces through coded themes.

Lynn Riggs's writing is crucial to censorship issues. Although it would take until the late 1990s for his queer themes to become visible, his work influenced creative Indigenous writers and contributed to two-spirit activism. In *The Cherokee Night*, Riggs embraced finding a primary sense of communal belonging and prioritized questions of tribal sovereignty. These notions served as the basis for two-spirit organizing and the emergent work of gay, lesbian, and two-spirit American Indians who authored their open affirmations of same-gender desires. Riggs had no formal political involvement with censorship. Unlike Cutting and Johnson, who held varying degrees of power and privilege in society and operated within the white male power structure of the federal government, Riggs relied on writing about his queer belonging in Santa Fe to validate his queer and gender-variant existence.[102]

Riggs grew up on a farm in the Cherokee Nation near present-day Claremore, Oklahoma. He cared deeply about his ancestral land—thirteen of his plays are set in the territory—but his homeland also caused him great pain. He struggled to reconcile his identities of mixed-race Cherokee and asegi/two-spirit and experienced feelings of abjection, isolation, fragmentation, assimilation, and cultural erasure. According to Qwo-Li Driskill (non-citizen Cherokee), there are several ways to describe two-spirit people in Cherokee. Some Cherokee people apply the term *asegi udanto* "to people who either fall outside of men's and women's roles or who mix men's and women's roles"; some also use the term *asegi* as a term similar to *queer*. Traditionally, asegi did not necessarily have a special tribal place but were considered "'a part of the circle,' a part of the larger whole of Cherokee community and lifeways." As the Cherokee people endured settler violence and "civilization" efforts that restructured numerous elements of their culture, including gender and sexuality, asegi lost their place within the circle. "Colonial heteropatriarchal genders and sexualities become internalized and legally inscribed in Cherokee communities during the periods between the late eighteenth century and the Removal" in 1838, argues Driskill.[103] Because asegi had been erased from Cherokee cultural practice when Riggs came of age, he had no one in his community to openly model or discuss his same-gender desires.

Ultimately, Riggs left the Cherokee Nation for less restrictive environs. Riggs and his siblings, upon their mother's passing, had inherited a land allotment, with their non-Cherokee father serving as the guardian. At the age of eighteen, Riggs mortgaged his portion of land to attend the University of Oklahoma and, later, during a tough financial time, sold it. He never lived there on his own, severing the Cherokee primacy of lived connections to the land. Instead Riggs searched for a new home, a place to live his truth. In thinking about his journey, Riggs confessed, "Actually, I have done little in life except try to discover who I am and what my relation to the world I know consists of. In the world itself I have never really felt at home."[104]

Queer belonging, locating a place to make a home, became a literary subtext for Riggs. He imagined the Southwest as a geographic space for being queer, a theme he alludes to in his poem "The Arid Land," published in *Laughing Horse*. In it, Riggs anticipates finding love in the desolation and defiance of the desert landscape. His poem traces his own transformation from envisioning the desert as a wasteland to a place of potential love. He first describes the desert as "treeless," "arid," and "desolate"; "buzzards circled there." Yet he embraces the promise of the desert, its "sky" and "defiance." He writes, "we yet may love / this so sunny land."[105] Riggs wrote these words four years since his sexual migration to Santa Fe. Riggs came out as a gay man in 1923 in Santa Fe, where he fell into a vibrant queer artists' culture. In 1925 his literary work took him to New York City and then Paris on a Guggenheim Fellowship, but he often thought of Santa Fe as a place he belonged. New Mexico offered him an expansive definition of inclusion that included queer and Indigenous people. Nurtured by his mentor Witter Bynner, Riggs did indeed come to love "this so sunny land." He discovered love both in Santa Fe's embrace of him as a gay man and with Ramón Naya (born Enrique Gasque-Molina), a Mexican painter and dramatist. Betty Kirk Boyer, one of Riggs's closest friends, recalled that "Santa Fe, I believe, was the true love of his [Riggs's] life, it was Home, it was his Source." Riggs's biographer also suggests that although Riggs lived other places from 1930 to 1934 (he commuted from Santa Fe to Hollywood and New York), "Santa Fe was still where Riggs felt the healthiest, happiest, and most free."[106] Riggs occasionally vacationed in Mexico, where he met Naya. The professional and intimate partners made a home together in Santa Fe and later Greenwich Village, New York.

Ramón Naya poses in front of his paintings in the home he shared
with his partner, Lynn Riggs, in Santa Fe. Photograph
courtesy of Claremore Museum of History.

Riggs largely kept his intimate relationship with Naya private, which
Naya struggled with at times. Naya wrote in one letter to Riggs that the
privacy of their relationship bothered him, though he was trying to understand: "I'm tired of 'little steps.' . . . I realize the necessity for such things
. . . and I don't resent you as much as you think. . . . The more I learn the
technique of living in a sophisticated society, the more I understand you
and the less I resent you."[107] Because Riggs was private about his sexuality,
the couple spent most of their time in their home. Their friend Spud Johnson called them "hermits." Johnson also recounted that the couple was so

in love that they stopped socializing, "drinking and smoking—and even writing and painting" and instead ensconced themselves in the sanctuary of their home.[108] Good friends knew that Riggs and Naya were together. The couple felt comfortable hosting friends in their Santa Fe home. Accustomed to spending time together, when apart, Naya complained. "I am going through an awful period about you. It's the negative side of being in love," wrote Naya while he was away in Mexico. He continued, "I'm a romantic, I guess, but I can't help it. I just miss you too much for my own good."[109] The deep bond they shared helped Riggs embrace his homosexual desires.

Riggs reflected on some of his identity struggles in his plays, most notably *The Cherokee Night*, which he considered his most serious and significant work. Native studies scholar Craig Womack (Creek/Cherokee) first interpreted *The Cherokee Night* through queer and Indigenous lenses, understanding it as "an emergence story for an Indian gay man."[110] Riggs conceived *The Cherokee Night* during his Guggenheim Fellowship year (1928–29) in Paris. He finalized the play in 1930 while summering in Provincetown, Massachusetts, a notable queer art colony. *The Cherokee Night* premiered at the Hedgerow Theatre near Philadelphia in June 1932 to a largely white, upper-middle-class audience, typical of theater attendees in the early to mid-twentieth century.[111] Riggs continued to direct the play at the University of Iowa in 1932 and at Syracuse University in 1934, and in the summer of 1936, it enjoyed a short ten-day run in New York City at the Federal Theatre. It briefly circulated in print in 1936 and was brought back into print in 1999. Riggs received mixed reviews from critics, but the play has grown in significance since it resurfaced in the nineties and became part of queer Indigenous scholarly conversations.[112]

The play's opening scene is set in Claremore Mound, a former site of an Osage/Cherokee battle haunted by its violent past.[113] Through seven nonlinear vignettes (one for each of the Cherokee clans), the mixed-race Cherokee characters wrestle with the dissolution of Cherokee culture and search for a place to belong.[114] *The Cherokee Night* grapples with mixed-race identity, Cherokee-white relations, problematics of assimilation, and connection to and loss of ancestral lands.[115] The play contains a multiplicity of meanings. Riggs acknowledged that "the play has a meaning beyond the story, even beyond the [Cherokee] theme."[116] While a Native theme

Lynn Riggs and Ramón Naya with a friend in their Santa Fe home.
Photograph courtesy of Claremore Museum of History.

is prominent, nuances of searching for a queer heritage, heteronormative assimilation, and internalized self-hatred are intensely coded.

The idea of keeping secrets and hidden lives come through in several of the characters. Womack posits that one of the characters, Gar Breeden, is an autobiographical depiction of Riggs. Gar goes on a quest "to find out if anyone still remembers how to be Cherokee." He flees to the mountains, like Riggs fled to Santa Fe, and encounters a strange cult called the Tribe. Gar explains his quest to the tribal leader as a repressed secret: "Listen! It's all shut up in me, it's drivin' me crazy." This is similar to how Riggs defined his mental breakdown to Bynner, a fixture in the queer art colony. Gar goes on, "They's no place for me anywhere, see! . . . Don't belong in Claremore. No place for me anywhere!" Womack argues that since Gar's Cherokee identity is well established, he is "the most Indian" of the play's characters, that Gar's quest is about reconciling his queer identity with Cherokee survivance and a subtle way for Riggs to process his individual struggles.[117]

The Cherokee Night is a site of queer resistance to censorship. On the one hand, Riggs felt restrained by cultural norms. *The Cherokee Night* and "The Arid Land" expressed queer inclinations in nearly imperceptible ways. On the other hand, Riggs defied censorship by including subtly discernable queer themes. The creative work of Native queer people has been instrumental to two-spirit identities and movements. Scholars initially attributed mid-1970s poems and the essay "Tinseled Bucks: A Historical Study of Indian Sexuality" by Maurice Kenny (Mohawk) as the first explicit and contemporary Native two-spirit writing. They continued to search for stories of those who navigated sexual and gender variance in earlier time periods. One of the first bibliographies of two-spirit literature, by conference panelists of the first two-spirit studies panel at the Native American Literature Symposium in 2003, featured three of Lynn Riggs's works—*The Cherokee Night* and two collections of poetry, *The Iron Dish* and *The Cream in the Well*.[118] Diversified queer cultural expressions proved to be an important method of resistance to censorship of queer voices.

THREE

Land of Entrapment

*The Formation and Consequences
of the Security State,
1945–1960s*

Morris Kight, born in Proctor, Comanche County, Texas, explored his same-sex desire when he moved to Fort Worth to attend Texas Christian University. During his college years, he studied public administration and was "somewhat active as a gay person."[1] He graduated in 1941, at the height of World War II. In spite of his post-graduation plans, he was required to register for military service. At the start of the war, the US Selective Service excluded men with "homosexual proclivities," but Kight was careful to conceal his sexual orientation.[2] He worried more about fulfilling his military service "without wielding a gun." Kight, a member of the nonviolent War Resister League, looked for a noncombatant service assignment. In February 1941, he applied to the National Youth Administration, an agency that provided vocational training to recent graduates, and fulfilled his requirement for military service.[3]

By June he had received a letter of acceptance and moved to Albuquerque for his assignment with the United Pueblos Agency (UPA), an organization that encompassed all nineteen Pueblo Nations in New Mexico and operated under the US Bureau of Indian Affairs.[4] Kight relished the work, which consisted of a public administration class, administrative work for the UPA, and evenings laboring in the field to build a well. He described the job as the "finest thing to ever happen in my life—besides being gay, which is the other good thing that happened."[5]

After Kight had worked there for a year, Sophie D. Aberle, superintendent of the UPA from 1934 to 1944, wrote to the commissioner of Indian Affairs recommending "Mr. Kight's separation" because "although his work was sufficiently satisfactory to continue him throughout the entire period of the Program, we do not believe that he is fitted for permanent appointment in the Service." Aberle cited "personality weaknesses," code for homosexuality, as the reason.[6] Wounded by the dismissal, Kight realized he needed to do a better job of hiding his sexual orientation.

Kight finished his compulsory military service in the US Marine Corps Reserve in Dallas, then returned to Albuquerque, where he attempted to lead a heteronormative public life and a secret gay life. He married Stanlibeth Peters in 1950 and became a father. He opened a real estate office and purchased and managed the Rio Grande Duke City Hotel (later renamed the New Mexican Hotel), a business that abetted his clandestine sexual activities.[7] Kight, though not an artist himself, helped to establish a thriving creative community in postwar Albuquerque that served as "the nexus of artistic innovation" in the state. He served as president of the New Mexico Art League, co-directing in the summer of 1951 the first all-Albuquerque art exhibition, which became an annual event.[8] Kight showcased the city's artful culture by hosting a radio program called *This Enchanted City*, for which he interviewed local artists and promoted their exhibitions. He also handled press releases and bookings for two local theater companies, and he joined the Old Town Players. The theater companies brought in actors from California, who exposed Kight to homophile literature and introduced him to the idea that queer people were "an oppressed cultural minority" deserving of equal rights.[9]

At night, Kight participated in an underground gay world through bars. Gay bars in the city developed in connection to an influx of military and scientific personnel tied to the nascent nuclear weapons industry, a demographic shift that pushed queer culture underground. Kight described Albuquerque's gay bar scene as "furtive" but generally felt safe patronizing them since the police took little notice of establishments with coded names, such as the Hitch'n Post, or oblique signs—"Rear Entry Only."[10] Kight's business thrived, he socialized with the fine arts crowd, and he found willing same-gender sexual partners at gay bars. His marriage provided a cover for his covert gay life.

Eventually, Kight grew tired of secrecy. He indulged more frequently in alcohol, and arrests piled up for disorderly conduct. He began making passes at men outside of gay bars, including an unwelcome advance at Calvin Horn, a member of the New Mexico legislature. Her suspicion confirmed, Kight's wife left the marriage. Kight, once a prominent businessman and art promoter for the city, became a pariah.[11] Albuquerque's art community discouraged queer presentation and banished Kight, who had been one of its central organizers and champions. Kight spent most of his time with his lover Edwin Steinbrecher at the new San Felipe Hotel, which he had recently acquired. In September 1956, a mysterious fire broke out and destroyed the hotel. Kight suspected arson and with Steinbrecher fled Albuquerque for Los Angeles, a city he had learned in reading homophile publications possessed a more vibrant gay scene.[12]

Kight's time in postwar Albuquerque illustrates three themes: secrecy, heteronormative citizenship, and mobility. Northern New Mexico had a history of laissez-faire attitudes toward queerness that engendered the blossoming of a semi-open white queer creative culture in the twenties and thirties. By the forties and fifties, the flourishing queer artistic culture eroded when New Mexico transitioned to a US national security space, ushering in a homophobic environment and forcing queer culture underground. New Mexico stimulated its economy and growth through its embrace of the military-industrial complex that stemmed from "the best-kept secret of the war"—the Manhattan Project. The project entailed a collaboration between the US government and industrial and scientific sectors in an effort to develop an atomic bomb. Los Alamos, approximately thirty miles northwest of Santa Fe, housed an undercover weapons laboratory and city, known during the war as Project Y.[13] Physicists and engineers at Project Y designed and assembled the world's first atomic bomb. Security measures inculcated a climate of secrecy that permeated the state and prevailed long after the war ended.

The concept of secrecy, the rationale for the security state itself, dominated the period after 1945 and served as a means of political and social control toward nonnormative sexuality. Secrecy replaced sexual privacy rights.[14] Sexual privacy—the right to keep certain information personal—had afforded some queer people a measure of security. In contrast, sexual secrecy mandated the necessity of concealing sexual proclivities to protect oneself from social, legal, and economic consequences. Forced secrecy, or "closeting," brought legal mechanisms that invalidated privacy rights, including security investigations designed to exclude "undesirables" from government employment and sodomy criminalization. In both examples, the government sought to pry secrets out of queer people and punish them. "The idea of the closet, therefore, is not just the idea that deviant gender or sexuality must be secret . . . but is more centrally a complex product of society and the law, which in the 1950s sought to enforce compulsory heterosexuality as a pervasive public policy," argues historian William Eskridge.[15] Eskridge asserts that the government and society insisted on hiding sexual nonconformity as a condition of citizenship.

The security state empowered government and professional authorities to impose and regulate heteronormative conceptions of citizenship.[16] During the Cold War era, the US federal government institutionalized the hetero-homo binary through policies that explicitly privileged heterosexuals and rationalized such policies by claiming that "homosexuals" threatened the security of the nation.[17] By 1943 every military branch had hardened exclusionary polices toward homosexuals, and in 1946 gay men and lesbians were purged from government employment in an event known as the Lavender Scare. Both developments demonstrate how the federal government defined the American citizen and citizenship rights as heterosexual, often in the name of national security interests.[18] The federal government's policies, the Department of Defense's military practices and security program, and the security measures of the new Atomic Energy Commission (AEC), which regulated and controlled nuclear science and technology, all sought to prepare for the long-term safety of the nation. In so doing, government agencies codified practices that excluded queer people.

The AEC, an agency I add to queer history's evaluation of state-sponsored homophobia, both supports and contradicts the field's current findings. Similar to the federal government and Department of Defense, the AEC formulated security clearance guidelines that regarded homosexuals as national security threats. But in comparison to other federal agencies and the military, which purged large numbers of alleged homosexuals from government service, the AEC's actions against queer people were fairly anemic. It rarely used the category of "homosexual" to deny security clearances to suspected gay men and lesbians, even when the hetero-homo binary became an organizing category of federal policy. In fact, the AEC had the lowest number of clearance denials of all government agencies. On average in the 1950s and 1960s, the AEC investigated twenty thousand Q-clearances (the highest level of access to classified information) per year. Between 1956 and 1963, the AEC only denied Q-clearances to twenty-eight people.[19] Some AEC supervisors argued that invasive interrogation tactics, used to ensure that future employees would guard government secrets, prevented qualified individuals from being hired. In letting suspected lesbian and gay men pass through security clearances because their "services were essential," the AEC sent a subtle message that consensual sexual activities did not affect one's ability to perform highly classified work. Furthermore, on the ground at Los Alamos, northern New Mexico still possessed a lingering social tolerance for gender and sexual difference, which emboldened some queer employees to resist heteronormative standards. While most studies have focused on the national context of the hetero-homo binary, multisited research helps to explain where homosexual exclusions solidified and how and why resistance patterns took shape.[20]

In the midst of heteronormative ideologies, gay men and lesbians organized to resist gay oppression. World War II marked a watershed for queer life in America; it mobilized queer people to leave home, settle in new places, and contribute to the visibility and growth of queer cultures and politics.[21] The most studied form of resistance is the founding of political organizations designed to fight homosexuals' second-class status, which included the birth of the gay male–oriented Mattachine Society (initially called Mattachine Foundation) in Los Angeles in 1950, followed by ONE, Incorporated in 1952, and the first lesbian organization, the Daughters of Bilitis, in San Francisco in 1955. These groups are collectively known as the homophile movement.[22] However, the regional composition of local queer culture, state laws, and police enforcement meant that some queer people benefited more from postwar queer mobility, visibility, and civil rights activism than others.

In the American West, Colorado, for example, saw the war give rise to a strong gay bar culture that resulted in a politicized homophile community. New Mexican gay men and lesbians remained virtually untouched by homophile politics, with the exception of accessing their publications, as Morris Kight did. However, they devised other forms of pursuing community and national belonging. Because the presence of the military-industrial complex stunted the growth of queer art culture, queer New Mexicans joined a broad swathe of gay people in implementing other strategies of self-defense and defiance.[23] They passed as straight, migrated to cities, and constructed an underground queer culture that consisted of bars, primarily in Albuquerque, and the circulation of male homoerotic photographs and stories through a clandestine pornographic market. These practices should not be seen as repressive but as avenues of accommodation *and* resistance that both reproduced and contested the privilege of heterosexuality. Passing, often referred to by gay men and lesbians of this era as "wearing a mask," limited exposure.[24] Queer scientist Claude R. Schwob wore such a mask while working at the Los Alamos National Laboratory. Strategic discretion was critical to postwar queer life, yet his private production and circulation of gay male erotica allowed homoeroticism to thrive in the midst of the Cold War.

Geographic mobility functioned in multifaceted ways. World War II uprooted millions of Americans, including geographic movement toward the centers of an advancing nuclear industry centered in the American West.[25] New Mexico's population swelled from the rise of the nuclear complex that brought migrants to weapon design, testing, and training establishments spread across nine counties. An influx of inhabitants to areas near Los Alamos, Sandia Laboratories and Kirtland Air Force Base (Albuquerque), Holloman Air Force Base (Alamogordo), Cannon Air Force Base (Clovis), and the White Sands Missile Range, a missile testing site that encompasses five counties, transformed the demographics of the state.[26] As a result, the state's population increased from just over 530,000 in 1940 to more than 950,000 by 1960.[27] The two counties with the largest percentage increase, Bernalillo and Otero, were home to Sandia Laboratories and Kirtland and Holloman Air Force Bases.[28]

The newcomers introduced novel cultural proclivities: an appreciation for high-technology enterprises over artistic sensibilities and heteronormative conceptions of settlement—homeownership, men as the primary breadwinners, and the nuclear family ideal—that excluded queer people.[29]

Nuclear workers in New Mexico, who adhered to such ideals, disrupted an oasis in the desert for queer refugees that had offered a measure of isolated protection for them to discover and live their inner emotional lives. As evidenced by Kight's time in the city of Albuquerque, gay men and lesbians confronted growing hostility toward queerness during the war and postwar years.

Nonetheless, queer individuals disrupted the heterosexual context of postwar migration by using mobilization to their advantage. Some gay residents found the state's homophobic climate restrictive and migrated to places such as New York, San Francisco, and Los Angeles, where they believed nonnormative identity might be more accepted. In continuing to evaluate the role of geographic queer mobility, this chapter ends with the migration narrative of R. C. Gorman (Diné/Navajo). Shortly after his honorable discharge from the Navy in 1955, Gorman made a sexual migration to San Francisco to come out as a gay man and embark on a career in art. Paradoxically, Gorman, a gay artist, felt compelled to launch his creative endeavors outside of New Mexico, a state that had once been a haven for queer creatives.

The Invasion of the Security State

In 1943 New Mexico became part of the federal government's apparatus for the management of national security when the US Army Corps of Engineers claimed land on the Pajarito Plateau for one of the Manhattan Project's key scientific laboratories. At first, scientists worked at thirty-seven installations and thirteen university laboratories across the United States. Later, the project centralized to three key sites, including Los Alamos, New Mexico, the site for the design and construction of an atomic bomb. The other two key sites were Oak Ridge, Tennessee, which provided the project's major industrial facilities, and Hanford, Washington, which housed nuclear reactors. The Manhattan Project also encompassed more than a hundred smaller sites.[30]

From its inception, Los Alamos was intertwined with issues of power, secrecy, and surveillance. Project Y's existence centered on manufacturing "devastation on an unimaginable scale."[31] The social, cultural, and political regulation connected to the project produced and maintained official practices of secrecy. Covert operations installed hierarchies of power and repression within the community of Los Alamos and extending to local communities of color as well as the nearby queer art culture. Elsewhere, scholars have documented the effect of "radioactive colonialism" after the discovery of uranium on nearby Pueblo nations, four-hundred-year-old Nuevomexicano villages, and the Navajo Nation.[32] Surrounding communities of color, particularly Nuevomexicano residents of Española and the four northeastern Pueblo nations—Santa Clara, San Ildefonso, Cochiti, and Jemez—that border Los Alamos, disproportionately bore the brunt of land dispossession so that the United States could build weapons facilities. They faced economic inequalities that divided the northern Rio Grande valley denizens into the hyper wealthy and very poor as well as environmental inequities through weapons testing and nuclear waste that remain ongoing.[33] Geographic movement toward the centers of the nuclear complex and the reconfiguration of space that took place in postwar New Mexico also affected queer people's lives and identities.

In 1943 Dr. Claude Rene Schwob, a gay man and professor of chemistry at St. Peter's College in Jersey City, New Jersey, enlisted in the US Army.[34] Like other gay men and lesbians who joined the military, Schwob felt a patriotic duty to serve his country and hid his sexual identity to enlist. His expertise in chemistry, a bachelor's, master's, and doctorate in the subject from Fordham University, led to his work on the Manhattan Project, where he developed methods of isolating and measuring the activity of radioisotopes and researched counting techniques, corrosion studies, and physical properties of special materials in an effort to prepare for the development and deployment of a nuclear bomb. Schwob conducted his research first at the Carnegie Institute of Technology (now called Carnegie Mellon University) in Pittsburgh, then the Metallurgical Laboratory in Chicago, before moving to Los Alamos in April 1945.

By the time Schwob arrived, the classified research site and atomic city housed close to five thousand Nobel Prize winners, military personnel, engineers, scientists, maintenance workers, domestic laborers, and other personnel critical to the laboratory's operation. Nuevomexicanos from nearby Sandoval County were among the first workers at the site, working as lab assistants, janitors, plumbers, and landscapers.[35] Women were also

Claude Rene Schwob worked for the Manhattan
Project in Los Alamos, New Mexico, where he helped to
develop and deploy a nuclear bomb. Despite the highly
restrictive and secretive nature of his work, he found
ways to embrace his gay identity, including a hobby
of male homoerotic photography. Claude R. Schwob
Papers (2003–12), courtesy of Gay, Lesbian,
Bisexual, Transgender Historical Society.

key to the nuclear enterprise. Over time, women employed as scientists,
technicians, nurses, teachers, secretaries, and clerks made up roughly 30
percent of the labor force.[36] Working mothers relied on the labor of Pueblo
women for childcare and house cleaning. The city provided domestic jobs
to women from San Ildefonso and Santa Clara Pueblos.[37] Pueblo women's
labor was equally critical to the day-to-day operations of the Manhattan
Project; they assisted with the care of close to one thousand babies born
between 1943 and 1949.[38] Family obligations and the needs of a typical
suburban neighborhood suffused with the aim of the project, inventing and
constructing an atomic weapon.

However, not all the women at Los Alamos married and had families.

A few privately identified as lesbian and dared to engage in lesbian relationships. Though additional research is needed about queer workers in the military-industrial complex, Atomic Energy Commission records document the existence of lesbians employed by the Manhattan Project who interacted with members of the Women's Army Corps (WAC). The homosocial military auxiliary service restricted married women's participation and thus attracted lesbians and bisexual women.[39] Fiona, a member of the WAC and a lesbian, was stationed at Los Alamos from 1944 to 1945 and befriended a group of lesbians employed there. Among them were Bonnie, who took a job as a clerk while her friend, and a later intimate partner, Hillary, who worked as a nurse. Beyond friendships, Fiona developed a romantic relationship with her WAC lieutenant. Not until the end of the war did the WACs develop formal policies for investigating lesbianism among soldiers. Instead, the military implemented "informal means" to deal with "unconventional" women.[40] In Fiona's case, to break up her lesbian attachments, the WACs transferred her out of Los Alamos. Lesbians at Los Alamos, although they had to hide their lesbianism, cultivated a subculture for mutual recognition, socialization, and sexual encounters. The model Cold War community came to symbolize an idealized white, patriarchal, heterosexual, middle-class neighborhood of American families despite its long dependence on the labor of women, communities of color, and queer people who concealed their sexual identity.

At Project Y, secrecy's hegemony began upon arrival. When Bob Porton arrived in November of 1944 to work in the recreation division, he remembers that within several days, "we were given an orientation lecture and then a security lecture. . . . I made a vow to myself right then and there that as long as I was going to be assigned here, there were two things: one was I was never going to ask any questions and two, I was never going to shoot off my mouth on anything at all because he kept talking about the great need for secrecy." Porton felt proud to be a part of the experimental scientific community. He unquestioningly accepted covertness as part of his new life. His only knowledge of Project Y was that work being conducted at Los Alamos would help to shorten the war, and "that was good enough" for him.[41] The intelligence officer charged with giving the security lecture informed all military and civilian employees about the classified nature of the project without revealing specifics of the mission. Jane Wilson, whose husband headed the Experimental Nuclear Physics Division, recalled that "we were a secret project, probably the most secret project which has ever existed in the United States. That one fact dominated our existence."[42]

Thirty miles from Project Y, in Santa Fe, secrecy altered the sexual landscape that gay men and lesbians had created in the 1920s. For instance, when Los Alamos employees began using La Fonda Hotel in connection to Project Y, queer artists lost one of their social hubs. Project Y established the Santa Fe office of the Manhattan Project one block from La Fonda at 109 Palace Avenue. Dorothy Scarritt McKibbin, who began working as a secretary at the office in March of 1943, welcomed new recruits, issued passes, and arranged transport to "the Hill," the coded name for Los Alamos.[43] Many new arrivals, weary from travel, replenished at La Fonda and waited for their escort to the Hill, "yet, the visitors had to maintain silence about what they were doing there—security was a prime consideration."[44] Once settled into life at Los Alamos, scientists and their families often ventured down from the Hill for rest and relaxation at La Fonda. Undercover agents monitored Los Alamos residents at La Fonda, fearing they might loosen up too much and reveal the project's top-secret goal.[45] Surveillance and constant influxes of strangers made it difficult for lesbians and gay men to gather at the hotel. Secrecy also prompted queer artists to reevaluate living in northern New Mexico and pushed them toward sites with more vibrant gay and lesbian cultures.

By 1945 New Mexicans and the many residents of Los Alamos who knew little about the exact nature of work at the lab surmised that the appearance of more experts and personnel meant that the team was close to accomplishing its covert mission. J. Robert Oppenheimer, director of Project Y, had recruited Enrico Fermi in August 1944 to head the Special Projects Division, later renamed Experimental Nuclear Physics Group. To help guide the project to its final goal of detonating an atomic weapon, Oppenheimer hired more members to Fermi's division, including Claude R. Schwob, a radio chemist. Schwob remembered that Oppenheimer "picked the group he wanted to solve the knotty problems presented by the manufacture of the bomb. . . . It was a privilege and an honor to be included." Schwob described his work "in large part original and of a type never attempted before."[46] Oppenheimer commended Schwob for his "work in the preparation and development of a novel method of testing the atomic bomb, and subsequently helping carry through this test with eminently satisfactory results." The army agreed that Schwob was a model sergeant. At the end of his first month at Los Alamos, they awarded Schwob a good conduct medal for exemplary behavior, efficiency, and fidelity in the army.[47]

Schwob carried out his role as a scientist working on the top-secret Manhattan Project with a secret of his own. He wore a straight mask that allowed him to pursue his scientific career while he participated in an underground gay life. Like other gay men from this era, Schwob moved between different lives. While working at Los Alamos, Schwob corresponded with a lover, Carl "Carlo" Greene, who served overseas. Greene wrote letters like this one to Schwob: "Spent a wonderful day walking over the cliffs and browsing in this old village. Found many things of interest, which you would like.—Why can't you be with me? It has been a glorious weekend—only one thing missing." In another letter, Greene again expressed his yearning to be with Schwob: "It is a cold rainy day, but so very comfortable by the fire. Don't you love to hear wood cracking? I do, but an open fire on a cold autumn day, music, and tea makes me dream and long for other days, other places, and someone." Greene does not identify his "someone," but his next sentence clarifies that his longing was for Schwob, "This is a sorewy [sic], disconnected letter, am trying to be with you." He ends the letter with "all my love, Your C."[48] Such sentiments could easily be misconstrued as friendship, but historian Allan Bérubé reasons that searching for same-sex eroticism during wartime requires reading between the lines for subtle hints of desire between men. Even while working *within* a highly secretive government agency, Schwob found ways to embrace his gay identity.[49]

At times, Schwob dealt with inquiries about his nonmarital status, as this article in the *Naval Radiological Defense Lab Newsletter* draws attention to: "Dr. Schwob is that *rara avis*—a bachelor. Perhaps, his vital interest in work and many diversified hobbies has kept him so busy he hasn't gotten around to thoughts of matrimony." Defending his bachelorhood, Schwob confirmed that he was "extremely busy with my work both during normal working hours and in the evening, with little time for diversion or recreation."[50] Schwob maintained one hobby that consumed much of his time—male erotic photography. He began taking nude photographs of men, a number of them soldiers, in the late 1930s. His photographic collection mostly contains male nudes without erections, which he took in the privacy of his residences with the consent of the participants.[51] He continued throughout his life and kept an extensive series of homoerotic pictures.

Arguably, Schwob's photographic erotica is a site of queer cultural production. Both skilled artists and amateurs produced explicit homoerotic art for private circulation in the gay world. One of the best known is *The Barn*, a series of highly explicit drawings by American artist Neel "Blade" Bates that were reproduced and circulated underground in the 1940s.[52] Images that emphasized an aesthetic approach to nude bodies were the most popular, indicating that while the photos piqued sexual interest, they also satisfied a deeper emotional hunger for belonging to a group who appreciated male beauty. Schwob's work followed this trend. He invites viewers to gaze at naked men, but he often places his subject in ordinary settings, which desexualizes the image. One nude man is sitting at a desk writing a letter. Another sits perched on the edge of a desk reading a letter. In a third image, a man stands casually in the nude smoking a cigarette, seemingly unaware of the photographer.[53] Some of Schwob's photos are sexual, with photographic subjects fondling and performing fellatio. Schwob and other gay men took great risks in creating and circulating what was deemed obscenity. Schwob faced a tremendous threat that put his livelihood in danger, and later he suffered an FBI investigation for his hobby.[54] Certainly, during his time at Los Alamos his erotic photography remained a closely guarded secret.

Queer erotic cultural production and circulation were central to building gay male culture in Cold War America.[55] Erotic images and queer-themed erotic literature built solidarity among many gay men; indeed, Schwob drew on an older tradition of gay photographers' producing erotic images and sharing them through an underground market.[56] Another producer of clandestine pornography argues that the underground industry was all "that we had. . . . Everybody who could get his hands on them [would circulate them]. Some people tried their hands at writing these stories, and some of them were really good. It was all male oriented and homosexual." Through erotica, gay men expressed their interest in other men's bodies and felt that others shared the same excitement. In so doing, it promoted a collective identity and laid the groundwork for the physique magazine industry, which became the primary gay media outlet in postwar America.[57] Schwob's collection reveals extraordinary openness and a lack of shame regarding homoerotic desires.

Back in his professional life, Schwob completed tasks mainly related to testing the bomb. As a result of his successful work, he "was chosen as one of the men to assist in testing the first nuclear bomb at Alamogordo, New Mexico." On a flat stretch of high New Mexico desert in the early morning hours of July 16, 1945, Schwob witnessed, along with 424 others, the detonation of the plutonium "Gadget," the first atomic explosion in history.[58] Schwob, a gay man, had made a significant contribution to the bombs the United States would detonate on two Japanese cities three weeks later. On August 6, 1945, Paul W. Tibbets Jr. piloted the *Enola Gay* and dropped an atomic bomb over Hiroshima, destroying the city and killing an estimated 135,000 people.[59] President Harry Truman, on that same day, then announced the nation's use of an atomic weapon and revealed the purpose of the Manhattan Project. Los Alamos figured prominently in newspaper articles about the atomic attack on Japan.[60] Shortly after, the army honorably discharged Schwob. Like most involved in developing nuclear energy, he continued to work for nuclear enterprises, first at Carnegie Institute of Technology as an assistant professor of chemistry and later at the Naval Radiological Defense Lab in San Francisco. Nonetheless, Schwob grappled with the implications of an atomically armed world. His subsequent research focused on nuclear safety.[61] Atomic culture intruded into American life and forever altered the world.

Atomic Energy Commission

The continuation of atomic energy research after the war made places such as Los Alamos National Laboratory permanent institutions within American society.[62] In December of 1945, Senator Brien McMahon introduced S. 1717, which created the Atomic Energy Act and confirmed civilian control of nuclear energy through the Atomic Energy Commission, composed of five commissioners, a general manager appointed by the president, and three major advisory committees. On January 1, 1947, the AEC assumed control of two facilities in New Mexico for weapons research—Los Alamos and Sandia.[63] The terms of conducting US nuclear science, under the newly drafted Atomic Energy Act, meant embedding secrecy as a constitutive element in the nuclear complex. Official practices of secrecy, including developing policies for keeping secrets and identifying security risks, resulted in a problematic form of identity politics for queer people operating within and beyond the US nuclear complex.

The act required that the AEC adopt security mechanisms over access to restricted data and nuclear materials by mandating a personnel security clearance program directed by the AEC, with support from the Civil Service Commission and Federal Bureau of Investigation. The AEC designed its personnel security clearance program to assure that only those who could be trusted were placed in top-secret positions.[64] After the formation of the AEC, Colonel Charles H. Banks, an intelligence officer under Lieutenant General Leslie Groves (former director of the Manhattan Project), proposed a formal security questionnaire. The Personnel Security Questionnaire inquired into issues of "character, associations, and loyalty." In addition, Los Alamos security officer Thomas O. Jones drafted a regulation that established three types of security clearances: P, S, and Q.[65] The AEC required background investigations of all employees, but persons who worked with special nuclear material—design, manufacture, or data—needed a Q-clearance and a fuller investigation. The AEC published its Security Clearance Procedures on September 12, 1950, and Personnel Security Clearance Criteria for Determining Eligibility on November 17, 1950.[66] These two documents established uniform standards that were applied in determining and processing eligibility for clearances.

All prospective applicants filled out the Personnel Security Questionnaire; answers then were compared against the established uniform standards. The AEC broke down its criteria standards into two categories. Category A represented derogatory information that established a security risk, such as having "aided or abetted" an "act of sabotage, espionage, treason, or sedition." The manager of operations could use category A information to deny a security clearance or refer the case to the director of security in the Washington, DC, office. In comparison, category B included "those classes of derogatory information where the extent of activities and the attitudes and convictions of the individual must be weighed."[67] Homosexuality fell under category B. Former general counsel to the AEC James Green interpreted category B as not constituting "a series of inflexible standards requiring denial of clearance to any individual whose investigation develops information—even reliable and substantial information—falling within them. An individual may properly be granted clearance in certain cases even if he is a homosexual."[68] It is worth noting that the AEC's inclusion of homosexual as a possible but not definitive security risk predates the federal government's Executive Order 10450, which President Dwight D. Eisenhower issued to expand the government's security apparatus from a few federal agencies to the entire federal workforce, including the AEC. Importantly, the executive order listed "sexual perversion" as a condition for firing a federal employee and denying employment to potential applicants. The federal government promulgated systematic exclusion of gay men and lesbians; any evidence of homosexual tendencies or conduct was sufficient reason for expulsion.[69] In contrast, the AEC considered homosexuality to be a *possible* risk factor.

After the passage of EO 10450, the AEC received pressure to update their practices to match with the Eisenhower provisions. The AEC resisted. "As we discussed May 6 [1953], Executive Order 10450, in the opinion of this office requires no change in the Atomic Energy Commission's present program," argued Deputy Attorney General William Rogers, because "the program of the Atomic Energy Commission exceeds the minimum standards of the Executive Order 10450."[70] But shortly after, Chairman Sterling Cole of the Joint Committee on Atomic Energy Commission, which advised the AEC, wrote to AEC Chairman Gordon Dean to reveal "that the Commission has granted 'Q' clearances to eight individuals as to whom FBI field investigation reports contain substantial evidence of homosexuality."[71] The AEC had a lesbian problem.

Between 1943 and 1953, a "group of girls at Los Alamos who were closely associated and who were considered to be Lesbians" came to the attention of the Joint Committee on Atomic Energy. The women's close relationships to each other as well as three other women who worked at the Hanford site in Washington raised concerns. While both employed at Hanford, Anne and Bonnie had started dating and lived together. After their breakup, Anne moved in with another woman named Denise, while Bonnie returned to Los Alamos and lived with her friend Hillary, who became her lover. The group of friends and lovers (Anne, Bonnie, Gina, Fiona, and Hillary), as well as a few other women (Cat, Denise, and Elaine), all had played together on a traveling baseball team. During one of the games, members from the other team reported to a site manager at Hanford that Elaine "had rigorous quarrels with another woman" who was known to have shared a room with a rumored lesbian, named Cat.[72] Their domestic arrangements and heated arguments aroused alarm. The publicity surrounding the Eisenhower security program's aggressive stance toward homosexuality, which received nationwide media coverage, prompted concerned citizens and employees to write letters and report information to implicate suspected queer people. For women, most investigations into lesbianism were based on rumors rather than any concrete evidence of homosexual activities. Their appearance, romantic attachments, and social ties were often scrutinized for evidence of lesbian tendencies.[73] Mere suspicion about Elaine's sexuality led to an FBI investigation that implicated seven other women who were, at first glance, guilty by association.

A closer interrogation revealed that some of their original clearance investigations contained derogatory information indicating possible homosexual tendencies. Yet the AEC had granted them clearances. In her original file, Gina's former neighbor and classmate had described her as "very mannish in appearance."[74] Likewise, an informant reported that both Hillary and Bonnie "appeared to be sour on men." Los Alamos's director of security determined that such tendencies did not warrant denying a Q-clearance to Hillary, Bonnie, and Gina. He reported that the information was not "sufficiently strong as to leave no question that the employee has been a lesbian." Additionally, at that time (pre-1953), the New Mexico site handled such cases primarily as a private matter rather than as a security matter.[75] Similarly, in 1950 the AEC had flagged the file of Dr. Louis Ridenour for his "personality problem," code for homosexuality. Despite the warning, the AEC concluded that Ridenour's "services were essential and that there was no question as to his loyalty." After a discussion, the AEC "granted Q-clearance to Dr. Ridenour" and requested an interview "to supplement material in his personnel security file."[76] Now, the Joint Committee on Atomic Energy impressed upon the AEC to change its practice urging that *any* indication of a homosexual tendency should result in expulsion.

Other scholars have uncovered a few instances where AEC employees were dismissed for "sexual perversion." According to authors Charles Johnson and Charles Jackson, the Tennessee Eastman Company, which operated the Y-12 plant at the Oak Ridge site, terminated the employment of two "sexual perverts." An informant "quietly" notified the company in 1946 about a "sexual pervert" working for the site, and the company terminated the employee "believed to be a sexual deviate." They also mention that in early 1945, when the sodomy arrest of Mr. Ford, a cement finisher, came to light, Ford was fired.[77] These two cases indicate that proof of sexual activity may have disproportionately affected gay men from employment discrimination. As low-skill workers, they might have also been deemed easily replaceable. The security state system created hierarchical structures of power that privileged educated Anglo-American professionals over manual laborers.

The white-collar suspected lesbians underwent a reinvestigation that consisted of a personal interview, one of the most common techniques used to detect homosexuality.[78] Interrogators tried to get an admission of guilt and names of other lesbians. The eight accused lesbians resisted the security process by vouching for each other's proper sexual morality during their individual interviews. Denise went on record to state that both Anne and Cat were persons of "good moral character." Elaine also attested to Cat's "good moral character" and argued that Cat kept "good associations." Fiona, a former WAC, defended Gina, stating that she "never engaged in any kind of immoral act and lived a very clean life." These women served as character references for one another and formed a chain of solidarity to fight the antigay policy. Nonetheless, all of the women except Hillary were subjected to a further reinvestigation process, and Anne, Cat, and Bonnie also had their Q-clearances put on hold. Charges against Hillary, since she was no longer employed by the AEC, were dropped.[79] What happened to the women during the second reinvestigation is lost to the historical record.

In the summer of 1953, the AEC capitulated to reopen additional security investigations. AEC commissioners publicly denied any relationship between their reinvestigation and Executive Order 10450 but privately expressed fears that the AEC might be perceived as "weak" if it failed to address the lesbian problem.[80] To bolster the public perception of heightening their security measures, the AEC devised a reinvestigation process. To start, the AEC implemented reevaluation on a selective basis. Employees faced a second inquiry if new derogatory information arose, if they had transferred locations or changed positions, and/or it had been three years since their initial investigation, which constituted about 16 percent of the workforce. The AEC asked these employees to fill out a supplemental personnel questionnaire that targeted information concerning memberships to subversive associations. In their vetting, they found 448 cases of non-substantially derogatory information (category B) and 15 cases with substantially derogatory information (category A). While a fair number of employees, 6,200 of 37,000, participated in the reevaluation process, the AEC only revoked two security clearances from the fifteen cases with substantially derogatory information.[81]

For comparison, before the Eisenhower administration issued EO 10450, about one hundred federal employees per year either resigned or were fired due to "sexual perversion." After the executive order, the number increased to around four hundred per year.[82] While the security state accelerated practices that regulated nonnormative sexuality, the AEC, to some extent, offers a counternarrative. To be sure, the AEC drafted a policy that produced the category "homosexual" as a potential security risk factor and did so before EO 10450. But it rarely used the category to deny security clearances to suspected gay men and lesbians. Collectively, the AEC had fewer clearance denials than all other government agencies.[83] From the existing AEC records, it is difficult to ascertain how many might have been denied due to sexual identity. But early examples, such as giving a high-level Q-clearance to a "very mannish in appearance" woman, Gina, illustrates that suspicion of lesbianism did not automatically make one a security risk.

The AEC exercised subtle forms of resistance to the enforcement of sexual norms—keeping sexual identity as category B, a low security risk. Additionally, some experts in the fields of science and global national security began to publicly criticize the Eisenhower security program's determination that homosexuality posed a high security risk in a special issue of the *Bulletin of Atomic Scientists* devoted entirely to critiquing loyalty-security policy.[84] German-born professor of American foreign policy Hans Morgenthau condemned the Eisenhower security program's obsession with sexuality. He went on to question the logic of a "sexual pervert" being "most obviously conducive to treason." "That the homosexual is peculiarly prone to commit crimes under the threat of blackmail is hardly doubted by anyone who faces the problem for the first time. Yet neither the histories of diplomacy and of treason nor the recollections of practitioners of diplomacy, insofar as I could ascertain, contain an instance of a homosexual having committed an act of treason under the threat of blackmail," argued Morgenthau.[85] Raymond Aron, a French political commentator, questioned the rationale behind the "determination of whether this person [homosexual] possesses characteristics or performs actions which constitute a danger to the state."[86]

Collectively, nearly twenty authors argued that protecting sensitive information from espionage is imperative but cautioned against broad definitions of security risks and urged the careful weighing of risk factors. Most looked to the AEC as a model. J. G. Beckerley, who served as the director of the classification for the AEC from 1949 to 1954, wrote, "I had ample opportunity to learn how delicately and sparingly these controls must be exerted."[87] During Beckerley's time as director, the AEC security clearances cases were "weighed in the light of all the information, and a determination must be reached which gives due recognition to the favorable as well as the unfavorable concerning the individual."[88] The AEC's counterexample, pitted against other state security punitive protocols, illustrates how the Eisenhower administration actively worked to structure exclusions of queer people while some AEC directors worked against it. Anti-homosexuality took work to develop and promote. The federal government made heteronormativity an enforced standard that linked an idealized marital heterosexuality to issues of protecting the nation. At the same time, working within the confines of Cold War nationalism, queer people and some experts worked to downplay differences between straight and gay citizens. Experts emphasized the value of scientific expertise over disqualifying someone for sexual proclivities, a nudge toward workplace equity for queer people.[89]

Finally, the location of many AEC employees in the state of New Mexico, and the American West generally, matters. Historian David Johnson argues that "the effects of the Lavender Scare were most acute in the gay and lesbian community of Washington D.C."[90] In DC, besides gay men and lesbians' employment within the nation's capital, the visibility of a gay enclave contributed to the Lavender Scare's local manifestation. Gay men used Lafayette Park, the epicenter of Washington's gay world, as a cruising site in the early twentieth century. Over time a YMCA, restaurants, and gay bars sprang up in the area and created an urban subculture of gay sociability. The visibility of gay men and lesbians who frequented this area contributed to the government's crackdown on homosexuals. In contrast, New Mexico had few demarcated areas for gay men and lesbians to gather, other than a few gay bars that developed in a scattered pattern rather than being concentrated in a gay neighborhood.[91] In this way, urban gay enclaves worked against gay men and lesbians, and the lack of such in New Mexico worked in their favor. The earlier integration of the queer population in northern New Mexico and the subsequent dispersal of its queer culture helped to prevent a mass purging of homosexuals from AEC employment. When a few lesbians congregated together at the Los Alamos and Hanford sites, they became targets of homophobia.

To be sure, New Mexican gay men and lesbians still felt the effects of national attention to homosexuals as security risks during the Cold War era. Ultimately, the security state institutionalized heteronormativity, which posed a constant threat to queer people. As the cases of the eight lesbians illustrate, the security procedures did not end with the granting of a clearance. The AEC's security program, the federal government's program, and the Department of Defense's military security program shared the practice of enforcing security protocols, which involved ongoing investigations to assure compliance and applying sanctions if rules were violated.[92] Part of this process implicated workers in the nuclear complex to report on problems or suspicions of colleagues and even neighbors, friends, and family. The system of secrecy acted as a mechanism of social control.[93] Take the example of Jon Hull, a gay man who worked as an engineer at Kirtland Air Force Base. Hull passed initial Department of Defense security screenings in 1976 but had his clearance revoked after an instructor of a security class reported to the Air Force Office of Security Investigations that Hull was gay. As a result, the Air Force suspended Hull's access to classified information in May of 1982. Hull requested a hearing and hired an attorney. Although the air force reinstated his clearance on May 1, 1986, the long and stressful ordeal taxed Hull's relationship with his partner and created a hostile work environment as Hull faced harassment from other employees after his sexuality became public knowledge.[94] As Hull's experience demonstrates, the structure of postwar security clearances continued well into the 1980s and placed gay men and lesbians in a constant state of anxiety over whether their sexual identity would be uncovered at any point in their careers.[95]

Even those with lower security clearances still felt the effects of national attention to homosexuals throughout the Cold War era. For example, a lesbian named Terri could not get promoted at Sandia because the mandatory security check would have exposed her sexuality.[96] Like Terri, many lesbians and gay men worked in security state industries. Lesbian Vangie Chavez worked in an unclassified position at Western Electric Company and was approved for a P-clearance, for employees with no access to restricted data or high security areas.[97] Chavez hid her sexual orientation, explaining that "It was not safe to be out. There was nothing good about being out in a workplace environment or anywhere for that matter. We had to lead double lives. We had the life in the workplace and then we had our lives around our lesbian culture and friends. They were distinct." At work events, Chavez impersonated a straight woman and pretended to have boyfriends, asking gay male friends to pose as her significant others.[98]

Secrecy provided a structural means of controlling knowledge and imposing heteronormativity, and the repercussions of silence had lasting psychological, political, and economic consequences for lesbians and gay men. Chavez suffered a mental breakdown. "I believe that the suppression of all the emotions that I did not know what to do with and had no one to talk with caused my emotions to burst and the majority of that was related to my sexuality," Chavez remembers.[99] Russell Gray, a gay activist, recalls a certain amount of paranoia among gay men and lesbians in New Mexico that lasted well into the 1980s. Gray believes that secrecy inhibited the formal development of gay and lesbian civil rights organizations in the state.[100] New Mexico's military-industrial complex institutionalized a hostile climate toward queer people, stimulating the practices of masking and migrating.

Queer Responses to the Security State

New Mexico acquired a new identity as the cradle of nuclear science innovation. Part of this transition entailed the coterminous entrance of hundreds of thousands of heteronormative migrants and eventual exodus of some queer residents. As illustrated through the narratives of Morris Kight and Claude Schwob, a few queer migrants were drawn to the state's new economic opportunities. But even for Schwob and Kight, both men carefully rethought where they could spend the remainder of their lives. After working on the Manhattan Project, Schwob took an assistant professorship of chemistry at Carnegie Institute of Technology. Within a year, he was promoted to associate professor. He disliked life in Pittsburgh, though, and by 1948 he determined to find a new job in San Francisco, a growing gay mecca. He took a position at the US Naval Radiological Defense Lab in the city. Schwob spent the remainder of his professional life in San Francisco, a place congenial to his hobby of producing erotica. A decade later, Kight's attempt at a heteronormative life crashed and burned in postwar Albuquerque. He found a vibrant queer culture in Los Angeles, where he cultivated a deep interest in gay civil rights activism. In 1969 alone, Kight cofounded three LGBT organizations: Gay Liberation Front, the Christopher Street West gay pride parade, and the Gay and Lesbian Community Services Center.[101]

New Mexico retained its reputation as an art center, but the addition of scientific sensibilities significantly altered the queer art culture. Upon returning to his home twelve miles from Los Alamos after serving in World War II, modernist painter Cady Wells realized that the nuclear age had forever disrupted his private life. Wells addressed his fear of the security state and a growing sense of homophobia in a letter to his friend E. Boyd, discussing the firings of homosexuals from federal employment. He put his adobe home up for sale "to get away from atomic energy," and, though he was unsuccessful at selling his house, he spent less and less time in Santa Fe, choosing instead to build a second home on Saint Croix, Virgin Islands.[102] Wells exercised his class privilege and ensconced himself in private locations to escape from homosexual persecution. Other queer artists and writers also moved away. In 1955 writer Myron Brinig sold his house in Taos and moved back to New York City. Albuquerque native Lester Q. Strong abandoned living in New Mexico after attempting to cope with its "overwhelming presence of the military," which forced him to keep his sexual identity a secret. Strong left for New York, where he became an author and editor focusing on gay culture and the arts.[103]

Aspiring queer artists and writers from the American Southwest sought out larger cities as spaces for alternative gender and sexual possibilities and fulfilling creative aspirations. A notable example is R. C. Gorman (Diné/Navajo).[104] Gorman marked the beginning of his professional art career and rise as an artist recognized internationally for his depictions of strong Navajo women only when he left the Navajo Nation and migrated to San Francisco. World War II spurred the greatest internal migration in American history; "an influx of tens of thousands of lesbians and gay men (as well as individuals bent upon 'exploring' their sexuality)" moved "into major urban areas across the United States."[105] This queer internal migration overlapped with a mass exodus of American Indians from reservations and rural regions to western cities. Native men who had enlisted in the military accelerated the movement of Native peoples to urban areas. Importantly, even though many Native people migrated to metropolises, they maintained connections to their ancestral lands through Native hubs, locational nodes that fostered community and belonging between urban spaces and tribal cultures, as Gorman would do. Gorman's decision to leave the Navajo reservation began with his own enlistment in the navy in 1951.[106] The navy honorably discharged Gorman in 1955 at Moffett Field (between Mountain View and Sunnyvale, California), at the rank of seaman.[107] His decision to stay in San Francisco after learning that the city held greater possibilities for gay men and lesbians solidified his career path as an artist.

Gorman arrived in the city during the San Francisco Renaissance, a movement sparked by informal gatherings in the North Beach District that permitted artistic radicals to produce a dynamic burst of art and literature.[108] Between 1955 and 1968, Gorman immersed himself in the San Francisco creative sphere—the cultures of artists, art movements, sexual freedom, and Native art hubs—that fundamentally shaped him as an artist, urban Indian, and gay man.[109] Rarely do discussions of San Francisco's renaissance include Native American artists, but Gorman participated in the city's bohemian art scene: his first solo show was at the Coffee Gallery, an epicenter for poetry, jazz, and art in North Beach.[110] The Coffee Gallery engendered racially mixed spaces for the display of art outside of mainstream venues, which often withheld endorsement of modern Native American artists. In contrast, the San Francisco Renaissance fostered an atmosphere conducive to producing cultural work that challenged conventional standards and nonconformist lifestyles. The blossoming alternative culture welcomed the art of an unknown Navajo artist.

Gorman's connections to artistic Native hubs also proved vital for the promotion of his art. Urban Native Americans, in response to their underrepresentation in the mainstream art market, formed organizations and venues devoted to supporting the validation and value of Indian art and artists. In particular, Gorman benefited from the 1964 establishment of the American Indian Historical Society in San Francisco. The society, founded

R. C. Gorman (Diné/Navajo) and his friend Ronald Rutt.
The back of the photo reads: "This is Rutt and Me. That hut in
the back is called a quonset hut. (Yes he is wearing my ring and
bracelet—that was just for the picture because he likes them.)"
After serving in the Navy together, Rutt and Gorman remained
lifelong friends. Virginia Dooley Papers (MSS 844 BC c.1,
box 3, folder 12), Center for Southwest Research, University
Libraries, University of New Mexico.

by Rupert Costo (Cahuilla), his wife, Jeannette Henry-Costo (Cherokee),
and thirteen other Native Americans of various nations, sought to improve
education, cultural exchange, and communication among Indians. The organization's academic emphasis meant it prioritized Indian arts in its activities, and its headquarters included an art museum.[111] The inaugural museum
exhibition, scheduled for July 15–August 15, 1967, featured the paintings
of R. C. Gorman and his renowned father, Carl N. Gorman. According to
local coverage, R. C. Gorman showed "boldly designed abstracts," while
Carl Gorman displayed "traditional water colors."[112] The American Indian
Historical Society committed to Native art and artists—R. C. Gorman and
his father first among them—by allocating space to display their work.

Artistic Native hubs helped to promote Gorman's art, but the evolution of his artistic style is inseparable from the exploration of his homosexuality. To express his queer identity more freely, Gorman moved off the Navajo reservation. San Francisco's queer subculture permitted Gorman access to gender variance, sexual knowledge, and space to "accept himself," which according to Gorman was the "biggest accomplishment" he made.[113] Gorman met Clifton Koltz on March 11, 1963. After developing a romantic relationship, they lived together at 4135 Army Street #10 in the Castro, a gay neighborhood.[114] Queer culture in San Francisco encompassed a broad demography, including spaces for fairies, gender-conforming homophile activists, gender-bending hippies, and underrepresented members—drag queens, transsexuals, and street youth—who practiced gender transgression through style and performance. Gorman was exposed to a variety of gender presentations, particularly as part of the bohemian art world and living in the Castro. Gorman often embodied the characteristics and performativity of the "fairy" by relishing theatricality, embracing a flamboyant style, and at times assuming the performativity of a woman, linking their sexuality and gender personas. Gorman, in their private correspondence, often referred to themself as a woman and called their partner, Koltz, their husband.[115]

Gorman likely used Navajo understandings of gender in combination with urban queer influences to form their identities. Gorman's homosexuality and flexible conceptions of gender led them to seek a deeper connection to the women subjects in their paintings.[116] Gorman's unique style emerged from their application of the confessional nature of expressionism to painting their interior realm, and beginning in the late sixties, a lyrical representation of Navajo women dominated Gorman's work. Throughout his career, interviewers asked Gorman why he painted women. Gorman's answer to this question is more complex when their queer identity is taken into account. In a letter to gallery owner John Manchester, Gorman explained: "It's me. I am every, fat, nude woman I draw."[117] Gorman's self-representation, depicted on canvas as Navajo women, challenged the Western binary construction of male/female. For his representations of Navajo women, Gorman gained worldwide acclaim after he exhibited at *Masterworks from the Museum of the American Indian* in 1973 at the Metropolitan Museum of Art in New York City. Thereafter, news media outlets including

By the mid-sixties, Diné artist R. C. Gorman gained national recognition for his art. Influential art critic for the *San Francisco Chronicle* Thomas Albright positively reviewed Gorman's series *Fragments*—abstract canvases based on Navajo rugs and pottery designs. One piece from the series, an acrylic on canvas titled *Homage to Spider Woman*, is shown behind Gorman in this promotional photograph. Virginia Dooley Papers (MSS 844 BC c.1, box 3, folder 12), Center for Southwest Research, University Libraries, University of New Mexico.

the *New York Times* sometimes referred to him as the "Picasso of American Indian Art."[118]

Unfortunately, Gorman's visits with his family, particularly his father, became strained after he disclosed his sexual identity.[119] This suggests that it likely would have been extremely difficult to publicly express a queer identity on the Navajo reservation.[120] During Gorman's coming of age in the 1930s, governmental efforts at assimilating Navajo and Pueblo people grew more intense (especially the imposition of Christianity), and gender variance classification receded as part of the public culture of Navajo society. In the postwar years on reservations, invisibility further enveloped many queer American Indians. The situation worsened when Native peoples were subjected to a heteronormative standard of citizenship formed both by the United States and some tribal nations.[121] A mutual contact outed Gorman to his family, forcing him to write home and divulge his sexual identity. "I am a homosexual. It's unfortunate only in that I myself did not tell you," Gorman wrote. Speaking from his heart in a meticulously crafted letter, Gorman explained his own coming to terms with his sexual orientation:

"One mistaken notion that many people have is that all homosexuals are suffering terribly and that they want to be cured. At first I might have felt that way but which way or to whom was I to turn?"[122] Gorman had turned to San Francisco, a city rumored to be a safe harbor for homosexuals in search of sexual knowledge. Once he arrived, he read books to learn about his sexual desire. He also visited a doctor and consulted friends. Many women and men who identified as homosexual often first sought information on homosexuality and then looked for kindred spirits before coming out to the larger public.[123] Gorman joined tens of thousands of gay men and lesbians who used movement as a foundational act in the process of self-identifying as gay in twentieth-century America. By the 1950s, a visible mass of sexual migrations had reshaped the cultural landscape of the nation.

Gorman made a reverse migration in 1968, returning to the American Southwest, where he ultimately felt he belonged. In addition, Gorman knew his artistic style sold well in the Southwest, as evidenced by his lucrative shows at the Manchester Gallery, so he could earn a living wage there. Thus Gorman became part of a smaller trend of gay men who left cities for rural settings. Tellingly, once Gorman moved to Taos, he seldom mentions his sexuality in the historical records he left behind. His reticence indicates one consequence of the increased scrutiny of gay artists that came on the heels of the security state and suggests that the locational specificity of his life influenced his navigation of sexual identity. Gorman, being a gay man, was limited in where he could publicly express homoeroticism. As his career grew and as he considered moving away from an urban gay mecca, he began to treat his sexuality as an open secret, a strategy many artists employed. Koltz and Gorman parted ways shortly after their move to Taos. Gorman then lived a public life as a straight man. The security state had forced the once-thriving queer art culture of New Mexico behind a veil of secrecy and in the process transformed what had been fairly amiable heterosexual and homosexual relationships into a homophobic environment. Then the state of New Mexico affirmed the heteronormative order, increasing punishments for sodomy and deepening an atmosphere that insisted on the concealment of sexual identity. Because of the insidious nature of secrecy, gay men and lesbians struggled to challenge these transitions.

FOUR

"What to Do about Homosexuals?"

Open Secrets and Sodomy Law, 1953–1963

Only a smattering of early figurative paintings from abstract artist Agnes Martin's experimental self-expression phase exists; Martin destroyed most of them.[1] A few nude portraits survived only because her then–lesbian partner, Lenore Tawney, hid them. One is a nude of a woman that Martin painted in 1947 in Taos, New Mexico, where her career as an artist began.[2] A half-portrait of a woman with golden-toned skin displays uneven broad shoulders and exposed breasts. Her head, tilted toward her right side, is flanked by long brown hair and short bangs. Thin, discerning eyebrows highlight very dark brown eyes that look almost black. The portrait is both alluring and slightly off-kilter. Art critic Nancy Princenthal posits that it "may have been an academic exercise" in figurative painting with a "Mexican or perhaps Native American" sitter.[3] Queer art historian Jonathan D. Katz infers that it is a self-portrait. He argues that the blushing high cheekbones in the portrait match the painter's.[4] Is *Nude* a self-expression of Martin's sexual nonconformity or an example of a middling painter feeling her way into the nuanced and renowned artist she would become?

"Art is the concrete representation of our most subtle feelings," answered Agnes Martin in a 1995 interview about how to define their body of works. Martin, known for their grid-based aesthetic, became an influential painter in the male-dominated genre of abstraction. They described their geometric

A rare figurative work by Agnes Martin. Agnes Martin,
Nude, 1947, oil on canvas, 20 × 16 in. Courtesy
of Harwood Museum of Art, Taos.

conceptions as emotional works: "I am simply painting concrete representation of abstract emotions such as innocent love, ordinary happiness. I
do want an emotional response. And I paint about emotions, not about
lines."[5] Throughout her life, Martin never publicly acknowledged her sexual
orientation but engaged in discrete lesbian relationships and later in life
embraced an asexual existence. She made strategic decisions to contain
personal information, including purging nude paintings that she did not
want seen. And yet, in several significant ways, as her description of her art
and *Nude* painting begin to reveal, Martin signaled her sexual and gender
variance through her creativity.

Martin's work offers another layer when it is placed in the context of its
production—Cold War New Mexico. Queer cultural producers, who still
sojourned to Santa Fe and Taos to make art, witnessed and endured the
pervasive silencing of same-sex desire. Beginning in 1946, Martin lived
intermittently in New Mexico for ten years, then returned in 1967 and
stayed until their death in 2004. The state gained another permanent artistic resident in 1949 when renowned artist Georgia O'Keeffe settled in
Abiquiú. That same year, after serving as a WAC, Janet Lippincott moved
to Taos to study art. She lived there with her lover Margaret Hibbard, but
the couple were rarely together in public. Lippincott "always dodged being
upfront about their sexuality." The art world classified the personalities of
these artists as unique calling Martin the "art nun," Lippincott a "loner,"
and O'Keeffe a "feminist."[6] I understand them as queer artists who ensconced themselves in the protective isolation of the desert and harnessed
the open-secret strategy.

The once semi-open queer art colony in northern New Mexico shifted
toward what scholar D. A. Miller has called an "open secret."[7] From the
mid-1940s through the mid-1960s, queer makers utilized an informal structure that discouraged explicit sexual labels but encouraged thinly percep-
tible indications of same-gender attraction. The strategy protected artists'
public reputations and preserved their careers, and for most, discretion
in public became a protective necessity.[8] After the 1960s, artists reared in
the open secret culture often continued to keep their intimate life private.
Nationwide, the attacks on queer people that stemmed from the construction of the security state and the perception of "homosexuals" as security
risks transformed queer openness in the art world. Pervasive homophobia,

concern about gay people in the arts, and ramping-up of criminal punishments for same-sex behavior, particularly sodomy laws, eroded visible networks of support for queer artists. Art critics and media outlets drew heightened attention to a queer presence in the arts and openly criticized queer lifestyles.[9] As historian Michael S. Sherry argues, "agitation about homosexuals in the arts became more frenzied and conspicuous in the early 1960s" and peaked mid-decade. "Queer artists of almost any aesthetic were attacked as creators of the twisted and the artificial," explains Sherry. Sherry, along with scholars Gavin Butt, Jonathan D. Katz, and Kenneth Silver, has analyzed the open-secret strategy largely from the standpoint of gay male artists in the post–World War II United States.[10] By contrast, I address the contexts in which queer women and other non-male artists operated in the post–World War II art world and extend the discussion to the music industry through an exploration of ranchera singer and Latina lesbian Genoveva (Geneva) Chávez.[11]

A significant disadvantage of the open secret in New Mexico's art circles was the loss of political clout for gay citizens. When the New Mexico legislature debated the state sodomy law, the second gay civil rights issue in the state, a silent public discourse meant that there was no queer constituency that rallied behind repeal efforts. A few lawmakers considered decriminalizing sodomy, influenced by sexologist Alfred Kinsey's liberalized view of human sexual behavior and the American Law Institute's (ALI) Model Penal Code (MPC).[12] In 1957 New Mexico's legislature began to reform its criminal law, including sexual offenses. Four years later, the New Mexico House of Representatives passed the *first* piece of legislation, House Bill 17, to remove criminal punishments for consensual same-sex sodomy.[13] It passed such a measure using sexual privacy argumentation that had emerged, in part, from the state's influential community of queer artists and transnational allies who had opposed censorship during the decency debates of 1929–30.

However, after the bill's passage in the House, members of the Catholic church and other constituents pushed back, insisting that the state regulate and control homosexuality through the threat of criminal punishment. Under the pressure of powerful social and cultural conservatives, the state of New Mexico—as did much of the United States during this period—codified a heteronormative order. The state government voted to keep the state's sodomy law intact and increased the fine to five thousand dollars and the prison sentence from a maximum of one year to ten years.[14] Both the reinforcement of the state sodomy law and open-secret strategy aided the national security state in imposing secrecy on queer people, keeping them an invisible class denied citizenship rights and thereby making it difficult for them to form community, organize, and contest heteronormative power structures. Antihomosexual laws punished gay people for coming out, having public relationships, and participating in the workforce and politics as gay citizens. Because of increased legal repression in the 1950s and 1960s, queer people lived under the shadow of regulations and societal norms that rendered them criminals. However, the reassertion of the sodomy law posed a greater threat to gay men, whom sodomy laws were most often used to apprehend and prosecute (although they could be used to deny or remove children from the custody of a lesbian parent).[15] For this reason, in the open-secret era in New Mexico, queer women led the endeavor to covertly nurture lesbian artistic support structures and foster queer artistic endeavors.

"What to Do about Homosexuals?"

A debate over the state's sodomy law furthered discriminatory conversations about queer people and legally justified homophobia. New Mexico, like many states, increased penalties for sodomy convictions due to heightened anxieties about homosexuals during the Cold War. States weaponized sodomy laws to target and punish queer people, particularly men. Before the Cold War, New Mexico had rarely employed its sodomy law to police same-sex desire; not until 1953 did the New Mexico Supreme Court have its first published sodomy case.[16] Fred Bennett and Earnest Briton, who were confined in the Quay County jail under a charge of burglary, were apprehended for unnatural sex acts (fellatio) on May 17, 1951. They both pled guilty but later petitioned the court, claiming that their plea was under a misapprehension of sodomy law. They were guilty of oral sex rather than in violation of the state's statute that prohibited anal sex. Since the state sodomy law retained the broad common-law definition of the "abominable crime of sodomy" without specifying its sexual acts, Bennett and Briton reasoned that oral sex was outside the scope of sodomy law.[17] New Mexico Supreme Court

Justice James Compton wrote the court's opinion on the case, *Bennett v. Abram*. He called same-sex oral sex "even more sensual and filthy than the offense" of anal penetration. He recommended that the legislature redefine *sodomy* to include oral sex and adopt the following language from the *Manual for Courts-Martial of the U.S. Army* (1949): "Sodomy consists of a person taking into his or her mouth or anus the sexual organ of any other person or animal or placing his or her sexual organ in the mouth or anus of any other person or animal. Any penetration, however slight, is sufficient to complete the crime of sodomy. Both parties may be principals." At the next session of the legislature, in 1955, New Mexico lawmakers added the new language to the existing sodomy statute and increased the penalty for conviction from a maximum of one year in prison to ten.[18]

But, a few years later, lawmakers considered legalizing sodomy influenced by Alfred Kinsey's liberalized view of human sexuality and the American Law Institute's Model Penal Code. By the 1950s, a growing number of postwar sexual liberals, including members of the legal profession, reconsidered whether sodomy should be criminally punished, in light of new scientific and medical research. Kinsey, a pioneer in the scientific study of sex, published groundbreaking works commonly referred to as the Kinsey reports, revealing that Americans engaged in a variety of sexual activity. He proposed a spectrum of sexualities on a seven-point scale ranging from exclusive heterosexuality to exclusive homosexuality and argued that most Americans' sexual behavior resided between the two extremes. Documented and verified through quantitative data, Kinsey showed that traditional ideals about sexual morality conflicted with people's actual behavior.[19] He suggested that his findings extend beyond scientific circles into the realm of law enforcement.[20] Based on Kinsey's assertion that laws criminalizing sexual behavior were unenforceable and misguided, some legal professionals began to reevaluate punishment of private, consensual homosexual and heterosexual sex acts and argued in favor of decriminalization.[21]

In the 1950s the ALI, a national nongovernmental association composed of elected judges, professors, and lawyers, embarked on a ten-year project to codify and reform US criminal law, known as the Model Penal Code. ALI then encouraged states to revise their criminal codes, including decriminalizing consensual sexual behavior, according to the organization's

Model Penal Code. Law professor Herbert Wechsler of Columbia University served as the reporter (the coordinator of the project), and a number of committee members, including Louis B. Schwartz of the University of Pennsylvania School of Law, who headed the sexual offenses section, prepared the principal work on the MPC.[22] Committees then debated this work and brought a draft to the full ALI membership during the annual meeting in Washington, DC. In May 1962 ALI published the finalized MPC, which eliminated the criminalization of consensual same-sex sexual behavior.[23]

After the MPC was finalized, most states established criminal reform commissions; a few—Connecticut, Georgia, Kansas, Illinois, Minnesota, New Mexico, and New York—had responded to earlier drafts.[24] In 1957 the New Mexico legislature created the Criminal Law Study Committee to examine the state's criminal code, including sexual offenses.[25] It conducted four years of research in an attempt to rework and revise the antiquated, contradictory, and often confusing New Mexican criminal laws, which dated back to 1846. The committee, in cooperation with the attorney general, then recommended changes and drafted new legislation, retaining existing criminal laws wherever possible and amending only when existing law was "unclear, unnecessary, a duplication or outmoded."[26]

The Criminal Law Study Committee relied on the recommendations laid out in all seven MPC drafts, Wisconsin's comprehensive criminal code revision, which predated the MPC (1955), Minnesota's revision study (1957), and Illinois's proposed criminal code (1958) to amend New Mexico's criminal laws.[27] The MPC section entitled "Deviate Sexual Gratification" relied on Kinsey's understanding of sexual expression: "the sexual impulse finds expression in a variety of ways other than heterosexual copulation. Substantial numbers of males and females find themselves drawn to members of their own sex." In the first draft, the MPC advisory committee suggested amending the sodomy provision stating that "no harm to the secular interests of the community is involved in atypical sex practice in private between consenting partners." Scholar Marie-Amelie George calls the statement "radical . . . in light of the fact that every state at that time criminalized these acts."[28] Even so, the chief reporters and ALI membership equivocated on whether or not to overturn the sodomy legislation. The second draft continued to criminalize sodomy but demoted the crime to a misdemeanor. Ultimately, in the final version passed in May 1962, the membership of ALI instituted a new legal paradigm that deregulated most private and consensual sexual behavior, including laws pertaining to homosexuals.[29]

In 1961 New Mexico became the first state legislature to decriminalize sodomy, heeding the ALI's recommendations.[30] By 1963 New Mexico's legislature would reverse its decision, reinstating sodomy as a crime and voting to increase the fine from one thousand dollars to five thousand dollars. Fifteen years after the publication of the MPC, only Illinois and Connecticut eliminated consensual sodomy as a crime.[31] The other southwestern state, Arizona, refused to consider reforming its homosexual sodomy law, which already had a penalty of five to twenty years in prison, one of the harshest in the nation, and instead added a five-thousand-dollar fine to the prison term.[32] Why the New Mexico House of Representatives passed the decriminalization of sodomy first relates to the state's earlier establishment and support of queer culture, particularly its embrace of sexual privacy. But the state government's ultimate decision to uphold sodomy as a crime underscores a growing antihomosexual undercurrent that supplanted sexual privacy rights.

When initially reconceptualizing its sodomy law, the New Mexico legislature disavowed the state's role in regulating consensual sex acts and sought to challenge the social condemnation of homosexuality. This is most strongly demonstrated in the progressive language it used to define sodomy. In its drafts, the ALI employed the term "deviate sexual conduct" to refer to sodomy, while other states, such as Wisconsin, defined sodomy as "sexual perversion."[33] Even Kinsey chose to rely on existing language when discussing sodomy laws: "Sodomy laws are usually indefinite in their description of acts that are punishable; perversions are defined as unnatural acts contrary to nature, bestial, abominable, and detestable." New Mexico replaced the term "sodomy" with "variant sexual practice" to refer to oral and anal sex for both same-sex and heterosexual couples.[34] Adopting this neutral terminology nudged toward the possibility of sexual equality. The phrase "variant sexual practice" likely stemmed from lawmakers' familiarity with sexological works outside of the Kinsey reports. Thanks to relaxed censorship regulations, sexological literature freely circulated beyond the medical profession.[35] Sexologists extensively discussed sexual variations by the second half of the nineteenth century: from Richard von Krafft-Ebing's *Psychopathia Sexualis*, first published in 1887, to psychiatrist

George H. Henry's *Sex Variants: A Study of Homosexual Patterns*, published in 1941. Henry defined the "sex variant" as someone who has an emotional experience with others of his or her own sex.[36] Some early gay activists, including the Mattachine Society, welcomed the term in an effort to liberalize Americans' sexual ideals.[37] Lesbian librarian Jeannette H. Foster published a groundbreaking study on lesbian literature entitled *Sex Variant Women in Literature: A Historical and Quantitative Study* in 1956. Foster selected "sex variant" "because it is not as yet rigidly defined nor charged with controversial overtones," arguing that it simply means "differing from a chosen standard," heterosexuality, a "western Christian culture of marriage and parenthood."[38] Because the social meaning of *sodomy* crystalized as thoroughly homosexual (and therefore stigmatized) during this period, replacing the term with *variant sexual practice* broadened it to include a range of sexual activities between consenting adults.

The Criminal Law Study Committee eradicated legal sanctions related to same-sex acts between consenting adults under Article 13, Section 13-7, encompassed in the omnibus criminal law revision House Bill 17 (HB 17). Like other postwar sexual liberals, committee members justified legalizing sodomy by invoking sexual privacy rights. They argued that acts conducted in private posed little harm to society. Staff member Ed Stockly, a Los Alamos attorney, in anticipation of criticism about legalizing sodomy, noted that "members of the committee may not approve of some things they have made to be no longer a crime. But when such things do not hurt society or persons involved in the legal sense, they do not constitute a crime." Stockly further countered moral objections by pointing out that "changes in the code reflect present practice of district attorney and changes in society as shown in such studies as the Kinsey reports."[39] Additionally, Chairman Mayo T. Boucher, an attorney and Valencia County Democrat, defended decriminalizing sodomy on the grounds that "district attorneys are never able to prosecute in cases involving mutual consent among adults."[40] Such discussions extended notions of sexual privacy from arenas of sexual speech to sexual acts.

The House of Representatives passed HB 17, which included the decriminalization of sodomy, with a 37–28 vote in January 1961. However, the legislature's legalization of sodomy produced a heated debate.[41] The first wave of controversy occurred in the Catholic community. Roman Catholicism has long been the dominant religion in New Mexico, followed by Protestantism. In the 1960s, around 39 percent of residents identified as Catholic, while the national average was 23.6 percent. Archbishop of Santa Fe Edwin V. Byrne seethed with shock and dismay that such a "perverse code" had made it through the House, stating, "It proposes a drastic departure from ordinary and common decency, to say nothing about the moral law and public order."[42] Byrne focused solely on the provision that decriminalized sodomy, even though HB 17 revised and systemized all aspects of New Mexican criminal law. The executive committee of the Archdiocesan Council of Catholic Men backed the archbishop's denunciation, ordering the legislature to oppose the legalization of sodomy. Other states, most notably New York, also faced Catholic opposition to decriminalizing state sodomy statues.[43]

Attention to the sodomy provision agitated many New Mexicans, who began to insist that the state regulate and control homosexuality through the threat of criminal punishment and, unlike state lawmakers, linked sodomy to "sexual perversion." Letters to the editor poured in to state newspapers protesting the sodomy provision, such as this one from Mrs. Vera Padilla: "It shocks me greatly, as I'm sure it will the majority of New Mexicans. The legalizing of sodomy, one of the greatest sins of perversion and degeneracy, by our House of Rep, is sure to bring nothing but sorrow and shame." She goes on to explain how the existing regulation of homosexuals works: "Those people who practice sodomy, until now have had to hide their ideas and practices to a certain extent. Now they will be able to flaunt their relationships and ideas without fear of punishment."[44] Padilla's comment speaks to the growing climate of secrecy imposed on gay men and lesbians. According to Padilla, forcing homosexuals to conceal their sexual identity kept the social and moral order intact.

Chairman Boucher commented that "my mail has been about equally split between those for and against the proposal," indicating that some New Mexicans supported the change, but the press favored publishing articles and letters to the editor that overwhelming represented the opposition.[45] The Santa Fe New Mexican published only one letter to the editor that supported the measure. Nancy Mainville wrote, "Many people here feel that our city [Santa Fe] is already a 'very warped place in which to live.' Most of us, fortunately, are glad of the general tolerance. . . . I admire the moral courage of whoever proposed that bill. I shall be proud of our state if it passes." Mainville's comment acknowledged Santa Fe as "the city different," a city that cultivated a reputation as a sanctuary for misfits, including queer people.[46] Mainville reminded Santa Feans of their bohemian sensibility as a way to encourage HB 17's passage.

Since Spud Johnson had ceased publication of his little magazine *Laughing Horse*, northern New Mexico lacked a mouthpiece for queer people. Johnson authored two editorial columns called the "The Horse Fly" and "The Gadfly" for local newspapers and occasionally as a freestanding paper into the 1960s, but his later articles rarely engaged with queer issues.[47] Not until 1972, when lesbian couple Marion Love and Betty Bauer founded *The Santa Fean*, did the area regain a queer editorship.[48] Instead, statewide, the New Mexico press stigmatized sodomy by linking it to homosexuality. A now open and public conversation about homosexuality emboldened journalists to inject their own religious and moral arguments. In small towns like Clovis, an agricultural community in the eastern part of the state, the local paper invoked the Bible: "Sodom was destroyed . . . and if we do not have a spiritual and moral awakening in the United States with accompanying rugged individual independence, we will go the same way, make no mistake about it." Clovis columnist David Baxter believed that homosexuals symbolized the nation's moral decline and indicated the need for better state protections.[49]

The press's negative portrayal of homosexuals combined with existing religious beliefs eroded New Mexicans' laissez-faire attitudes toward their queer neighbors. The local media regurgitated the dominant discourse—homosexuals were sexual perverts who threatened the safety of the nation—and thus reshaped ideas about lesbians and gay men. Before the debates instigated by the criminal code reform, New Mexicans had formed their own opinions on the state's queer population and, given queer people's integration in 1920s and 1930s, earlier opinions had been far more favorable than those after the advent of the security state.[50]

In part because of earlier favorable conditions, queer New Mexicans never formed a homophile organization that could have rallied in support of the decriminalization measure. Rarely had the state government enforced its sodomy law, and as in the Pacific Northwest cities of Portland and Seattle, police harassment of queer people in Albuquerque and Santa Fe was minimal, so there simply did not seem to be an urgent reason to organize.

The nascent homophile movement grew most notably in populous cities where queer people faced harsh discriminatory treatment by the state government or harassment by police. New chapters of the Mattachine Society formed in New York (1957), Washington, DC (1957, 1961), Mattachine Midwest (1965), Florida (1966), and Denver (1957), the only chapter in the American West outside of California.[51] In western states with large land masses but small populations, such as Nevada, queer people were isolated, making political building more challenging. Although Mattachine chapters spread to large cities, historian Lillian Faderman points out that the organization "never grew larger than a few hundred members nationally at any given time." Likewise, the Daughters of Bilitis, founded in San Francisco, developed chapters in New York, Philadelphia, Boston, Chicago, Los Angeles, and Fanwood, New Jersey, that collectively consisted of a few hundred members. Due to a strong, albeit small, homophile presence in California, activists launched a legislative challenge to their state sodomy law, which resulted in its repeal in 1975.[52] Another avenue for organization stemmed from bar culture that developed in cities such as Denver, Colorado, and Buffalo, New York.[53] New Mexico never contained a political consciousness through bar-based culture in the 1950s and 1960s. Finally, the imposed secrecy that enveloped queer people during this period made it difficult to form community and organize in opposition to heteronormative structures of power. Formalized organization in the state lay a decade in the future.

However, like other queer people in states without bar-based resistance or formal political organizing, New Mexicans could connect to early activism through homophile publications. Homophile groups published their own journals and newsletters that circulated nationally, albeit with a limited reach, including ONE Magazine (1953–67), Mattachine Review (1955–66), and The Ladder (1956–72). Letters to the editor in the Mattachine Review reveal that this publication reached queer New Mexicans.[54] The Daughters of Bilitis and Mattachine initially fostered an interest in reforming sodomy laws, as evidenced by their avid reporting on sodomy law repeal in the homophile press. The first issue of The Ladder, the Daughters of Bilitis's publication, included as one of its goals "investigation of the penal code as it pertains to the homosexual, proposal of changes to provide an equitable handling of cases involving this minority group, and promotion of these changes through due process of law in the state legislatures."[55] Mattachine shared this vision, arguing that "sexual activities between two willing and consenting adults should not be a legal matter governed by public law but rather a matter of individual personal morals."[56]

Support for the New Mexico measure surfaced in the burgeoning homophile press. The Mattachine Society congratulated the New Mexico legislature for being the first state "to revise sex laws along lines advocated by the American Law Institute."[57] Mattachine desired that New Mexico set a legal precedent, establishing the right for homosexuals to behave as they wished in private, without fear of criminal consequences. Getting rid of sodomy laws would break down a legal barrier and grant greater freedom in intimate private lives. Because New Mexico had rarely enforced its same-sex sodomy law and cultivated a reputation as a state where queer people could live peacefully and privately, the Mattachine Society hoped the state would pave the way in legalizing sodomy.

By the end of February of 1961, statewide New Mexico newspapers reassured readers that the bill was doomed to fail. Boucher rapidly yielded to pressure to remove the sodomy clause.[58] In an article entitled "What to Do about Homosexuals?" in May 1961, the *Mattachine Review* reported the defeat of HB 17, explaining that although state legislatures, bar associations, and psychiatrists overwhelmingly concurred that punitive laws against consensual sex acts needed to change, religious opposition had prevented New Mexico's attempt to make such changes. The Mattachine Society even wrote a letter to the Roman Catholic archbishop of New Mexico, Edwin V. Byrne, seeking clarification on the church's opposition and arguing that consensual sodomy statutes should be eliminated. Francis A. Tournier of Santa Fe replied on Byrne's behalf but did not provide a clear answer. Tournier only confirmed that the prelate's protest caused the Senate to "shelve the entire criminal code revision."[59] HB 17 had cleared the House of Representatives on January 30, 1961, but was killed by a Senate committee on March 11. Lawmakers ordered the Criminal Law Study Committee to continue its work for an additional two years, and in 1963 the committee proposed a revised criminal code that not only failed to decriminalize sodomy but in fact increased the fines related to sodomy charges from one thousand to five thousand dollars.[60]

The larger paradoxical culture of both leniency toward private same-sex relationships and heightened fears against gay personhood influenced the impetus and outcome of HB 17. While some legal experts in the state had recommended the separation of sexual morality from criminal punishment, religious authorities and vocal residents demanded its integration. A public outcry from the Catholic church and constituents forced legislators to consider their demand and concede to antigay attitudes. The debate over sodomy demonstrates that New Mexicans correlated homosexuality with sodomy even though it criminalized a diverse set of nonreproductive sexual acts.

In 1929 the queer art community had rallied in support of sexual politics during the decency debates, assisting in the breakdown of strict federal obscenity standards and in turn bolstering sexual discourse. By the postwar era, queer art and literary colonies had lost political power. Their reticence on decriminalizing sodomy spoke volumes about their contemporary place in society. The continuation of the sodomy statute ensured second-class status for sex and gender-variant people. New Mexicans feared that removing criminal punishment for "perverse" acts would erode the social order and lead to a dangerous moral reorientation, an issue that had seemed of little concern a few decades before. Here, the system of secrecy, the foundation for the security state, aided in the reassertion of a policy that mandated homosexuals hide. The mere threat of arrest kept queer people in stark silence. In response, many sunk deeper into the shadows as a means of self-preservation, while others embraced queer lives elsewhere.

"First Lady of the Santa Fe Fiesta"

The open-secret lifestyle had a deeper history in Nuevomexicano communities. Queer Nuevomexicanxs had long adhered to what I call a "culture of privacy," an arranged system of privacy toward sexual identity and behavior as long as individuals used discretion in public places. Nuevomexicanos employed silence as a cover for exploring sexual indiscretions outside the bounds of normative sex. Latina lesbian and ranchera singer Genoveva Chávez melded the culture of privacy and open-secret strategy to navigate her successful career in mariachi music in both Los Angeles and Santa Fe. Chávez's life affords the opportunity to consider the open-secret strategy from a Latina perspective. Her narrative, analyzed in tandem with existing queer Latinx history, which is still largely unwritten, suggests that the mu-

Geneva Chávez, who professionally used the name Genoveva Chávez,
developed a successful career in mariachi music in both Los Angeles and
Santa Fe. Chávez was known for serenading audiences with soulful Spanish-
language ballads at the Santa Fe Fiesta. A public silence about Chávez's
lesbianism has suppressed the acknowledgment of a Latina lesbian's
contribution to the musical culture of mariachi. Courtesy of Palace of the
Governors Photo Archives (NMHM/DCA), HP.2008.25.016.

sic industry served as an avenue for queer exploration and community for Latinx people.[61]

Lyric folk songs and stories, soulful ranchera melodies, and lively mariachi music comprise some of the vibrant musical traditions of Nuevomexicanos.[62] Spanish-language songs and stories have sustained cultural ties and invigorated spaces for an evolving Nuevomexicano identity. Folk songs and stories created in the early 1900s even willingly addressed what most Nuevomexicanos shrouded in secrecy—homosexuality.[63] Oral performance and musical expression offer a source for excavating the stories of queer Latinx people, particularly in the postwar era, when Nuevomexicanos claimed authority over their cultural production.[64] Grasping the significance of the region's musical traditions, "passed from musician to musician through oral culture," Ruben Cobos, a professor, folklorist, and musician, captured the stories and songs of Nuevomexicanos in northern New Mexico and southern Colorado between 1944 and 1974. Of the 591 musical and spoken samples Cobos recorded, seven discuss male homosexuals. While understandings of gender and sexuality among US Latino populations encompass a continuum of experiences—historical, religious, cultural, and lived—those seven stories provide a window into the integration of American and Latin American sexual systems, as well as local understandings of queer people.[65] In the Nuevomexicano culture of privacy around sexuality in general and homosexuality in particular, music served as a space to address sexual topics and, for Genoveva Chávez, a nurturing site for her lesbian and creative expression.

In the spoken Spanish anecdote "El hombre que fue pa Juarez," a man tells his friend that there are virgin girls in Juarez, Mexico. The friend decides to go to a Juarez brothel and asks the madam for a virgin. By misunderstanding, she sends him an effeminate homosexual man.[66] "El pirujo," a similar humorous story, describes a homosexual going to a bar and asking for a beer. The bartender, sensing the man is gay, tells him to ask for it with balls; the homosexual responds literally, asking the bartender for a beer with balls.[67] These two stories and others in the collection, written and performed by men, cast gay men in a hierarchal structure that privileges heterosexuality and masculinity. Both stories portray homosexuals as effeminately gendered and therefore insufficiently masculine. In the second story, the gay protagonist confronts the hegemony of heteronormative sexuality.

The bartender displays open hostility toward him, refusing to serve him a beer because he is *pirujo* (gay) and emasculating him. To be sure, stories and songs often spoke to an exaggerated sense of masculinity associated with strength, sexual potency, and prowess.[68] Nonetheless, such narratives cautioned individuals against expressing gender and sexuality outside of these cultural norms or else risk ridicule and ostracism from their community.

In the postwar period, these anecdotes continued to circulate and shape conceptions of queer people. They aided the concealment and suppression of nonnormative sexual liaisons, which prevented open acknowledgment of Nuevomexicanx homosexual identity. Further complicating the recognition of queer Nuevomexicanxs, scholar Tomás Almaguer affirms that "Chicano men who embrace a 'gay' identity (based on the European-American sexual system) must reconcile this sexual identity with their primary socialization into a Latino culture that does not recognize such a construction: there is no cultural equivalent to the modern 'gay man' in the Mexican/Latin-American sexual system."[69] Tellingly, local Nuevomexicanos developed their own terminology. Bennett Hammer, a gay man who moved to New Mexico in 1967 to study bilingual Spanish-English education, learned of a local Spanish phrase for queer men: "There is a phrase in Spanish in [northern] New Mexico the way parents say, mainly mothers, Spanish mothers, say that their son is queer . . . *Mejor solo que mal acompañado*, meaning 'poorly accompanied or poorly paired.' That is their way of saying 'my son is queer.'"[70] The phrase expresses the sentiment that it is better for a gay Latino man to remain unpartnered than be in a gay relationship. Latina lesbian Carla Trujillo, born in New Mexico, describes the imposition of public sexual conformity. She recalls that mothers "whispered the warnings, raised the eyebrows, or covertly transmitted to us the 'taboo nature' of same-sex relationships."[71] Chicana lesbian Nadine Armijo, who established a lesbian household across the street from her family in Corrales, also spoke about her mother's refusal to utter the word *lesbian*. Only once, during a fight, did she acknowledge her daughter's lesbianism by name.[72]

Growing up gay as a young person in Santa Fe, Genoveva Chávez faced a conflict between a growing consciousness of her sexual difference and the postwar imperative of heteronormativity. She found an outlet through music. Chávez was born in Santa Fe in 1942 to a Nuevomexicano family with deep musical roots. Both her father, Henry, a guitarist, and her mother,

Ruby, a vocalist, performed with Rhythm Kings, a popular mariachi band. At the age of five, Genoveva Chávez began singing at weddings and other family celebrations. She learned the lyrics to ranchera music by listening to records and the radio, singing "Mal Hombre" along with Lydia Mendoza and "Cuando el Destino" with Lola Beltrán.[73]

In 1958, at the age of sixteen, Chávez began performing at the Santa Fe Fiesta, serenading audiences with soulful Spanish-language ballads accompanied by mariachi music. Fiesta, an annual event funded by the city and a major tourist attraction, celebrates the Spanish reconquest of the city from Pueblo control in 1692. The three-day event romanticizes portrayals of a Spanish cultural heritage over other forms of Latino history and culture, with the exception of lively mariachi music, a Mexican tradition that rings throughout the days and nights of Fiesta. Indigenous to Jalisco, an agricultural state of western Mexico, the mariachi ensemble, known for featuring violins, guitars, and, later, trumpets, became a symbol of Mexican identity to large Mexican American communities in California, Texas, and parts of the Southwest.[74] In the United States, mariachi groups, composed almost exclusively of men, first appeared in cantinas, bars that served rural and blue-collar men. The music spread beyond cantinas, enlivening outdoor plazas, restaurants, and family celebrations. The genre commercialized in the 1940s and 1950s and merged with música ranchera, country music that touched deep emotional chords, particularly through lyrical love songs played on the radio and in cinema.[75] The most popular vein of Mexican music, ranchera helped to popularize Spanish-language music with white audiences through touring musical shows. Such shows featured a big-name singer, where a few women, most notably Lydia Mendoza, found an opportunity to perform.[76]

Shortly after graduating from Santa Fe High School in 1960, Chávez, who idolized the careers of Mendoza and Beltrán, moved to Los Angeles to pursue a musical career. During the day, Chávez worked; at night, she sang in East LA nightclubs.[77] Eventually, she landed a better gig performing on a cruise ship, the *Love Boat*, that sailed from Los Angeles to Acapulco, Mexico, and later inspired a popular TV show by the same name. Her tour on the *Love Boat* led to recording with notable stars.[78] She later performed with several mariachi groups and famous Mexican musical stars, including Lucha Villa, Lola Beltrán, Vicente Fernández, and José Alfredo Jiménez and recorded with the labels Lobo Records, Dimsa, Music Records, and Casanova Records. Despite her success, she always returned to her hometown to perform in the Santa Fe Fiesta.[79]

Another reason for Chávez's migration to Los Angeles was to locate spaces to explore her lesbian identity. By 1960 Los Angeles contained a considerable number of nightspots for lesbians. Latina lesbians often frequented working-class, racially mixed lesbian bars such as Tulley's in Pico Rivera, a working-class suburb about fifteen miles east of East Los Angeles. Redhead in East LA opened in 1960 and catered specifically to Latina lesbians.[80] The greater East LA area was a geographic stronghold for Latino culture. Latina lesbians, through lesbian bar culture in Latino neighborhoods, congregated and developed bonds informed by Latino cultural values and expressed through Latina lesbian cultural vernacular.[81] As a queer singer and musician who performed in East LA nightclubs, it is likely Chávez used bar culture as opportunities to socialize with other queer Latinas. In contrast, not until the 1970s did Chicana lesbians create space for themselves in New Mexico's gay bar scene.

Eventually, Chávez moved back to Santa Fe, likely because of her systemic lupus erythematosus diagnosis, which hampered her successful music career. She lived the remainder of her life with her partner, Dorothy Rivera, and continued to perform at Fiesta.[82] A Santa Fe resident recalled that "Fiesta was not official until Genoveva took the microphone and, with great joy, serenaded the crowd with her heart-felt canciones." Chávez is sometimes referred to as the "First Lady of the Santa Fe Fiesta" for her annual Spanish-language musical performances. Others whispered about her "secret" partnership: "Genoveva Chávez she was a singer, a famous singer in northern New Mexico. There is a recreational center named after her. She was with her partner for thirty years, everyone knew, but you didn't talk about it," remembers white lesbian Linda Siegle.[83] Chicana lesbian Ana Castillo, a native of Chicago who moved to New Mexico, remembers being frustrated by her attempts to discuss lesbian sexual desire with other Latinas "how I wanted, needed to talk." In an anthology that gave voice to Latina lesbians, she said, "because of the strict social attitudes toward open sexual expression, most lesbians of our [Mexican] culture have not politicized their desires nor declared them openly as a way of life." Instead, Chicana lesbians operated "covertly so as to not risk losing social status and financial security."[84] The open secret enforced public silence about individuals' sexuality and has suppressed the acknowledgment of queer creatives, such as Chávez, who left an indelible mark on American musical cultures. While a lesser-known singer on the national scene, Chávez was beloved in her hometown and one of the earliest local women superstars of mariachi. Not until the late 1960s and 1970s were Latina women encouraged to perform mariachi music.[85] The city of Santa Fe recognized Genoveva Chávez's musical contributions when it opened a new community center in January 2000 and named it in her honor. Of the many remembrances published in newspapers about her life, only one mentions her long-term partner.[86] Silences around Chávez's sexual identity have allowed her music to go unrecognized as a contribution from a Latina lesbian.

Open Secrets

Likewise, only recently have abstract artist Agnes Martin's contributions as a queer maker been acknowledged.[87] Martin navigated the world as a poor, queer artist who experienced serious mental health episodes, eventually being diagnosed with paranoid schizophrenia in 1962.[88] To address poverty, grapple with same-gender desires, and ease mental distress, Martin embraced periods of itinerancy and solitude, finding in them a calming, emancipatory effect. She chose to live in New Mexico for much of her life in part for its low cost of living, relative isolation, and queer art circles. Martin, similar to Chávez, employed the open-secret strategy to explore their nonconforming gender and sexual ideals in the white bohemian art world. Martin also benefited from two significant queer mentors—renowned artist Georgia O'Keeffe and gallery owner Betty Parsons.

Martin first moved to Albuquerque in 1946 to join the University of New Mexico's Fine Arts Department after receiving a scholarship.[89] Studying art for one year, she devoted herself to figurative painting and earned a second scholarship to attend the Harwood Museum's Art Field School in Taos. She spent the next decade teaching art at the University of New Mexico and the John Marshall School, both in Albuquerque, while she experimented with various art styles. She continued to paint portraits and added representational landscapes and abstract canvases to her repertoire.[90] Martin had met Daphne Cowper, an English and drama student at UNM, in

Post-painterly abstract artist Agnes Martin worked, painted,
and socialized within the constellation of Albuquerque, Santa Fe,
and Taos as well as their rural environs. Pictured here in the Ledoux
Street Studio, Taos, Martin spent half their life in New Mexico.
By 1967 Martin had rejected the label *woman* and embraced an
asexual existence. Photograph courtesy of the Harwood Museum
of Art and Mildred Tolbert Archive, Taos.

1946. They developed an intimate partnership, and after Martin's summer in Taos, the couple lived together. They built an adobe home on Avalon, a secluded patch of land near Fifty-Second and Central Avenue, where they resided for three years. They kept the nature of their relationship private; its secretive restrictions ultimately led to its unraveling.[91]

Martin worked, painted, and socialized within the constellation of Albuquerque, Santa Fe, and Taos as well as their rural environs. She benefited, in particular, from her contact with Georgia O'Keeffe and Betty Parsons. Scholars have long debated O'Keeffe's sexuality. Biographer Benita Eisler claims that O'Keeffe and Rebecca "Beck" Strand had a sexual affair when they traveled together to New Mexico in 1929 and concludes that O'Keeffe was bisexual. Others cling to O'Keeffe's heterosexuality.[92] Queer activist and Distinguished Professor of the Humanities Sarah Schulman pushes back on the hesitancy to explore "desire and emotions of erotic feeling" in artists such as Agnes Martin and Georgia O'Keeffe, arguing that scholars should move away from the need to pin down an identity category of "lesbian" or "bisexual." Schulman urges scholars to grapple with the "nuance, complexity, contradiction, vagueness, ambivalence, [and] confusion" of artists' emotions and actions. She writes, "Lesbians give each other meaning in private, and it is too easy to keep the secret. It doesn't have to be clean, neat, safe, compartmentalized, or expected. Show it all and let the chips fall where they may."[93]

O'Keeffe was married to photographer and art dealer Alfred Stieglitz, though the couple spent long periods of time away from each other.[94] Initially, Stieglitz's extramarital affair with Dorothy Norman, his secretary and gallery manager, precipitated O'Keeffe's desire for time away from her husband. O'Keeffe traveled alone to Maine in May 1928. She made annual trips to Santa Fe in the summers between 1929 and 1931 and in 1932 visited Canada by herself. She realized that time apart benefited her creativity and insisted on continuing her solo annual excursions to New Mexico. Throughout her marriage, O'Keeffe's personal correspondence reveals sexual attraction to other men as well as elements of romantic entanglements in her correspondence with women, particularly lesbian and aspiring writer Maria Chabot. The two met in 1940, when O'Keeffe was fifty-three and Chabot twenty-six, at the home of Mary Wheelwright, a well-known gathering point for "a growing colony of lesbian women" in Alcalde, north of

Santa Fe.[95] After Chabot's final breakup with on-and-off intimate partner Dorothy Stewart, Wheelwright invited Chabot to stay with her. Chabot found her new living situation disagreeable. In a letter to Stewart, she wrote "had she [Mary Wheelwright] been a man she would have been a Dictator." O'Keeffe offered a solution: come live with her instead. In summer and fall from 1941 through 1944, Chabot lived with O'Keeffe at Ghost Ranch as her assistant and companion. They produced a large body of correspondence, which if read through a queer lens illustrates same-gender companionship and a reimagining of gender identities within their relationship.[96]

In one telling letter, on May 8, 1942, Chabot wrote to O'Keeffe anticipating their time together at Ghost Ranch. She teased, "Do you think you could keep me away?" Chabot relayed in the letter that her mother fretted over the meaning of her relationship with O'Keeffe, asking, "does this woman look upon you as a servant or a friend?" Chabot answered, "neither." Chabot's relationship with O'Keeffe began as an economic arrangement: O'Keeffe gave her a place to live, a quiet space to write, and a small salary in exchange for assisting with household management tasks. By the second year, in this same letter, Chabot refused O'Keeffe's offer of payment, writing, "Don't you know you don't pay for the good things of life?" Chabot described her time with O'Keeffe as "enlightened" and shared that "what I like about you is your damned independence." Chabot wished to be "just as independent."[97]

Beyond their living arrangement, Chabot and O'Keeffe frequently went camping together, especially near the Bisti Badlands in northwestern New Mexico, a stark landscape with undulating white, black, and red hills. A few references to women, particularly lesbian-identified, imply that couples used camping and backcountry trips for privacy. Indeed, Santa Fe artist and author Walter Cooper claims Agnes Sims "took various girlfriends on back-country auto trips in her modified roadster," which she equipped with a bed in the back of the car, covered with a canvas top.[98] Kristina Wilson, who had a romantic relationship with Agnes Martin in the mid-fifties, revealed in an oral history that "camping gets you into a lot of trouble." Time together in the natural landscape held special meaning to O'Keeffe and Chabot. To remind O'Keeffe of their time together in the Bisti Badlands, Chabot gifted her a black stone shaped liked the area, though she had initially hesitated to give the gift: "I carried it miles and swore I'd not send it to you, my conscience got the better of me." Chabot exhibited a much stronger attachment to O'Keeffe. Their relationship was fraught with this tension, and it ended dramatically in the fall of 1949. O'Keeffe asked Chabot not to return the following summer to Ghost Ranch, then worked to keep Chabot at bay. After years of remaining distant friends, O'Keeffe penned a coded disclosure about the role Chabot played in her life in an inscription in Chabot's copy of her autobiography *Georgia O'Keeffe*: "For Maria Chabot who . . . has dreamed other dreams with me here near the cliffs and the red hills," a nod to their camping endeavors together.[99]

Determining if O'Keeffe engaged in sexual relationships with women may not be possible, but what is evident is that O'Keeffe developed and embodied the notion that northern New Mexico offered creative women independence and belonging.[100] O'Keeffe sought a distinct space for creative activity and served as an ongoing inspiration for women creatives, many of them queer, to seek a place in which to nurture their self-expression. Women made room for other women. They socialized and lived with each other. They took back-country auto trips and camped together. They assisted one another with forging artistic career paths. Historian Flannery Burke has argued that women held the power in the Taos art colony, which operated under an inequitable gendered, racialized, and classed hierarchy. Gay men made up the middle rungs, while powerful women such as Georgia O'Keeffe secured a place above them. To be sure, gay men provided companionship and support for white women. O'Keeffe, for example, socialized with Spud Johnson and called upon him when she needed a travel companion. Johnson, who begrudgingly spent a considerable amount of leisure time with women, continually complained in his journal and correspondence about the area having "too many women & no men."[101] Amid his frustration with a social life dominated by women he nurtured a private misogyny. In the social matrix of northern New Mexico's queer culture, gay men and lesbians developed a preference for a gender-stratified queer environment.

O'Keeffe had been spending long stretches of time at her Ghost Ranch property and her newly acquired summer home in Abiquiú, about two hours from Albuquerque, when artist Agnes Martin arrived in New Mexico to teach. Martin visited O'Keeffe in Abiquiú, though there is little documentation of their meetings, except for a few of Martin's recollections.[102] Although their friendship was short-lived—Martin claims O'Keeffe "forgot me when she got old"—it embodied the importance of queer mentorship and women-centered support in an art world dominated by men. According to Sarah Lowndes, "O'Keeffe offered a model to other artists (including Martin) of how to live and work in isolation in New Mexico, yet still remain connected to the New York art world." O'Keeffe, after her first trip to New Mexico in 1929, every year returned to spend up to six months painting and living a secluded life in the high desert, without her husband, then exhibited her works in New York City at her husband's gallery.[103] Martin charted a similar course, immersing herself in the isolation of the desert with pilgrimages to New York to stay connected to its art world. After O'Keeffe's husband passed away in 1946, she took a few years to settle his estates, then moved permanently to northern New Mexico. Similarly, once Martin established a market for her art, she "felt free to leave" New York City and settled in the desert.[104] After dealing with poverty for most of her life, Martin achieved critical success in the 1960s and commercial success thereafter, which brought her some stability and comfort. She chose to settle down in Cuba, then Galisteo, and back in Taos, where she died in 2004.

Queer cultural producers taught each other how to self-actualize. Art made New Mexico a queer haven, but queer culture took root because participants nurtured and ascribed significance to queer creative networks. Although the vibrancy of queer art and literary colonies began to fade by World War II, those who stayed settled into creating alternative domestic arrangements. Women artists such as O'Keeffe created communities in which women could live independently of men. Maria Chabot resided, at various points in her life, with Dorothy Stewart, Mary Wheelwright, and Georgia O'Keeffe. This is particularly remarkable given the context of the time, "an historical moment when marriage seemed inescapable and building a life with a woman nearly impossible."[105] Same-sex partners established households together and hosted small gatherings of gay and lesbian artists and writers. While Bynner bashes, a staple for queer socialization, ended in the 1940s, Bynner and his partner, Robert Hunt, who continued to live together in Santa Fe, occasionally entertained visiting gay writers such as author Christopher Isherwood.[106] Isherwood also stayed with O'Keeffe in Abiquiú for a ten-day visit in 1950. Likewise, partners Agnes Sims and Mary Louise Aswell built a life together in Santa Fe and hosted notable gay guests, including authors May Sarton and Truman Capote. Partners Laura Gilpin and Elizabeth Forster, after thirty years of living apart, in 1945 decided to live together in Santa Fe.[107] Others formed queer marriages, a term attributed to gay composer Virgil Thomson that referred to flexible unions that were quietly sexually open but bounded by strong emotional fidelity and a desire for and commitment to the domestic rituals of marriage. Clifford McCarthy, after the death of his companion Bronson Cutting, entered a "queer marriage" with lesbian Eleanor Bedell, owner of a Native American art store and an interior designer.[108]

In the 1950s Martin met another mentor, New York gallerist and lesbian artist Betty Parsons, who was visiting Taos.[109] Parsons often roamed the North American West, even though she owned and operated a midtown New York City gallery. The Betty Parsons Gallery, which she opened in September 1946, helped bring abstract expressionism to the forefront of the art world by featuring the artwork of Jackson Pollock, Mark Rothko, Ad Reinhardt, and others. The gallery also became a creative haven for artists who received less recognition, particularly women and queer artists; Parsons sought out and promoted the work of many gay, lesbian, and bisexual artists during a time when the art world remained dominated by straight men.[110] Parsons herself had relationships with other women and gender-variant artist Agnes Martin.[111] While visiting Taos, Parsons attended an exhibition, *The Ruins in Ranchos de Taos*, at a cooperative gallery and there admired one of Martin's semi-abstracts called *Autumn Watch* (1954). Intrigued by the painting, Parsons urged Martin to move to New York to further her career, but Martin demurred, explaining that she lacked the financial means to make such a move. The two met again in 1957. This time, Parsons offered to represent Martin if she moved to New York and bought five of Martin's paintings, enabling her to relocate. Parsons gave Martin her first solo show of oil paintings at her gallery in December 1958. After the successful show, Parsons broadcast in promotional material that "Agnes Martin is one of the most interesting painters I have found in the last ten years."[112]

As part of the open-secret strategy, most participants kept their sexuality private outside of these networks, but rarely were nonnormative sexual and gender identities and behaviors kept from those inside such networks. Within queer art circuits participants encoded queer revelations for each other. They crafted a distinct way of reading literature and art underpinned by a knowledge of euphemistic queer recognition. In an announcement card for her second exhibition at the Betty Parsons Gallery, Martin quoted a line from a lesbian love poem written by Gertrude Stein: "In which way are stars brighter than they are. When we have come to this decision. / We mention many thousands of buds. And when I close my eyes I see them."[113] The intimate theme of the poem is not readily evident in the passage Martin selected, but as scholar Brendan Prendeville has pointed out, the lines that follow immediately after are declarative of lesbian intimacy:

If you hear her snore
It is not before you love her
You love her so that to be her beau is very lovely. . . .
She is very lovely and mine which is very lovely[114]

Anyone familiar with Stein's work would know to read Martin's selection as a nod to lesbianism. Martin, by citing a Stein quotation, subtly invoked an insider discourse about queerness that circulated among lesbian artists and queer creatives. Stein's entire poem was originally published in the *Little Review*, a magazine run by two lesbians that often featured lesbian writers. Lesbians who connected to queer creative networks through little magazines and art exhibitions became skilled at locating queerness within spaces of high culture. Such networks, built in the 1920s, remained entrenched during the early Cold War as the need for secrecy increased. As historian Lillian Faderman has argued, in the context of the Cold War, being covert "became one of the chief manifestations of lesbian existence for an entire generation."[115] Clandestine references and secrecy defined lesbian culture for many women.

This structure of queer identification was also mobile. Movement and diaspora were factors in many queer lives and allowed queer people to hold on to their structures of identification when they moved through art communities across the United States and Europe. Martin found solidarity and support in the bohemian enclave of Coenties Slip, New York City (near present-day Battery Park) and the art colonies of New Mexico. Parsons, too, moved through multiple lesbian art circles. Small professional and social networks cultivated creative spaces for queer artists that often connected large art centers to bohemian communities, including Greenwich Village, Provincetown, and Taos. Advertisements associated the bohemian art enclaves with each other. A brochure from the 1950s called Albuquerque the "Greenwich Village of the West" while a *New York Times* article referenced

Taos as the "Provincetown of the Desert."[116] The materials alluded to New Mexico as queer friendly, and some readers may have interpreted the headlines as such.

Not until 2010 did scholars write a more nuanced accounting of Martin's life. Fiercely guarded and committed to the open-secret strategy, Martin had asked friends to keep her sexuality and diagnosis of paranoid schizophrenia private until she passed away. They respected her wishes and did not disclose these aspects of her identity during her lifetime. In 2012 her friend and gallerist Arnold Gilmecher published a book about their relationship and divulged that Martin suffered "from schizophrenia and from time to time required hospitalization." At the 2012 symposium accompanying the posthumous exhibition *Agnes Martin: Before the Grid* at the Harwood Museum of Art in Taos, resident Kristina Wilson presented a paper that publicly declared that she had a romantic relationship with Martin in the mid-fifties.[117] Wilson described the atmosphere of queer artists in northern New Mexico as "very secretive" and elaborated that Martin was "in denial" and experienced "tremendous conflict" and "guilt" about her sexuality. Historians Jonathan D. Katz's and David Ward's inclusion of Martin's *Nude* (1947) in the exhibition *Hide/Seek: Difference and Desire in American Portraiture* (2010–11) at the Smithsonian's National Portrait Gallery helped to publicize Martin's lesbianism. It is important to note, however, that later in life, Martin rejected the label "lesbian."[118] In 1967, when Martin moved back to New Mexico, they embraced a new understanding of their gender and sexuality, which they expressed by refusing the nomenclature "lesbian," no longer identifying as a woman, wearing unisex clothing, and abstaining from sexual relationships with others. Scholars Ela Przybylo and Danielle Cooper caution against understanding Martin as a lesbian and instead posit that they lived an asexual life, due to Martin's public disavowals of erotic pleasure.[119] The intersecting lives of Mary Wheelwright, Dorothy Stewart, Maria Chabot, Georgia O'Keeffe, and Agnes Martin reveal queer nuance and complexity during the open-secret era. Queer mentorship and cultural production continued, but because of its covert nature, it failed to translate to an open community with political power, an absence deeply felt during the second gay civil rights issue in the state—decriminalizing sodomy law. It would take another wave of sexual migrants to awaken a modern gay civil rights movement.

FIVE

Land of Entwinement

Rural and Urban Queer Lives

Rosanne Baca, who was born in Gallup and raised in multiple cities in New Mexico, eventually settled in Albuquerque. At the age of twenty-eight, she moved in with her twenty-three-year-old partner, Gloria Gonzagowski, a transition she characterized as "happy, content, settled." Baca described spending most of her time at home and a few nights a week dancing to disco, playing pool, and drinking with friends at Cricket's, a working-class Latina lesbian bar. Although she identified as a Chicana and acknowledged a strong Chicana power movement at the University of New Mexico (UNM) in Albuquerque, she chose "not to be involved." Instead, she searched for lesbian-centered places and activities. She picked up *Sister Lode*, a local feminist journal for "news, arts, and ideas," and *Seer's Catalogue*, an underground newspaper, at the feminist bookstore Full Circle Books, looking for articles on "gay life."[1] While thumbing through *Sister Lode*, she found a summer solstice event on lesbian land called Arf in Tesuque, about ten miles north of Santa Fe, and attended for several years. Still, she yearned for more: "If they [lesbians] had a rally or a group meeting, I would be there."[2]

Baca was cognizant of the three hubs for queer people in 1970s New Mexico—a social hub through bar culture, a political hub connected to UNM, and a bohemian hub that entwined rural and urban spaces, particularly in the northern part of the state. By the mid-1960s, Albuquerque possessed a handful of gay bars, where lesbians and gay men socialized in a mixed-gender environment. Initially, the only public space for lesbians to gather was Cricket's, a private women's club located on Fourth Street in the predominately working-class Latino west side.[3] Chicanas created space for themselves at Cricket's. No bar catered specifically to the state's queer and two-spirit Indigenous people.[4]

Since Albuquerque's gay bar culture was purely social, residents lacked a platform for a shared sexual political consciousness. Formalized gay liberation politics actualized on the UNM campus in 1971 with the advent of Gay Liberation (GL-NM), the first gay political organization in the state, and the inauguration of the Women Studies program (WMST) in 1972.[5] GL-NM only lasted two years, and Juniper, a subsequent iteration also formed by students in 1974, similarly collapsed within three years.[6] WMST, in contrast, has provided the lesbian community with a long-standing institutional base.[7]

Baca felt she could best articulate her lesbianism through overlapping rural-urban lesbian hubs. Nationwide, lesbian feminists spearheaded a Lesbian Nation movement that rejected narratives, customs, and politics that privileged a white, male, middle-class urban experience.[8] They brought the vision of a lesbian nation to fruition, establishing women-only cultural institutions, rural and urban communes, businesses, and periodicals all over the United States as a way to denounce patriarchy. Some constructed physical lesbian feminist places; others cultivated discursive spaces for their own politics and poetics through the burgeoning lesbian press. New Mexico was a vital conduit of the Lesbian Nation, particularly lesbian land. A small group of mainly white lesbian feminists constructed utopic rural communes in Northern California in the late 1960s, then in southern Oregon and northern New Mexico.[9] New Mexico had several intentional lesbian communities, including Arf and Oquitadas Feminist Farm.

New Mexican lesbians also subscribed and contributed to feminist publications as a way to explore and participate in the Lesbian Nation. Nationally circulating publications such as *Amazon Quarterly* (1972–75), *Country Women* (1973–80), *Lesbian Connection* (1974–present), and *Maize: A Lesbian Country Magazine* (1983–present) shared a feminist philosophy, critiqued urban queer culture, and worked to create an ethic of lesbian solidarity without spatial demarcation. The production of do-it-yourself periodicals, argues historian Martin Meeker, "provided a powerful conduit through which information about lesbianism could travel into places and on a scale unheard of in previous decades."[10] Importantly, these periodicals, to some extent, reached and included queer women of color and set the stage for some of the earliest articulations of Latina lesbianism.

Borrowing from lesbian separatist strategies, notable gay activist Harry Hay and other gay men dissatisfied with urban gay neighborhoods created their own movement called the Radical Faeries in 1979. Hay moved to New Mexico in 1970 and looked to both the lesbian land model and Native two-spirit traditions to fuel his new theories on gay men's sexuality and spirituality. Hay conceptualized the Faerie Nation while living in an adobe compound on the Pueblo of Ohkay Owingeh, a sovereign Native nation. He set out to provide gay men with physical spaces—rural retreats and natural sanctuaries—for finding spiritual fulfillment outside of Christianity and cultivated a sense of queer belonging rooted in Indigenous gender and sexual diversity. The Radical Faeries began with an inaugural conference held in Benson, Arizona, at the Sri Ram Ashram Desert Sanctuary. At their first gathering, they committed to forming a permanent land community for gay men and developing sanctuaries, which now exist throughout Canada, Europe, Australia, Thailand, and the United States, including one in the Zuni Mountains of New Mexico that still operates today.[11] But unlike Lesbian Nation, Faerie Nation failed to initially attract queer Latinx and Indigenous people due to Hay's essentialist and primitivist views, which shaped the beginning of the movement, though it later evolved to become more inclusive of other genders and orientations, as well as people of color. Hay's motivating desire to emulate and embody Indigenous gender and sexual diversity constituted a form of settler-colonial power that displaced queer Native agency. In turn, Native gay and two-spirit people sought distinction from non-Native sexual minorities. Urban migration fueled their movement for queer politics by and for Native people.

New Mexico's queer hubs were bolstered by the growth of the gay population when a new wave of sexual migrants that included LGBTQ+ students, lesbian feminists, back-to-the-landers, radical gay liberationists, and queer artists and writers moved to and within the state in the 1970s. Some of the sexual migrants gravitated to Albuquerque, the site of UNM, while queer creatives selected the northern New Mexican cities of Santa Fe and Taos. Santa Fe and Albuquerque also gained new Native residents from Cochiti, Isleta, Jemez, Laguna, Ohkay Owingeh, Sandia, San Felipe,

Santa Ana, Santo Domingo, and Zia Pueblos as well as To'hajiilee, a small Diné community, who elected to live near Albuquerque but remain close to homelands.[12] Lesbian feminists, back-to-the-landers, and radical gay liberationists choose surrounding rural environs. Oral histories indicate that the state's queer Latinx population primarily moved within the boundaries of New Mexico or to neighboring states for brief periods of time. An examination of queer mobility into and within New Mexico suggests that the state provided both urban spaces and rural outposts for cultivating a sense of self and engendering gay liberation politics. The modern gay liberation movement (1963–80), a period of radical queer resistance and activism, achieved unprecedented mass mobilization that spread well beyond urban queer meccas.[13] The movement fomented social change by emphasizing coming out, advocated for a rethinking of sexual and gender politics, and enriched coalition politics by allying with other radical, leftist, and countercultural politics. According to historian Marc Stein, "Much of the social and political work of gay liberation took place in affiliated consciousness-raising groups, coffeehouses, collectives, and communes."[14] The formation of Lesbian Nation and Faerie Nation on the ground in New Mexico illustrate this impulse. Queer institution building, through three interconnected hubs, organically established gay liberation politics in multiple places throughout the state rather than in an urban epicenter.

Lesbian Nation

Thousands of mostly young people flocked to northern New Mexico as part of the back-to-the-land movement, a migration that elaborated on and expanded the region's long-standing bohemianism. The movement resonated in the Taos area, which witnessed the founding of more than a dozen communes in the late 1960s. "Northern New Mexico, with its vast spaces and open skies, Indian occupants, and tradition as a mecca for artists, became a particularly potent magnet for counterculture communitarians from throughout the nation and even the world," affirms historian Sherry Smith. Most communes, which strove for a self-sufficient life close to nature, were short-lived. The tide of counterculture migrants, Smith claims, ended "by 1971," when "Taos fever appeared to have dissipated."[15] But Smith's assertation discounts lesbian feminists' movement to New Mexico throughout the

1970s, followed by the Radical Faeries. While historians have written about "the hippie invasion," few have included the narratives of queer people who came to partake in their own bohemian experimentation.[16]

Lesbian utopic rural communes were part of the Lesbian Nation—physical places and discursive spaces for women experiencing displacement from American culture to cultivate a bounded identity of patriarchal resistance. Lesbian feminist and author Jill Johnston named the abstract concept in a series of stream of consciousness essays called *Lesbian Nation: The Feminist Solution*, published in 1973.[17] The birth of lesbian feminism, which overlapped with but was distinct from women's liberation and the gay rights movement, is often associated with the most well-known and well-read text—the Radicalesbians position paper, "The Woman-Identified Woman"—though multiple lesbian feminisms and texts produced around the country emerged before and after the Radicalesbians' manifesto.[18] The paper defined lesbianism beyond a singular focus on sexual identity to include a political identity. Johnston, drawing from "The Woman-Identified Woman," bemoaned the difficulty in declaring a lesbian identity that embodied more than a connection to deviant sexual acts. Johnston claimed, "There was no lesbian identity. There was lesbian activity." "Identity was presumed to be heterosexual unless proven otherwise and so for all social purposes we were all heterosexual," she extrapolated. She maps out how heteronormative forms of intimacy are embedded in discourse, marriage and family, law, employment, and politics, which caused lesbians to construct identities in accordance with norms established by the dominant culture. Lesbians, by contrast, had no institutional matrix for their nonnormative intimacies. Johnston proposed a solution in *Lesbian Nation*, a call to construct women-only spaces to dismantle heteronormativity and create a set of lesbian ideas and practices. "The best thing to do was retreat and get your own shit together and to build lesbian nation from the grass roots out of your own community of women. I couldn't agree more with that," Johnston wrote. Her book called for both feminists and lesbians to embrace separatism as a method to combat gendered vulnerabilities linked to the exigencies of patriarchy.[19]

A zone of contact within the Lesbian Nation was lesbian land, also referred to as lesbian feminist land, lesbian intentional communities, lesbian separatist land, and the women's land movement. Some lesbian feminists seized the opportunity to transform natural spaces into a radical, women-centered alternative culture. Southern Oregon and an area along the I-5 corridor that stretched down the California Coast and up to Seattle (popularly known as the Amazon Trail) has been identified as the core of the lesbian land movement. Almost all academic works on rural lesbian separatism focus on this region because of its connection to the beginnings of a lesbian land hub.[20] While lesbian land was centered here, it grew to encompass a larger geographic area, including New Mexico and eventually extending into multiple states and to Canada, France, and Germany.[21]

Participants themselves often reference New Mexico as a conduit in the web of lesbian lands. Bethroot Gwynn, who created Fly Away Home outside of Myrtle Creek, Oregon, in 1976 and continues to live there as of 2013, explains: "It's northern California, Oregon, and New Mexico that you can think about as kind of a triangle for women who were doing spirituality, living on land. . . . There was a lot of travel among those places."[22] Other lesbian landers noted the interconnectedness between land communities. Juana María Paz spent 1978 and 1979 living on and moving through women's lands: "I have lived at La Luz in California, OWL Farm in Oregon, visited ARF in New Mexico, Cabbage Lane and Rainbow's End in Oregon and spent time at Rainbow Land and Sassafras in Arkansas." Similarly, Jae Haggard built houses on "Lesbian Lands in several states" before forming a community called Outland in Serafina, New Mexico, with then-partner Lee Lanning.[23]

As fluid and porous entities, these lands created circles of community and a mobile lesbian landscape that intersected rural and urban living. Thyme Siegel described her coming-out process within a lesbian feminist community in Oregon she called "Lesbian Village," which included urban spaces like Full Moon Rising (a women's forestry cooperative in Eugene), Gertrude's Café, Mother Kali's Books, and the rural lesbian communities of OWL Farm and Cabbage Lane. Siegel joined a community of migratory country and urban lesbians. In her writings, she emphasized the importance of movement: "The phenomenon of migratory lesbians in the country was not limited to northern California and Oregon. A network developed which encompassed Arizona, New Mexico, Minnesota, Wisconsin, Michigan, Missouri, Vermont, New York, Arkansas, Kentucky, Carolinas, Tennessee, West Virginia and Florida."[24] Similar to Oregon's Lesbian Village, Santa Fe

MAIZE
A LESBIAN COUNTRY MAGAZINE   FALL 97

Photograph by Jae Haggard, editor of *Maize: A Lesbian Country Magazine*, of a lesbian lander relishing the wondrous women's land of New Mexico. Courtesy of Jae Haggard and Lesbian Herstory Archives.

had a small-scale lesbian community that included a women's center called the Gathering, women's health services, a feminist media collective, a rape crisis line, a women's press, and a lesbian alliance group. Santa Fe's lesbian establishments supported the needs of lesbian landers who lived in "large, spread out" communities grouped by "special intentions of the dweller." Some included "living with nature as a primary goal" while others "aimed for a common ground of creative endeavors, such as with the artists or separatists."[25] Hooked into the growing Lesbian Nation, connected through word of mouth, periodicals, and women-run establishments, lesbian communitarians easily located and moved through a network of lesbian land and urban lesbian feminist institutions.

White lesbian activist Elaine Mikels established the initial lesbian land venture in New Mexico—Oquitadas Feminist Farm. She first moved to New Mexico in 1969 when her niece, Lisa Law, a photographer of and a participant in the counterculture movement, invited her to take care of an adobe home and farm on ten acres in Truchas. Mikels accepted the invitation and left city life for the country. As an ex-urbanite, Mikels honed rural skills, learning how to split wood, raise farm animals, garden, build structures, drive tractors, and so forth—all skills that promoted her self-sufficiency in a rural setting. She shared her newfound adeptness with other urban-to-rural migrants by contributing articles to *Country Women*, a "feminist country survival manual and a creative journal" from northern California, and *Maize: A Lesbian Country Magazine*, focused on "lesbian experiences and strategies in urban/country relations and community building" distributed out of northern New Mexico.[26] Collectively, these publications showed great numbers of lesbians that it was possible to live independent feminist lives in the country. In an article that describes her transformation, Mikels wrote that she had acquired "a taste for the countryside" and relished procuring rural skills traditionally viewed as masculine. "I became inspired by the self-reliant spirit of a woman of my own age who was farming and building her own structure," wrote Mikels. Invigorated by working the land at Truchas and encouraged by two lesbian friends, Bea and Ellen, who had moved from San Francisco to Taos and built their own adobe house, Mikels sought out her own property. She found a house and a small piece of land ten miles north of Taos.[27]

Mikels favored her self-selected queer country identity, but she felt isolated from other lesbians. When she met a lesbian named Gayle from Albuquerque, the two decided to turn Mikels's property into lesbian land, calling it Oquitadas Feminist Farm. The *New Mexico Daily Lobo*, the UNM student paper, promoted the venture and pointed to the farm as a model of building women's culture. Other feminist events even borrowed the term "Oquitadas" to invoke "a symbol of the feminist spirit." Two feminists in Albuquerque conceived a show "of theatre, music, poetry and dance by, for and about women" and named it Oquitadas.[28] The *New Mexico Daily Lobo*'s support of Oquitadas illustrates the interconnectedness of rural and urban feminist endeavors. Additionally, Mikels and Gayle recruited other women to join by posting announcements in the aforementioned lesbian publications. Eleven lesbians from Oregon heeded the call.

Despite the promise of the endeavor, tensions immediately arose. Some of the new collective members wanted freedom to be themselves in safe, private places and to experiment with erotic lesbian expression, including public nudity, polyamorous relationships, and various degrees of public sexual acts. Having lived in New Mexico, Mikels was sensitive to the conservative Latino Catholic population who were their neighbors. The north-central part of the state contained a sizable number of Latino Catholics, and lesbianism within these communities was censured. Mikels feared open displays of same-sex affection might instigate "acts of vandalism by young Hispanic men who resented the influx of hippie-type Anglos and lesbians." Her niece, Lisa Law, encountered "not always harmonious" interactions with Latino neighbors.[29] Counterculture migrants experienced firsthand the fissures in northern New Mexican communities, which divided over issues of race and ethnicity, sexual openness, and class, particularly the complexities of landholding. During the countercultural movement, some Taoseños resented that hippies rejected a middle-class lifestyle, which insulted their aspiration to achieve a higher socioeconomic status. Mikels was also cognizant of how locals monitored their public sexual expression and wished to respect their customs. Mikels, herself, "had settled in quietly in this village of 200 inhabitants, maintaining as well as I could, a low profile, allowing my neighbors to get to know me as a person, not necessarily sharing with them many of my ideas." She felt her fellow separatists were "low on sensitivity to" the surrounding population. Reflecting back on the conflict, Oquitadas resident Pelican Lee admitted, "We [not including

Mikels] knew nothing of respecting ways other than our own."[30] Mikels grasped queer country customs; the newcomers to the feminist farm did not. Mikels built a separate house on the property to help alleviate some of the conflict, but the situation failed to improve, and she asked the women to leave. Oquitadas folded.

Lesbian intentional communities, as Oquitadas demonstrates, disrupted rural cultural norms, remained small, and often failed. The women who moved from Oregon lesbian land to New Mexico worked to extricate themselves from mainstream institutions and build a new one that prioritized lesbianism. Lesbian separatists' vision of an open sexual culture clashed with residents long tied to the area who maintained a private view toward sexuality. The Nuevomexicano mindset of privacy toward sexual matters facilitated an implicit acceptance of lesbianism, provided its practice remain private. Rural Chicana lesbians needed an environment where many types of sexual expression—overt, covert, and even celibacy—would be welcomed. Some lesbian landers neglected to see how pushing overt lesbianism might exclude local Latina lesbians, who needed space for different lesbian expressions and who had less privacy since they lived near or with family members. Furthermore, rurality produced its own forms of queer identity. Like many queer people living in hinterland areas, Mikels attempted to gain acceptance by being one of the locals.[31] She understood the importance of community connectedness as part of the infrastructures of rural life. She first worked to claim local status, endearing herself to neighbors, before sharing her lesbian feminist ideas. The lesbian newcomers disregarded such notions and felt Mikels was "too closeted" because many of the locals did not know of her lesbianism.

Nevertheless, lesbian land endeavors continued, and subsequent ventures were more successful and flexible than Oquitadas. Arf established a new haven for lesbian feminist migrants and locals; it remains a lesbian land community as of this writing.[32] The women who started Arf have opted to keep their identities private, but they discussed the establishment of the property in the book *Lesbian Land*. In 1977 a group of lesbians hiked on a trail with a spectacular view of the Sangre de Cristo mountains, steep rising peaks covered with pine, piñon, oak, and cedar trees. Later, they purchased twenty-five acres nearby as women's land. The protection of the mountains gave them seclusion, an essential element to the founders. Conceptually, they envisioned a village structure where each person had her own housing structure and communally the group shared a garden, ritual space, and a bathhouse. A woman identified as Sarah elaborated, "We're all pretty private people here. None of us wanted to live as a group, as a collective."[33]

The women practiced collective ownership of Arf. Four of the founders organized as a legal collective, purchased the property for seventy-five thousand dollars, and handled the deed and taxes, while the other two made up the living collective and had a say in day-to-day decisions. Ellie, an elementary school teacher with a regular salary, contributed the most toward buying the land and in turn was given an existing house on the plot. In contrast, Rose, part of the living collective, did not want any permanent ties to Arf and lived in a tipi. Collective ownership, practiced extensively throughout the lesbian land movement, allowed women to own land who probably would not have been able to afford it as sole buyers. In this way, lesbian landers rejected the system of capitalism by transforming relations of ownership.[34]

Arf's fluid social structure—"a constantly changing animal and human population"—encouraged a highly transient population, one that Thyme Siegel witnessed when she traveled to New Mexico. Pelican Lee, who knew Siegel from Oregon's land community, had written to Siegel on many occasions, encouraging her to visit. In her journal entry, Siegel reflected on the multiracial, environmentally friendly, politically minded, mobile population of women at Arf and in the surrounding area. She met Zaceté, who wore "punk dyke attire—a chain tight around her neck like a leash and a leather jacket with 'Arf Scorpions'"; Raven, a Jewish lesbian with a physical disability who resided down the road from Arf in Chimayo; and Deja and her son both of Haitian descent. Lee confirmed that Arf was "one of the few women's lands that welcomes boy children, plenty of boys, and lesbian mothers."[35] Additionally, lesbians such as Rosanne Baca traveled to Arf for special events. Siegel's depiction of lesbian land in New Mexico challenges scholars' portrayal of the movement as exclusively white. Some women of color participated in separatist rural life; others launched critiques against the racial norms of lesbian separatist utopian ideals.[36]

Lesbian land drew sexual migrants to the hinterlands of New Mexico, contributing to the state's long history of queer mobility. Lesbians migrating to rural areas left a legacy of selecting landscapes and building communities suited to their needs and sexual identification. Many viewed their day-to-day living, queering the household form itself, as a political statement. Additionally, lesbian landers brought lesbian feminism, a political identity and approach to queer politics, to fruition in rural spaces. They also supported and circulated multi-issue intersectional politics of lesbian feminism to wider audiences through a flourishing of do-it-yourself (DIY) publications.

Lesbian Feminist Print Culture

Forming the Lesbian Nation was discursive as well as structural. Lesbians, by 1975, had created more than fifty DIY publications to address their concerns.[37] Woman-centered cultural production furthered the promises of gender and sexual liberation and "centrally defined lesbianism in the 1970s."[38] For those who were less mobile, periodicals served as an entry point to Lesbian Nation.

Gloria from New Mexico discovered the lesbian feminist literary journal *Amazon Quarterly* (AQ) through an advertisement in the mainstream feminist magazine *Ms*. Her subscription to both illustrates the overlapping constituencies of feminism and lesbianism, although she preferred AQ. Like many lesbians, Gloria gravitated toward AQ because of its literary focus. Editors Laurel Galana and Gina Covina started the Oakland-based magazine in 1972 to connect "artists and writers who were working out of a sensibility similar to ours." AQ used queer cultural production, including visual media, poetry, fiction, and criticism, as a means to transform patriarchal culture. Galana and Covina also sought to link isolated, community-based lesbian networks with a nationally bounded one. AQ, which had the widest circulation of a lesbian periodical in the era, compiled a directory of women-run "centers, projects, organizations, services, and individual contacts" in thirty-three states. The published directory pointed lesbians in New Mexico to the state's rape crisis center on the UNM campus and the publication *Santa Fe Women's Community*.[39]

Lesbian Connection (LC) also reached lesbians in New Mexico. One of the aims of LC—the longest-running lesbian periodical to date—was to provide a larger geographic platform for the lesbian feminist movement. Taking the concept of Lesbian Nation seriously, LC built a database of lesbian networks through its directory called "Contact Dykes"—"a lesbian who is willing to have her name and or address and or phone number published so other lesbians can contact her for information, and lesbians traveling through can talk to a friendly dyke." Contact dykes, many of whom identified as rural women, assisted other lesbians with travel to their area. They recommended lesbian friendly spaces and sometimes offered their own home as a place to stay. The magazine listed contact dykes in Albuquerque, Santa Fe, Farmington, Las Cruces, and Roswell, and the rural areas of Ojo Caliente and Mesilla. Contact dykes epitomized the spread of lesbian feminism outside queer meccas, as Joan Nestle explains: "'Contact Dykes' became a wonderful service because it offered us [lesbians] 'safe houses' virtually everywhere in the country. It opened the whole country to us!" The program became so popular it warranted its own directory in the early 1980s; it still exists in 2022.[40]

Malflora Valverde, who lived in Rowe, a small village of fewer than three hundred residents (with a Latinx majority) on the Santa Fe Trail, authored one of the first letters to the editor to appear in *LC* from a New Mexico lesbian: "Dear Amazons: I have been reading and enjoying your newsletter for a year. I especially like the nationwide feeling and connection with other lesbians. . . . We're sort of isolated in northern N.M. with amazon friends 70 and 100 miles away." Valverde continues, "I would like to hear more from third world dykes and where we're at."[41] Valverde's brief letter demonstrates her own and other lesbians marginalization in rural northern New Mexico. New Mexico, geographically the fifth-largest state, at that time represented only 1 percent of the country's population. Since 1945 the once-remote desert state experienced unfettered growth, its population bolstered by a consistent migratory stream of newcomers, particularly in Alamogordo, Carlsbad, Clovis, Hobbs, Farmington, Las Cruces, Rio Rancho, Roswell, and Santa Fe. Nonetheless, the state maintained a mix of culturally vibrant cities and extremely rural spaces. As late as the 1970s, New Mexico contained some seventy towns and villages, not including Indigenous Pueblos, with a population of under six thousand and classified as rural in the US census.[42] The dearth of population in the hinterlands and the even smaller percentage of out lesbians in such environs made feelings of remoteness more intense. Reading publications like *LC*, rural New Mexican lesbians imagined themselves as part of a national lesbian community; they entered into a culture of lesbian readers, writers, and artists where they held cultural power. From its inception, the Ambitious Amazons, the creators of *LC*, nurtured a grassroots network of lesbians. They created a lifeline to women, like Valverde, who lived in isolated communities.

Valverde's letter further reveals the diversity of New Mexican lesbians when she inquiries about struggles for "third world dykes" and includes herself in this category. To some extent, lesbian periodicals connected people from different backgrounds. According to Rodger Streitmatter, "The [lesbian] publications demonstrated a strong commitment to Third World lesbians."[43] Although the majority of editors and writers were white, periodicals such as *LC* committed to inclusivity by publishing reader content and implemented equalitarian outreach by making the magazine free to all lesbians.[44] To keep costs down, they asked other lesbians to reproduce and distribute *LC*.

When Valverde authored her letter, only one lesbian magazine existed by and for lesbians of color.[45] In 1974 Reverend Delores Jackson founded Salsa Soul Sisters: Third World Women Inc., the first organization dedicated to lesbians of color in New York City. Salsa Soul Sisters, which grew out of the Black Lesbian Caucus of the Gay Activist Alliance, consisted primarily of African American lesbians but was inclusive of Latinas, Asian American, and Indigenous women who identified as lesbian, gay, bisexual, or same-gender-loving. In 1976 Salsa Soul Sisters launched a monthly periodical called the *Salsa Soul Gayzette* (1976–85) and one year later founded *Azalea: A Magazine by Third World Lesbians* (1977–83).[46] However, both had a limited circulation and distribution contained within major cities, as well as relatively short lives. It does not appear that Valverde read the *Salsa Soul Gayzette* or *Azalea*. Instead, she continued to read and write to *LC*. *LC*'s aim of reaching lesbians everywhere made the magazine accessible to her, which she continually expressed: "Sure feels good to be 'connected' with lesbians nationwide out here in rural New Mexico." In a third letter, she asked again about lesbians of color, imploring them to contact her and participate in a survey about their personal experiences negotiating racial and sexual identity. Her subsequent letters reveal that several years later, she still searched for information on lesbians like herself.[47]

Some of the earliest representations of Chicana lesbianism can be found in the Chicano movement publications: *El Grito* (1968–74), produced at the University of California, Berkeley, and *El Grito del Norte* (1968–73), based in Española, New Mexico. Both publications included content on Chicana feminism, which emerged out of women's work in the Chicano movement and a longer tradition of gender community-based activism. *El Grito* published the work of five women writers: Clara Lefler, Leticia Rosales, Estela Portillo, Diana Pérez, and Diana de Anda.[48] Non-lesbian author Portillo published content with stereotypical tropes of lesbianism.[49] Likewise, an early portrayal of Chicana lesbianism can be found in activist Enriqueta Vasquez's series of articles in *El Grito del Norte*. Vasquez supported Chicana feminism by questioning women's subordination, advocating for women's critical role in the Chicano movement, and imagining a Chicano community that fostered women's untapped potential. She also called for a distancing of Chicanas from the women's liberation movement, arguing, "we have to come up with some of our own answers" and warned not to use the "white women's liberation movement" as "a home base for working for our people." To Vasquez, white women's liberation signaled "man-hating" and "lesbianism." She linked lesbianism to white culture and explicitly condemned it: "One of the greatest strengths of Raza is that of our understanding and obedience to nature and its balance and creation. This same awareness makes us realize that it takes a male and a female to make a whole. One sex cannot have total fulfillment without the other."[50] Chicana lesbians faced marginalization and oppression from both Chicana feminists and men hostile to feminism within the Chicano movement. Anti-lesbian sentiment often kept Chicana lesbians within the movement from coming out.[51] Out Chicana lesbians such as Rosanne Baca stayed away from Chicano/a politics. Chicana lesbians looked to connect with each other through lesbian print culture, which began to offer an avenue toward visibility and a platform for developing a Chicana lesbian feminist discourse.

In *Sister Lode*, an Albuquerque-based feminist publication, native Nuevomexicana Juanita Sanchez decried that "virtually nothing is written that addresses Chicana lesbianism," a void she filled by publishing in *Sister Lode*. In June 1978 around fifteen women formed a collective to "gather, provide and disseminate current and relevant information, data and literature which concern wimmin as a whole and in particular as members of the community."[52] They created *Sister Lode* and distributed one thousand free copies of each issue. Sanchez, a member of the commune, produced graphics and poetry for the community-based, lesbian-oriented periodical. Sanchez published a poem entitled "Sculpturing the Brown Woman" that intersects lesbianism, art, and Chicana identity:

> I think
> > of her
> Image
> > becomes shape
> Form
> > moulded into strength.[53]

In the poem, the sculptor is literally creating a brown woman and giving her representation. The artist's construction is thoughtful and intimate. She ponders her endeavor, then imbues her with strength. Her female brown body is not commodified for male sexual desire but rather lovingly shaped by a woman artist. At the end of the poem, there is also a blurring of art and lesbianism as the sculptor and sculpture become one.

Next, Sanchez published a drawing entitled "Kindling" of two women's faces looking away from each other, separated by a burning candle, and enclosed in a circle. The image is reminiscent of some "pro-lesbian" pulp covers, with a subtle butch-femme feel.[54] One face, with cropped hair and prominent lips, is turned forward; the other is in profile with flowing, long hair. The pairing of women companions signifies their sexual preference, and the candle between them suggests a stirring awareness of a newly ignited passion.[55] Sanchez recasts lesbianism as positive and powerful.

By 1984 Sanchez's contributions grew political. She raised the need to bring together Native and Latina lesbians to form a group: "As the years have gone by since my coming out, I have noticed that there has been an expressed need for Hispanic and Native American Women to gather and trade ideas, personal stories, philosophical ideologies or just to 'platicar.'"[56] Sadly, there is no evidence that such a group was ever organized. Nonetheless, Sanchez's engagement with *Sister Lode* aided her exploration of lesbian feminism. She continued to develop a Chicana lesbian political discourse through her writing in an anthology devoted exclusively to Chicana lesbianism.[57] Chicana lesbians wrote about their lesbianism in DIY lesbian print culture and experienced lesbianism through their engagement with women-centered places. Their voices amplified lesbian visibility and complicated lesbian politics and identity by critiquing their lack of representation. I suspect there are many more voices to uncover.

Faerie Nation

On Ohkay Owingeh Pueblo, gay activist Harry Hay conceptualized a grassroots spiritual movement of gay men that embraced gender and sexual politics and back-to-the-land principles called the Radical Faeries.[58] Hay, a well-documented figure in the gay liberation movement, rose to prominence in the 1950s as the force behind the creation of the first major homophile political group—the Mattachine Society. As one of the founders of the homophile movement, scholars largely agree, Hay helped to conceive of homophiles as an underrepresented minority deserving of equal rights protection.[59] Academics have also investigated Hay's later role in creating the Radical Faeries. Hay's biographer Stuart Timmons defines the Radical Faeries as "a mixture of a political alternative, a counter-culture, and a spirituality movement, the Faeries became Harry's 'second wind' as a major figure in gay culture and found him enmeshed in a new kind of organizing—a networking of gentle men devoted to the principles of ecology, spiritual truth, and, in New Age terms, 'gay-centeredness.'"[60]

Hay theorized his "second wind" of queer politics in part by borrowing from Tewa worldviews, including kwidó (two-spirit) practices and lesbian feminist politics connected to the women's land movement in New Mexico.[61] Radical Faeries founders (all non-Native queer people) implemented a mobile practice of gay men retreating into nature to connect with Indigenous spiritual roots. They used pre-colonial Native gender systems for their own cultural formation and political purposes. Scholars have acknowledged that Hay culturally misappropriated from Native American traditions. Scott Morgensen, for example, critiques the "racial and colonial formation as a network of white men who appropriated Native culture to enliven their sexual subjectivities." But he tempers his critique by also showing how, by the 1990s, the Radical Faeries movement sought to collaborate with Native gay and two-spirit people who "hold Radical Faeries to a closer relationship by educating them with distinctive understandings of how queerness, indigeneity, and settler colonialism shape their interrelated lives."[62] Broadly, Morgensen and others have relied on Hay's research on the "berdache"—a derogatory anthropological term that referred to an American Indian man who assumed the dress, social status, and role of a woman—to examine Hay's inspiration for his political theories as well as ethnographic research, conducted at Faerie events, to study the continuing movement.[63] In so doing, they miss examining the specific context of northern New Mexico, where Hay visited beginning in 1956 and lived from 1970 to 1979. I take a historical approach in looking closely at Hay's spatial territory—the Tewa-speaking pueblos of San Ildefonso, Pojoaque, and Ohkay Owingeh, countercultural communes, and lesbian land.

Moreover, few studies have addressed the ways Faeries used lesbian feminists' theories and conceptions of living on the land in New Mexico to build an alternative gay men's movement.[64] Similar to lesbian feminists, Radical Faeries aimed to create a Faerie Nation—"one made of invisible borders defined as much by a state of mind"—a strikingly analogous notion to Lesbian Nation.[65] Additionally, Faerie culture is "explicitly oriented to circulation." "The circulation of people, knowledge, and practices plays an important role in the world-making practices of this movement," argues Elizabeth Povinelli. Faerie culture owes a lot, conceptually, to lesbian feminism: Hay borrowed from lesbian feminist theories and practices without crediting women and applied them to a group that has branded itself as gender transformative.[66]

Three central theoretical questions on homosexuality had preoccupied Hay since he had assisted with the founding of the Mattachine Foundation in 1950: "Who are we? Where did we come from? and What are we for?" Hay, in helping to birth identity politics for gay men and lesbians, began to answer "who are we" and "what are we for" in conjunction with two other homophile organizations—the Daughters of Bilitis and ONE, Inc.[67] Although Hay had a prominent role in developing the Mattachine Society, his involvement with it was cut short once his communist ties came to light. In 1953 a new contingent ousted Hay, took over the group, renamed the organization Mattachine Society, and deescalated its political agenda. Rejected by the homophile movement for his communist affiliation and abandoned by the Communist Party for his queerness, Hay turned inward.

He spent his time studying and researching homosexuality, attempting to answer "where did we come from?" for close to ten years.[68]

Hay fixated on the "berdache" as the key to unlocking a queer past.[69] By the twentieth century, anthropologists who studied practices of gender variance and sexual diversity in tribes applied *berdache* as the standard term for a man who had sexual and domestic relations with another man in tribal societies, which Hay discovered by reading V. F. Calverton's compendium *The Making of Man: An Outline of Anthropology*.[70] Anthropology foregrounded Native American gender and sexuality diversity as the cornerstone for queer activists, like Hay, to make correlations between contemporary queer identities and historic divergences from Western sex and gender norms. Hay believed that Indigenous cultures in which gender differences were integral to the tribe's structure could be used as models for contemporary gay men to recognize and appreciate a universal gayness.[71] He understood the "berdache" as having a clearly defined set of social functions—artistic, creative, and spiritual—that nurtured a queer sensibility. Influenced by the writing of anthropologist Ruth Benedict, who studied the Zuni Pueblos, Hay ventured to New Mexico to conduct anthropological observation and interview two-spirit people.[72]

Hay and his then-partner Jørn Kamgren began taking summer trips to visit the pueblos of New Mexico.[73] On their first excursion in 1956, they met Enki, who lived on San Ildefonso Pueblo, one of six Tewa-speaking Río Grande Pueblos.[74] Enki told Hay about *kwidó*, a Tewa word for "individuals who are both man and woman" and who possess a reputation for artistic excellence. Hay searched for a kwidó to interview but found no one willing to identify as such.[75] Hay may have had difficulty finding such individuals because open markers of kwidó status had been abandoned. Unbeknownst to Hay, the people of the Tewa world have additional gender characteristics kept private from non-Tewa people. Tewa culture possesses a concept called *kwi-sen* (woman-man), which indicates the equal importance of men and women to community well-being. Kwidó and kwi-sen are gender conceptions defined by qualities beyond gender—social roles, religion, kinship, and economies. Gender-variant people of the Tewa world perform specialized duties not meant for public display, and their roles are not open for public discussion.[76]

A dialogue about two-spirit roles for Native people took place in 1975 with the founding of Gay American Indians (GAI), the first such organization by and for Native Americans headquartered in San Francisco.[77] Cofounders Barbara Cameron and Randy Burns sought "first and foremost a group for each other" and to educate Native people "that there *are* gay Indians." GAI reclaimed tribal formations of gender and sexual variance for Native people. Burns explained that "In the Indian community, we are trying to realign ourselves with the trampled traditions of our people. Gay people were respected parts of the tribes." Two-spirit roles, as they are now often called, encompass "religious, economic, and social dimensions." Burns asserts, "It's not just a sexual thing."[78] Many who affiliated with the organization, including Paula Gunn Allen, also pointed out significant differences between two-spirit traditions and contemporary gay roles: "Simple reason dictates that lesbians did exist widely in tribal cultures, for they exist now." Allen is careful to qualify her statement by adding, however, that "the concepts of tribal cultures and of modern, western cultures are so dissimilar as to make ludicrous attempts to relate the long-ago women who dealt exclusively with women on sexual-emotional and spiritual bases to modern women who have in common an erotic attraction to other women." Allen avoids conflating sexual orientation and two-spirit identity and cautions against understanding two-spirit roles as a universal category that represents Native peoples now and prior to contact. Both Hay, who later became involved with GAI, and GAI began referencing historical foundations of gender and sexual diversity in American Indian societies to contest notions of heteronormative citizenship. But GAI did not invite non-Natives to identify with two-spirit traditions. GAI encouraged Native people to unearth their tribal histories of gender and sexual variance and to come out through the Native urban queer community and, if possible, "the Indian community."[79]

Many queer-identified Native people left reservation life in the 1970s to embrace sexual identity. "For many gay Indians, the path to a positive self-image begins with a break from reservation and family," Erna Pahe (Diné/Navajo), chair of the GAI Board of Directors, explained. To be clear, Pahe also expressed that gay Navajo people could live quietly on parts of the reservation: "If you're secluded like in Snake Flats or Chinle, it ain't going to make any difference to anybody. If you get into Window Rock, which is the capital with a big population, and you have an elementary school, a high school, and you have a lot more education Indians who have lived in Flagstaff and heard the criticisms—when you do get into big populated areas like that there's quite a bit of discrimination." At the age of twenty-two, Pahe moved to San Francisco, came out as gay, and took a leadership role in GAI. She chose to migrate because it permitted her to be "vocal" and visible instead of living "very quietly" on isolated parts of the Navajo Nation.[80]

In contrast, Hay made an urban-to-rural migration when he relocated to an adobe home on private land in Ohkay Owingeh Pueblo in May of 1970 with his new partner, John Burnside. While there were a number of factors that influenced their decision to move—they had several friends that lived in the state and the couple wished to ease the financial burden of living in Los Angeles—Hay claimed that his strongest drive stemmed from finding information on spirituality and gender at some of the nearby Pueblos and to help "Gay Indian and Chicano brothers . . . enter the New World of 'Gay Lib.'"[81] Hay envisioned using rurality and critiques of urban capitalism as venues to ally with people of color and colonized peoples. Hay believed he could lead a gay liberation movement inclusive of gay Latino and Native men. His patronizing proclamation to bring gay liberation to New Mexico lacked an understanding about forms of gay resistance that already existed, such as urban relocation and migration of Native queer people, which had proved essential for gay American Indian leaders like Erna Pahe.[82] Nor did Hay take into account how centuries-long experiences of colonialism had shaped sexual privacy practices in rural areas.

While living in New Mexico, Hay worked to ally with Latino and American Indian people through his involvement in multiple grassroots issues. He volunteered to assist with the bilingual newspaper *El Grito del Norte*, aimed at a Chicano movement readership, and took a leading role in a water rights campaign (popularly known as the El Llano Canal Project) to prevent the federal government from damming the Rio Grande. He also networked with gay men and lesbians in an attempt to form a cohesive movement for their civil rights in the state. Back in Los Angeles, Hay and Burnside had founded a small gay liberation organization called the Circle of Loving Companions in 1965. The Circle, one of many groups comprising the growing gay liberation movement, functioned as a nonhierarchal service organization that, mainly through research, attempted to add insights into what it meant to be and live as a gay person. In thinking through their evolving queer theories and politics, the Circle came to adopt Indigenous gender and sexual knowledge for the cause of gay liberation. Hay listed the Circle as a public gay organization in northern New Mexico, hoping to recruit new members; only a few New Mexicans joined. Alejandro Lopez saw the listing, joined, and befriended Hay and Burnside. The other two local New Mexicans who affiliated with the Circle, John Ciddio and his partner, Pat Gutiérrez, had met Hay through the water rights campaign.[83]

Because the Circle remained small, Hay began to work in conjunction with local gay liberationists, particularly lesbian feminist Katherine Davenport and an organization called the Lambdas de Santa Fe, formed in 1977 to address violence against and harassment of patrons at the Senate Lounge, a gay bar in Santa Fe.[84] That same year, Albuquerque celebrated its second gay pride parade. Hay, along with gay liberation leaders in the state, Kris Dodds (Metropolitan Community Church of Albuquerque), Dan Butler (Gay Co-Op), and Katherine Davenport, addressed the crowd at a post-parade rally.[85] Hay's speech explored how "all Gays, women and men alike, had to learn to look at their world through the Hetero window using hetero-evolved language and hetero-male-evolved patterns of thought." As a result, gay men and lesbians needed to relearn how to view their world through the gay window—a shared perspective that linked all gay men and women together. He further called for cross-pollination with other oppressed groups: "Blacks, Chicanos, and Native Americans could share with us numerous ways for successful collectivization" and help gay people "to find words and models to communicate our rich heritage with others."[86] While Hay intersected with gay liberation politics, his pride speech and political style fell flat with the local community. "The gay window idea sounds just a little mystical," commented Bill after the rally. Alejandro Lopez, Hay's friend and a member of the Circle, acknowledged Hay's "powerful and illuminating presence" but also felt that Hay "seemed to appear from a realm quite different from gay people in New Mexico."[87]

Other than these intersections with gay liberation and connecting with John Ciddio and Pat Gutiérrez in Española Valley, Hay's presence in the state never brought large numbers of queer men of color into gay liberation politics. And at times his sexual openness clashed with traditional values in the area. Hay recalled that he and Burnside were asked not to attend a fundraiser for the El Llano Canal Project because locals worried that

Partners John Ciddio and Patrick Gutiérrez joined
Harry Hay's gay liberation organization the Circle of Loving
Companions. According to Hay, Ciddio and Gutiérrez defied local
Nuevomexicano sexual customs and were an openly gay couple
in the Española Valley. Courtesy of San Francisco
History Center, San Francisco Public Library.

On June 28, 1977, Albuquerque celebrated its second
gay pride parade. Harry Hay, along with gay liberation leaders
in the state Kris Dodds, Dan Butler, and Katherine Davenport
addressed the crowd at a post-parade rally. Courtesy of ONE
National Gay and Lesbian Archives, Los Angeles.

the two men would dance together.[88] Like the lesbian landers who pushed for sexual openness at Oquitadas, Hay's open homosexuality disrupted a conservative Nuevomexicano way of expressing sexual orientation. Gay male Latino men in New Mexico straddled the border of admittance and disavowal.[89] Bobb Maestra, for example, born in Santa Fe in 1957, grew up in "a large Hispano family." His upbringing influenced how he viewed his sexual identity as "a very private thing, even though I am open about it." He started coming out in the mid-1970s when he moved to Albuquerque, discovered the gay organization Juniper, and determined to "meet gay people because" he didn't "know any." Through Juniper and pride events, Maestra met an array of gay men and women. He claimed, "That's when my whole life turned around, and I became gay and comfortable with it and started being a gay man."[90] Hay's ideas about solidarity with gay Latino men, through notions of rurality and critiques of urban capitalism, contrasted with gay Latino men's lived experiences and needs. Maestra explored his homoerotic openness in the state's largest city.

Undeterred by the small enrollment in the Circle, Hay carried on with his evolving theories on "where did we come from?" Surrounded by dozens of land communities in the vicinity of Taos, Hay found inspiration. Hay made friends with two lesbian landers, Lily and Hawk. They started a discussion group where Hay learned about the structure of New Mexico lesbian land and retreats held in the mountains.[91] Northern New Mexico offered a secluded place available to lesbian land residents and the larger local lesbian population to gather. For instance, inhabitants opened up Arf for feminist events, such as the summer solstice, and advertised in local feminist publications.[92] Lily and Hawk shared the structure of temporary rural retreats with Hay. While the discussion group only lasted six weeks, the idea of convening a conference in nature, which lesbians did frequently in New Mexico, provided fodder for Hay's Radical Faerie vision.[93] His plan included a network of natural sanctuaries for retreats that would dot the nation.

Hay was also influenced by an earlier encounter with twenty-nine-year-old Richard Tapia (Pojoaque Pueblo), whom he had met and sexually propositioned in the summer of 1961. Tapia rebuffed Hay's sexual and romantic advances, but Hay continued to pursue a relationship anyway.[94] In subsequent letters Hay sent to Tapia, he relayed how his time in Pojoaque, north of Santa Fe, and with Tapia had awakened an idea about a new gay consciousness. Hay wrote about how Tapia, as a tribal member of Pojoaque Pueblo, possessed a unique relational perspective: "when Tewa people speak of themselves and the world of nature and creatures of which they are a part . . . the universe appears to him to be a vast net of correspondences agreeing among themselves in an organic fashion." Hay believed that Tapia's Tewa worldview—a state of balance or state of harmony between the human and natural environments—might influence gay consciousness.[95] A return to this kind of life could be extended to gay men by encouraging them to embrace their roles as spiritual and cultural leaders. Tewa worldviews convinced Hay that the next phase of gay liberation lay in creating separate communities that shared an ethos of *gi woatsi tuenji* (we are seeking life), a Tewa concept that signifies actualization and fulfillment.[96] Hay kept pages of notes on the Pojoaque Pueblo and drafts of letters to Tapia, which indicates the importance of the relationship to Hay and the ideas that stemmed from it.

While Hay began to advocate for urban gay men to frequent gatherings at temporary rural retreats, he at once actively discouraged gay American Indians from moving to cities. Hay remained convinced that Native men like Tapia had to reject "the door of the white man's cities," which works to "destroy utterly the Pueblo man AND his traditions."[97] For Tapia, Tewa society was organized to achieve balance and harmony between dialectic forces, a process that entails "seeking life," avoids stasis, and embraces movement.[98] Tapia, like many Native people in New Mexico, sometimes resided in Pojoaque with family and other times lived outside his ancestral lands in Albuquerque. Since the beginning of the twentieth century, Native people had moved to the urban centers of Gallup, Albuquerque, and Santa Fe for jobs, education, or personal reasons. Others resided on or near Native nations but traversed into towns and cities for work. Cyclical migration back and forth between the city and reservation had long been a survival strategy for Native people.[99] The city of San Francisco, for example, played a key role in shaping gay American Indian politics, but so did movement back home and working with tribal communities to advance sexual and gender equality. At one point, Tapia desired to move to California, an idea Hay opposed. According to Hay, being "indigenous" meant living on ancestral lands. Hay's reductive thinking tapped into deep-seated mythological notions about American Indians' reverence for the natural world and romanticized notions of the Puebloan past. Non-Natives often assume that Pueblo nations have remained largely unchanged for thousands of years.[100] On the contrary, only by adapting to evolving circumstances and environments did Puebloan communities survive, and for two-spirit and gay-identified Natives, migration into cities supported their identity and political formation.

After meeting Tapia, Hay wrote about gay identity as a "minority of common spirituality," a fundamental shift from his earlier understanding of gay people as a political group deserving of rights.[101] Relying in part on a Tewa worldview, which he later reduced to a sweeping Native consciousness, Hay began to conceptualize gay identity and relationships as "subject-subject." In 1976 Hay wrote a position paper called "Gay Liberation: Chapter Two," which he deemed imperative to crystalizing his new theory. He argues that the dominant mode of forming gay identity is derived from how heterosexuals perceive each other as objects. He proposed that gay men should establish subject-subject relationships to form egalitarian bonds of love with each other and nature: "Humanity must expand its experience from persons (subjects) thinking objectively . . . to thinking subject to SUBJECT." He further argues that this way of thinking was inherent to *all* gay people because they possess qualities of creativity, similar to two-spirits, that guided their ability to change their perception of relationships. Hay posited that "homophiles" are "descendants of the berdache." He ends his paper with a second section, a "call to action," a reawakening of gay liberation to "regenerate itself into the gay fairy family."[102]

Hay's writings contained the theme of escaping heterosexual hegemony: "To even begin to prepare ourselves for a fuller participation in our Gay subject-SUBJECT inheritance, we must, both daily and hourly, practice throwing off all those Hetero-imitating habits."[103] Hay believed gay men needed to discover homosexuality without the imposition of heterosexual norms. He advocated creating sanctuaries to achieve such a goal. Much of what Hay proposed as novel, separatism, had already been circulating among lesbian feminists for several years. Condescendingly, Hay wrote a preface to his paper stating that it was crafted from "the Gay Masculine point of view" which "is quite different from Gay Feminine Consciousness" and, "insofar as it is known to the writer, the Gay Woman have not addressed themselves to the matters about to be discussed."[104] Here, he discounts the influence of lesbian feminist theories and practices that contributed to his theoretical breakthrough. Hay articulated a gay male version of separatism and insisted on *his ownership* of such ideas.

Hay's theories on gay consciousness never rallied local support from "Gay Indian and Chicano brothers" but did influence notable lesbian feminist Judy Grahn and a larger cohort of white urban gay men outside of New Mexico who became invested in Hay's gay consciousness, including Arthur Evans, Don Kilhefner, and Mitch Walker.[105] Together, they informed a new gay male liberationist consciousness, which rejected gay assimilation, sometimes through urban-to-rural migrations, and instead celebrated the differences that separate gay people from heterosexuals.[106] As gay neighborhoods developed in American cities, some gay men retreated from what they viewed as "gay ghettos." For decades cities had aided gay men with exploring their homoerotic feelings by offering anonymity and urban outlets. But as the 1970s progressed, a few began to leave cities, some carried by the back-to-the-land movement. Though they hardly constituted an organized group, rural gay men had established several rural collectives and an anti-urban queer publication called *RFD* (1974–present).[107]

Through these networks Don Kilhefner and Mitch Walker connected with Hay. Kilhefner traveled to New Mexico to visit Hay, and while "sitting on the banks of the Rio Grande for long hours at a time, we engaged in vigorous and far-reaching discussions about what was working and what was not working with the ten-year-old gay liberation movement. We both saw the slow encroachment of bourgeois gay assimilation—with its lack of vision, imagination, and audacity—as having a suffocating effect."[108] From its very beginnings, the modern gay liberation movement contained divergent views on strategy, organization, and the scope of its political agenda, particularly the tension between those who sought a radical undercurrent of social constructions of sexuality and gender against those who desired entry into the existing political and economic order. A small cohort embarked on a new direction of gay liberation by calling a conference of like-minded gay men to confer in nature.

In their call for the first Radical Faeries event, advertised in *RFD*, Hay, Kilhefner, Walker, and Burnside proposed "an annual fairy-like gathering of the Rainbow Family Tribe."[109] The men organized a rural gathering in

Benson, Arizona, at the Sri Ram Ashram Desert Sanctuary. Around two hundred urban men attended to explore their gender, sexuality, and spirituality as gay men. Hay proclaimed at the Arizona conference that gay men were shedding "the ugly green frog-skin of Hetero-male imitation," and Faeries adopted the phrase as the group's mantra.[110] During Faerie gatherings, men discovered who they might be and how they might perform through talk, walk, and dress if removed from the shadow of heterosexuality and safe from the threat of homophobia. They tapped into their consciousness during faerie circles, which mixed, according to Scott Morgensen, "quasi-Indigenous rituals with gay translations of feminist neo-paganisms to honor gay men's effeminate ties to the land."[111] The most important ritual that occurred at the first gathering, and all subsequent ones, is the heart circle. Participants, seated in a circle, "speak from the heart" when passed a talisman. The process invoked feminist consciousness-raising, and the talisman tied gay subjectivity to indigeneity. Radical Faeries used indigenized and feminist tools to unleash their inherited sexual and gender nature in the remote terrain of southeastern Arizona.

In universalizing the Radical Faerie identity to a shared gay Indigenous spirituality, Hay reduced rather than expanded an understanding of Native gender and sexual practices. He also ignored the roles of female two-spirits. GAI took on these issues when they launched their history project.[112] The hinterland migration and the politics it spurred did not always mix well with the structures of rural life or among those born and raised in Indian Country or small Nuevomexicano villages who were used to carefully monitoring their public displays of same-sex affection and gender variance. Queer politics still had work to do in terms of advancing gay rights for all southwestern residents. Thus, it was necessary to create multiple hubs for queer exploration, each performing a different cultural and political function and moving at a pace conducive to change for diverse residents.

SIX

Offending Moral Decency

*The 1969 "Love-Lust" Controversy
and Gay Liberation*

In March 1969 African American teaching assistant Lionel Williams discussed second-generation Beat poet Lenore Kandel's "Love-Lust Poem" on the pleasures of heterosexual oral sex with his students in an introductory English course at the University of New Mexico. The event, which came to be known as the "Love-Lust" controversy, triggered a statewide public conversation over the proper place of sex in society.[1] UNM students, staff, and faculty and legislators, parents, church parishioners, and members of civic organizations who perceived the erotic "Love-Lust Poem" as a threat to the moral fabric of society opposed sexual liberalism and championed its censorship. Faculty and students, the nucleus of "Love-Lust Poem" defenders, challenged sexual conventions of whiteness, maleness, and heteronormativity and in their protest efforts opened forums for debating new sexual standards on campus and in public. Literary writers such as Kandel also helped to secure a place for frank sexual speech in America, and educators such as Williams defended the right to disseminate permissive content. New Mexico newspapers and the UNM student paper *New Mexico Daily Lobo* reported on the unfolding controversy, illustrating how the event created an exchange of views on sexual knowledge.[2] The "Love-Lust" incident brought the expression of private heterosexual sexual acts to public attention, weakening the state's reticence on sexual discourse.

The spotlight on sexual content at UNM brought to light another discussion in Williams's class when he invited adjunct instructor Kenneth Pollack to give a guest lecture on homosexuality. Surprisingly, Pollack's discussion of various male homosexual acts culled from the sexually graphic magazine *Screw* never triggered as much outrage as did the class's discussion of the "Love-Lust Poem."[3] Instead, Pollack's lecture emboldened queer visibility on campus. It inspired the formation of the first gay liberation organization in the state—a chapter of the Gay Liberation Front, which formed in 1970.[4] Additionally, lesbians combined feminist politics and lesbian culture when they united with straight women to establish a women's studies program, one of the first such programs in the United States.[5] Lesbians had a substantial presence in establishing, shaping, and maintaining the program.

By opening a public sexual discourse in New Mexico, the "Love-Lust" incident broke down the climate of secrecy and surfaced intertwined notions of gender relations, sexual equality, and racial disenfranchisement. To start, the "Love-Lust" incident reveals virulent racism against African Americans. New Mexico's racial system is often misrepresented as relations between whites, American Indians, and Latinos, a framing that excludes the state's African Americans. Albuquerque, a city with a small African American population—under 3 percent—still clung to myths about Black male sexuality.[6] Williams's racial identification complicated his ability to convey unconventional sexual narratives. Some politicians and prominent New Mexico citizens defined Williams as a threat to white female virtue. They tapped into a deep-seated mythology of Black male hypersexuality and its danger to white women.[7]

"Love-Lust" drew attention to the entanglement of race and sexuality prompting queer people of color to publicly claim their identities. Gender and sexuality among residents of New Mexico encompassed a spectrum of experiences further complicated by race and ethnicity. Queer Latinx people faced a lack of representation within Latino culture as well as LGBTQ+ organizations. Latina lesbians continued to dismantle barriers of invisibility using cultural activism. In this chapter, I examine spaces of Latina feminism that emerged as Latina women gained equal access to education. The passage of the 1965 Higher Education Act opened up equal opportunity for low-income and students of color in collegiate education.[8] As a result, by the late 1960s, a growing number of Latino/a students attended colleges across the Southwest, their numbers peaking in 1975. Extending need-based financial assistance shifted racial and gender demographics on the campus of UNM, ushering in new forms of activism, including what was then called Chicana feminism.[9] Chicana feminists who explored their lesbianism served as change agents for mitigating homophobia in Latino political organizations and racism in academia. These practices spread beyond campus as Latinx queer people increased their influence on queer politics particularly through queer art, film, and music. Latina lesbian couples from New Mexico, for example, agreed to appear in the documentary film *Word Is Out: Stories from Some of Our Lives*, the first full-length gay and lesbian documentary by LGBTQ+ filmmakers that would reach a wide audience.[10]

Nationally, *Word Is Out* highlighted the visibility of queer people; locally, the "Love-Lust Poem" sparked the birth of a queer political hub at the state level. Queer New Mexicans first focused on coming out, the cornerstone of the new gay liberation movement.[11] Many gay men and lesbians asserted their sexual identity through everyday cultural subversions. Cultural activism disentangled notions of sinfulness and criminality from queerness and was essential in building an inclusive sexual freedom movement. It inaugurated an era of queer creative production by Black, Native, Latinx and Asian and Pacific Islander feminist, lesbian, queer, gay, bisexual, and transgender artists. Some queer activists participated in formalized politics and advocated for overturning state sodomy laws and passing protective gay rights legislation. Activists debated among themselves how to achieve these aims.[12] Like queer activists across the country, they wrestled with the questions of prioritizing assimilation versus rejecting institutions and seeking more radical change.

The "Love-Lust" Controversy

In early March of 1969, a freshman English class discussed the following passage from Beat writer Lenore Kandel's "Love-Lust Poem."

I want to fuck you
I want to fuck you all the parts and places
I want you all of me

all of me

my mouth is a wet pink cave
your tongue slides serpent in
stirring the inhabited depths.[13]

Teaching assistant Lionel Williams dispersed six mimeographed poems from Kandel's collection *Word Alchemy* to his two sections of English 102. A few days later, Williams asked his students to analyze the "Love-Lust Poem," considering "what the words mean to the author, and how the poem affects the reader."[14] Williams rolled up the sleeves on his freshly ironed shirt, perched on the edge of an open student desk, leaned toward his class, and waited for their response. "I think this is one of the most honest poems I have ever encountered," offered one woman student. Another challenged that it was a "dirty poem." Undergraduates debated Kandel's subject matter and questioned her vulgar language. With twenty minutes of class left, Williams interjected to address Kandel's application of confessional poetry, a technique employed to explore deeply personal matters.[15] Armed with new information, students critiqued her work as an example of modern literature. Class ended without anyone realizing that their section on the "Love-Lust Poem" would generate a statewide dialogue on sex.

Kandel's unabashed eroticism reflected a new generation of Americans willing to publicly defy polite society's conventional views on women's sexuality, and not without challenge.[16] Her sexually explicit language about women's sexual pleasure faced censure both in New Mexico and California. In April 1967 San Francisco's municipal court had categorized Kandel's *The Love Book* as obscenity because the jurors perceived Kandel's writing as a violation of moral ethics.[17] Nonetheless, Kandel continued to subvert decency standards by publishing new erotic poetry in her next book, *Word Alchemy*, which sent similar shockwaves through New Mexico.

Williams selected Kandel's poetry from *Word Alchemy* to suit his 102 courses' theme of intimacy of expression. Students read a range of texts from classics such as William Shakespeare's *The Tragedy of King Lear* to modern works like Joseph Heller's *Catch-22*.[18] Specifically, Williams used Kandel's poetry to reflect on how sex is a natural part of human expres-

Lobo Photo by Sharon Snyder

Lionel Williams·

Lionel Williams, English teaching assistant under fire from the State Legislature for distributing material to his students, alleged to be obscene, is shown discussing questions that have been raised about the poem, "Love Lust" with his class.

In 1969 this UNM classroom served as a significant site for opening a public dialogue that challenged gendered and heteronormative sexual conventions but not racialized ones. Here, teaching assistant Lionel Williams engages his students in a conversation about lust, power, and the human condition. Courtesy of *Daily Lobo* Newspaper Collection, Center for Southwest Research, University Libraries, University of New Mexico.

sion. "When you read a poem by Lenore Kandel, you are not advocating eroticism. You are talking about the poet's intimate expression of love and desire," observed Williams, who refused to classify the "Love-Lust Poem" as obscene. He articulated that he wanted students to consider "if a woman's intimate desire for love, in the form of oral sex, is perceived differently, and why or why not?" Williams admitted that he assigned the poem as a way to contest the sexual double standard, "the suggestion that women can't be exposed to things that men can."[19] He attempted to create an environment that pushed students past comfort zones to think critically about society's gender and sexual norms.

After Williams's English 102 class discussion of Kandel's work, a woman student brought home a copy of "Love-Lust Poem."[20] Her outraged father, Charles W. Soltis, a member of the chamber of commerce, sent the "inappropriate" course material to Republican senator William A. Sego of Berna-lillo County on the grounds that his daughter should be shielded from such explicit sexual descriptions. In response, Senator Sego raised the issue at the March 21 meeting of the Senate Finance Committee during a hearing on the university budget and argued that UNM was teaching pornogra-phy, submitting a copy of "Love-Lust Poem" as evidence. Senator Sego's classification of the poem as pornography signaled his displeasure with its sexual content rather than its obscene language.[21] Senator Harold Runnels from Lea County, chairman of the finance committee, further roused legis-lators and demanded an investigation of higher education in the state. The committee suggested reappropriating forty thousand dollars of university funding to form and finance the Legislative University Investigating Com-mittee, which would be tasked with inspecting irregularities at UNM and serving as a governmental censorship board to review classroom materials, a measure that became known as House Bill 300.[22] One day later, the House of Representatives debated "Love-Lust Poem," proposing a resolution that insisted the university regents fire Williams. On the House floor, Repre-sentative Brad Prince of Albuquerque decried, "The poem is smut and I'd knock his block off if he showed such a thing to my college-age children."[23] Public officials passed the resolution by a vote of 47–12, which stated that Williams "offended the very foundations of decency in New Mexico by the distribution of pornographic materials to students in classrooms in his capacity as instructor. The activities of this instructor have placed him outside the accepted standards of decent citizens of New Mexico."[24] State officials, followed by many citizens of New Mexico, demanded to address what they saw as Williams's transgression of moral decency, sexual propri-ety, and pedagogical standards.

UNM president Ferrel Heady capitulated to political pressure and offi-cially suspended Williams and Pollack—after the guest lecture on homosex-uality came to light. After the two teaching assistants were suspended, Pres-ident Heady asked Joseph Frank, as department chair, to find replacements. Frank refused. Consequently, Heady relieved Frank of his duties as chair on March 27. When the suspensions became public knowledge, discord over "Love-Lust Poem" intensified. Letters from inside and outside the university offer a glimpse into New Mexico public opinion about obscenity, sexuality, and academic freedom. Close to fifteen thousand New Mexicans sent letters and telegrams to New Mexico governor David Cargo denouncing the use of sexually overt materials at the university.[25] Concerned parents, church parishioners, civic organizations, UNM faculty, and others conveyed support for the suspensions. President Heady received mail mainly from those who supported his position. Chalmer R. Myer of Gallup, New Mexico, father of two UNM undergraduates, wrote, "I support investigation of campus activities. . . . I support final removal of undesirable professors who promote foul teaching." Myer argued that academic freedom entailed a responsibility not only to students but also to the "larger community." Similarly, Mesa Lodge No. 27 of the Independent Order of Odd Fellows of Albuquerque applied a singular definition of the state's moral heritage to all New Mexican institutions and residents. Lodge members drafted a resolution to Governor Cargo. First, the resolution expressed outrage that professors "presented material completely without regard to the high level of moral standards existing in the state," asked for the endorsement of stricter standards to ensure "that the teaching staff is of the highest moral character," and concluded that students should never "be subjected to coercion by peddler[s] of pornographic filth."[26]

Many organizations enumerated citizens who desired to defend New Mexican morality. Twenty-four Southern Baptist churches and missions in Chaves and Eddy counties (in the southeast corner of the state), with a total membership of 6,219, wrote a collective letter to "oppose the lewd 'Love Lust' poem."[27] Some groups even called for UNM to cease operation because of the scandal: "We, Members of Torrance County Farm and Livestock Bureau, send you this letter to tell you how we feel about this issue. In the past the University of New Mexico has allowed certain material to be taught to English students, Freshmen English Students, and has required that these students study subject matter, which to many of them, and to us, is repulsive. . . . Many people in this area [think] it would be better to close the University than to allow this display of weakness to be broadcast any longer."[28] The majority of more than ten thousand letters pronounced that Williams and Pollack had offended moral decency by exposing college students to "pornographic filth." A coalition gathered around Heady and the legislature, advising each to regulate sexual knowledge. The "Love-Lust" controversy provoked a public declaration of conservative sexual values across the entire state of New Mexico.

Galvanized erotica opponents, then, turned to obscenity statutes as a means to contain sexuality and punish violators. The Albuquerque Police Department's Vice Squad deployed the city's obscenity ordinance to seize sixteen copies of Kandel's *Word Alchemy* from the Yale Street Grasshopper Book Store on Friday, March 28. In Albuquerque, before the "Love-Lust" scandal, residents had been able to purchase both of Kandel's publications, *The Love Book* and *Word Alchemy*, without harassment.[29] Largely, the New Mexico legislature permitted citizens the right to privacy when it came to obscenity. In 1969 the year of the "Love-Lust" event, every state in the nation enforced an obscenity law except New Mexico.[30] New Mexico had first considered an obscenity law in the winter of 1956, when Governor John F. Simms (1955–57) organized the Government Advisory Committee for Decency. Harry Corcoran, a resident of Albuquerque, chaired the committee, and former state police captain A. H. Hathaway served as its lead investigator. Hathaway inquired into the production and merchandising of indecent materials while Corcoran worked on drafting an obscenity law.[31] The committee's timing corresponded with the legislature's reexamination of the state's criminal code.

Ultimately, an obscenity statute was not encompassed in the omnibus criminal law revisions (House Bill 17). Instead, the New Mexico legislature encouraged local governments to adopt ordinances prohibiting the dissemination of obscenity in their communities. Both the city of Albuquerque and the Bernalillo County Commission passed anti-obscenity ordinances in the 1960s. Although rarely utilized, the ordinances made it unlawful for anyone to sell or exhibit obscene writing or pictures in the city or county. Oddly, these two ordinances did not apply to UNM. According to New Mexico's district attorney Alexander F. Sceresse, "Our state has no obscenity statute. Our city and county do, but the county has no jurisdiction over the university, and the city's jurisdiction is limited and questionable."[32]

Using the city ordinance, police arrested Yale Street Grasshopper Bookstore owner Philip Mayne, a husband and father of four, and employee Stephen Stroh. Mayne had been arrested once before for selling Robert M. Rimmer's *The Harrad Experiment*, William S. Burroughs's *Naked Lunch*, Michael McClure's *The Beard*, and the anonymous memoir *My Secret Life* but had sold Kandel's work for two years without incident. Mayne's initial arrest and conviction were the first time the city used the obscenity ordinance to confiscate books. After Mayne's second arrest, Municipal Judge

Harry D. Robins warned Albuquerque residents that until the municipal court trial determined if the poem was obscene, those who distributed it might be guilty of violating the "lewd, immoral or obscene acts" ordinance, which prohibited "manufacturing, promoting, distributing or possessing any obscene publication." Mayne's second arrest never resulted in a conviction because the Albuquerque court ruled that "Love-Lust Poem" did not meet the local standard for obscenity.[33]

Sex animated the most passionate debate over "Love-Lust Poem," but race heightened the fervor. Despite both Pollack's and Williams's suspensions, outraged citizens and media outlets demonized Williams, a Black man married to a white woman. TV reports and several newspaper articles featured images of Williams teaching in a classroom of mainly white women. Williams even received hate mail that threatened sexualized racial violence.[34] For the alleged crime of exposing young women to pornography, some insisted Williams deserved physical harm. Blatant racism, invocations of racial stereotypes, and fear of Black male sexuality drove white public attitudes toward Black men in the 1960s and 1970s. The decades gave rise to the image of the hypermasculine Black man and combined with the older stereotypical conception of Black men as hypersexual. Attempts to establish "whiteness" as inherently better than "blackness" rested on stressing the sexual difference of African Americans. White Americans upheld the sexual mores of whites as moral and degraded Black sexual mores as immoral to justify racial control over Black populations.[35] The distribution of "obscene" material by a Black instructor added racial fury to the fires of the "Love-Lust" ordeal.

Calls for violence against Williams not only came as anonymous threats but were also published in the *Albuquerque Journal*. The newspaper reported on a business luncheon at the Alvarado Hotel during which Albuquerque insurance executive Robert P. Tinnin declared, "If Williams had passed this kind of filth out to my daughter, I don't think we would have to worry about Lionel Williams today." Tinnin's son and daughter attended UNM, yet he only became alarmed over the spread of sexual filth to his daughter. In the growing market of erotica, men wrote and produced most materials for an audience of other men.[36] Male-centered narratives asserted men's sexual autonomy. In contrast, "Love-Lust Poem" was erotica penned by a woman, intended for audiences of any gender, and celebrated women's sexual autonomy. Tinnin's anxiety toward women's and racial-sexual equality verged to the point of hysteria. He demanded the university close or at least be "completely fumigated." By calling for the prohibition of sexual themes in higher education, Tinnin and his supporters argued for the suppression of academic freedom to uphold a traditional moral order enforced by white men.

Students raised the race issue in their protests against Williams's suspension. Barbara Brown Simmons, a founding member of the UNM Black Student Union started in 1967, claimed President Heady fired Williams because "he is a black man." She alleged that other English faculty taught Kandel's work, but when Williams did the same he faced attacks. Mary Riege, a teaching assistant in the sociology department, supported Brown Simmons's assertions, explaining that trouble ensued "when the legislature learned a black man was teaching what they thought was a filthy poem to their white daughters." The Black Student Union organized a march on the administration building. On April 1 several hundred students joined the Black Student Union with signs that referenced the "Love-Lust" controversy's racial implications. A photograph of the march captures a student holding a sign that reads "Break the Chains" and displays two fists breaking the bonds of slavery. During the event, seventeen Black Student Union members and United Mexican American Students met with President Heady, Academic Vice President Chester Travelstead, and Vice President for Student Affairs Harold Lavender. They presented a list of demands, the first of which stated, "Williams was suspended because he's a black man discussing a sexual issue" and should "be immediately reinstated." Other demands included hiring more African American professors and including Black student representation in the process of establishing a Black studies department. Williams was the only African American teaching assistant at UNM. Black faculty remained virtually nonexistent until the 1976–77 academic year, when the university recruited two African American professors.[37] Despite the Black Student Union's attention to the entanglement of race and sexuality, a candid dialogue about Black sexuality never surfaced outside the university.

Collectively, student organizations on campus conducted the largest demonstration in the university's history in support of Williams and Pollack. The intersectional issues of race, gender, and sexuality drew feminists, gay men, lesbians, Chicana/os, Black student activists, and others. Around 1,500 participants gathered on the mall in front of the student union building to voice their opposition to the suspensions on Friday, March 28, two days after President Heady announced them.[38] Visiting Assistant Professor Robert Creeley spoke first, reading excerpts from Walt Whitman and D. H. Lawrence, illustrating that sexual themes have always been pervasive in literature. Various students and faculty addressed the crowd, and English Assistant Professor Gene Frumkin read "Love-Lust Poem." Protestors moved into the student union building for a twenty-four-hour teach-in on erotica and "theology of sex." Students formed the Ad Hoc Committee for a Free University, which called for a boycott of classes and instead arranged for students to attend sessions on "Love-Lust Poem."[39]

In addition to the rally, students deployed a variety of protest tactics. In Williams's class, undergraduate David Levine wrote and circulated a petition that proclaimed, "We, the undersigned, support Lionel Williams's right of academic freedom and his right to due process. We furthermore think that if UNM is to be a free University that [the] state legislature should not control the material taught by teachers." English department teaching assistants released a similar declaration calling for due process and the reinstatement of the instructors. Student disapproval carried on in other forms, some of which resulted in arrests. Overall, students applied constant pressure on Heady to rescind the suspensions. Their open discussions of sexuality became a part of UNM's public culture. Student and faculty defiance of censoring "Love-Lust Poem" ended the invisibility of sexual matters on campus and attempted to remake the university as a place to contemplate new sexual ideals.[40]

Although Heady had ruled on the issue, he was required to follow American Association of University Professors' procedures, which stipulated that graduate students, before official dismissal, had the right "to be heard before a duly constituted committee." Heady convened a Special Advisory Committee consisting of Faculty Policy Committee Chair Hubert Alexander, Graduate Dean and Vice President of Research George Springer, and Chairman of the Committee on Academic Freedom and Tenure John Green to conduct an "informal" hearing on the matter beginning on April 1. Law professor Leo Kanowitz provided academic counsel for the two instructors. The Special Advisory Committee spent five days hearing evidence from eighty witnesses. Among them were Williams and Pollack, students who had taken their courses, vociferous legislative critic Senator Runnels, and psychologist Karl Koening. The hearing focused on whether sexuality was an appropriate theme for an English class to ascertain "if there had been a deliberate attempt to overemphasize the themes of sex" and "whether any students might have been harmed" through verbal sexual assault.[41]

Williams's and Pollack's testimonies, evidence from witnesses, and seventy-five letters from UNM administrative offices persuaded the committee that neither Williams's or Pollack's courses were "overbalanced toward sex" and therefore the questionable materials were "not inappropriate in terms of the educational objectives being pursued." The committee deemed that Pollack's session on homosexuality was "dubious" but dismissed his guest lecture as "the sole occasion of anything questionable in his behavior." Furthermore, according to the committee report, "none of the students interviewed felt that he or she had been attacked or harmed in any way." Most students' testimonies revealed enthusiasm and interest in the course material selections. A first-year student who attended the protest rally reacted strongly in favor of the poem: "When I first got the poem I was shocked by it. I'll admit it. But then in the class discussion, I started to open up to it . . . and I think Williams really opened up my mind."[42] Testimonials and textual evidence persuaded the committee that "Love-Lust Poem" and the articles on homosexuality were "unoffensive" to student sensibilities. The committee concluded the hearing with the release of a thirty-seven-page report to the university community and the general public that found "no justification for accusing . . . [Williams and Pollack] of 'verbal sexual assault'" and recommended the immediate reinstatement of the teaching assistants with the caveat that the English department closely supervise them.[43] Within a few days, President Heady complied with the recommendations. UNM took a tentative step toward curriculum development in the humanities that informed students about the complexities and importance of sexual expression.

Technically, the "Love-Lust" controversy ended with the conclusion of the hearing and Williams's and Pollack's reinstatement as teaching assistants and Frank as chair of the English department.[44] But the issue continued to agitate people who believed that public discussions about sex were inappropriate. Some legislators pursued the passage of the general appropriations bill HB 300, which established, in part, a Legislative University Investigating Committee to investigate the state's universities and appropriated forty thousand dollars to finance it for the next two fiscal years. Governor David Cargo signed HB 300 into law on April 10. In its first year, the committee took testimony from voluntary faculty and administrators in a series of hearings, then hired investigator William O'Donnell, a former vice president of New Mexico State University, to review witness testimonies, conduct interviews, and file an official report with recommendations for improvement. In essence, the Legislative University Investigating Committee extended the Special Advisory Committee hearing's role to research campus issues, particularly those related to sexuality. The "Love-Lust" event played a prominent role in O'Donnell's report, which warned that UNM had become too liberal and predicated a sharp decrease in student enrollment as a result of the poem incident. Students recognized the shift as well. *New Mexico Daily Lobo* journalist Jon Bowman argued that 1969 marked the year UNM transitioned from a conservative public university to a radical campus.[45]

At the end of the academic year, Pollack's teaching assistant position ended, and he moved to New York City. Frank, UNM's English department chair, resigned and accepted a position as chair at the University of Massachusetts. Williams finished his graduate education over the summer and accepted a job at Sonoma State University. Those most directly involved in the controversy left UNM and the issue behind them, but with the floodgates open, public conversations on sexuality prevailed. To kick off the 1969–70 academic year, the Student Organizing Committee announced in the *New Mexico Daily Lobo* that Wednesday, September 17, 1969, would be University Purification Day—an event that aimed to defy the Legislative University Investigating Committee's attempt to "purify" UNM. Purification Day featured rock bands, four-letter-word bingo, poetry readings, and a march against censorship. Students were encouraged "to bring their favorite dirty book." During the spring semester, the Student Organizing Committee also invited Lenore Kandel to campus. The Legislative University Investigating Committee immediately responded and passed a unanimous motion to ask the Board of Regents and President to cancel Kandel's poetry reading. UNM took no such action, and on May 1, 1970, Kandel read twenty-seven of her works, including the "Love-Lust Poem" to a rapt audience of three thousand. She departed with a standing ovation and hearty cheers.[46] The "Love-Lust" controversy left an indelible mark on UNM.

Gay Liberation and Lesbian Feminist Politics

Although Pollack's conversation on homosexuality took a back seat to the "Love-Lust Poem" discussion, its importance manifested after the scandal died down. Pollack had brought visibility to gay people and issues. In response, during the 1970–71 academic year, the *New Mexico Daily Lobo* and KUNM Radio featured interviews with five gay-identified students and offered the first student reporting on homosexuality. Inspired by the events around the "Love-Lust" controversy and growing radicalism on the UNM campus as well as the larger context of the sexual revolution, including the Stonewall Riots and gay liberation movement, the student newspaper and radio station began regular reporting on gay and lesbian issues. Additionally, a handful of gay and lesbian students founded Gay Liberation in the fall of 1970. After receiving a charter from the university on February 16, 1971, the organization welcomed gay, bisexual, and heterosexual students to join. Nationwide, by 1974, close to 175 gay student groups dotted university and college campuses.[47]

GL-NM modeled itself on the Gay Liberation Front, a radical group that embraced sexual politics and committed to solidarity with students from underrepresented backgrounds.[48] GL-NM's constitution declared disseminating sexual knowledge as the organization's main focus: "to provide a forum for the discussion of the issues pertaining to human sexuality and related matters, in particular male homosexuality and lesbianism." The new organization petitioned the university to establish a homosexuality course and a space in the student union to house periodicals and literature on the topic. It also held its own weekly classes, and at the invitation of instructors, members made presentations on sexual liberation in college and high school courses.[49] The "Love-Lust" controversy helped pave the way for studying sexuality.

GL-NM further aimed to raise visibility of the gay student population. On September 24, 1971, it coordinated guerrilla theater and short speeches at the mall on the campus of UNM.[50] The lyrics they sang displayed same-sex desire in a public space: "I was embarrassed and ashamed to tell anyone / About the gay feelings I had / So I'd masturbate in bed each night, / And think about the bodies of the boys in my gym class."[51] Similar to Kandel's confessional poetry, queer students increased sexual candor by composing confessional music. Personal sexual revelations, disclosed in public, challenged sexual taboos. The demonstration pushed heterosexual students to confront homosexuality in public, though it would take much more than street theater to gain equality.

During the 1971–72 academic year, GL-NM President Mark Youtzy expanded the group's aims to self- and social acceptance as well as combating legal problems. The organization moved beyond campus politics and attempted to break down structural barriers for New Mexican gays. They mailed questionnaires to legislators asking for their support on the repeal of the state sodomy law and implementation of fair housing and employment practices for sexual minorities. They even went as far as advocating the abolition of "all laws and institutional practices of the U.S. governments—federal, state, and local—that in any way discriminate against persons because of actions expressive of their sexual natures." GL-NM put pressure on politicians to recognize state and national level civil rights for gay men and lesbians.[52] GL-NM moved Albuquerque from a city with no institutional gay and lesbian political structure to one with a radical, political presence. The sodomy law was repealed in 1975 when New Mexico joined twelve states in revising sodomy laws, lifting criminal punishments for consenting adults to engage in oral and anal intercourse. However, by this time GL-NM had dissolved; nationwide, GLF groups collapsed by 1973. Those that formed on college campuses often renamed themselves.[53] Albuquerque's GL-NM followed suit and the organization changed its name to the Gay People's Union. This second reincarnation withered away but was followed by Juniper in 1974 and the Gay Co-op in 1976.[54]

In contrast, the formation of the Women Studies program at UNM, one of the earliest in the nation, provided a long-standing institutional base for lesbians. The Ad Hoc Committee that had helped to organize the "Love-Lust" demonstration on campus had also formed a free university, "a student-sponsored, and student-run alternative to departmental offerings."[55] On college and university campuses nationwide, before women's studies coalesced into an organized academic entity, women faculty and students first offered courses inclusive of women often under the auspices of the free university. UNM's first women studies course followed suit. At UNM the idea for a class taught entirely from a women's perspective arose during a consciousness-raising group formed in the summer after the "Love-Lust" controversy. Graduate students and staff Diane Brown, Marilee Dolan, Gail Baker, Lucia Valeska, and Mary Maxine taught The Second Sex: Explorations in the Revolution of Women from Economic, Political, and Historical Points of View as a free university class in the winter of 1970. The course, open to anyone, attracted forty women and jumpstarted the idea for a university program.[56]

After the course, Brown, Dolan, Baker, Valeska, and Maxine organized a conference on campus to brainstorm about a permanent women's studies program, including "what should it be and whom should it serve." The featured speaker at the conference was lesbian poet and native New Mexican Judy Grahn, whose presence foreshadowed the prominent role lesbianism would play in shaping the program. After the final panel of the conference, all attendees met and decided by consensus to establish a collective that would pursue the establishment of a women studies program for the 1971–72 academic year.[57]

From WMST's inception at UNM, the program's structure and course offerings committed to a "multi-cultural feminist education. . . . within the context of furthering its analysis of and struggle against women's oppression." A less-acknowledged function of the program is that it served overlapping needs of feminism and lesbianism.[58] Lesbians used the program as a base camp for mobilization to promote greater visibility, find each other, claim a new public place, and build a sexual political consciousness that has served generations of LGBTQ+ students. WMST functioned as an entry point for women, lesbians in particular, to generate a variety of meeting spaces meant to encourage feminist lesbian identity, feminist activism, and sexual politics. From its inception, the program gained an informal reputation as a lesbian hub, and lesbians pushed to include a critique of heterosexuality as a foundation of the program.

Both lesbians and Chicana feminists left a mark on UNM's women studies program by institutionalizing identarian political struggles. Self-identified Chicana feminists influenced the formation of WMST by creating a class on their feminist experiences called La Mujer Chicana (The Chicana Woman). In designing coursework, WMST members discussed the pedagogical implications of the various divisions of knowledge—race, class, sexuality, nation, and so forth. Alesia Kunz, one of the core founders of WMST, recalled, "Every ism there was we talked about it."[59] However, the proposal for a cross-cultural feminist class arose from outside of the collective. The idea germinated in an organization called Las Chicanas—an informal rap group of Chicana activist students. According to Erlinda Gonzales-Berry, the faculty advisor for the group, Las Chicanas formed due to its members' dissatisfaction "with 'women's auxiliary role' in the activities of the Chicano Center on campus" and a reluctance "to become involved in the women's movement."[60] Members felt situated between these two social movements. Las Chicanas conducted consciousness-raising sessions to explore feminisms within their own cultural context. Member and graduate student Beverly "Beva" Sanchez Padilla first approached the Chicano studies department with the proposal for the La Mujer Chicana class. When Chicano studies rejected it, Padilla turned to WMST. WMST included La Mujer Chicana as one of its initial courses and asked Padilla and Gonzales-Berry to coteach it.[61] With the introduction of the class, Las Chicanas forged a bridge between white feminists and emerging Chicana feminists.

By its second year, WMST had committed to challenging heterosexism through the introduction of a new class Lesbian Feminism in America. WMST hired lesbians Jennifer Woodul and Kate Winter, both from Siren, a local women's organization in Albuquerque, to coteach the class in fall of 1974.[62] Woodul brought to the class her experiences from the women's liberation movement, including her involvement with a separatist lesbian feminist collective, The Furies in Washington, DC, and her protest of lesbians' treatment in the movement during the Lavender Menace action on May 1, 1970.[63] Perhaps due to Woodul's notoriety, a record-breaking seventy-five students and community members attended the class. Graduate instructor Ann Nihlen remembers the class as a place where lesbians embraced their sexual orientation: "Many of them took it because they were working on issues in their lives with men and personal issues. Many women came out."[64] The academic space publicly affirmed the legitimacy of lesbian sexuality, a fairly radical proposition for the first decade of women's studies. Most women's studies courses offered at universities and colleges were rarely advertised with the word *lesbian*. In December of 1971, the National Advisory Council on Women's Educational Programs commissioned Florence Howe and Carol Ahlum to assess the state of women's studies programs. They compiled and published a list of 610 women's studies courses taught between 1969 and 1972, and of these, only three class titles contained the words *lesbian* or *gay woman*, while thirteen contained *sexuality*.[65] WMST's Lesbian Feminism in America course validated lesbian identities and represented lesbianism as central to a new feminist space: the classroom.

In light of the "Love-Lust" ordeal, some UNM personnel remained uncomfortable with the teaching of sexual content in the classroom. Using the word *lesbian* in the title of the class elicited strong reactions from some men in the faculty and administration. During the 1974–75 academic year, Nathaniel Wollman, the dean of the College of Arts and Sciences, launched an attack against the entire WMST's program. Wollman claimed that some WMST classes, including Lesbian Feminism in America, had not received formal approval and criticized the department for its low "academic quality," threatening to withdraw credit. At the same time, an opinion piece in the *New Mexico Daily Lobo* written by Stephen Beckerman, a professor in the Department of Anthropology, accused WMST of systematically discriminating against heterosexual men and women by denying their enrollment in Lesbian Feminism in America.[66]

In response, an out and radical lesbian feminist, P. M. Duffy-Ingrassia, rose up to protest the attack on WMST. Duffy-Ingrassia not only contested the accusations; she launched an effective counterattack. Because Dean Wollman and Professor Beckerman had used the student newspaper as their forum for questioning the legitimacy of the program, Duffy-Ingrassia organized a sit-in protest at the *New Mexico Daily Lobo* office. Thirty women from WMST occupied the office on Friday September 19, 1974, to demand the publication of a special edition on WMST so they could present an opposing view. The women occupied the office for several days, which caused the staff to negotiate a resolution. Staff promised to publish a special issue on oppression if they received enough articles from those on campus who felt oppressed. While the special issue never came to fruition, WMST remained front-page news for several weeks, and lesbian feminists filled the letters to the editor section with favorable depictions of WMST. More importantly, Duffy-Ingrassia arose as a prominent lesbian on campus whose activities kept constant attention on lesbian issues. A few examples include Duffy-Ingrassia's participation in establishing the first feminist/lesbian coffeehouse in Albuquerque, her campaign and election—as an out lesbian—for homecoming queen in 1976, and workshop presentation on "Lesbians, Non-Lesbians and Women's Studies" at the 1977 National

Women's conference in Houston.[67] Starting with the demonstration, Duffy-Ingrassia opened up additional spaces for lesbians to come together.

The public outing of WMST as a lesbian space produced an unintended rift with ethnic studies. After Dean Wollman published his critique of WMST, he announced his intention to withdraw academic credit from both ethnic and women studies programs if they failed to meet academic standards. Immediately, all three ethnic studies directors distanced their own programs from the WMST controversy. Harvey Paymella, coordinator of the Native American studies program, commented on the Lobo sit-in, in the student paper: "we have nothing to do with it. This was an individual effort." African American Studies Director Charles Becknell declared he had previously secured Dean Wollman's support for Black studies and their "situation is cleared up." Finally, although Duffy-Ingrassia had called specifically for Chicano participation at the protest because WMST and many Chicanas had a good working relationship Chicano Studies Director Antonio Mondragon refused to participate. Collectively, ethnic studies directors objected to their being lumped in with WMST and left the program to defend itself.[68]

Even the Las Chicanas group, which had found support through WMST, distanced itself from the program because of its association with lesbianism. The La Mujer Chicana class continued to be taught, but Las Chicanas published a statement in the student newspaper, affirming the group's position as committed to the Chicano movement: "It is easy for you as white women to say 'Let's get it together and become sisters,' but is it possible? NO! We cannot be 'sisters.' . . . We as Chicanas choose to work in a United Effort within the Chicano Movement."[69] The controversy surrounding WMST's now-public association with lesbianism caused discomfort for some Chicana students, especially in light of lesbian-baiting within the Chicano movement. In Chicano activism, "merely being a feminist meant that you would be called a lesbian," and men Chicano activist leaders sometimes used lesbian-baiting as a weapon to silence Chicana activists and keep them in a subordinate position.[70] Fear of being labeled a lesbian cultivated an environment in which Chicana lesbians could not proclaim their identity. Politically active lesbian Chicanas typically kept their sexual identity private while socially active and out Chicana lesbians tended to shy away from political activity.[71] When Las Chicanas rejected

WMST's validation of lesbians, it kept Chicana lesbians silent and in the margins. On the other hand, white feminists held a more privileged position in society that better allowed them to publicly declare a lesbian status. In an attempt to tone down radicalness as well as capitulate to university pressure, WMST renamed Lesbian Feminism in America to Heterosexism in Society the next semester, ending the controversy. Nonetheless, divisions between WMST and Chicana feminists persisted until ethnic studies and WMST formed a solidarity coalition, spearheaded by Ann Nihlen, in 1981.[72]

Word Is Out

Chicana lesbians who were silenced within campus politics found agency in connection to the Mariposa Film Group's *Word Is Out: Stories from Some of Our Lives* (1977), which featured twenty-six intimate queer stories told directly to the camera. The film is remarkable for bookending the narrative with a Latina lesbian couple from Corrales, New Mexico. Peter Adair and his crew aimed to make a work of cultural activism that sought to change millions of minds about who gay people were and how gay people fit in to society. Adair described the project as a "powerful voice in altering American attitudes towards homosexuality" as well as "a piece of art and a piece of social activism." One reviewer of both *Word Is Out* and documentary *Gay USA* agreed, "there is no question that, if seen by large numbers of people, these films could prove to be highly effective tools for social change."[73] *Word Is Out* argues that gay people have a place in American society. With themes of inclusion and positive representations of lesbian and gay experiences, it framed gay rights as a fight for equal dignity and belonging to the mainstream institutions of love, marriage, and family.

In 1973 aspiring documentarian Peter Adair, who grew up on the Navajo Nation, started filming interviews with his gay and lesbian friends in San Francisco. Adair learned his autoethnographic approach, in part, from the influence of his father John Adair, a visual anthropologist who studied the Pueblo of Zuni and Navajo Nation. From 1953 to 1960, John Adair joined the Cornell-Navajo Field Health Research Project at Many Farms, on the Navajo reservation.[74] Peter Adair credits this experience with shaping his early filmmaking: "Being in the minority, and sometimes the only white kid around, started me looking at everything from the eyes of an outsider." Adair's initial vision for his interviews "began as a teaching film which would basically present a series of positive role models." The project was also personal. "When I realized I was gay, I made a film about it," Adair recounted.[75]

At a time when honest conversations about gay and lesbian experiences were rarely covered in documentaries, Adair decided to expand the project into a full-length gay and lesbian documentary by LGBTQ+ filmmakers, primarily funded by gay people and businesses. He enlisted the help of his sister Nancy Adair because "he wanted a lesbian to interview gay women."[76] As the project grew, the duo placed a recruiting advertisement in an alternative San Francisco paper. Six people heeded the call, including Andrew Brown, Lucy Massie Phenix, Veronica Selver, and Rob Epstein, who became a renowned queer filmmaker. The group named themselves the Mariposa Film Group and shared equal credit for their contributions.[77]

An early cut of the documentary highlighted the narratives of eight queer people—Pat Bond, Whitey Fladden, Elsa Gidlow, Pam Jackson, Tede Mathews, George Mendenhall, Rusty Millington, and Rick Stokes. After screening this footage to gay audiences, the collective responded to feedback about a lack of racial diversity and geographic representation.[78] Importantly, the filmmakers then prioritized representing a diversity of voices including African American, Asian American, and Latinx interviewees who were encouraged to tell their own stories in their own way. There is also a subtle openness to sexual identities beyond gay and lesbian and gender variance, such as the film's only genderqueer participant, Tede Mathews. In total, the Mariposa Film Group interviewed more than two hundred queer people from California, Massachusetts, New Mexico, North Carolina, Pennsylvania, and Washington, DC, about their identity concerns and gay sociality. By consensus, the collective added another sixteen interviewees, four of whom lived in New Mexico—Nadine Armijo, John Burnside, Harry Hay, and Rosa Montoya.[79]

Word Is Out debuted on December 1, 1977, at San Francisco's Castro Theatre as a benefit in support of the campaign against the Briggs Initiative (Proposition 6), which would have prohibited gay and lesbian people from teaching in California public schools. It then screened across the country in gay metropolises and at LGBT film festivals and was broadcast on PBS television in October 1978. The television broadcast likely reached viewer-

The Mariposa Film Group (*left to right*): Lucy Massie Phenix, Nancy Adair, Peter Adair, Rob Epstein, Andrew Brown, and Veronica Selver. Photograph by Janet Cole. Courtesy of the Peter Adair Papers, James C. Hormel LGBTQIA Center, San Francisco Public Library, the Mariposa Film Group, and Milliarium Films.

ship in the low millions, though exact numbers are not available. Because it aired on TV, Adair made it palatable for mainstream audiences, avoiding "dirty words" or showing "nudity." He also promised to not promote a "Gay Lib rhetoric." Mainstream presses positively reviewed it, while gay presses were more critical because the documentary shied away from discussions of sex and politics.[80] For example, the film never explores Harry Hay's Radical Faeries movement or his earlier political work with the homophile movement.

Nonetheless, many viewers loved it. The Mariposa Film Group received more than a thousand letters, primarily from those who watched it on PBS.[81] "I saw the documentary, The Word is Out, just last week on Chicago's educational channel 11. I want you to know that I was thrilled with the program. It was the very best portrayal on the topic of same-sex love that I have ever witnessed," wrote Shirley R. Simeon. Rex Wilkinson found the participants' "frankness and sincerity" refreshing. He appreciated the "broad cross-section of our so-called sub-culture." "Instead of hoping that my parents were not watching the program as I often feel when there is something on TV about being gay, I actually hoped that they were watching!" confessed Wilkinson. He felt the film would bring comfort to his parents because of its central focus on love. Straight audiences responded as well. Dana Bewer, who identified as "fifteen years old and straight," wrote, "I have just finished viewing your program of gays and found it very informative. I am glad to see that homosexuals were finally given a chance to speak out." Bewer conveys that gay people "are no different from anyone else."[82]

The film opens with a scene of Nadine Armijo sitting on her white iron-framed bed, a pair of rosary beads hanging from it. She pets her dog, Louisa. The shot closes in on Armijo's face as an off-screen voice (Veronica Selver) asks, "Were you always . . . gay?" "Always? Hmm . . . I don't think so. Well maybe, I don't know. It's hard to say," ponders Armijo. Then, she breathes, looks directly at the camera, and asserts, "Yeah, I've been gay."[83] With these words, Armijo invites the audience to hear her story.

Word Is Out is divided into three parts, though the subject matter frequently overlaps. Part 1, "The Early Years," focuses on older participants and life in the closet; part 2, "Growing Up," considers exploration, particularly finding a partner and entering a community; and part 3, "From Now On," is an assessment of contemporary queer lives as well as projections about the future. In the final two sections, interview subjects are joined by their partners, a structure that privileges stable relationships to send the message that queer partnerships are just like straight ones. Love is love, a political argument that has defined mainstream LGBTQ+ activism for four decades, is highlighted in the film and foreshadows the marriage equality movement that took shape in the early 1990s.[84]

In part 2 of the documentary, Nadine Armijo and Rosa Montoya sit side by side on their bed, answering questions about their lesbian relationship. Armijo details their home-centered life together: "We don't go out much like to the bars. We stay here. Rosa studies. I read. We go for walks. We play ball. Go fishing sometimes. Play with the dogs. Take her to the park. Sometimes I go horseback riding or I go pick apples with my cousin. I help him pick apples. They have a big orchard."[85] In the close-knit village community where Armijo's family possessed deep roots as apple orchard farmers, the couple lived across the street from Armijo's parents. The homebound

Word Is Out omitted from the film Hay's approach to gay liberation, which was vocally against assimilation. Courtesy of the Peter Adair Papers, James C. Hormel LGBTQIA Center, San Francisco Public Library.

Nadine Armijo, sitting comfortably on her bed, tells part of her story in the first scene of *Word Is Out*. Courtesy of the Peter Adair Papers, James C. Hormel LGBTQIA Center, San Francisco Public Library.

lesbian couple negotiated their sexual identity within family and church structures. Despite Corrales's close proximity to Albuquerque, Armijo and Montoya spent most of their time in the small village.[86]

Their story is revealed in a domestic space (the bedroom), yet it is devoid of explicit depictions of sex. Their relationship is desexualized by focusing on scenes of homemaking. Still, Armijo and Montoya discuss and display physical intimacy. Veronica Selver asks, "Are you affectionate with each other when others are around?" "No, we're not. We are hardly affectionate with each other," Montoya promptly replies. Armijo gently corrects her, "Yes, we are. But not in front of other people." Armijo and Montoya felt compelled to monitor their public sexual expression. They never engaged in physical or emotional affection with each other in front of other people, even in their own home.[87] The final scene of the twenty-six participants reenters the intimate space of Armijo and Montoya's bedroom. It ends with Armijo and Montoya lying on their bed, hands clasped, whispering to each other. What they whisper is barely audible, but the powerful sexual attraction and emotional connection between the two women is palpable.[88]

Tellingly, comments critical of racial injustices in the pre-interview stage were left out of the final version. While it is difficult to gauge how the Mariposa Film Group made such decisions, racial critiques ran counter to the final film's amicable tone. The documentarians left out Armijo's tension with her family and her linking it to Chicano culture. In her longer interview, which didn't make it into the final film, Armijo narrates her coming-out process. She first expresses her inability to communicate her lesbian desires to her family, whom she describes as "typical Chicanos" who believe "that it is really bad to be gay."[89] She narrates her self-imposed exile from Corrales when she temporarily moved to Albuquerque to meet other lesbians. Armijo's mother confronted her about the reason she had left and condemned her for breaching her commitment to the family. This was the only time her mother had ever used the word *lesbian*. Armijo returned to Corrales after a few years, and even though she moved into a house across the street from her parents and siblings with her lover, she revived her religious and familial obligations by attending Mass and family dinners on a weekly basis. Her relatives ignored the sexual aspect of her relationship and accepted her partner, Montoya. Silence allowed Armijo room for sexual exploration. According to sociologist Mary Gray, in rural towns, residents partially tolerated homosexuality if it existed quietly and did not interfere with one's commitment to family and community.[90] Due to such constraints, the couple created a home-centered life, but their peaceful domestic setting is unsettled by the fuller picture of their struggle to discuss and express their lesbianism.

By agreeing to appear in film, Armijo and Montoya boldly challenged the censure of their same-sex expression. The Mariposa Film Group pre-interviewed another Latina lesbian couple, Cecilia and Marilyn. While Cecilia and Marilyn's domestic relationship is strikingly similar to Nadine and Rosa's—Cecilia and Marilyn lived together "two doors away from" Cecilia's family, and neither of them had ever come out to their families—Cecilia and Marilyn's interviews have a much stronger political tone and critique of racialized power in New Mexico. Cecilia was born in Los Alamos to Norte Nuevomexicano parents and attended UNM with the assistance of the Higher Education Act. The founder of Las Chicanas asked Cecilia to join the organization. She described Las Chicanas as the "first feeling of community that I ever had" and felt empowered by the "career oriented women." Although Cecilia "identified as straight" when she began attending meetings, she met her future lesbian partner Marilyn through the organization. Marilyn began attending UNM in 1969 but did not find community in the feminist organizations she joined on campus. She saw a flyer in the Student Union Building "on Women's Liberation pertinent to Chicanas" and became a member of Las Chicanas.[91]

Although they met through Las Chicanas, it wasn't until they saw each other at the Chicana lesbian bar Cricket's that their relationship began. "One night I went to Cricket's. I wasn't sure if Cecilia was gay until I saw her dancing close with another woman so I asked Cecilia to dance," remembered Marilyn. The two privately developed a lesbian relationship, which they kept hidden from Las Chicanas due to anti-lesbianism in the group. Cecilia commented that most members "expressed disgust for lesbians." Marilyn agreed, recalling one meeting where members discussed how "most lesbians are unhappy and tended to be alcoholic." Yet the couple continued to participate in Las Chicanas because they desired to explore all three of their identities: "gay, Chicana, and feminist." Marilyn was careful to qualify, "I don't think I have ever been totally successful at it. I don't know if this is the proper solution, but I find myself, a lot of the time, avoiding a lot of the

Chicano men. Being a bit put off by white feminist women . . . in a limbo. There is a lot of racism that white women are not aware of. [They] have a condescending attitude about Chicana women, especially the academic white women." She goes on, "But I also feel that way about Chicano men. I try to extrapolate from all the movements without trying to compromise myself."[92]

The interviewer then asked the couple about separatism as a solution. Cecilia had experimented with a separatist phase in which she had lived on lesbian land, but she had several complaints. She found it to be "too much time together," disliked the "hippy-dippy town without anything going on but playing pool," and noted that radical dykes held prejudices against bisexuals. Marilyn disagreed with the concept of a physical Lesbian Nation, finding it "ridiculous," but said, "if you are talking about a mental Lesbian Nation where you have a strong affinity and solidarity with other lesbians, I definitely feel that." Cecilia expressed that within the Lesbian Nation Chicana lesbians lacked visibility, which is why she agreed to be in the film.[93]

Word Is Out provided another venue for articulations of Latina homoeroticism. The documentary's more conservative focus on stable queer partnerships created a platform for Latinas to discuss living in long-term lesbian partnerships. While not all Latina lesbian couples fit this mold, embracing a conventional model of domestic life for gay people permitted Latinas to fit into existing cultural tropes of marriage and family. Furthermore, Latina lesbians, rather than Latino gay men, first achieved visibility in a cultural context and created a path for gay Latino men to follow.[94] Beginning in the 1980s an explosion of discussions, publications, films, and other creative works centering Latina lesbianism emerged, with a substantial number produced by Nuevomexicanas. Also, New Mexico proved to be a state that cultivated Latinx queer households. *The Gay and Lesbian Atlas*, based on the 2000 census records, ranks New Mexico first in the nation for the highest concentration of Latinx same-sex couples and second for the highest concentration of lesbian couples.[95] Queer Latinx couples have found spaces of belonging in the state.

The narrative in *Word Is Out* helped to foster an image of gay people as stable and respectable, a strategy that has long aided gay liberation politics. In so doing, it created a space for some queer people of color to find visibility and respectability. In contrast, the "Love-Lust" controversy broadened the sweep of explicit sexual discourse, generating a more open discussion about identities and behaviors that challenged gendered and heteronormative sexual conventions but not racialized ones. The "Love-Lust" controversy and *Word Is Out* both characterized 1970s gay rights activism. "Love-Lust" defenders advocated for a radical transformation of sexuality, while *Word Is Out* participants reflected a mix of dissidence, pushing the conventional limits of gay visibility, and assimilation, seeking access to mainstream American society. The goals and tactics of gay liberation were shaped along these lines. As gay men and lesbians in New Mexico embraced visibility, protested their second-class treatment, and galvanized New Mexicans' opinions toward supporting same-sex rights, they constituted a political force that relied on cultural activism and the formalized structures that grew from cultural debates to move New Mexico toward a position that began to ensure civil rights for gay men and lesbians.

CONCLUSION

"We Never Go Away"

we never go away
even if we're always
leaving
because the only home
is each other

PAULA GUNN ALLEN
"Some Like Indians Endure"

The first anthology devoted to the queer cultural productions of two-spirit and gay American Indians, *Living the Spirit* (1988), begins with Paula Gunn Allen's poem "Some Like Indians Endure." Allen's poem is also the leading work in a 2011 collection by two-spirit writers.[1] The poem captures how both lesbians and Native Americans have survived by finding home in each other, homes formed in part by acts of coerced and voluntary mobility. Allen, through poetry, makes a powerful political statement about survivance in the face of ongoing settler colonialism and asserts the existence of contemporary two-spirit American Indians.[2] Her poem's enduring legacy, from its initial publication in 1988 to its most recent in 2011, showcases the significance of Native two-spirit and queer people's creative work as a form of defiance against settler colonialism and heteropatriarchal regimes.

Allen blazed a path for pantribal two-spirit people to unite, imagine, and create queer places of belonging. She penned some of the earliest and most notable pieces of Native American two-spirit literature. By 1988 contributors to *Living the Spirit* joined Allen in defining two-spirit roles, reaffirming gender variance in their Native nations, and supporting pantribal "groups and societies for gay Indians." In 1984 GAI began recording Native histories of gender and sexual variance as part of its history project, a collective act of resistance that culminated in the seminal text *Living the Spirit*. Cofounder of GAI Randy Burns and Chair of the GAI Board of Directors Erna Pahe spearheaded the endeavor in collaboration with white anthropologist Will Roscoe, who coordinated and edited the volume. Writers, artists, and activists used historical accounts of two-spirits, such as the life of Hastíín Klah, as well as their own contemporary experiences and artistic representations of growing up gay on-and off-reservation to illuminate a queer two-spirit heritage by and for Native people.[3]

To accompany Allen's poem, photographer Hulleah J. Tsinhnahjinnie (Taskigi/Diné) contributed a photo from her 1984 series *Metropolitan Indian*. In the photo, an American Indian wearing tribal regalia stands next to a motorcycle in front of "painted ladies," Victorian rowhouses in San Francisco's gay neighborhood. Tsinhnahjinnie's image connects two-spirit people to urban cities and tribal homelands. Urban Indian, modern, queer, and mobile are themes that run throughout the anthology. *Living the Spirit* informed and grew an activist movement that understood two-spirit people as modern mobile subjects who remain tied to tribal nations. Tsinhnahjinnie's photography and Allen's writing also reflect this book's themes of queer cultural production, mobility, and activism, and both women are grounded to their ancestral lands in the American Southwest.

New Mexico remains a center of queer creativity. Long before *Living the Spirit*, two-spirit artists such as Klah produced the state's earliest pieces of queer art—individual acts of resistance in response to the deepening of settler colonialism and suppression of two-spirit roles. Klah's return to their homeland enabled them to embrace a nádleehí status and occupations as both a feminine weaver and masculine ceremonial singer. Queer creative energy shifted from cultural traditions tied to homelands to outsider's claiming queer belonging in the wide-open terrain of New Mexico. Fueled by transience, queer art and literature flowed from urban centers to peripheries; wayward lives found solace in the desert landscapes. In the process, the queer population blended in. Their integration fostered characteristics of bohemian rebellion against the status quo, gender transgression, and sexual freedom.

However, during World War II, New Mexico embraced a new identity as a security state. The development of modern nuclear weapons marred the region physically and culturally, leaving a scar on queer cultural aesthetics. Queer cultural makers quietly persevered. Using knowing winks, allusions, and euphemisms, makers navigated homophobic environments. Others mobilized to escape Cold War ideologies of normalcy in favor of entering nascent gay meccas linked to large urban centers. Queer people asserted a right to be mobile and used geographic mobility as a tool of resistance against heteronormative confines.

By 1969 stirrings of sexual and gender discontent awakened a new creative burst that was more insistent, explicit, and political. Nationally, gay liberation promoted a politics of visibility by encouraging people to come out, an ethos that manifested in art and in urban life. During gay liberation, artists became emboldened to make explicit art about their sexual identity, and LGBTQ+ art historians began to unearth the work of queer artists that had gone unnoticed.[4] Historians should do the same. The desire to creatively document depictions of queer identity and culture is another form of sexual politics that emerged during the course of the twentieth century, formed, in part, by geographic movement to places conducive to producing queer representations.

Queer cultural production has helped to document the historic lives of queer people, and in turn such works have fundamentally altered societal conceptions of love, marriage, and family and have redefined notions of citizenship and equality. This project has acknowledged the prominent role native New Mexicans, transplants, migrants, and temporary residents of the state have played in crafting a new identity politics focused on cultural activism, which queer people used to form communities and engage in politics even without a consistent urban geographic constancy and density. Queer cultural production, as this book has demonstrated, served as a spark for advancing gay civil rights.[5] The queer art circles of northern New Mexico generated opportunities for dialogue about sexual censorship and engaged in a political battle that advocated for fewer restrictions on the dissemination of sexual information. When the security state stifled queer creative expression, queer people struggled to partake equally, in politics as evidenced by the failed attempt to decriminalize sodomy in 1963. By the end of the sixties, an erotic poem triggered a statewide public conversation about sexual conventions of whiteness, maleness, and heteronormativity and opened new forums for debating sexual standards on campus and in public, including the first gay liberation organization in the state. At the same time, the University of New Mexico's Women Studies program originated and served as a base camp of mobilization for lesbian activism. Many continued activist work for lesbian feminist and gay causes long after their involvement with WMST.

From 1970 onward, New Mexico took a formal political role in national and regional gay liberation politics. In the 1979 competitive search for co-executive director, the National Gay Task Force (NGTF), an association founded in 1973 that brought together 850 local gay organizations, hired Lucia Valeska, who had been active in WMST and the Gay People's Union on the UNM campus.[6] The *Lesbian Tide* endorsed Valeska's appointment because she "brings to this well known and generally conservative organization a strong background in both the feminist and lesbian feminist movement." NGTF hired Valeska, whom they dubbed the "Desert Dyke," to promote greater lesbian visibility and to help form a national gay liberation movement by engaging gay men and lesbians who lived outside gay urban meccas. Valeska spent twelve years in New Mexico and spoke from experience when she noted that "gays who live outside of a large urban center with a lot of resources face very different situations than those in large cities. They need ways of staying in touch with each other, they need a different approach to dealing with harassment, and with political growth." Valeska's appointment signaled NGTF's willingness to engage in an interconnected vision of liberation and solidarity, but the organization carefully paired her with a conservative counterpart. Her codirector, Charles Brydon, was a West Coast gay activist who worked within existing political arenas to advocate for change. Those who worked with Valeska in New Mexico described her as "in your face," while those close to Brydon understood him as someone who always seemed "to be wearing a conservative sports jacket even when he was not."[7]

During her time with NGTF, Valeska fought to include the demands of the working class, underserved communities, and lesbians, though personality and political conflicts hindered her effectiveness. Valeska also struggled with transitioning from local-level grassroots activism to national politics. Brydon quit NGTF in August 1981, and Valeska resigned November 1,

1982, amid charges against incompetency, mismanagement, and failure to cooperate with other national gay organizations.[8] NGTF felt Valeska had steered the organization far off course. East Coast activist Virginia "Ginny" Apuzzo replaced Valeska in an effort to reestablish NGTF's place in the "mainstream."[9] NGTF's evolution embodied the shift toward limited rights achieved through institutional channels: court systems, corporations, and Congress. The variegated interests of New Mexican gay men and lesbians fell by the wayside. But Valeska's appointment and priorities demonstrate the potential for an ideologically inclusive and geographically broad gay movement, though the people she invoked remained on the margins.

Regionally, gay activists began to come together for similar reasons to connect local grassroots movements with the fight in a national gay rights agenda.[10] Bill Conrad, a gay activist from Phoenix, Arizona, and Russell Gray, a native New Mexican born and raised in Las Cruces, both conducted human rights workshops, a training on how gay men and lesbians could advocate for their protection in the workplace, housing, and public accommodations in their respective states. The two men corresponded about their efforts. Gray had recently helped to form Common Bond in 1981, which served as an umbrella group to create statewide services for gay men and lesbians.[11] Shortly after Conrad learned about Common Bond he attended a Las Vegas, Nevada, gay pride celebration program—a human rights seminar hosted by the president of the Las Vegas Gay Academic Union, Michael Loewy. Realizing the significant overlap between their endeavors, Conrad suggested that he, Loewy, and Gray get together to discuss starting a broad Southwest conference on gay activism and leadership. Loewy, Conrad, and Gray organized Empowering Each Other, the first Desert and Mountain States Lesbian and Gay Conference, which was held in Las Vegas in March 1985. The conference served as a mobilizing force for sharing activist strategies among southwesterners. Henceforth, the desert and mountain states of New Mexico, Arizona, Utah, Nevada, and Colorado (plus Wyoming as of 1987) cooperated to build a regional identity for gay civil rights until 1991, when interest waned. Key organizer Loewy shared that these states "all had something in common—the [repressive] political climate of Arizona and Nevada and New Mexico. We felt so isolated in our communities—California didn't even know that we existed."[12]

White gay men led these endeavors. In New Mexico, from its inception,

Common Bond faced critiques from New Mexicans about its lack of racial and gender diversity in both its makeup of members and political goals.[13] The organization asserted its political power and differentiated itself from intersectional feminist and gay liberation causes. Without polyvocality within the organization, Common Bond mainly represented the interests of its membership.

Because formal gay civil rights in the 1980s catered to white gay New Mexican men, cultural activism remained a vital forum for queer people of color and lesbians. The 1980s also ushered in an era of critical interventions from queer people of color. Anthologies, in particular, served as alternative sites of queer knowledge production for underrepresented subjects. The groundbreaking cultural works of *Living the Spirit, Chicana Lesbians, Lesbian Art in America*, which includes a significant number of artists of color, and others paved the way for inclusive notions of queerness that have served the sexual equality movement since. I end this book where it began: by evaluating the significant role art and mobility had in shaping queer cultural and political formation through the narratives of women and nonbinary individuals because they were historically driving actors in the queer history of New Mexico, and their stories present a fuller picture of the LGBTQ+ past.

A fresh wave of queer creatives descended in northern New Mexico in the late 1970s and early 1980s. Harmony Hammond, for example, a central figure in the feminist art movement in New York City who championed lesbian art and activism, accepted a one-semester visiting professorship at the University of New Mexico in 1978. Hammond, a white lesbian, met other lesbians through Women Studies and collaborated with the program to sponsor an exhibition called *Lesbian Visual Art*, a public validation of lesbians' role in shaping American art culture. In turn, the landscape of New Mexico inspired Hammond's art. Roadtripping in a Volkswagen bug, she explored every corner of the state, sparking her affection for the flat-topped mesas and hills, steep mountains, and vast deserts. Although she initially returned to New York, by 1984 Hammond had permanently moved to New Mexico with her teenage daughter and then-partner Judith Daner.[14]

In an interview, Hammond explained that she "didn't come here [New Mexico] for a community of artists"; rather, she "liked the wide-open space," "cultural mix" and "outlaw sensibility," elements she linked to an earlier history of queer women. "There's something about this big space that gives everybody room to be who they think they are. Historically that's been true for women. If they didn't fit into the social structures on the East Coast, and they didn't have money to go to Europe, they went west. . . . Many were bisexual or lesbian," Hammond articulated.[15]

Hammond settled in Galisteo, a tiny outpost near Santa Fe where queer painter Agnes Martin resided until 1992. Hammond, while living and working there, researched and wrote the influential book *Lesbian Art in America: A Contemporary History*.[16] Through her contacts "both within the art world and in lesbian communities outside the art world," she highlighted the artistry of thirty lesbian makers and contextualized lesbian art history post-1970. Hammond asked each artist "if there was a woman artist who had really influenced them" and discovered that "many artists named 'the lesbian artist Agnes Martin.'" Surprised by this response, Hammond understood that "At this point, there was no writing out there anywhere, no way, no how, about any of Agnes's lesbian affairs, involvements, or relationships. There's still not a lot out there, but back then, there was nothing. As someone who does know a little bit about Agnes's life, I knew that these women who were stating that 'the lesbian artist Agnes Martin' influenced them didn't know anything specific about her personal or sexual life other than the absence of the usual heterosexual narrative." Martin had long coded her gender and sexual variance in her art shows. When Martin resettled in New Mexico, they reached a new understanding of themself as asexual and nonbinary.[17] Martin became a pioneer of a particular selfhood and art—resistance to heteronormative and binary gender labels—that inspired a new generation of queer artists. Martin's life and work further solidified New Mexico's reputation as a place of sexual and gender transgression and creative potential even though these aspects of their life went unrecorded.

Hammond worked with more than three hundred artists to write the history of lesbian art post-Stonewall. *Lesbian Art in America* has a bicoastal framing, since visibility for lesbian artists emerged first in New York and California. A group of feminists in New York City established the Feminist Art Institute and the magazine *Heresies: A Feminist Publication on Art and Politics* (1977–93), which Hammond helped to develop. On the West Coast, the Woman's Building in Los Angeles allocated a space for lesbian art, as did the journal *Chrysalis: A Magazine of Women's Culture* (1977–80). But the book's next strongest geographic representation is New Mexico. Out lesbians Maxine Fine, Joan Watts, Lor Roybal, Bernadette Vigil, and Ada Medina, to name a few, all lived and worked in northern New Mexico. Watts's work specifically links lesbianism to the New Mexican landscape, influenced by O'Keeffe and Martin. Watts, who moved to the state in 1986, focused her art on recreating sexual slots, "sensuous, rounded contours found in the northern New Mexico landscape." Watts's work connotes a relationship between lesbianism and southwestern nature and light.[18]

As Hammond highlights, queer cultural producers by the 1980s redefined their content to be less abstract and more political and to engage directly with sexual themes. An important element of this shift was the emergence of working-class artists and artists of color. Hammond discusses the work of photographer Hulleah J. Tsinhnahjinnie, who was raised on and around the Navajo Nation in an artistic family.[19] Her father, Diné artist Andrew Van Tsinhnahjinnie, deeply influenced her decision to study art. First interested in painting, she attended the Institute of American Indian Arts in Santa Fe. By 1978 she turned to photography and earned a bachelor of fine art at the California College of Arts and Crafts in Oakland. Tsinhnahjinnie identifies as "two spirited" because "my community would have a hard time dealing with the label [*lesbian*]. . . . I also believe that lesbian would be a white descriptor for who I am."[20] She raises questions about multiple identities, in particular indigeneity in connection to gender, sexual identity, and other forms of self-identification.

Tsinhnahjinnie, who migrated to the San Francisco Bay Area from New Mexico, vocalized her politics of visibility through both lesbian-centered anthologies and *Living the Spirit*, in which she published four photographs and four graphics. Since its publication, the anthology has fostered the cultural renewal of two-spirit roles and facilitated political activism among two-spirit and LGBTQ+ Native people. Tsinhnahjinnie describes her photography as activism: "we carry the dreams of our ancestors, dreams of a day when there will be historical truth, cultural survival, religious freedom, environmental respect and first Nation sovereignty. Among those who have taken the responsibility to translate these dreams, to be message carriers, are the first Nation artists."[21] Particularly for historically underrepresented communities who were often shut out of formalized political structures, creative expression served as an arena for activism.

Chicanas also found room for conveying their lesbianism through creative and critical writings. Native Nuevomexicana Juanita Sanchez, who first published Chicana lesbian content in the do-it-yourself feminist publication *Sister Lode* in 1978, continued to develop a Chicana lesbian political discourse through her writing. Sanchez authored two poems for an anthology devoted exclusively to Chicana lesbianism, edited and compiled by Carla Trujillo. *Chicana Lesbians: The Girls Our Mothers Warned Us About*, published by Third Woman Press in 1991, collects works of fiction, poetry, and essays that center on questioning gender boundaries and sexual identity in a Chicano/a cultural context.

Influenced by her upbringing in Las Vegas, New Mexico, and later working-class communities in Northern California, which she described as "the uncertainties of growing up queer in a patriarchal culture," Trujillo recalls spending "an earlier part of my life working to bring to light the voices of the invisible"—Chicana lesbians. Trujillo also felt personally hindered and "overwhelmed by the poundage of culture, class, and religious doctrine" during her coming of age. To cope, she read the works of Cherríe Moraga, Gloria Anzaldúa, and Juanita Ramos.[22] When she published *Chicana Lesbians*, Trujillo joined a network of lesbians of color whose cultural creativity functioned as a form of resistance. *Chicana Lesbians*, now in its third printing, won the Lambda Book Award for Best Lesbian Anthology in 1992 and continues to influence Latina lesbian creative and critical works.[23]

Such works inspired me to write this book. Researching and writing about the lives of queer New Mexicans pushed me beyond the conventionally founded modes of historical inquiry into the realms of art and literature, which I supplemented with personal narratives, government documents, and print media sources. Anthologies guided me to an imagining of radical, decolonial queer critiques that demand centering nonwhite, nonmale frameworks and experiences. Stories and voices embedded in anthologies and oral histories have been my most critical teachers.

Much of this history is scattered in various archives, personal collections, and people's memories. I often felt like I was putting together a puzzle without knowing what the final image would look like. I have striven to offer a composite portrait of queer lives in twentieth-century New Mexico, but I am missing some pieces. I hope my research inspires others to ask more questions, to offer different perspectives, and to ponder things I may have missed. New Mexico has a long and rich history of queer cultural expression and sexual politics that flourished long before a formalized gay liberation movement coalesced in 1969. New Mexico's queer past brims with untold stories.

NOTES

INTRODUCTION

1. Walter Cooper, *Unbuttoned: Gay Life in the Santa Fe Arts Scene* (North Charleston, SC: self-published), 83.

2. Sims's former home and studio, on the corner of Canyon Road and Camino Escondido, is now Gallery 901. Notable exhibitions of her works include *Agnes Sims Remembered Magic*, New Mexico Museum of Fine Art, August 15–November 1, 1987; *American Indian Rock Drawings*, Brooklyn Museum, October 9, 1952–January 4, 1953; *Man and Magic, Work of Agnes Sims*, McNay Art Institute, 1972; and *Painting Today and Yesterday in the United States*, Santa Barbara Museum of Art, June 5–September 1, 1941.

3. Elizabeth I. Hanson, *Paula Gunn Allen* (Boise: Boise State University Press, 1990), 6; Jocelyn Y. Stewart, "Champion of Native American Literature," *Los Angeles Times*, June 7, 2008, http://articles.latimes.com/2008/jun/07/local/me-allen7.

4. Franchot Ballinger, Brian Swann, and Paul Gunn Allen, "A MELUS Interview: Paula Gunn Allen," *MELUS* 10, no. 2 (1983): 6.

5. Paula Gunn Allen, interview, July 16, 1985, transcript, box 1, folder 1, Will Roscoe Papers and Gay American Indians Records, 1987-04, Gay, Lesbian, Bisexual, Transgender Historical Society, San Francisco (hereafter Roscoe Papers); Allen quoted in Will Roscoe, "Gay American Indians: Creating an Identity from Past Traditions," *The Advocate*, October 29, 1985, p. 46, box 1, folder 28, Roscoe Papers.

6. The term *two-spirit* is an Indigenous created and defined term. See, for example, Qwo-Li Driskill, ed., *Queer Indigenous Studies: Critical Interventions in Theory, Politics, and Literature* (Tucson: University of Arizona Press, 2011); Brian Joseph Gilley, *Becoming Two-Spirit: Gay Identity and Social Acceptance in Indian Country* (Lincoln: University of Nebraska Press, 2006); Sue-Ellen Jacobs, Wesley Thomas, and Sabine Lang, eds., *Two-Spirit People: Native American Gender Identity, Sexuality, and Spirituality* (Chicago: University of Illinois Press, 1997); and Mark Rifkin, *When Did Indians Become Straight? Kinship, the History of Sexuality, and Native Sovereignty* (New York: Oxford University Press, 2011).

7. Paula Gunn Allen, "Beloved Women: Lesbians in American Indian Cultures,"

Conditions 3, no. 1 (1981): 65–87; Tara Prince-Hughes, "Contemporary Two-Spirit Identity in the Fiction of Paula Gunn Allen and Beth Brant," *Studies in American Indian Literatures* 10, no. 4 (1998): 9–32; Lisa Tatonetti, "Indigenous Fantasies and Sovereign Erotics: Outland Cherokees Write Two-Spirits Nations" in Driskill, *Queer Indigenous Studies*, 157; and "The Emergence and Importance of Queer American Indian Literatures; or, 'Help and Stories' in Thirty Years of SAIL," *Studies in American Indian Literatures* 19, no. 4 (2007): 143–70.

8. Nadine Armijo, film interview 1991.1.34.23, VHS tape, box 58, Peter Adair Papers (GLC 70), LGBTQIA Center, San Francisco Public Library (hereafter Adair Papers).

9. Nadine Armijo and Rosa Montoya, film interview transcript, box 43, folder 6, Adair Papers.

10. Armijo, film interview.

11. *Word Is Out: Stories of Some of Our Lives*, directed by Peter Adair and Lucy Massie Phenix (1977; New York: Oscilloscope Laboratories, 2010), DVD.

12. *Word Is Out* is a "gay and lesbian" film. The makers and participants identified as either "lesbian" or "gay." However, there is nuance and flexibility within the binary identifications that allow for explorations of bisexual, transgender, and genderqueer experiences of the film's subjects.

13. To the best of my knowledge, the first documentary film on homosexuality is *The Rejected*, a made-for-television broadcast produced for KQED in San Francisco, which aired on September 11, 1961. See Andrew Lester, "The Rejected: Homophile Activists in the Spotlight," *Notches* (blog), January 27, 2016, http://notchesblog.com /2016/01/07/the-rejected-homophile-activists-in-the-spotlight/.

14. *Word Is Out.*

15. Geoffrey W. Bateman, "Queer Wests: An Introduction," *Western American Literature* 51, no. 2 (2016): 132. For a critique of gender in LGBT history, see Margot Canaday, "LGBT History," *Frontiers: A Journal of Women Studies* 35, no. 1 (2014): 11–19.

16. Critical mobilities scholars have argued that mobility is increasingly seen as a right. See, for example, Mimi Sheller, "Mobility," *Sociopedia.isa* (2011): 6, DOI: 10.1177/205684601163.

17. For a historiographical discussion of queer oral history, see Nan Alamilla Boyd and Horacio N. Roque Ramirez, introduction, *Bodies of Evidence: The Practice of Queer Oral History* (New York: Oxford University Press, 2012), 2–7.

18. LGBT Educational Archives Project, Facebook, www.facebook.com/LGBTArchives/. See the oral histories series in the Bennett Hammer LGBT Collection, MSS 975, Center for Southwest Research, Zimmerman Library, University of New Mexico, Albuquerque (hereafter Hammer Collection). Roughly half of the interview participants agreed to donate their oral histories to the archive.

19. For a further discussion of my methodology, see Jordan Biro Walters, "Uncov-

ering Queer Voices in New Mexico through the Process of History" (paper presentation, American Historical Association Annual Meeting, New York City, January 2–5, 2015), https://www.academia.edu/17277206/Uncovering_Queer_Voices_in_New _Mexico_Through_the_Process_of_Oral_History.

20. In particular, I draw on interviews conducted by Lester Strong and Peter Adair, gay men who grew up in New Mexico and returned in the 1970s to interview New Mexican gay men and lesbians. Peter Adair conducted oral histories for the Mariposa Film Group's *Word Is Out*. Strong, who worked as a part-time freelancer in New York City, visited his hometown with his gay partner in the summer of 1979. He completed five interviews to write an article on the city's gay and lesbian population and establishments and returned to Albuquerque several times to conduct further interviews with Latino gay men. See Adair Papers; Lester Strong, "Hometown Revisited: Gay Liberation Reaches the Provinces," *Gay Community News*, September 12, 1981; and Lester Q. Strong Papers, Manuscripts and Archives Division, New York Public Library (hereafter Strong Papers). I also draw on interviews in the Women's Studies Oral History Collection at the University of New Mexico and Voices of the Manhattan Project, a joint project by the Atomic Heritage Foundation and the Los Alamos Historical Society.

21. See Kath Weston, "Get Thee to a Big City: Sexual Imaginary and the Great Gay Migration," *GLQ* 2, no. 3 (1995): 253–77.

22. See, for example, Colin R. Johnson, *Just Queer Folks: Gender and Sexuality in Rural America* (Philadelphia: Temple University Press, 2013).

23. "[While] there was frank and affirmative [queer] writing from the century's start . . . it was usually published abroad or by marginal presses or remained private and unpublished" (Claude J. Summers, ed., *The Gay and Lesbian Literary Heritage: A Reader's Companion to the Writers and Their Works, from Antiquity to the Present* [New York: H. Holt, 1995], 30).

24. Jonathan D. Katz, *Hide/Seek: Difference and Desire in American Portraiture* (Washington, DC: Smithsonian, 2010), 16, 14.

25. Canaday, "LGBT History," 12. Queer of color methodologies, worldmaking, and resistance are discussed in José Esteban Muñoz, *Disidentifications: Queers of Color and the Performance of Politics* (Minneapolis: University of Minnesota Press); Nayan Shah, "Queer of Color Estrangement and Belonging," in *The Routledge History of Queer America*, ed. Don Romesburg (New York: Routledge, 2018), 262–75.

26. Elyssa Ford, *Rodeo as Refuge, Rodeo as Rebellion: Gender, Race, and Identity in the American Rodeo* (Lawrence: University Press of Kansas, 2020), ch. 5; Dennis McBride, *Out of the Neon Closet: Queer Community in the Silver State* (North Charleston, SC: self-published, 2017), ix; María Polletta, "No LGBT History in Arizona? Think Again," azcentral, February 9, 2017, https://www.azcentral.com/story/news/local /phoenix/2017/02/09/no-lgbt-history-arizona-think-again/97239296/; Rebecca

Scofield, *Outriders: Rodeo at the Fringes of the American West* (Seattle: University of Washington Press, 2019), ch. 4.

27. In understanding cultural activism, I have been influenced by Douglas Crimp, *AIDS: Cultural Analysis / Cultural* Activism (Cambridge, MA: MIT Press, 1988); and Begüm Özden Firat and Aylin Kuryel, *Cultural Activism: Practices, Dilemmas, and Possibilities* (New York: Rodopi, 2011).

28. Maurice Kenny, "Preface: Paula Gunn Allen As I Knew Her," in *Weaving the Legacy: Remembering Paula Gunn Allen*, ed. Stephanie A. Sellers and Menoukha R. Case (Albuquerque: West End Press, 2017), 5; Roscoe, "Gay American Indians," 46, box 1, folder 28, Roscoe Papers.

29. For more on the importance of internal sexual migrations in postwar America, see Allan Bérubé, "Behind the Spector of San Francisco," in *My Desire for History: Essays in Gay, Community and Labor History*, ed. John D'Emilio and Estelle B. Freedman (Chapel Hill: University of North Carolina Press, 2011), 54–61; Peter Boag, "Gay Male Rural-Urban Migration in the American West," in *City Dreams, Country Schemes: Community and Identity in the American West*, ed. Kathleen A. Brosnan and Amy L. Scott (Reno: University of Nevada Press, 2010); and John Howard, "Place and Movement in Gay American History: A Case from the Post-World War II South," in *Creating a Place for Ourselves*, ed. Brett Beemyn (New York: Routledge, 1997), 211–25.

30. An example is *Gay New York*, one of the most influential books in the field of LGBT history. George Chauncey devotes only a few pages to sexual migrations. Rather than focus on the process of migration, Chauncey uncovers the development of a gay male world in New York *after* migrants had already moved in. George Chauncey, *Gay New York: Gender, Urban Culture, and the Makings of the Gay Male World, 1890–1940* (New York: Basic, 1994), 135–36, 245–46, 271–73.

31. For an excellent feminist and postcolonial study on migration, see Sara Ahmed, Claudia Castada, Anne-Marie Fortier, and Mimi Sheller, eds., *Uprootings/ Regroundings: Questions of Home and Migration* (Oxford: Berg, 2003).

32. Gayle S. Rubin defines *sexual migration* in "Thinking Sex: Notes for a Radical Theory of the Politics of Sexuality," in *Pleasure and Danger: Exploring Female Sexuality*, ed. Carol S. Vance (Boston: Routledge, 1984), 286. Rubin's article served as a catalyst for interdisciplinary scholarship on queer mobility, of which I have been most influenced by Andrew Gorman-Murray, "Rethinking Queer Migration through the Body," *Social & Cultural Geography* 8, no. 1 (February 2007): 105–21, https://doi.org /10.1080/14649360701251858; Hiram Perez, "You Can Have My Brown Body and Eat It, Too!," *Social Text* 23, no. 3–4 (Fall/Winter 2005): 171–91, doi:10.1215/01642472-23- 3-4–84-85-171; Jasbir K. Puar, "Circuits of Queer Mobility: Tourism, Travel, and Globalization," *GLQ* 8, no. 1 (2002): 101–37; and Nathan Titman, "The Drift of Desire:

Performing Gay Masculinities through Leisure, Mobility, and Non-Urban Space, 1910–1945" (PhD diss., University of Iowa, 2014), 9–11, https://iro.uiowa.edu/esploro /outputs/doctoral/The-drift-of-desire-performing-gay/9983777397902771

33. Some examples include Miriam Frank, *Out in the Union: A Labor History of Queer America* (Philadelphia: Temple University Press, 2014); E. Patrick Johnson, *Sweet Tea: Black Gay Men of the South* (Chapel Hill: University of North Carolina Press, 2011); and Daniel Winunwe Rivers, *Radical Relations: Lesbian Mothers, Gay Fathers, and Their Children in the United States since World War II* (Chapel Hill: University of North Carolina Press, 2013).

34. Chauncey, *Gay New York*, 132; Pippa Holloway and Elizabeth Catte, "Rural," in Romesburg, *Routledge History of Queer America*, 184.

35. An exception is Nan Alamilla Boyd's excellent cultural study *Wide-Open Town: A History of Queer San Francisco to 1965* (Berkeley: University of California Press, 2003), which brings together a diverse and transient milieu of San Francisco's queer and transgender communities to illustrate the flourishing of sexual cultures before World War II. Boyd traces how and why San Francisco is a queer city. The title of my book is a play on Boyd's and extends insights of the wide-open town to the desert landscape.

36. Judith Halberstam, *In a Queer Time and Place: Transgender Bodies, Subcultural Lives* (New York: New York University Press, 2005), 36–37; Scott Herring, *Another Country: Queer Anti-Urbanism* (New York: New York University Press, 2010), 15–17.

37. Christopher Hommerding, "As Gay as Any Gypsy Caravan: Grant Wood and the Queer Pastoral at the Stone City Art Colony," *Annals of Iowa* 74, no. 4 (2015): 378–412, https://doi.org/10.17077/0003-4827.12233; Daniel Hurewitz, *Bohemian Los Angeles and the Making of Modern Politics* (Berkeley: University of California Press, 2008); Karen Christel Krahulik, *Provincetown: From Pilgrim Landing to Gay Resort* (New York University Press, 2007); Esther Newton, *Cherry Grove, Fire Island: Sixty Years in America's First Gay and Lesbian Town* (Boston: Beacon, 1993).

38. Joseph Traugott, *New Mexico Art through Time: Prehistory to the Present* (Santa Fe: Museum of New Mexico Press, 2012), 13.

39. Natalie Hegert, "An Art 'City Different': What Santa Fe Has to Offer," *HuffPost*, April 28, 2017, https://www.huffpost.com/entry/an-art-city-different-what-santa -fe-has-to-offer_b_59036a03e4b084f59b49f879.

40. Jonathan Batkin, *Pottery of the Pueblos of New Mexico, 1700–1940* (Colorado Springs: Taylor Museum of the Colorado Sprints Fine Arts Center, 1987); Dwight P. Lanmon, "Pueblo Man-Woman Potters and Pottery Made by the Laguna Man-Woman, Arroh-a-och," *American Indian Art Magazine*, Winter 2005, 72–85; Will Roscoe, "We'wha and Klah: The American Indian Berdache as Artist and Priest," *American Indian Quarterly* 12, no. 2 (1988): 127–50, https://doi.org/10.2307/1184319; and Will

Roscoe, "Discovering Two-Spirit Artistry in the History of Pueblo Pottery Revival," February 2017, http://www.willsworld.org/PuebloTwoSpiritPottery-WEB.pdf.

41. Juanita Ramos, ed., *Compañeras: Latina Lesbians, An Anthology* (New York: Routledge, 1987) is one of the earliest anthologies of Latina lesbian writers. Tara Burk, "LGBTQ Art and Artists," in *LGBTQ America: A Theme Study of Lesbian, Gay Bisexual, Transgender and Queer History*, ed. Megan E. Springate (Washington, DC: National Park Foundation, 2016), www.nps.gov/subjects/tellingallamericansstories/lgbtqthemestudy.htm.

42. I defined queer cultural production by consulting Gavin Butt, *Between You and Me: Queer Disclosures in the New York Art World, 1948–1963* (Durham, NC: Duke University Press, 2005); Judith Halberstam, *The Queer Art of Failure* (Durham, NC: Duke University Press, 2011); and Catherine Lord and Richard Meyer, *Art and Queer Culture* (London: Phaidon, 2013). A queer subject can be straight or gay if they practice and embrace identities that deviate from the ideals of the heterosexual family and understand "sexuality as constitutive of the self." See Christina B. Hanhardt, "Queer History," *American Historian*, May 2019, https://www.oah.org/tah/issues/2019/may/queer-history/.

43. On Sims's lesbianism, see Cooper, *Unbuttoned*, 83–90; Michael Ettema, "New Beginnings on Canyon Road," *Canyon Road Arts* 2 (2005–2006): 68–73, http://www.canyonroadarts.com/links/New%20Beginnings%20on%20Canyon%20Road.html; Lois P. Rudnick, ed., *Cady Wells and Southwestern Modernism* (Santa Fe: Museum of New Mexico Press, 2009), 38; and Joan Schenkar, *The Talented Miss Highsmith: The Secret Life and Serious Art of Patricia Highsmith* (New York: Macmillan, 2010), 143.

44. Truman Capote wrote, "Did you know Santa Fe is the dyke capital of the United States?" in *Answered Prayers: The Unfinished Novel* (New York: Vintage, 1994), 149–50.

45. Butt, *Between You and Me*, 65, 11.

46. For general studies on the entanglement of art and homosexuality, see Lord and Meyer, *Art and Queer Culture*; and Christopher Reed, *Art and Homosexuality: A History of Ideas* (New York: Oxford University Press, 2011).

47. Mary Bernstein, "Nothing Ventured, Nothing Gained? Conceptualizing Social Movement 'Success' in the Lesbian and Gay Movement," *Sociological Perspectives* 46, no. 3 (September 1, 2003): 353–79, https://doi.org/10.1525/sop.2003.46.3.353; James Button, Barbara A. Rienzo, and Kenneth D. Wald, "The Politics of Gay Rights at the Local and State Level," in *Politics of Gays Rights*, ed. Craig A. Rimmerman, Kenneth D. Wald, and Clyde Wilcox (Chicago: University of Chicago Press, 2000), 269–89. Marc Stein identifies five major federal policies that have advanced LGBT equality and contends that that there is more to achieve. Marc Stein, "Law and Politics: 'Crooked and Perverse' Narratives of LGBT Progress," in Romesburg, *Routledge History of Queer America*, 317–18, 320–26.

48. Following Flannery Burke, I define the twentieth-century American Southwest as the states of Arizona and New Mexico. Flannery Burke, *A Land Apart: The Southwest and the Nation in the Twentieth Century* (Tucson: University of Arizona Press, 2017), 7. For queer scholarship on New Mexico, see chapter 1, n4. As an example of LGBT history in Arizona, see Carolyn Evans, "Remembering the 307: A Call for LGBTQ Historic Preservation in Arizona," *Journal of Arizona History* 62, no. 2 (2021): 229–47.

49. On themes of mobility and rootedness, I have been influenced by Burke, *A Land Apart*; James F. Brooks, "The Southwest," in *The Oxford Handbook of American Indian History*, ed. Frederick E. Hoxie (New York: Oxford University Press, 2016); and Sarah Deutsch, *No Separate Refuge: Culture, Class, and Gender on an Anglo-Hispanic Frontier in the American Southwest, 1880–1940* (New York: Oxford University Press, 1989).

50. For a discussion of sexual regulation at the US-Mexico border, see Celeste R. Menchaca, "Staging Crossings: Policing Intimacy and Performing Respectability at the U.S.-Mexico Border, 1907–1917," *Pacific Historical Review* 89, no. 1 (February 1, 2020): 16–43, https://doi.org/10.1525/phr.2020.89.1.16.

51. See Robin Henry, "Queering the American Frontier: Finding Queerness and Sexual Difference in Late Nineteenth-Century and Early Twentieth-Century Colorado," in *Queering the Countryside: New Frontiers in Rural Queer Studies*, ed. Mary L. Gray, Colin R. Johnson, and Brian J. Gilley, 290–308 (New York University Press, 2016).

52. Susan Lee Johnson, *Roaring Camp: The Social World of the California Gold Rush* (New York: W. W. Norton, 2000); Peter C. Boag, *Re-Dressing America's Frontier Past* (Berkeley: University of California Press, 2011).

53. Judith Boyce DeMark, ed., *Essays in Twentieth-Century New Mexico History* (Albuquerque: University of New Mexico Press, 1994), 3; "Southwest Region—Tribes Served," Bureau of Indian Affairs, accessed January 31, 2019, https://www.bia.gov/regional-offices/southwest/tribes-served.

54. Burke, *A Land Apart*, 67, 196; DeMark, *Essays in Twentieth-Century New Mexico History*, 6.

55. For example, the San Juan Pueblo council formally changed its name in December 2005 to Ohkay Owingeh, the tribe's original name in Tewa. Martin Salazar, "San Juan Pueblo Tries to Change Name," *Albuquerque Journal*, September 18, 2005.

56. See Phillip B. Gonzales, "The Political Construction of Latino Nomenclatures," *Journal of the Southwest* 35, no. 2 (Summer 1993): 158–85. I am aware of the criticisms of the term *Latinx*, primarily that the gender-neutral noun is disrespectful to the Spanish language (and seldom used by Latinos). I have chosen to use *Latinx* in a current context to support evolving and fluid understandings of identities and *Latino* or *Latina* in an historical context and if a gendered term is appropriate. Marisa Peñaloza, "Latinx is a Term Many Still Can't Embrace," National Public Radio, October 1, 2020, https://

www.npr.org/2020/10/01/916441659/latinx-is-a-term-many-still-cant-embrace; A. K. Sandoval-Strausz, email message to author, January 9, 2022.

57. On the identifier Nuevomexicano, see Michael L. Trujillo, *Land of Disenchantment: Latino/o Identities and Transformations in Northern New Mexico* (Albuquerque: University of New Mexico Press, 2009), 12.

58. Not all members of tribal nations agree about an historical presence of two-spirits. I follow the lead of activists and scholars who have reconstructed archival evidence of two-spirits and developed its robust tradition that exists today. For a list of tribal nations with two-spirit roles, see Will Roscoe, ed., *Living the Spirit: A Gay American Indian Anthology* (New York: St. Martin's Press, 1988), 217–22. I added the Pueblo of Tesuque to this list after Tracy Brown, "'Abominable Sin' in Colonial New Mexico," in *Long before Stonewall: Histories of Same-Sex Sexuality in Early America*, ed. Thomas A Foster (New York University Press, 2007), 51. According to *Living the Spirit*, the Mescalero Apache Tribe has two-spirit roles, but I was unable to find enough research to include them here.

59. About the translation of *nádleehí*, a term with no singular definition, Martha Austin-Garrison (Diné/Navajo), a Diné College Navajo language professor, explained, "'Nádleeh' is a verb meaning 'it changes.' There are three different noun-making enclitics *-í* or *-ii* or *ígíí* that are used, but essentially they all mean 'the one who is'" (email to author, January 16, 2020). See also Epple, "Coming to Terms," 267–90; Harlan Pruden and Se-ah-dom Edmo, "Two-Spirit People: Sex, Gender and Sexuality in Historic and Contemporary Native America," http://www.ncai.org/policy-research-center/initiatives/Pruden-Edmo_TwoSpiritPeople.pdf; "PBS Documentary Explores Navajo Belief in Four Genders," *Indian Country Today*, November 5, 2013, https://newsmaven.io/indiancountrytoday/archive/pbs-documentary-explores-navajo-belief-in-four-genders-r3dVknNYZEenpPY95jd1ig/; Navajo Nation Human Rights Commission, "Status of Navajo Women"; Roscoe, *Changing Ones*; Wesley Thomas, "Navajo Cultural Constructions of Gender and Sexuality," in Jacobs et al., *Two-Spirit People*, 157–69; and Nibley and Martin, *Two Spirits*.

60. Navajo Nation Human Rights Commission, "The Status of Navajo Women and Gender Violence: Conversations with Diné Traditional Medicine People and a Dialogue with the People" (Saint Michaels, AZ, 2016), 53.

61. Hurewitz, *Bohemian Los Angeles*, 3, 4–8.

ONE "Going Santa Fe"

1. Ruthling quoted in Rudnick, *Cady Wells and Southwestern Modernism*, 39–40.

2. Since the 1990s, there have been a number of biographies on queer bohemians, mostly white gay men, within the Taos and Santa Fe art colonies. See Flannery Burke, "Spud Johnson and a Gay Man's Place in the Taos Creative Arts Community," *Pacific*

Historical Review 79, no. 1 (February 1, 2010): 86–113; Heather Hole, *Marsden Hartley and the West: The Search for an American Modernism* (Yale University Press, 2007); James Kraft, *Who Is Witter Bynner? A Biography* (Albuquerque: University of New Mexico Press, 1995); and Sharyn Rohlfsen Udall, *Spud Johnson and Laughing Horse* (Albuquerque: University of New Mexico Press, 1994). A few include discussions of queer women, see Arrell Morgan Gibson, *The Santa Fe and Taos Colonies: Age of the Muses, 1900–1942* (Norman: University of Oklahoma Press, 1983); and Rudnick, *Cady Wells and Southwestern Modernism*; Mabel Dodge Luhan and Lois Palken Rudnick, *The Suppressed Memoirs of Mabel Dodge Luhan: Sex, Syphilis, and Psychoanalysis in the Making of Modern American Culture* (Albuquerque: University of New Mexico Press, 2012); *Utopian Vistas: The Mabel Dodge Luhan House and the American Counterculture* (Albuquerque: University of New Mexico Press, 1998).

3. Burke discusses gay cruising in both Taos and Santa Fe in "Spud Johnson and a Gay Man's Place," 98–99.

4. Margaret D. Jacobs was one of the first scholars to discuss Anglo-American women and Pueblo Indians attitudes toward sexuality within the context of the dance controversy in *Engendered Encounters: Feminism and Pueblo Cultures, 1879–1934* (Lincoln: University of Nebraska Press, 1999), 106–48.

5. Janet Lecompte, "The Independent Women of Hispanic New Mexico, 1821–1846," *Western Historical Quarterly* 12, no. 1 (1981): 17–35; Pablo Mitchell, *Coyote Nation: Sexuality, Race, and Conquest in Modernizing New Mexico, 1880–1920* (Chicago: University Of Chicago Press, 2005); Pablo Mitchell, *West of Sex: Making Mexican America, 1900–1930* (Chicago: University of Chicago Press, 2012); Emma Pérez, "Queering the Borderlands: The Challenges of Excavating the Invisible and Unheard," *Frontiers: A Journal of Women Studies* 24, nos. 2–3 (2003): 122–31.

6. Because I make the argument that Klah could, to some extent, embrace a nádleehí status, I refer to Klah with they/them pronouns.

7. For the spelling and translation of hataałii, I relied on Farina King, "Diné Doctor: A Latter-day Saint Story of Healing," *Dialogue: A Journal of Mormon Thought* 54, no. 2 (2021): 81–86.

8. Jennifer Nez Denetdale, "Naal Tsoos Saní: The Navajo Treaty of 1868, Nation Building and Self-Determination," in *Nation to Nation: Treaties between the United States and American Indian Nations*, ed. Suzan Shown Harjo (Washington, DC: Smithsonian, 2014), 121–22; Lloyd L. Lee, ed., *Navajo Sovereignty: Understandings and Visions of the Diné People* (Tucson: University of Arizona Press, 2017), 3; and Peter Iverson, *Diné: A History of the Navajos* (Albuquerque: University of New Mexico Press, 2002), 55.

9. The Navajo people were the only tribal nation to escape the Indian Removal Act through a treaty. See Denetdale, "Naal Tsoos Saní," 116–32.

10. Franc Johnson Newcomb, *Hosteen Klah: Navaho Medicine Man and Sand Painter* (Norman: University of Oklahoma Press, 1964), 60.

11. Ahson and Hoksay noticed that their child used their left hand more readily than the right and gave them the name Klah ("left-handed"). *Hastíín* or *hosteen* is a term of respect similar to *mister*. In the literature Klah's name has been spelled Hastíín Klah, Hastiin Klah, and Hosteen Klah.

12. For the location of Klah's family, see Harriet Koenig, *Acculturation in the Navajo Eden: New Mexico, 1550–1750* (self-published, 2005), 263.

13. Michelle Kahn-John and Mary Koithan, "Living in Health, Harmony, and Beauty: The Diné (Navajo) Hózhó Wellness Philosophy," *Global Advances in Health and Medicine* 4, no. 3 (May 2015): 24, https://doi.org/10.7453/gahmj.2015.044; Gill Witherspoon, "The Central Concepts of the Navajo World View," *Linguistics* 119 (1974): 41–59. In understanding Navajo worldviews, I have been most influenced by Jennifer Nez Denetdale, *Reclaiming Diné History: The Legacies of Navajo Chief Manuelito and Juanita* (Tucson: University of Arizona Press, 2007).

14. I use the term *nation* because the treaty "represents the birth of the modern Navajo Nation." Although the United States then acknowledged the Navajo people as sovereign, the Navajo people began using the term "Navajo Nation" between 1950 and 1969. They passed a resolution to make their national status official in 1969, although not everyone agreed on the turn toward a Western-style government. Before the development of a Navajo nationalist ideology, the Diné political organization was composed of local bands that typically consisted of forty families. Denetdale, "Naal Tsoos Saní," 116; Jennifer Nez Denetdale, foreword to Lee, *Navajo Sovereignty*, vii–ix; Iverson, *Diné*, 136.

15. Newcomb, *Hosteen Klah*, xv, 60. Frances "Franc" Johnson Newcomb's biography *Hosteen Klah* is the primary source on Klah's life. Newcomb, a white woman, became a member of the community around the Navajo Nation, became conversant in Diné Bizaad, and received her Navajo neighbors' permission to conduct oral histories with the Klah family. Her narrative covers two centuries of Diné history through the lens of one family's experiences and its entwinement with Anglos. While I was initially skeptical about using Newcomb's work, it stands out as culturally sensitive compared to the majority of ethnographic Indigenous biographies. However, I am aware of her presence in the text and at times question and critique Newcomb's interpretations. Newcomb's background is outlined in William H. Lyon, "Gladys Reichard at the Frontiers of Navajo Culture," *American Indian Quarterly* 13, no. 2 (1989): 139–43, https://doi.org/10.2307/1184055; and Susan Berry Brill de Ramírez, *Women Ethnographers and Native Women Storytellers: Relational Science, Ethnographic Collaboration, and Tribal Community* (Lanham, MD: Lexington, 2015), 25–28.

16. Newcomb, *Hosteen Klah*, 53. I found Farina King's (Diné/Navajo) #DinéDoctorSyllabus particularly helpful with understanding Diné experiences with healing. See Farina King, *Diné Doctor History Syllabus*, accessed June 22, 2022, https://farina king.com/dinedoctorhistorysyllabus/.

17. Peggy V. Beck, Anna Lee Walters, and Nia Francisco, *The Sacred: Ways of Knowledge, Sources of Life* (Tsaile, AZ: Navajo Community College Press, 1977), 28; James C. Faris, *The Nightway: A History and a History of Documentation of a Navajo Ceremonial* (Albuquerque: University of New Mexico Press, 1990), 7, 86.

18. Although the scholarship on Navajo weaving has primarily been produced by non-Navajos, I relied on Navajo-authored texts and oral histories and Navajo perspectives in published accounts or exhibitions. For scholarship on Navajo men as weavers, see, for example, Museum of Indian Arts and Culture, *Weaving in the Margins: Navajo Men as Weavers* (Albuquerque: Museum of New Mexico, 1999). The hataałii occupation has been dominated by men. During Klah's lifetime, Newcomb noted only one medicine woman: "Here at last I was seeing a real Navajo medicine woman" (Franc Newcomb, "Medicine Woman," Newcomb Original Notes, n.d., Frances Johnson Newcomb Collection, Wheelwright Research Library, Wheelwright Museum of the American Indian, Santa Fe). See also Ruth Roessel, "Navajo Medicinewomen," in *Women in Navajo Society* (Rough Rock, AZ: Navajo Resource Center, 1981), ch. 7; Maureen Trudelle Schwarz, *Blood and Voice: Navajo Women Ceremonial Practitioners* (Tucson: University of Arizona Press, 2003).

19. In 2016 the Navajo Nation Human Rights Commission recognized four genders in traditional Navajo society. Navajo Nation Human Rights Commission, "Status of Navajo Women," 14. See also Lydia Nibley and Russell Martin, *Two Spirits*, video (Independent Lens, 2010).

20. In terms of sexual partners, a nádleehí could have sexual relationships with women or men or remain celibate. Carolyn Epple, "Coming to Terms with Navajo 'Nádleehí': A Critique of 'Berdache,' 'Gay,' 'Alternate Gender,' and 'Two-Spirit,'" *American Ethnologist* 25, no. 2 (May 1998): 279.

21. I feel Reichard's definition of *nádleehí* is inaccurate, since "one-who-has-been-changed" connotes a fixed category rather than a fluid, situational one. Gladys A. Reichard, "Individualism and Mythological Style," *Journal of American Folklore* 57 (1944): 19; Louise Lamphere, "Gladys Reichard among the Navajo," *Frontiers: A Journal of Women Studies* 12, no. 3 (1992): 79–115, https://doi.org/10.2307/3346644.

22. Some white anthropologists and philanthropists further speculated that Klah was intersex. Newcomb wrote that while Klah was recuperating from a horse-riding accident, Klah's family discovered "he was a hermaphrodite [intersex]" (Newcomb, *Hosteen Klah*, 97). Anthropologist Gladys Reichard also identified Klah as intersex but attributed it to infant emasculation as a result of the family's being attacked by Utes on the return home from Bosque Redondo (Reichard, "Individualism and Mythological Style," 23). I conclude that there is not enough evidence to understand Klah as intersex, but ample evidence shows Klah was recognized as nádleehí.

23. Examples of Klah's sandpainting textiles are preserved at the Arizona State Museum, Tucson; the Art Institute of Chicago; Heard Museum, Phoenix; Kennedy

Museum of Art, Ohio University, Athens; and the Wheelwright Museum of the American Indian, Santa Fe, although not all display their works because some Navajo disapprove of sharing religious ceremonial knowledge. I visited the Kennedy Museum of Art on May 20, 2021, to view a sandpainting textile in storage; the textile was unfinished at the time of Klah's death but completed by their nieces: Hosteen Klah, Gladys Manuelito, and Irene Manuelito, *The Skies from the Shootingway Chant*, 1935–37, synthetic and undyed wool.

24. Klara Kelley and Harris Francis, *A Diné History of Navajoland* (University of Arizona Press, 2019), 24. The reason why Klah evaded the compulsory education clause in the Navajo Treaty of 1868 remain unclear. Navajos strongly resisted that clause, and early attempts to set up day schools failed. The first permanent boarding school was established on the Navajo reservation in 1883, when Klah was sixteen.

25. Unnamed Navajo elder quoted in Willard W. Hill, "The Status of the Hermaphrodite and Transvestite in Navaho Culture," *American Anthropology* 37 (1935): 274.

26. Newcomb, *Hosteen Klah*, xvi, 89, 145, 201, 97; Ramírez, *Women Ethnographers*, 25–28; Reichard, "Individualism and Mythological Style," 23.

27. Will Roscoe, "Was We'wha a Homosexual? Native American Survivance and the Two-Spirit Tradition," *GLQ* 2, no. 3 (June 1995): 200, https://doi.org/10.1215/10642684-2-3-193.

28. Epple, "Coming to Terms," 270; Roscoe, *Changing Ones*, 41–42.

29. Although an imperfect term, I use *cross-dress* following cross-dressing histories such as Clare Sears, *Arresting Dress: Cross-Dressing, Law, and Fascination in Nineteenth-Century San Francisco* (Durham, NC: Duke University Press, 2015).

30. Scholars have been unable to identify the female Navajo weaver or even agree on whether two weavers demonstrated their craft or just one. See Hubert Howe Bancroft, *The Book of the Fair: An Historical and Descriptive Presentation of the World's Science, Art, and Industry, as Viewed through the Columbian Exposition at Chicago in 1893: Designed to Set Forth the Display Made by the Congress of Nations, of Human Achievement in Material Form, So as the More Effectually to Illustrate the Progress of Mankind in All the Departments of Civilized Life* (San Francisco: Bancroft, 1893), 26, https://catalog.hathitrust.org/Record/100206082; St. Sukie de la Croix, *Chicago Whispers: A History of LGBT Chicago before Stonewall* (Madison: University of Wisconsin Press, 2012), 10; and Jeanne Weimann, *The Fair Women: The Story of the Women's Building as the World's Columbian Exposition, Chicago, 1893* (Chicago: Academy Chicago, 1981), 404.

31. There were two earlier recorded attempts of sandpainting weaving made in the Chaco Canyon area, but the artist(s) remain unknown. Thus, Klah is credited as the first. See Leatrice A. Armstrong, *Mary Wheelwright: Her Book* (Santa Fe: Wheelwright Museum of the American Indian, 2016), 118; and Roscoe, *Changing Ones*, 51.

32. Roscoe, *Changing Ones*, 41–42.

33. Hill, "Status of the Hermaphrodite," 273, 279.

34. Thomas, "Navajo Cultural Constructions of Gender," 166.

35. Roscoe, *Changing Ones*, 41–2.

36. Elsie C. Parsons, "Isleta, New Mexico," in *Forty-seventh Annual Report of the Bureau of American Ethnology, 1929–1930* (Washington, DC: Government Printing Office, 1932), 246.

37. The June 2001 murder of F. C. Martinez (Diné/Navajo) at age sixteen, one of the youngest victims of a hate crime in modern history, is case in point. Martinez, a self-identified two-spirit resident of Cortez, Colorado, was murdered by Shaun Murphy after they left the Ute Mountain Roundup Rodeo in Farmington, New Mexico. Murphy pleaded guilty to second-degree murder and was sentenced to forty years in jail. The documentary *Two Spirits* details the life and death of Martinez. More recently, the Navajo Human Rights Commission addressed the problem of violence against Navajo women and the Navajo LGBTQI community in the report "Status of Navajo Women."

38. Photograph of Hasteen Klah by Dane Coolidge, n.d., box 2, folder 21, Leland Clifton Wyman Papers on Navajo Myths and Sandpaintings, MSS 650, Center for Southwest Research, Zimmerman Library, University of New Mexico, Albuquerque (hereafter Wyman Papers); Marian E. Rodee, *Old Navajo Rugs* (Albuquerque: University of New Mexico Press, 1981), 103.

39. Ann Lane Hedlund, *Navajo Weaving in the Late Twentieth Century: Kin, Community, and Collectors* (Tucson: University of Arizona Press, 2004), 94.

40. Anderson Hoskie, "Hataal: Navajo Healing System," *Leading the Way: The Wisdom of the Navajo People* 11, no. 6 (June 2013): 2–4; Roscoe, "We'wha and Klah," 135.

41. Wade Davies, *Healing Ways: Navajo Health Care in the Twentieth Century* (Albuquerque: University of New Mexico Press, 2001), 4. Klah described this process in a narrative reproduced in Faris, *Nightway*, 201. Klah also explains how the bear gods instructed medicine men to create images in sand in Hasteen Klah, "Male Bear Ceremony or Mountain Chant," recorded by Inez Barrington and Arthur Newcomb, 1927, box 1, folder 22, Leland Clifton Wyman Papers on Navajo Myths and Sandpaintings, MSS 650, Center for Southwest Research, Zimmerman Library, University of New Mexico, Albuquerque.

42. Dane Coolidge and Mary Roberts Coolidge, *The Navajo Indians* (New York: AMS Press, 1980), 106.

43. Beck et al., *The Sacred*, 27.

44. Elayne Zorn, "Hastiin Klah (1867–1937), Navajo (Diné) Weaver," in *Encyclopedia of Native American Artists*, ed. Deborah Everett and Elayne Zorn (Westport, CT: Greenwood, 2008), 102.

45. Gladys Amanda Reichard, *Navajo Shepherd and Weaver* (Glorieta, NM: Rio Grande Press, 1984), 38; Newcomb, *Hosteen Klah*, 67. For general studies of Navajos and tourism markets see Erika Marie Bsumek, *Indian-Made: Navajo Culture in the*

Marketplace, 1868–1940 (Lawrence: University Press of Kansas, 2008); and Colleen M. O'Neill, *Working the Navajo Way: Labor and Culture in the Twentieth Century* (Lawrence: University Press of Kansas, 2005).

46. Sarah M. Nelson, *Handbook of Gender in Archaeology* (Lanham, MD: Rowman Altamira, 2006), 440.

47. Navajo Nation Museum, *Diné Dah'Atl'ó (Men Who Weave): A Revival in Diné Bikyah*, (Cortez, CO: Southwest Printing, 2004), 10.

48. Teresa María Montoya, "Woven Kin: Exploring Representation and Collaboration in Navajo Weaving Exhibitions" (master's thesis, University of Denver, 2011), 115, 123, https://digitalcommons.du.edu/etd/443.

49. Zorn, "Hastiin Klah," 117; Armstrong, *Mary Wheelwright*, 119.

50. Jonathan Goldberg, "Photographic Relations: Laura Gilpin, Willa Cather," *American Literature* 70, no. 1 (1998): 63–95, https://doi.org/10.2307/2902456; Hunter Drohojowska-Philp, *Full Bloom: The Art and Life of Georgia O'Keeffe* (New York: W. W. Norton, 2004), 355; Molly H. Mullin, *Culture in the Marketplace: Gender, Art, and Value in the American Southwest* (Durham, NC: Duke University Press, 2001), 83.

51. Mary Cabot Wheelwright, "Journey towards Understanding," 8, unpublished manuscript, folder 1, Mary C. Wheelwright Autobiography and Related Materials, MSS 773 BC, Center for Southwest Research, Zimmerman Library, University of New Mexico, Albuquerque.

52. Armstrong, *Mary Wheelwright*, 7, 93–94, 52, 226, 251.

53. Traugott, *New Mexico Art through Time*, 101.

54. Mary Wheelwright quoted in Roscoe, *Changing Ones*, 54; Hasteen Klah, recorded by Mary C. Wheelwright, *Navajo Creation Myth: The Story of Emergence* (New York: AM Press, 1980).

55. This problem remains ongoing. See Alisa Blackwood, "Navajo Nation Hopes to Revive Traditional Medicine," *Los Angeles Times*, July 11, 1999, https://www.latimes .com/archives/la-xpm-1999-jul-11-me-54883-story.html.

56. Anthropologist Will Roscoe claims "Klah's assistant died unexpectedly in 1931," while Newcomb states that Begay quit and left the reservation. Will Roscoe, "Hastiin Klah," in *Encyclopedia of Lesbian, Gay, Bisexual and Transgender History of America*, ed. Marc Stein (New York: Charles Scribner & Sons, 2003), 117; Newcomb, *Hosteen Klah*, 117.

57. Armstrong, *Mary Wheelwright*, 131, 136; Nancy J. Parezo and Karl A. Hoerig, "Collecting to Educate: Ernest Thompson Seton and Mary Cabot Wheelwright," in *Collecting Native America, 1870–1960*, ed. Shepard Krech and Barbara A Hail (Washington, DC: Smithsonian Institution Press, 1999), 219, 222–23; Washington Matthews, *Navaho Legends* (New York: Houghton Mifflin, 1897); and Washington Matthews, *The Night Chant, a Navaho Ceremony* (New York: Knickerbocker, 1902).

58. Zorn, "Hastiin Klah," 101.

59. Klah, *Navajo Creation Myth*; Mary C. Wheelwright, *Hail Chant and Water Chant*, vol. 2 (Santa Fe: Museum of Navajo Ceremonial Art, 1946).

60. Roscoe, *Changing Ones*, 55; Rayna Green, "Review Essay: Native American Women," *Signs* 6 (Winter 1980): 261.

61. Faris, *Nightway*, 28, 176–77.

62. I compared Klah's narrative of the Nightway ceremony, reprinted in Faris, *Nightway*, 177–229, to Wheelwright's published version. See Hosteen Klah, "Tleji or Yehbechai, Myth, Retold in Shorter Form from the Myth by Mary C. Wheelwright," *Bulletin No. 1* (Santa Fe: Museum of Navajo Ceremonial Art, 1938).

63. By the 1970s, Navajo healers founded the Diné Hataałii Association (formerly the Navajo Medicine Men's Association) to reclaim authority over their religious practices and "protect, preserve and promote Diné cultural wisdom, spiritual practice, and ceremonial knowledge." See Chip Colwell, *Plundered Skulls and Stolen Spirits: Inside the Fight to Reclaim Native America's Culture* (Chicago: University of Chicago Press, 2017), 175; and "About D.H.A.," Diné Hataałii Association Inc., updated November 2012, https://dhainc.org/about-d-h-a/.

64. Armstrong, *Mary Wheelwright*, 199, 235, 243.

65. Will Roscoe, "Sexual and Gender Diversity in Native America and the Pacific Islands," in Springate, *LGBTQ America*.

66. Klah's remains would later be buried on the museum's grounds. Mary Louise Grossman, "The Wheelwright Museum," *American Indian Art Magazine*, Summer 1977, 86.

67. Wheelwright, *Navajo Creation Myth*, 14.

68. The emotional toll of his restless lifestyle began to weigh on Hartley. In the summer of 1937, he returned to his birthplace, Maine, where he produced critically successful landscapes of Maine and nude figures of men. He found, in his late-life return to Maine, some sense of belonging. Hole, *Marsden Hartley and the West*, 140; Elizabeth Mankin Kornhauser and Ulrich Birkmaier, eds., *Marsden Hartley* (Hartford: Wadsworth Atheneum Museum of Art, 2002), 26, 207.

69. Donna M. Cassidy, Elizabeth Finch, and Randall R. Griffey, *Marsden Hartley's Maine* (Metropolitan Museum of Art, 2017), 33.

70. Hole, *Marsden Hartley and the West*, ix; Marta Weigle and Kyle Fiore, *Santa Fe and Taos: The Writer's Era, 1916–1941* (Santa Fe: Ancient City Press, 1982).

71. Marsden Hartley, Alfred Stieglitz, and James Timothy Voorhies, *My Dear Stieglitz: Letters of Marsden Hartley and Alfred Stieglitz, 1912–1915* (Columbia: University of South Carolina Press, 2002), 3.

72. Marsden Hartley to Alfred Stieglitz, October 23, 1914, in Hartley et al., *My Dear Stieglitz*, 164.

73. Katz, *Hide/Seek*, 26; Hole, *Marsden Hartley and the West*, 21; and Jonathan Weinberg, Charles Demuth, and Marsden Hartley, *Speaking for Vice: Homosexuality*

in the *Art of Charles Demuth, Marsden Hartley, and the First American Avant-Garde* (New Haven: Yale University Press, 1993), 3.

74. Sascha T. Scott, *A Strange Mixture: The Art and Politics of Painting Pueblo Indians* (Norman: University of Oklahoma Press, 2015), 50.

75. Marsden Hartley to Alfred Stieglitz, May 28, 1918, box 22, folder 531, Stieglitz/O'Keeffe Archive, Yale Collection of American Literature, Beinecke Rare Book and Manuscript Library, Yale University, New Haven, https://brbl-dl.library.yale.edu /vufind/Record/3862712.

76. Flannery Burke, *From Greenwich Village to Taos: Primitivism and Place t Mabel Dodge Luhan's* (Lawrence: University Press of Kansas, 2008), 26. Mabel Evans Dodge Sterne Luhan was married four times. She used various iterations of her name but primarily used the name Mabel Dodge in much of her public work, so I use that name here. According to Dodge's primary biographer, Lois Rudnick, Dodge discussed her lesbianism in an unpublished portion of her memoir *Intimate Memories*. See Luhan and Rudnick, *Suppressed Memoirs*, 32.

77. Burke, *From Greenwich Village to Taos*, 15, 29, 34, 40.

78. Tisa Joy Wenger, *We Have a Religion: The 1920s Pueblo Indian Dance Controversy and American Religious Freedom* (Chapel Hill: University of North Carolina Press, 2009), 149.

79. Complaints by missionaries about alleged immoralities in Hopi and Pueblo dances can be found in Charles Burke, "Segments from the Circular No. 1665 and Supplement to Circular No. 1665," Department of the Interior Office of Indian Affairs, April 26, 1921, and February 14, 1923 (Washington, DC), https://www.webpages .uidaho.edu/~rfrey/PDF/329/IndianDances.pdf.

80. Alfonso Ortiz, ed., *New Perspectives on the Pueblos* (Albuquerque: University of New Mexico Press, 1971), 139.

81. Scott, *A Strange Mixture*, 28–37. In relation to land and water, the *United States v. Sandoval* (1913) decision granted the federal government jurisdiction over Pueblo territory.

82. Scott, *A Strange Mixture*, 74–75.

83. See especially, Marsden Hartley, "Tribal Esthetics Dance Drama," *El Palacio* 6, no. 4 (February 8, 1919): 53–55. Marsden Hartley, "The Scientific Esthetic of the Redman," *Art and Archaeology* 13 (March 1922): 113; Marsden Hartley, "The Festival of the Corn," in *The Collected Poems of Marsden Hartley, 1904–1943*, ed. Gail R. Scott (Santa Rosa: Black Sparrow, 1987), 48–49. "Corn Dance" is a misnomer that Pueblos likely began using when tourists started attending dances. Hartley employs a descriptor that is comprehensible to an Anglo audience. A more accurate general term would be "Fertility Dance," but this designation might have led to further suppression of ceremonial practices. Hartley is correct in his explanation of the Corn Dance—it both promoted a successful corn harvest and ensured the fertility and well-being of the Pueblo world.

84. Spud Johnson, entry for February 4, 1934, unnumbered diary, box 17, folder 6, Spud Johnson Collection, Harry Ransom Humanities Research Center, University of Texas, Austin (hereafter Johnson Collection).

85. Both Jacobs and Wenger point to the writings of women such as Mary Austin and Mabel Dodge. See Jacobs, *Engendered Encounters*, 113–14, 116–24; and Wenger, *We Have a Religion*, 160–67.

86. Mary Austin, *The Land of Journeys' Ending* (New York: Century, 1924), 255–56; Jacobs, *Engendered Encounters*, 118; Alice Corbin Henderson, "The Dance-Rituals of the Pueblo Indians," *Theatre Arts Magazine* 7 (April 1923): 112; Elise Clews Parsons, *Taos Pueblo* (Menasha, WI: George Banta, 1936), 99.

87. Jacobs, *Engendered Encounters*, 13, 74 113–14, 142–44.

88. Cynthia L. Chavez, "Negotiated Representations: Pueblo Artists and Culture" (Ph.D. diss., University of New Mexico, 2001), 73–87.

89. Lujan quoted in Jacobs, *Engendered Encounters*, 130.

90. Mathew Martinez (Ohkay Owingeh Pueblo), "All Indian Pueblo Council and the Bursum Bill," *New Mexico History*, January 17, 2014, http://newmexicohistory.org/2014/01/17/all-indian-pueblo-council-and-the-bursum-bill/.

91. Vigil quoted in Jacobs, *Engendered Encounters*, 140. On the sexual symbolism in dances, see Wenger, *We Have a Religion*, 140–41.

92. Sophie D. Aberle, *Twenty-Five Years of Sex Research: History of the National Research Council Committee for Research Problems of Sex, 1922–1947* (Philadelphia: W. B. Saunders, 1953).

93. Sophie D. Aberle, "End of an Illusion," unpublished manuscript, 1983, 18–19, box 14, folder 22; and Sophie D. Aberle, "Pueblo of San Juan," 1927, 33, 35, 46–47, box 1, folder 17, Sophie D. Aberle Papers, MSS 509 BC, Center for Southwest Research, Zimmerman Library, University of New Mexico, Albuquerque.

94. Joseph H. Suina, "Pueblo Secrecy: Result of Intrusions," *New Mexico Magazine* (January 1992): 61–63.

95. Hurewitz, *Bohemian Los Angeles*, 7; Marc Stein, *Rethinking the Gay and Lesbian Movement* (New York: Routledge, 2012), 33.

96. James Kraft, introduction, in Witter Bynner, *Selected Poems: The Works of Witter Bynner*, ed. Richard Wilbur (New York: Farrar, Straus, Giroux, 1977), lvi.

97. Kraft, *Who Is Witter Bynner?*, 49.

98. Corbin met Bynner at a poetry lecture he gave in Chicago. Corinne P. Sze, "The Witter Bynner House," *Bulletin of the Historic Santa Fe Foundation* 20, no. 2 (September 1992): 4.

99. Riggs also exhibited physical symptoms of tuberculosis, perhaps related to his depression. Phyllis Braunlich and Lynn Riggs, eds., *Haunted by Home: The Life and Letters of Lynn Riggs* (Norman: University of Oklahoma Press, 1988), 6; and James H. Cox, "The Cross and the Harvest Dance: Lynn Riggs' and James Hughes' *A Day in*

Santa Fe," Quarterly Review of Film and Video 32, no. 4 (2015): 384, DOI:10.1080/105 09208.2014.968513.

100. Lynn Cline, *Literary Pilgrims: The Santa Fe and Taos Writers Colonies, 1917–1950* (Albuquerque: University of New Mexico Press, 2007), 127–28; Lynn Riggs to Witter Bynner, December 3, 1923, in Braunlich and Riggs, *Haunted by Home*, 7.

101. Winnek quoted in Jean G. Downey, "Marian Frances Winnek, 1883–1977" (unpublished manuscript, 1988), 5, J. V. Fletcher Library, Westford, MA; Elizabeth Willis DeHuff, review of *Juniper Hill* by Marian Winnek, *New Mexico Quarterly* 2, no. 4 (1932): 353–54.

102. Winnek quoted in Downey, "Marian Frances Winnek," 9, 33.

103. Myron Brinig, "Someone at the Door: Memoirs of an Outsider," unpublished manuscript, 82, 90–99, box 1, folder 2, Myron Brinig Memoirs, MSS864 BC, Center for Southwest Research, Zimmerman Library, University of New Mexico, Albuquerque. For biographical information on Myron Brinig, see Alan M. Wald, *American Night: The Literary Left in the Era of the Cold War* (Chapel Hill: University of North Carolina Press, 2012), 128; and Earl Ganz, "Myron Brining," LGBT Encyclopedia, accessed January 16, 2015, http://www.glbtq.com/literature/brinig_m,2.html.

104. Myron Brinig, *This Man Is My Brother* (New York: Farrar & Rinehart, 1932), 305.

105. Johnson discusses the club in his journal entry dated January 2, 1948, Diary 6, 1948–51, box 12, folder 3, Johnson Collection; and "The Rabble," *New Mexico Quarterly Review* 19 (Spring 1949): 72–75.

106. Haniel Long, "The Poets' Round-Up," *New Mexico Quarterly Review* 19 (Spring 1949): 72; Braunlich and Riggs, *Haunted by Home*, 14–19.

107. Walter Willard Johnson, *Horizontal Yellow: By Spud Johnson* (Santa Fe: Writers' Editions, 1935), 83–84.

108. Johnson was far from alone in his feelings. Historian Craig Loftin has uncovered similar sentiments in letters authored by gay men written to the editors of *ONE*, the first openly gay magazine in the United States, during the 1950s and 1960s. Craig M. Loftin, ed., *Letters to ONE: Gay and Lesbian Voices from the 1950s and 1960s* (Albany: SUNY Press, 2012), 1–2.

109. Spud Johnson, "Horizontal Yellow: Accounts, Records and Mailing List," 1935, box 14, folder 3, Johnson Collection.

110. Harold W. Hawk to Johnson, June 24, 1936, box 8, folder 2, Johnson Collection.

111. Bynner's literary career spanned fifty years, peaking in the 1920s. He published close to twenty books of poetry as well as poetic translations. He is most known for his Chinese translations. For example, see Kang-hu Kiang, *The Jade Mountain: A Chinese Anthology, Being Three Hundred Poems of the T'ang Dynasty*, 618–906, translated by Witter Bynner (New York: Knopf, 1929).

112. Although there were celebrated poets in the 1920s and 1930s who identified as gay—Hart Crane, W. H. Auden, and Edwin Denby for instance—gay themes

rarely emerged in their poetry. Roger Austen, *Playing the Game: The Homosexual Novel in America* (Indianapolis: Bobbs-Merrill, 1977), 35.

113. Kraft, *Who Is Witter Bynner?*, 91–92; Anthony Slide, *Lost Gay Novels: A Reference Guide to Fifty Works from the First Half of the Twentieth Century* (New York: Routledge, 2003); Witter Bynner, *Eden Tree* (New York: Knopf, 1931).

114. Positive reviews of Bynner's poetry prior to *Eden Tree* are numerous. A few examples include Babette Deutsch, "Bitterness and Beauty," *New Republic*, February 10, 1926, 338–39; Berenice Van Slyke, "Vildrac via Bynner," *Poetry* 24, no. 4 (July 1924): 223–25; and Louis Untermeyer, "A Christmas Inventory," *Bookman*, December 1925, 495–96. One critical review of Bynner's poetry after *Eden Tree* is Louis Forester, "The Two Bynners," *Poetry* 57, no. 3 (December 1940): 217–19.

115. Louis Untermeyer, "*Eden Tree* by Witter Bynner," *Saturday Review*, October 10, 1931, 186.

116. Kraft, *Who Is Witter Bynner?*, 58; Phoebe Dechart, "Community Theater: Santa Fe's Oldest Surviving Drama Group," *Santa Fe New Mexican*, March 19, 1978, 12–14.

117. Sze, "Witter Bynner House," 7; Paul Horgan, "About Witter Bynner (1881–1936)," Witter Bynner Foundation for Poetry, accessed January 15, 2020, https://www.bynnerfoundation.org/witterbynner/index.htm.

118. Spud Johnson, "Got Up As," *New Mexican*, June 4, 1961. Descriptions of Bynner's style are included in Cooper, *Unbuttoned*, 104; Kraft, *Who Is Witter Bynner?*, 35, 59; and Sze, "Witter Bynner House," 5.

119. Sze, "Witter Bynner House," 3. Krahulik outlines how queer fashion developed in the art colony of Provincetown in Krahulik, *Provincetown*, 85–89.

120. Richard Lowitt, *Bronson M. Cutting: Progressive Politician* (Albuquerque: University of New Mexico Press, 1992), 187; Rudnick, *Cady Wells and Southwestern Modernism*, 39; John La Farge, *Turn left at the Sleeping Dog: Scripting the Santa Fe Legend, 1920–1955* (Albuquerque: University of New Mexico Press, 2001), 121.

121. For the histories of plazas, see Daniel D. Arreola, *Tejano South Texas: A Mexican American Cultural Province* (Austin: University of Texas Press, 2002). For a history of New Mexico's plazas, see Chris Wilson and Stefanos Polyzoides, eds., *The Plazas of New Mexico* (San Antonio: Trinity University Press, 2011).

122. Peter Hertzog, *La Fonda: The Inn of Santa Fe* (Santa Fe: Press of the Territorial, 1964), 3; Chris Wilson, *The Myth of Santa Fe: Creating a Modern Regional Tradition* (Albuquerque: University of New Mexico Press, 1997), 138–39; Joseph Traugott, *Art of New Mexico: How the West Is One, The Collection of the Museum of Fine Arts* (Santa Fe: Museum of New Mexico Press, 2007), 93.

123. Hay and Sanchez quoted in La Farge, *Turn Left*, 203, 55. Barrows quoted in La Farge, *Turn Left*, 63. See also interviews that highlight La Fonda with Alice Henderson Rossin, Paul Frank, Samuel Adelo, J. I. Staley, Miranda M. Levy, and Margaret Larson in *Turn Left*, 244–52.

124. Hay quoted in La Farge, *Turn Left*, 207; Weigle and Fiore, *Santa Fe and Taos*, 136; Cooper, *Unbuttoned*, 85.

125. Sanchez and Campbell quoted in La Farge, *Turn Left*, 23, 342; Andreita Padilla quoted in Nan Elsasser, Kyle MacKenzie, and Yvonne Tixier y Vigil, *Las Mujeres: Conversations from a Hispanic Community* (Old Westbury, NY: Feminist Press, 1980), 26; Carol Lee Sanchez quoted in Judy Grahn, *Another Mother Tongue: Gay Words, Gay Worlds* (Boston: Beacon, 1984), 111.

126. On western wear and masculinity, see Elyssa Ford, "Becoming the West: Cowboys as Icons of Masculine Style for Gay Men," *Critical Studies in Men's Fashion* 5, nos. 1 & 2 (2018): 41–53; and Rebecca Scofield, "'Chaps and Scowls': Play, Violence, and the Post-1970s Urban Cowboy," *Journal of American Culture* 40, no. 4 (2017): 325–40, https://doi.org/10.1111/jacc.12805.

127. Clay Evans, "Gays in Santa Fe," *Santa Fe Reporter*, March 11, 1992, https://newspaperarchive.com/santa-fe-reporter-mar-11-1992-p-17/.

128. Cooper, *Unbuttoned*, 85; Mullin, *Culture in the Marketplace*, 73. Most gay men and women resorted to a number of subtle dress codes to identify themselves to other queer people. See Madeline D. Davis and Elizabeth Lapovsky Kennedy, *Boots of Leather, Slippers of Gold: The History of a Lesbian Community* (New York: Routledge, 1993); and Shaun Cole, *"Don We Now Our Gay Apparel": Gay Men's Dress in the Twentieth Century* (New York: Berg, 2000).

129. Since the late 1970s, the All Pueblo Council of Governors (formerly the All Indian Pueblo Council) and the state's Eight Northern Pueblos have boycotted the Fiesta. For an in-depth discussion of Santa Fe Fiesta's history, see Wilson, *Myth of Santa Fe*, 181–231.

130. Sarah Bronwen Horton, *The Santa Fe Fiesta, Reinvented: Staking Ethno-nationalist Claims to a Disappearing Homeland* (Santa Fe: School for Advanced Research Press, 2010), 41.

131. Traugott, *Art of New Mexico*, 95.

132. Sze, "Witter Bynner House," 6. For scholarship on Pasatiempo, see Rudnick, *Cady Wells and Southwestern Modernism*, 39; and Wilson, *Myth of Santa Fe*, 211–22.

133. "Mrs. Terresa Dorman Hostess at Gay Costume Party for Edward Hall," *Santa Fe New Mexican*, September 3, 1927, in Wilson, *Myth of Santa Fe*, 216.

134. Over time, Nuevomexicanos wrested control of the Fiesta from Anglos. Since 1945 a Latino president has presided over the Santa Fe Fiesta Council, and the council began to advertise Fiesta as a "tribute to the active preservation of Hispanic heritage in New Mexico." Horton, *Santa Fe Fiesta*, 42.

135. For an excellent discussion of race and power in New Mexico through the lens of the Santa Fe Fiesta, see Sarah Horton, "Where Is the 'Mexican' in 'New Mexican'? Enacting History, Enacting Dominance in the Santa Fe Fiesta," *Public Historian* 23, no. 4 (2001): 41–54, https://doi.org/10.1525/tph.2001.23.4.41.

136. Thomas, "Navajo Cultural Constructions of Gender," 157.

137. Qwo-Li Driskill, Daniel Heath Justice, Deborah A. Miranda, and Lisa Ta-tonetti, eds., *Sovereign Erotics: A Collection of Two-Spirit Literature* (Tucson: University of Arizona Press, 2011), 1.

TWO Decency Debate

1. Willard Johnson, "History of the Laughing Horse," *South Dakota Review* 6, no. 3 (Autumn 1968): 15–16; Frederick J. Hoffman, Charles A. Allen, and Carolyn F. Ulrich, *The Little Magazine: A History and a Bibliography* (Princeton, NJ: Princeton University Press, 1946), 7, 235–36 (this volume does not include *The Lark* but allowed me to place it in the historical context of other little magazines); Marvin R. Nathan, "San Francisco's Fin de Siècle Bohemian Renaissance," *California History* 61, no. 3 (Fall 1982): 196–209; Christine Scriabine, "Bruce Porter: San Francisco Society's Artful Player," *California History* 85, no. 3 (2008): 48–67, 70–72; and *The Lark*, nos. 13–24, May 1896–June 1897, www.google.com/books/edition/The_Lark/5Urs AAAAIAAJ.

2. A.P. (Chairman), "Better Books Committee," *Laughing Horse*, April 1922, in Udall, *Spud Johnson and Laughing Horse*, 105.

3. On *Laughing Horse* and censorship, see Donald A. Barclay, "'The Laughing Horse': A Literary Magazine of the American West," *Western American Literature* 27, no. 1 (1992): 47–55; Cline, *Literary Pilgrims*, 105–7; William M. Roberts, "The Laughing Horse: A Horse Laugh at the University," *Chronicle of the University of California* (Spring 2002), https://cshe.berkeley.edu/sites/default/files/chron5_excerpt_laughing _horse.pdf; Daniel Worden, "*Laughing Horse* Magazine and Regional Modernism in New Mexico," *Journal of Modern Periodical Studies* 5, no. 2 (2015): 203–5; and Udall, *Spud Johnson and Laughing Horse*, 118–21.

4. Paul S. Boyer, *Purity in Print: Book Censorship in America from the Gilded Age to the Computer Age* (Madison: University of Wisconsin Press, 2002), 132; D. J. Carlile, "A Dark and Wayward Book," *Los Angeles Times*, December 16, 2001, https:// www.latimes.com/archives/la-xpm-2001-dec-16-bk-carlile16-story.html; "Fantazius Mallare: A Mysterious Oath, by B. Hecht (Book Review)," *Psychoanalytic Review* 10 (1923): 235.

5. John Worthen, *D. H. Lawrence: The Life of an Outsider* (New York: Counterpoint, 2005), 281.

6. D. H. Lawrence, review of Ben Hecht's *Fantazius Mallare*, *Laughing Horse*, December 1922.

7. Quoted in Worthen, *D. H. Lawrence*, 275.

8. D. H. Lawrence, *Laughing Horse*, December 1922; B. M. Woods to President Barrows, December 20, 1922, in Roberts, "The Laughing Horse," 16.

9. Roy Chanslor wrote a letter to President David P. Barrows protesting his expulsion. He asserted that the obscenity charge was only a pretext for the real objection to the contents of *Laughing Horse*—criticism aimed at higher education and the University of California administration. See Roberts, "The Laughing Horse"; Upton Sinclair, "The Goose-Step: A Study of American Education," *Laughing Horse*, December 1922; Upton Sinclair to President Barrows, December 14, 1922, in *Laughing Horse*, 1923.

10. Johnson, "History of the Laughing Horse," 17.

11. Mary Austin to Spud Johnson, December 9, 1923, box 4, folder 8, Johnson Collection.

12. "The Tariff: Obscenity Bypath," *Time*, October 21, 1929, 18.

13. I have not reviewed Cutting's personal papers. His same-sex love correspondence is referenced in William J. Mann, *Kate: The Woman Who Was Hepburn* (New York: Macmillan, 2006), 553n146. Cutting's biographer Richard Lowitt argues that "Cutting was not gay" and concludes that Cutting's sexuality is not "worthy of undue attention" (Lowitt, *Bronson M. Cutting*, xi).

14. Boyer, *Purity in Print*, 213.

15. Margaret A. Blanchard, *Revolutionary Sparks: Freedom of Expression in Modern America* (New York: Oxford University Press, 1992), 135.

16. In understanding sexual privacy, I have been most influenced by Clayton Howard, *The Closet and the Cul-de-Sac: The Politics of Sexual Privacy in Northern California* (Philadelphia: University of Pennsylvania Press, 2019), 2, 5–6, 72–82, 86–87.

17. The roots of the movement for a new sexual ethic date back at least to the eve of World War I, when Americans embarked on the long-term process of sexual liberalization. In understanding the long sexual revolution and its relationship to the modern gay liberation movement, I have been most influenced by Jeffery Escoffier, "Pornography, Perversity and the Sexual Revolution," in *Sexual Revolutions*, ed. Gert Hekma and Alain Giami, 208 (New York: Palgrave Macmillan, 2014); Gert Hekma and Alain Giami, introduction, in Hekma and Giami, *Sexual Revolutions*, 8–10; and Joanne Meyerowitz, "The Liberal 1950s? Reinterpreting Postwar U.S. Sexual Culture," in *Gender and the Long Postwar: The United States and the Two Germanys, 1945–1989*, ed. Karen Hagemann and Sonya Michel (Baltimore, MD: Johns Hopkins University Press, 2014), 295–317.

18. Some examples of sexological, autobiographical, and fictional publications that circulated in the early twentieth century and discuss gender and sexual variation include Havelock Ellis, *Studies in the Psychology of Sex*, vol. 2, *Sexual Inversion* (Philadelphia: F. A. Davis, 1901); Oscar Paul Gilbert, *Men in Women's Guise: Some Historical Instances of Female Impersonation*, translated by Robert Bruce Douglas (John Lane: London, 1926); Earl Lind, *Autobiography of an Androgyne* (New York: Medico-Legal Journal, 1918); and Blair Niles, *Strange Brother* (New York: Liveright, 1931).

19. Black queer people during the 1920s and 1930s looked to magazine articles focusing on sexuality and homosexuality that circulated in both the mainstream press and the Black press. A. B. Christa Schwarz, *Gay Voices of the Harlem Renaissance* (Bloomington: Indiana University Press, 2003), 38.

20. Brett Beemyn, "The New Negro Renaissance, Bisexual Renaissance: The Lives and Works of Angelina Weld Grimke and Richard Bruce Nugent," in *Modern American Queer History*, ed. Allida Mae Black (Philadelphia: Temple University Press, 2001), 36–48; and Schwarz, *Gay Voices of the Harlem Renaissance*, 30.

21. Richard Bruce Nugent, "Smoke, Lilies, and Jade," *Fire!*, November 1926, 33–39.

22. Bruce Nugent and Thomas H. Wirth, *Gay Rebel of the Harlem Renaissance: Selections from the Work of Richard Bruce Nugent* (Durham, NC: Duke University Press, 2002), 13, 50, 1.

23. James F. Wilson, *Bulldaggers, Pansies, and Chocolate Babies: Performance, Race, and Sexuality in the Harlem Renaissance* (Ann Arbor: University of Michigan Press, 2010), 18.

24. Chauncey, *Gay New York*, 247; and Eric Garber, "A Spectacle in Color: The Lesbian and Gay Subculture of Jazz Age Harlem," in *Hidden from History: Reclaiming the Gay and Lesbian*, ed. Martin Duberman, Martha Vicinus, and George Chauncey (New York: NAL, 1989), 318–21. Garber extended the discourse of the Harlem Renaissance to include the participation of lesbian, gay, bisexual, and transgender voices.

25. Burke, *From Greenwich Village to Taos*, 97. In particular, Carl Van Vechten fetishized Black male bodies. See, for example, James Smalls, *The Homoerotic Photography of Carl Van Vechten: Public Face, Private Thoughts* (Philadelphia: Temple University Press, 2006).

26. Burke, "Spud Johnson and a Gay Man's Place," 95; Spud Johnson, entry for October 17, 1934, Diary 3, box 12, folder 3, Johnson Collection.

27. Historian Jonathan D. Katz notes that literary culture in Harlem was far less open than the city's art and music culture. Katz, *Hide/Seek*, 27–28.

28. A. Gabriel Meléndez, *So All Is Not Lost: The Poetics of Print in Nuevomexicano Communities, 1834–1958* (Albuquerque: University of New Mexico Press, 1997), 135.

29. On heteropatriarchy, see Mitchell, *West of Sex*, 104, 117–18. For an example of heteropatriarchy as a literary theme in Spanish-language newspapers, see Isidoro Armijo, "Sesenta minutos en los infiernos," *El eco del valle*, September 23, 1911.

30. Lynn Riggs, "The Arid Land," *Laughing Horse*, Autumn 1927; Craig S. Womack, *Red on Red: Native American Literary Separatism* (Minneapolis: University of Minnesota Press, 1999), ch. 8.

31. Rachel Potter, *Obscene Modernism: Literary Censorship and Experiment, 1900–1940* (Oxford: Oxford University Press, 2013), 20; Boyer, *Purity in Print*, 58.

32. Potter, *Obscene Modernism*, 39; Meyerowitz, "Liberal 1950s?," 311–12. The American Civil Liberties Union, created in 1920, also sought to protect writers against re-

strictions on freedom of speech and gradually adopted sexual speech and expression as part of its civil liberties domain. On the ACLU, see Leigh Ann Wheeler, *How Sex Became a Civil Liberty* (New York: Oxford University Press, 2013).

33. I derived my definition of "little magazines" from Suzanne W. Churchill and Adam McKible, "Little Magazines and Modernism: An Introduction," *American Periodicals* 15, no. 1 (2005): 1–5; Felix Pollak, interviewed by Mark Olson, in *The Little Magazine in America: A Modern Documentary History*, ed. Elliott Anderson and Mary Kinzie (Yonkers: Pushcart Press, 1978), 35; and Andrew Thacker, introduction, in *The Oxford Critical and Cultural History of Modernist Magazines*, ed. Peter Brooker and Andrew Thacker (New York: Oxford University Press, 2009), 1–28.

34. Eric Bulson, *Little Magazine, World Form* (New York: Columbia University Press, 2017), 1–3; Victoria Kingham, "Audacious Modernity: *The Seven Arts* (1916–17); *The Soil* (1916–17); and *The Trend* (1911–15)," in Brooker and Thacker, *Oxford Critical and Cultural History*, 403; and Alan Golding, "The Little Review (1914–29)," in Brooker and Thacker, *Oxford Critical and Cultural History*, 61–84.

35. Margaret Anderson, "Mrs. Ellis's Failure," *Little Review* (March 1915): 16–19; Holly A. Baggett, "'Someone to Talk Our Language': Jane Heap, Margaret Anderson, and *The Little Review* in Chicago," in Black, *Modern American Queer History*, 24–35; Margaret Anderson and jh (Jane Heap), *Intimate Circles: American Women in the Art*, Beinecke Rare Book and Manuscript Library, Yale University, online exhibition, July 28–October 18, 2003, http://brbl-archive.library.yale.edu/exhibitions/awia/gallery /anderson.html.

36. Golding, "The Little Review (1914–29)," 83.

37. John D'Emilio and Estelle B. Freedman, *Intimate Matters: A History of Sexuality in America* (New York: Harper & Row, 1988), ch. 10; "Sex O'Clock in America," *Current Opinion*, August 1913, 113–14; Maria V. Johnson, "'Jelly Jelly Jellyroll': Lesbian Sexuality and Identity in Women's Blues," *Women & Music* 7 (January 1, 2003): 31–52; Jana Evans Braziel, "'Bye, Bye Baby': Race, Bisexuality, and the Blues in the Music of Bessie Smith and Janis Joplin," *Popular Music and Society* 27, no. 1 (January 1, 2004): 3–26, https://doi.org/10.1080/0300776032000144896. Others such as Ethel Waters and Alberta Hunter concealed their lesbian inclinations.

38. British physician and psychologist Havelock Ellis described the culture of "sexual inversion" in American cities and tackled the topic of "female inversion" in *Studies in the Psychology of Sex,*, vol. 2, 172–201, 350–51. The most candid published writing with homosexual themes and characters of the 1920s include Robert McAlmon's poetry collections *Explorations* (1921) and *The Portrait of a Generation* (1926), Clarkson Crane's *The Western Shore* (1925), Richard Bruce Nugent's "Smoke, Lilies, and Jade" (1926), and Radclyffe Hall's *The Well of Loneliness* (1928).

39. Potter, *Obscene Modernism*, ch. 1.

40. Spud Johnson, *A Short History of Laughing Horses . . . And a Suggestion for Developing Thoroughbreds: A Pamphlet with a Purpose*, undated pamphlet, box 39, folder 26, Johnson Collection.

41. Udall, *Spud Johnson and Laughing Horse*, 154. Flannery Burke's biographical article on Johnson has the most coverage of his limited and often precarious finances. Burke, "Spud Johnson and a Gay Man's Place," 105.

42. Johnson, *Short History of Laughing Horses*; Spud Johnson, handwritten log of "Subscriptions and Exchanges for *Laughing Horse*," 1938, box 14, folder 4, Johnson Collection. From the records Johnson kept, I surmise he produced a few hundred copies of each issue, which was typical for a little magazine in the American West, although a few such as the *New Mexico Quarterly* had several thousand subscribers. See Sarah A. Fedirka, "'Our Own Authentic Wonderland': The Modernist Geographical Imagination and 'Little Magazines' of the American West," in Brooker and Thacker, *Oxford Critical and Cultural History*, 576–98.

43. *Laughing Horse* 8, 1923.

44. Doris Meyer, *Speaking for Themselves: Nuevomexicano Cultural Identity and the Spanish-Language Press, 1880–1920* (Albuquerque: University of New Mexico Press, 1996). Isidoro Armijo's short story "Sesenta minutos en los infiernos" was translated and republished in *Laughing Horse*: Isidoro Armijo, "Sixty Minutes in Hades," *Laughing Horse*, May 1924.

45. Spud Johnson to Henry Somers Janon, May 8, 1929, box 6, folder 6, Johnson Collection.

46. Charles Rembar, *The End of Obscenity: The Trials of Lady Chatterley, Tropic of Cancer, and Fanny Hill* (New York: Random House, 1968), 16; Justin D. Edwards, "At the End of *The Rainbow*: Reading Lesbian Identities in D. H. Lawrence's Fiction," *International Fiction Review* 27, nos. 1 and 2 (2000), https://journals.lib.unb.ca/index.php/IFR/article/view/7659/8716; D. H. Lawrence, *A Propos of Lady Chatterley's Lover* (London: Mandrake Press, 1930), 9.

47. Tariff Act of 1842, Pub. L, No. 566–67, 5 Stat. 548, section 28 (August 30, 1842); Boyer, *Purity in Print*, 208–10; Michael Harold Paulos, "'Smoot Smites Smut': Apostle-Senator Reed Smoot's 1930 Campaign against Obscene Books," *Journal of Mormon History* 40, no. 1 (2014): 67.

48. Robert W. Haney, *Comstockery in America: Patterns of Censorship and Control* (Boston: Beacon Press, 1960), 16; Potter, *Obscene Modernism*, 17; Rembar, *The End of Obscenity*, 20.

49. I have not been able to find the blocklist. Boyer and Paulos both reference it and cite Senator Bronson Cutting in the Congressional Record as their source, noting that further works were added to the list in April 1929. Boyer, *Purity in Print*, 99, 207–10; Paulos, "'Smoot Smites Smut,'" 67.

50. Acting Commissioner of Customs to Senator Bronson Cutting, May 6, 1929, box 6, folder 6, Johnson Collection.

51. Paulos, "'Smoot Smites Smut,'" 68.

52. Senator Bronson Cutting to Secretary of the Treasury, Andrew W. Mellon, May 15, 1929, box 6, folder 6, Johnson Collection; Secretary of the Treasury, Andrew W. Mellon to Senator Bronson Cutting, May 22, 1929, box 6, folder 6, Johnson Collection.

53. Boyer, *Purity in Print*, 208; Spud Johnson to Henry Somers Janon, Esq., May 8, 1929, box 6, folder 6, Johnson Collection. Johnson was one of the first people to face charges for obtaining copies of *Lady Chatterley's Lover*. Also in 1929 James A. DeLacey, owner of the Dunster House Bookshop in Cambridge, Massachusetts, and his clerk Joseph Sullivan, who sold the book, were found guilty on obscenity charges. Judge Arthur P. Stone sentenced DeLacey to four months in jail as well as a eight-hundred-dollar fine while Sullivan received two weeks' jail time and a two-hundred-dollar fine. DeLacey appealed to the Massachusetts Supreme Court in 1930, but the court upheld his conviction. See Dawn B. Sova, *Literature Suppressed on Sexual Grounds* (New York: Facts on File, 2006), 138–42.

54. Josh Lambert, *Unclean Lips: Obscenity, Jews, and American Culture* (New York: New York University Press, 2013), 68.

55. Boyer, *Purity in Print*, 99, ch. 5.

56. Wheeler, *How Sex Became a Civil Liberty*, 40–43.

57. Douglas A. Irwin, *Peddling Protectionism: Smoot-Hawley and the Great Depression* (Princeton, NJ: Princeton University Press, 2011), 2–3; Tariff Act of 1930, available via Cornell Legal Information Institute, https://www.law.cornell.edu/cfr/text/19/145.51.

58. Boyer, *Purity in Print*, 92–94, 214; Modris Eksteins, "*All Quiet on the Western Front* and the Fate of a War," *Journal of Contemporary History* 15 (1980): 353.

59. Cutting quoted in "Assails Exclusion of Remarque's Book," *New York Times*, July 29, 1929.

60. Leslie A. Taylor, "'I Made Up My Mind to Get It': The American Trial of 'The Well of Loneliness' New York City, 1928–1929," *Journal of the History of Sexuality* 10, no. 2 (2001): 268; Ernst quoted in *Morris Leopold Ernst: An Inventory of His Papers*, Harry Ransom Center, University of Texas, Austin, https://norman.hrc.utexas.edu/fasearch/findingAid.cfm?eadid=00602; and Morris L. Ernst and William Seagle, *To the Pure . . . A Study of Obscenity and the Censor* (New York: Viking, 1928), ch. 10.

61. Rochelle Gurstein, *The Repeal of Reticence: America's Cultural and Legal Struggles over Free Speech, Obscenity, Sexual Liberation, and Modern Art* (New York: Hill and Wang, 2016), 184; E. P. Walkiewicz and Hugh Witemeyer, eds., *Ezra Pound and Senator Bronson Cutting: A Political Correspondence, 1930–1935* (Albuquerque: University of

New Mexico Press, 1995), 16. Privacy defined as "the right to be left alone" arose from the legal framework of Judge Louis Brandeis and Samuel Warren in "The Right to Privacy," *Harvard Law Review* 4, no. 5 (December 15, 1890): 195, 197.

62. 71 Cong. Rec. S4339, daily ed., October 10, 1929, statement of Sen. Cutting.

63. Walter Barnett, "Corruption of Morals—The Underlying Issue of the Pornography Commission Report," *Law and the Social Order* 189 (1971): 189–243; William B. Lockhart and Robert C. McClure, "Obscenity in the Courts," *Law and Contemporary Problems* 20 (Fall 1955): 587–607.

64. 71 Cong. Rec. S4335, daily ed., October 10, 1929, statement of Sen. Cutting; Taylor, "'I Made Up My Mind,'" 265.

65. Boyer, *Purity in Print*, 221; 71 Cong. Rec. 4445–76, daily ed., October 11, 1929.

66. "Senate Eliminates 'Obscene' Book Ban," *New York Times*, October 12, 1929, ProQuest Historical Newspapers; "The Tariff," *Time Magazine*, 18; Boyer, *Purity in Print*, 222, 224.

67. John Hiltman, "Books in Legislation," *Publisher's Weekly*, January 24, 1931, 112; Lowitt, *Bronson M. Cutting*, 169.

68. Ezra Pound, "Honor and the United States Senate," *Poetry*, June 1930, 152; John Dewey, *Laughing Horse*, February 1930.

69. Bronson Cutting to Spud Johnson, January 1, 1930, box 6, folder 6, Johnson Collection.

70. Spud Johnson, "Laughing Horse Feeling Its Oats; Will Ha-Ha Book Censorship Idea," *Santa Fe New Mexican*, February 4, 1930, 4; Udall, *Spud Johnson and Laughing Horse*, 156.

71. Johnson, "History of the Laughing Horse," 17.

72. Carl Sandburg, *Laughing Horse*, February 1930.

73. Sherwood Anderson, *Laughing Horse*, February 1930.

74. Bronson Cutting to Spud Johnson, February 15, 1930, box 6, folder 6, Johnson Collection.

75. Boyer, *Purity in Print*, 226.

76. "Decency Squabble," *Time Magazine*, March 31, 1930.

77. 72 Cong. Rec. S5414, daily ed., March 17, 1930, statement of Sen. Smoot.

78. Donna I. Dennis, "Obscenity Law and the Conditions of Freedom in the Nineteenth-Century United States," *Law & Social Inquiry* 27, no. 2 (2002): 388.

79. 72 Cong. Rec. S515, daily ed., March 17, 1930, statement of Sen. Smoot; 72 Cong. Rec. S5494, daily ed., March 18, 1930, statement of Sen. Smoot.

80. 72 Cong. Rec. S5415–16, daily ed., March 17, 1930, statement of Sen. Smoot; Mann, *Kate*, 552n146.

81. 72 Cong. Rec. S5431, daily ed., March 17, 1930, statement of Sen. Blease.

82. 72 Cong. Rec. S5430, daily ed., March 17, 1930, statement of Sen. Heflin.

83. 72 Cong. Rec. S5494, daily ed., March 18, 1930, statement of Sen. Cutting.

84. 72 Cong. Rec. S5414, daily ed., March 18, 1930; Tariff Act of 1930, 19 U.S.C. § 1305, June 17, 1930.

85. Boyer, *Purity in Print*, 207, ch. 6 and 7.

86. Stein, "Law and Politics," in Romesburg, *Routledge History of Queer America*, 317.

87. Boyer, *Purity in Print*, 224; Taylor, "'I Made Up My Mind,'" 284; "'The Well of Loneliness' Has Been Pronounced Respectable by the United States Customs Court," *Publishers Weekly*, August 10, 1929, 545.

88. Bronson Cutting to Ezra Pound, December 9, 1930, in Walkiewicz and Witemeyer, *Ezra Pound and Senator Bronson Cutting*, 40.

89. While Pound served as editor of *The Little Review*, the US Post Office invoked Article 211 to block the distribution of the October 1917 issue, which contained the controversial story "Cantleman's Spring Mate" by Wyndham Lewis. Pound, then, publicly attacked Article 211 and lobbied to repeal it by authoring letters to various US officials. Walkiewicz and Witemeyer, *Ezra Pound and Senator Bronson Cutting*, 26.

90. By the mid-1930s, Pound embraced conspiracy theories about the economic causation of World War I and became a fascist sympathizer. According to Walkiewicz and Witemeyer, "From mid-1935 on, ugly and irrational statements about President Roosevelt and the Jews began to appear in Pound's public writing. . . . Had Cutting lived beyond May 1935, he would probably have received letters very different in tone." Anti-Semitism does not appear in Pound's correspondence to Cutting. Walkiewicz and Witemeyer, *Ezra Pound and Senator Bronson Cutting*, 4, 232–36.

91. Cline, *Literary Pilgrims*, 110.

92. Ezra Pound, "Small Magazines," *English Journal* 19, no. 9 (1930): 689–704.

93. Mark S. Morrisson, "Ezra Pound, the Morada, and American Regionalism," *Chicago Review* 55, no. 3/4 (2010): 37–45.

94. John E. Semonche, *Censoring Sex: A Historical Journey through American Media* (Lanham, MD: Rowman & Littlefield, 2007), 29; *Publisher's Weekly*, April 2, 1932, 1561.

95. William H. Pickens, "Bronson Cutting vs. Dennis Chavez: Battle of the Patrones in New Mexico, 1934," *New Mexico Historical Review* 46 (January 1971): 20. Jacqueline Kaye also notes that Cutting encountered "formidable" opposition from "Catholic lay societies, the Methodist Episcopal Board of Public Morals, the Lord's Day Alliance, the New York Society for the Suppression of Vice, the American Medical Association and the American Federation of Labor." Jacqueline Kaye, *Ezra Pound and America* (New York: St. Martin's, 1992), 169.

96. "Great Depression and New Deal in New Mexico 1929," *New Mexico History*, November 15, 2103, http://newmexicohistory.org/2013/11/15/great-depression-and-new -deal-in-new-mexico-1929/; Lowitt, *Bronson M. Cutting*, 308–16.

97. Barbara Harrelson, *Walks in Literary Santa Fe: A Guide to Landmarks, Legends, and Lore* (Layton, UT: Gibbs Smith, 2007), 30; Julia Keleher, "Los Paisanos," *New*

Mexico Quarterly 6, no. 1 (1936): 54–55, https://digitalrepository.unm.edu/nmq/vo16 /iss1/18; Lowitt, *Bronson M. Cutting*, 187; La Farge, *Turn Left*, 121.

98. For a general discussion on gay, lesbian, and feminist bookstores, see Bob Summer, "Bookselling as Cultural Politics: Twenty-Five Years after Stonewall, Gay and Lesbian Bookstores Are a Mainstay of the Movement," *Publishers Weekly*, June 27, 1994, 29–31.

99. Spud Johnson to Daniel Clifford McCarthy, n.d., box 4, folder 3, Johnson Collection; Patricia A. Klemans, "Being Born a Woman: Critical Essays on Edna St. Vincent Millay," *Colby Quarterly* 15, no. 1 (1979): 7–18; Edna St. Vincent Millay, *Fatal Interview: Sonnets* (New York: Harper and Brothers, 1931); Robert Godwin-Jones, *Romantic Vision: The Novels of George Sand* (Summa, 1995); Pratima Prasad, "Deceiving Disclosures: Androgyny and George Sand's Gabriel," *French Forum* 24, no. 3 (1999): 331–51; Spud Johnson, diary 3, box 12, folder 3, Johnson Collection.

100. Eve Kosofsky Sedgwick, *Between Men* (New York: Columbia University Press, 1985), 203.

101. John D'Emilio, *Sexual Politics, Sexual Communities: The Making of a Homosexual Minority in the United States, 1940–1970* (Chicago: University of Chicago Press, 1983), 131; Summers, *Gay and Lesbian Literary Heritage*, 33.

102. Perhaps because Riggs had no models for being asegi/two-spirit during his lifetime, he primarily understood himself as a gay man. Thus, I use he/him pronouns.

103. Qwo-Li Driskill, *Asegi Stories: Cherokee Queer and Two-Spirit Memory* (Tucson: University of Arizona Press, 2016), 6, 102, 160; Roscoe, *Changing Ones*, 250–51; Gregory D. Smithers, "Cherokee 'Two Spirits': Gender, Ritual, and Spirituality in the Native South," *Early American Studies* 3 (2014): 626–51.

104. Braunlich, *Haunted by Home*, 24, Riggs quoted on 174.

105. Riggs, "The Arid Land," in Udall, *Spud Johnson and Laughing Horse*, 235.

106. Braunlich, *Haunted by Home*, 13, 145; Betty Kirk Boyer to Dr. Arrell M. Gibson, November 26, 1967, box 5, folder 1, Johnson Collection.

107. Ramón Naya to Lynn Riggs, September 30, 1941, box 4, folder 89, Lynn Riggs Papers, MSS 61, Yale Collection of American Literature, Beinecke Rare Book and Manuscript Library, New Haven. The interracial relationship nature of their relationship, particularly Naya's immigration status, further complicated their bond. See Kayleigh J. T. Harrison, "The Private Life of Lynn Riggs," *Claremore Progress*, June 23, 2020, www.claremoreprogress.com/news/the-private-life-of-lynn-riggs/article _95832190-b589-11ea-a4f5-abgd26935fb5.html.

108. Spud Johnson to Patrick White, n.d., box 4, folder 2, Johnson Papers; Riggs and Braunlich, *Haunted by Home*, 151; Craig S. Womack, *Art as Performance, Story as Criticism: Reflections on Native Literary Aesthetics* (University of Oklahoma Press, 2014), 160.

109. Ramón Naya to Lynn Riggs, May 29, 1939, box 4, folder 89, Lynn Riggs Papers.

110. Womack, *Red on Red*, ch. 8. On October 20, 1930, Riggs wrote to his friend and agent Barrett H. Clark, that he hoped *The Cherokee Night* "will be my best play, it can be" (Riggs, *Haunted by Home*, 95).

111. Phyllis Cole Braunlich, "The Oklahoma Plays of R. Lynn Riggs," *World Literature Today* 64, no. 3 (1990): 392, https://doi.org/10.2307/40146628.

112. Jace Weaver, foreword, in Lynn Riggs, *The Cherokee Night and Other Plays* (Norman: University of Oklahoma Press, 2003), xiii, xviii–xix; Lynn Riggs, *Russet Mantle and the Cherokee Night: Two Plays* (New York: Samuel French, 1936); Riggs, *The Cherokee Night*; Tatonetti, "Emergence and Importance," 143–70; and Jace Weaver, *That the People Might Live: Native American Literatures and Native American Community* (New York: Oxford University Press, 1997) 101–3.

113. Riggs, *The Cherokee Night*, 111.

114. In using the term *mixed-race* I follow the lead of G. Reginald Daniel, "Editor's Note," *Journal of Critical Mixed Race Studies* 1, no. 1 (2014), https://escholarship.org/uc/item/5sg4b35k#page-4.

115. In understanding the Cherokee Nation, I have been most influenced by Tiya Miles's *The House on Diamond Hill: A Cherokee Plantation Story* (Chapel Hill: University of North Carolina Press, 2010); and Tiya Miles, *Ties That Bind: The Story of an Afro-Cherokee Family in Slavery and Freedom* (Berkeley: University of California Press, 2005).

116. Riggs, *Haunted by Home*, 95.

117. Riggs, *The Cherokee Night*, 221–23; Womack, *Red on Red*, 290, 296–300.

118. Daniel Heath Justice, Deborah A. Miranda, and Lisa Tatonetti, "Indigenous Literature with a Queer/LGBT/Two-Spirit Sensibility," https://cpb-us-w2.wpmucdn.com/sites.uwm.edu/dist/f/241/files/2016/11/Queer-LGBT-Two-Spirit-Bib-1agod1i.pdf; Driskill et al., *Sovereign Erotics*, 7.

THREE Land of Entrapment

1. "Biographical Documents," box 1, folder 2, Morris Kight Papers and Photographs, Co112010.008, ONE National Gay and Lesbian Archives, Los Angeles; "Interview with Morris Kight," in *Growing Up before Stonewall: Life Stories of Some Gay Men*, ed. Peter M. Nardi, David Sanders, and Judd Marmor, 15 (New York: Routledge, 1994).

2. Lillian Faderman, *The Gay Revolution: The Story of the Struggle* (New York: Simon and Schuster, 2016), 31.

3. Mary Ann Cherry, *Morris Kight: Humanist, Liberationist, Fantabulist* (self-published, 2020), 38, 40. Thanks to Mary Ann Cherry, who shared her research on Kight's time in New Mexico.

4. Kathlene Ferris, "Sophie D. Aberle and the United Pueblos Agency, 1935–1944"

(master's thesis, University of New Mexico, 2014), 11–12, https://digitalrepository.unm.edu/hist_etds/29.

5. Kight quoted in Cherry, *Morris Kight*, 40.

6. S. D. Aberle to Commissioner of Indian Affairs, September 11, 1941, in possession of author.

7. "Miss Peters, Morris Kight Wed at St. John's Cathedral," *Albuquerque Journal*, December 19, 1950; Cherry, *Morris Kight*, 48.

8. Traugott, *Art of New Mexico*, 150–51; All Albuquerque Artists Exhibition Catalog, June 1–July 5, 1951, in possession of author; "Can Albuquerque Be an Art Center?," *Albuquerque Journal*, May 1950; "Art News," *Albuquerque Journal*, April 15, 1951; "Art Winners to be Honored, *Albuquerque Journal*, December 14, 1951; and "Art League Elects Slate Head by Kight," *Albuquerque Tribune*, June 3, 1952.

9. Cherry, *Morris Kight*, 49; Nardi et al., *Growing up before Stonewall*, 19–20.

10. Nardi et al., *Growing up before Stonewall*, 17–18; Daniel L. Evans, "All Is Not Dead Here in the Desert: The Development of Albuquerque's Organized Gay Community, 1971–1991" (master's thesis, University of New Mexico, 1992), 14; Tom Barry, "Gay Bars, Gay People," *Seer's Catalogue*, August 8–22, 1975, 15; Cherry, *Morris Kight*, 50; and Linda Rapp, "Morris Kight (1919–2003)," *GLBT: An Encyclopedia of Gay, Lesbian, Bisexual, Transgender, and Queer Culture*, archived on October 24, 2014, https://web.archive.org/web/20141024110242/http://www.glbtq.com/social-sciences/kight_m.html.

11. Cherry, *Morris Kight*, 61–69.

12. "Fire Destroys Old San Felipe Hotel and Kight Family Museum," *Albuquerque Journal*, September 18, 1956. For further discussion of why Los Angeles attracted queer people, see C. Todd White, *Pre-Gay L.A.: A Social History of the Movement for Homosexual Rights* (Urbana: University of Illinois Press, 2009), 1–10.

13. The Manhattan Project was formally known as the Manhattan Engineer District and postwar was referred to in the press as "the best-kept secret." See "Atomic Bomb Held 'Best-Kept Secret,'" *New York Times*, August 9, 1945, http://blog.nuclear secrecy.com/wp-content/uploads/2013/03/1945-NYT-Best-Kept-Secret.jpg; Frenec Morton Szasz, *The Day the Sun Rose Twice: The Story of the Trinity Site Nuclear Explosion, July 16, 1945* (Albuquerque: University of New Mexico Press, 1984), ch. 1.

14. I agree with Sissela Bok's differentiation between secrecy and privacy, even though they overlap. See Sissela Bok, *Secret: On the Ethics of Concealment and Revelation* (New York: Pantheon, 1982), 10.

15. For a discussion of the closet, see Margot Canaday, *The Straight State: Sexuality and Citizenship in Twentieth-Century America* (Princeton, NJ: Princeton University Press, 2011), 169–73, 256; William N. Eskridge, *Gaylaw: Challenging the Apartheid of the Closet* (Cambridge, MA: Harvard University Press, 1999), quote from 7; and Eve

Kosofsky Sedgwick, *Epistemology of the Closet* (Berkeley: University of California Press, 1990).

16. I rely on Inderpal Grewal and Caren Kaplan's definition of "state," in *An Introduction to Women's Studies: Gender in a Transnational World* (Boston: McGraw-Hill, 2006), 151.

17. Margot Canaday, "Heterosexuality as a Legal Regime," in *The Cambridge History of Law in America*, vol. 3, ed. Michael Grossberg and Christopher Tomlins, 442–71 (New York: Cambridge University Press, 2008); and Jonathan Katz, *The Invention of Heterosexuality* (University of Chicago Press, 2007). I use the term *homosexual* to replicate the vocabulary of pre- and postwar American life. I do not wish to impose the present onto the past by replacing *homosexual* with *queer*. However, I do alternate between *homosexual*, *gay*, *lesbian*, and *queer*, paying attention to how individuals self-identified and to broaden the discussion of sexual identity.

18. Canaday further examines three "arenas where the meaning of American citizenship was most sharply articulated": immigration, the military, and welfare. See Canaday, *The Straight State*, 3.

19. Harold P. Green, "Q-Clearance: The Development of Personnel Security Program," *Bulletin of Atomic Scientists* 20, no. 5 (May 1964): 14.

20. See Anna Lvovsky, "Cruising in Plain View: Clandestine Surveillance and the Unique Insights of Antihomosexual Policing," *Journal of Urban History* 46, no. 5 (September 1, 2020): 980–1001, https://doi.org/10.1177/0096144217705495.

21. See, for example, Allan Bérubé, *Coming Out Under Fire: The History of Gay Men and Women in World War Two* (New York: Free Press, 1990).

22. On the rise of the homophile movement, see D'Emilio, *Sexual Politics, Sexual Communities;* Faderman, *The Gay Revolution*, part 2; Marcia M. Gallo, *Different Daughters: A History of the Daughters of Bilitis and the Rise of the Lesbian Rights Movement* (New York: Carroll & Graf, 2006); and Eric Marcus, *Making Gay History: The Half Century Fight for Lesbian and Gay Equal Rights* (New York: Harper Perennial, 2002), part 2.

23. Thomas Jacob Noel, "Gay Bars and the Emergence of the Denver Homosexual Community," *Social Science Journal* 15, no, 2 (April 1978), 59–74; Amanda H. Littauer, "Sexual Minorities at the Apex of Heteronormativity (1940s–1965)," in Romesburg, *Routledge History of Queer America*, 67–81.

24. When referring to how queer people navigated their concealment of sexual identity, I use the metaphor of "the mask" following the lead of historian Craig Loftin. Craig M. Loftin, *Masked Voices: Gay Men and Lesbians in Cold War America* (Albany: State University of New York Press, 2012), 10–11.

25. John M. Findlay and Bruce William Hevly, eds., *The Atomic West* (Seattle: Center for the Study of the Pacific Northwest, 1998).

26. Joseph P. Masco, *Nuclear Borderlands: The Legacy of the Manhattan Project in Post-Cold War New Mexico* (Princeton, NJ: Princeton University Press: 1999), 36; Barron

Oder, "From Western Frontier to the Space Frontier: The Military in New Mexico, 1900–1940," in DeMark, *Essays in Twentieth-Century New Mexico History*, 110–14.

27. Sigurd Johansen, "Changes in the Distribution of New Mexico's Population Between 1930 and 1970," Agricultural Experiment Station Research Report 222 (Las Cruces: New Mexico State University, 1972); US Census Bureau, *Census of Population*, 1950 (Washington, DC: US Department of Commerce, 1952); US Census Bureau, *Census of Population*, 1960 (Washington, DC: US Department of Commerce, 1963).

28. Johansen, "Changes in the Distribution," 3, table 1.

29. Lizabeth Cohen, *A Consumers' Republic: The Politics of Mass Consumption in Postwar America* (New York: Vintage, 2004), 137–43, 156–60, 166–70.

30. Peter Bacon Hales, *Atomic Spaces: Living on the Manhattan Project* (Urbana: University of Illinois Press, 1999), 1.

31. Jon Hunner, *J. Robert Oppenheimer, the Cold War, and the Atomic West* (Norman: University of Oklahoma Press, 2009), 115.

32. Herman Agoyo, "Who Here Will Begin This Story?," *Race, Poverty & the Environment* 5, no. 3/4 (1995): 37–38; Lucie Genay, *Land of Nuclear Enchantment: A New Mexican History of the Nuclear Weapons Industry* (Albuquerque: University of New Mexico Press, 2019); Masco, *Nuclear Borderlands*, ch. 3; María E. Montoya, "Dennis Chavez and the Making of Modern New Mexico," in *Telling New Mexico: A New History*, ed. Marta Weigle, Frances Levine, and Louise Stiver (Albuquerque: University of New Mexico Press, 2009); and Barbara Rose Johnston, Susan Dawson, and Gary Madsen, "Uranium Mining and Milling: Navajo Experience in the American Southwest," in *Indians and Energy: Exploitation and Opportunity in the American Southwest*, ed. Sherry L. Smith and Brian Frehner, 116 (Santa Fe: School for Advanced Research Press, 2010).

33. Burke, *A Land Apart*, 252.

34. Army of the United States, Certificate of Service, Claude R. Schwob, Private First Class, Company C, October 21, 1943, box 2, folder 6, Claude R. Schwob Papers, GLBT Historical Society, San Francisco, California (hereafter Schwob Papers); W. A. Noyes, Chairman, National Defense Research Committee, to Claude Schwob February 13, 1942, box 1, folder 16, Schwob Papers.

35. Burke, *A Land Apart*, 254.

36. Ruth H. Howes and Caroline L. Herzenburg, *Their Day in the Sun: Women and the Manhattan Project* (Philadelphia: Temple University Press, 1999), 13–14.

37. While Pueblo women economically benefited from these jobs, the work also depleted "Pueblo communities of needed leaders and active participants in communal work." See Burke, *A Land Apart*, 231, 253, 261; and Lucie Genay, "The Devil's Bargain: The Effects of Nuclear Revolution of New Mexican Culture of Work," *American Studies in Scandinavia* 46, no. 1 (2014), 77.

38. Burke, *A Land Apart*, 232; Hunner, *J. Robert Oppenheimer*, 94.

39. M. Michaela Hampf, "'Dykes' or 'Whores': Sexuality and the Women's Army Corps in the United States during World War I," *Women's Studies International* 27, no. 1 (January–February 2004): 13–30. While researching the Atomic Energy Commission records, I came across a case file on an investigation of eight lesbians employed by the AEC, five at Los Alamos and three at the Hanford site in Washington. The documents do not name the women; I created pseudonyms that correlate with their alphabetical case file.

40. Canaday, *The Straight State*, 181; Leisa D. Meyer, "The Myth of Lesbian (In) visibility: World War II and the Current Gays in the Military Debate," in *Modern American Queer History*, ed. Allida M. Black, 272 (Philadelphia: Temple University Press, 2001).

41. Bob Porton, interview by Theresa Strottman, January 11, 1992, transcript, Oral History: Manhattan Project Voices, Los Alamos, https://www.manhattanproject voices.org/oral-histories/bob-portons-interview.

42. Department of Energy, *Manhattan District History*, Book 7, Los Alamos Project, vol. 1 (Washington, DC: US Government Printing Office, 1947), 6.49; Wilson quoted in Burke, *A Land Apart*, 233.

43. Intelligence banned the name Los Alamos, which was never mentioned on birth certificates, drivers' licenses, or postal mail. Most residents called it "the Hill." Official documents listed the location as Box 1663, Sandoval County, Rural.

44. Henry Jack Tobias and Charles E. Woodhouse, *Santa Fe: A Modern History, 1880–1990* (Albuquerque: University of New Mexico Press, 2001), 143; Nancy Cook Steeper, *Gatekeeper to Los Alamos: Dorothy Scarritt McKibbin* (Los Alamos: Los Alamos Historical Society, 2003), 75; Eleanor Roensch, interview by Theresa Strottman, March 21, 1992, transcript, Oral History: Manhattan Project Voices, Los Alamos, https://www.manhattanprojectvoices.org/oral-histories/eleanor-roenschs-interview.

45. "Los Alamos, NM," Atomic Heritage Foundation, accessed March 8, 2015, http://www.atomicheritage.org/location/los-alamos-nm.

46. Job Application for the Naval Radiological Defense Lab and supplemental section, box 2, folder 9, Schwob Papers.

47. Dr. J. Robert Oppenheimer to Dr. Claude R. Schwob, October 1, 1945, box 2, folder 9, Schwob Papers; William Harmon, Special Order 90, April 14, 1945, box 2, folder 7, Schwob Papers.

48. Although most of the letters are undated, an address on a postcard that Greene sent to Schwob reveals that the two corresponded when Schwob worked at Los Alamos. Postcard and other undated letters to Claude Schwob from Carl Greene, undated, box 1, folder 7, Schwob Papers.

49. Bérubé, *Coming Out Under Fire*, 121. Historians are just beginning to uncover queer life in mainstream Cold War spaces. For an example, see Nicholas Syrett, "A Busman's Holiday in the Not-So-Lonely-Crowd: Business Culture, Epistolary Net-

works, and Itinerant Homosexuality in Mid-Twentieth Century America," *Journal of the History of Sexuality* 21 (January 2012): 121–40.

50. "Noteworthy NRDLERS," Naval Radiological Defense Lab Newsletter, 1950s, box 2, folder 11, Schwob Papers; draft of supplemental section to Job Application for the Naval Radiological Defense Lab, 18, box 2, folder 9, Schwob Papers.

51. Model release forms, box 1, folder 29, Schwob Papers.

52. Emmanuel Cooper, *The Sexual Perspective: Homosexuality and Art in the Last 100 Years in the West* (New York: Routledge, 2005), 233–34.

53. Claude Schwob, 1955, black and white photograph, box 3, folder 12, Schwob Papers; Claude Schwob, *Model B*, circa 1940s, black and white photographs, box 3, folder 24, Schwob Papers.

54. Exactly how Schwob shared his erotic photography collection with other gay men is unclear. One clue arises from an undated letter to a man named Tom, who wanted copies of Schwob's erotica. In his reply, Schwob admitted that the FBI had recently ransacked his erotica, at this time both film and photographs. He was still able to send Tom "surviving fragments" from his "criminal life." Claude Schwob to Tom, n.d., box 1, folder 3, Schwob Papers.

55. David K. Johnson, *Buying Gay: How Physique Entrepreneurs Sparked a Movement* (New York: Columbia University Press, 2019).

56. Beginning in the late nineteenth century, photography of the male nude was a feature of gay culture. By the 1920s, nude photos were widely marketed in the back of both art and physical culture magazines. In the post–World War II era, such images became a visible part of American culture through a commercial network of physique magazines. See Jason Goldman, "The Golden Age of Gay Porn," *GLQ* 12, no. 2 (2006): 237–58; Johnson, *Buying Gay*; and Thomas Waugh, *Hard to Imagine: Gay Male Eroticism in Photography and Film from Their Beginnings to Stonewall* (New York: Columbia University Press, 1996).

57. Steward quoted in Justin Spring, *Secret Historian: The Life and Times of Samuel Steward, Professor, Tattoo Artist, and Sexual Renegade* (New York: Farrar, Straus and Giroux, 2010), 85; Johnson, *Buying Gay*, 4.

58. Supplemental section to Job Application for the Naval Radiological Defense Lab, 14, box 2, folder 9, Schwob Papers; White Sands Missile Range Public Affairs Office, *Trinity Site, 1945–1995* (Washington, DC: Department of the Army, 1995).

59. The Manhattan District's estimated figure fails to account an additional sixty thousand delayed civilian casualties. "The Atomic Bombings of Hiroshima and Nagasaki: Total Casualties," Avalon Project, Yale Law School, Lillian Goldman Law Library, https://avalon.law.yale.edu/20th_century/mp10.asp.

60. Harry S. Truman, "Statement by the President of the United States," in "Primary Resource: Announcing the Bombing of Hiroshima," PBS, accessed August 27, 2014, http://www.pbs.org/wgbh/americanexperience/features/primary-resources

/truman-hiroshima/; "Los Alamos Secret Disclosed by Truman: Deadliest Weapons in World's History Made in Santa Fe Vicinity," *Santa Fe New Mexican*, August 6, 1945.

61. Supplemental section to Job Application for the Naval Radiological Defense Lab, 15, box 2, folder 9, Schwob Papers. See, for example, Claude R. Schwob and Raymond Nether, "A Monitoring Probe for Radiochemistry Laboratories," *Science* 106, no. 2753 (October 1947): 327.

62. Jon Hunner, *Inventing Los Alamos: The Growth of an Atomic Community* (Norman: University of Oklahoma Press, 2004), 126.

63. Only part of Sandia Base, its Z Division, was under AEC control. Hunner, *Inventing Los Alamos*, 125.

64. Chair, AEC Commission, Gordon Dean, to Director, Bureau of the Budget, Joseph M. Dodge, March 16, 1953, "Security and Intelligence-Investigation and Clearance," file 4-1, box 148, records of the Atomic Energy Commission, RG 326, National Archives and Records Administration College Park, Maryland (hereafter AEC Records); Atomic Energy Commission, "Report on Establishment of Standards and Specifications as to the Scope of Investigations," January 10, 1955, 2–3, box 148, file 4-1, AEC Records; Atomic Energy Act of 1946, Public Law 585, 79th Congress; William Henderson, "A Brief History of the U.S. Personnel Security Program," *Defense News*, June 29, 2009, http://news.clearancejobs.com/2009/06/29/a-brief-history-of-the-u-s-personnel-security-program/.

65. Report to the General Manager by the Director of Security on the appointment of an ad hoc committee to review AEC personnel clearance criteria and procedures, August 23, 1955, p. 22, box 148, file 4-1, AEC Records; Atomic Energy Commission, "Report on Establishment of Standards and Specifications," 2–3; Sandia National Laboratories, "The Origin of 'Q' and 'L' Clearances," accessed November 5, 2014, http://www.sandia.gov/fso/fso_conferences/2011_FSO_Conference/2011_FSO_OriginQandL.pdf. A P clearance was for employees who had no contact with nuclear information while an S clearance was for those who would visit AEC facilities but did not have access to restricted data. Later, in 1955, the classifications narrowed to two categories, L and Q.

66. "In the Matter of J. Robert Oppenheimer: Transcript of Hearing before Personnel Security Board, Washington, D.C., April 12, 1954, Through May 6, 1954," Avalon Project, Yale Law School, Lillian Goldman Law Library, http://avalon.law.yale.edu/20th_century/opp01.asp. In 1946 US Army Counter Intelligence Corps Major Bud Uanna established the criteria for the Q-clearance with thirteen levels of access, or "sigmas." See Masco, *Nuclear Borderlands*, 268; and "End of the Universal 'Q'–'L' Clearances Coming Soon for Many Sandians," *Lab News*, April 30, 1993, 1, 5.

67. Report to the General Manager, 29.

68. Harold Green, "The Unsystematic Security System," *Bulletin of Atomic Scientists* 11, no. 4 (April 1955): 122.

69. Executive Order 10450, "Security Requirements for Government Employment," *Federal Register*, April 27, 1953, 2489; E. Carrington Boggan, Marilyn G. Haft, Charles Lister, and John P. Rupp, *The Rights of Gay People: The Basic American Civil Liberties Union Guide to a Gay Person's Rights* (New York: Avon, 1975), 64; David K. Johnson, *The Lavender Scare: The Cold War Persecution of Gays and Lesbians in the Federal Government* (Chicago: University of Chicago Press, 2006), 129.

70. William P. Rogers to William Mitchell, June 8, 1953, box 149, file 4-1, AEC Records.

71. Chair, AEC Commission, Gordon Dean, to Sterling Cole, Chair, Advisory Committee to the Atomic Energy Commission, June 8, 1953, file 4-1, box 148, AEC Records.

72. Atomic Energy Commission, "JCAE Inquiry Relative to Certain Individual 'Q' Clearances," June 11, 1953, box 148, file 4-1, AEC Records.

73. Johnson, *The Lavender Scare*, 131; Canaday, *The Straight State*, 177; Robert Byron Genter, "'An Unusual and Peculiar Relationship': Lesbianism and the American Cold War National Security State," *Journal of the History of Sexuality* 28, no. 2 (May 2019): 250.

74. Case G is outlined in Atomic Energy Commission, "JCAE Inquiry," 4–5.

75. Atomic Energy Commission, "JCAE Inquiry."

76. Atomic Energy Commission, minutes, meeting 453, August 10, 1950, box 148, file 4-1, AEC Records.

77. "History," Eastman Chemical Company, accessed December 17, 2020, https://www.eastman.com/Company/About_Eastman/History/Pages/Introduction.aspx; Charles W. Johnson and Charles O. Jackson, *City behind a Fence: Oak Ridge, Tennessee, 1942–1946* (Knoxville: University of Tennessee Press, 1986), 148.

78. The other was a polygraph test, but polygraphs were only used briefly by the AEC at the Tennessee site. Johnson, *The Lavender Scare*, 128; Memorandum, "Use of the Polygraph on Individuals Having Continuous Physical Access to Nuclear Storage Facilities," July 19, 1951, box 148, file 4-1, AEC Records.

79. Atomic Energy Commission, "JCAE Inquiry."

80. Atomic Energy Commission, "Re-Evaluation of Personnel Security Files," December 31, 1953, box 148, file 4-1, AEC Records.

81. Atomic Energy Commission, minutes, meeting 840, March 20, 1953, box 148, file 4-1, AEC Records.

82. These figures are from David Johnson, who cautions that "the total number of men and women affected by the anti-homosexual purge is incalculable" (Johnson, *The Lavender Scare*, 166).

83. Ralph S. Brown, *Loyalty and Security Employment Tests in the United States* (New

Haven: Yale University Press, 1958), 181–82, appendix A; Green, "Q-Clearance," 9–14.

84. *Bulletin of Atomic Scientists* 11, no. 4 (April 1955).

85. Hans J. Morgenthau, "The Impact of the Loyalty-Security Measures on the State Department," *Bulletin of Atomic Scientists* 11, no. 4 (April 1955): 136.

86. Raymond Aron, "Realism and Common Sense in Security Policy," *Bulletin of Atomic Scientists* 11, no. 4 (April 1955): 111–12.

87. J. G. Beckerley, "The Impact of Government Information and Security Controls on Competitive Industry," *Bulletin of Atomic Scientists* 11, no. 4 (April 1955): 123.

88. John G. Palfrey, "The AEC Security Program: Past and Present," *Bulletin of Atomic Scientists* 11, no. 4 (April 1955): 131.

89. In terms of employment discrimination for queer people, it is important to note the activism of Dr. Franklin E. Kameny. After being fired from his federal government job in 1957, Kameny fought an eighteen-year battle to overturn the exclusion of homosexuals from federal employment. "Dr. Franklin E. Kameny," National Park Service, August 9, 2018, https://www.nps.gov/places/kameny-residence.htm.

90. Johnson, *The Lavender Scare*, 149.

91. Evans, "All Is Not Dead Here," 14.

92. Green, "Q-Clearance," 10–11.

93. For theorizing issues of social control, see Michel Foucault, *Discipline and Punish: The Birth of the Prison* (New York: Vintage, 1977); and Dany Lacombe, "Reforming Foucault: A Critique of the Social Control Thesis," *British Journal of Sociology* 47 (June 1996): 332–52.

94. Alan Stringer, "Gay Community Leader Regains Security Clearance," *Common Bond Ink*, June 1986.

95. Most federal agencies denied security clearances for gay men and lesbians until the 1980s. In August of 1995, President Clinton issued Executive Order 12968, which stated that the federal government may not discriminate on the basis of sexual orientation in access to classified information.

96. Terri quoted in Jack Kutz, *Grassroots New Mexico: A History of Citizen Activism* (Albuquerque: Inter-Hemispheric Education Resource Center, 1989), 110.

97. In 1949 the Atomic Energy Commission negotiated a contract with Western Electric Company to operate Sandia lab as a private corporation. See Roger Walker, "War-Oriented Facilities," in *Victory in World War II: The New Mexico Story*, ed. Monroe L. Billington, Gerald W. Thomas, and Roger D. Walker (Las Cruces: New Mexico State University, 1994), 138–41.

98. Vangie Chavez, interview by author, September 4, 2013, audio recording, box 1, folder 2, Hammer Collection.

99. Chavez interview.

100. Gray quoted in Kutz, *Grassroots New Mexico*, 112.

101. Morris Kight and Eric Marcus, "Morris Kight," *Making Gay History* (podcast), December 7, 2017, https://makinggayhistory.com/podcast/morris-kight/; and White, *Pre-Gay L.A.*, 193–95.

102. Rudnick, *Cady Wells and Southwest Modernism*, 55–56, 69, 75; Wells quoted in Daniel Lang, *From Hiroshima to the Moon: Chronicles of Life in the Atomic Age* (New York: Simon and Schuster, 1959), 141.

103. Earl Ganz, "Myron Brining," LGBT encyclopedia, accessed January 16, 2015, http://glbtq.com/literature/brinig; Strong, "Hometown Revisited."

104. Because Gorman, like Riggs, grew up during a time when it was difficult to express two-spirit identity but professed such a strong identification with the women subjects in his art, I have chosen to refer to him by he/him and they/them pronouns.

105. Weston, "Get Thee to a Big City," 255.

106. I borrow the term "Native hubs" from Renya K. Ramirez, *Native Hubs: Culture, Community, and Belonging in Silicon Valley and Beyond* (Durham, NC: Duke University Press, 2007). R. C. Gorman, *The Radiance of My People* (Houston: Santa Fe Fine Arts, 1992), 12.

107. Navy Discharge Papers, April 15, 1955, box 3, folder 9, Virginia S. Dooley Papers from Her Personal Life and Business Relationship with R.C. Gorman, 1916–2008, MSS 844 BC, Center for Southwest Research, University Libraries, University of New Mexico (hereafter Dooley Papers).

108. Michael Davidson, *The San Francisco Renaissance: Poetics and Community at Mid-Century* (New York: Cambridge University Press, 1989), xi–xii.

109. I offer a longer discussion in Jordan Biro Walters, "'So Let Me Paint': Navajo Artist R. C. Gorman and the Artistic, Native, and Queer Subcultures of San Francisco, California," *Pacific Historical Review* 88, no. 3 (2019): 439–67.

110. "The Coffee Gallery Presents Oils by Navajo Artist R.C. Gorman," December 1–31, 1959, box 3, folder 17, Dooley Papers.

111. Rose Delia Soza War Soldier, "'To Take Positive and Effective Action': Rupert Costo and the California Based American Indian Historical Society" (PhD diss., Arizona State University, 2013), ii, 117.

112. "Indian Society," *San Francisco Chronicle*, June 21, 1967, 48; "Indian art on display," July 26, 1967, in scrapbook, box 5, folder 16, Dooley Papers. On Carl N. Gorman's life, see Henry Greenberg and Georgia Greenberg, *Power of a Navajo: Carl Gorman, The Man and His Life* (Santa Fe: Clear Light, 1996).

113. R. C. Gorman to Carl Gorman, n.d., personal collection of Zonnie Gorman (half-sister of R. C. Gorman).

114. For a history of the Castro, see Josh Sides, *Erotic City: Sexual Revolutions and the Making of Modern San Francisco* (New York: Oxford University Press, 2009), 83–122.

115. See correspondence between R. C. Gorman and John Manchester, 1965–67,

box 10, folder 12, Dorothy Brett Papers, MSS494 BC, Center for Southwest Research, University Libraries, University of New Mexico.

116. On queer people of color creating alternative paths to queer identity, see Martin F. Manalansan, *Global Divas: Filipino Gay Men in the Diaspora* (Durham, NC: Duke University Press, 2003).

117. R. C. Gorman to John Manchester, February 18, 1965, box 10, folder 12, Brett Papers.

118. *Masterworks from the Museum of the American Indian, Heye Foundation* (New York: Metropolitan Museum of Art, 1973), front and back covers and 59; Denita M. Benyshek, "R. C. Gorman: The Picasso of American Indian Artists," *Collectors Mart*, September/October 1984, 46–53; Clyde Haberman, "Show by 'the Picasso of American Indian Artists' Opens," *New York Times*, May 4, 1979; Jamie Simon, "The Work of R. C. Gorman, the Picasso of American Indian Art," *Smithsonian Magazine*, January 25, 2011, http://www.smithsonianmag.com/smithsonian-institution/the-work-of-rc-gorman-the-picasso-of-american-indian-art-4736433/.

119. To be fair, Gorman and his father harbored lingering hurt feelings in addition to R. C. Gorman's disclosure of his homosexuality. For example, when Carl enlisted in World War II, R. C. resented his father's absence and the burdens he endured while his father was away, mainly raising his younger brothers and sisters. Zonnie Gorman in discussion with author, March 2010, and email correspondence, July 15, 2016.

120. Native scholar Jennifer Nez Denetdale (Diné/Navajo) has discussed how some Navajo youth left the Navajo Nation for urban areas to find queer community because of the backlash against non-heterosexual Navajos. Jennifer Denetdale, "Carving Navajo National Boundaries: Patriotism, Tradition, and the Diné Marriage Act of 2005," *American Quarterly* 60, no. 2 (2008): 289–94, https://doi.org/10.1353/aq.0.0007.

121. In understanding how the imposition of a modern state formation has reconfigured gender and sexuality structures and replicated American gender roles in the Navajo Nation, I consulted Jennifer Nez Denetdale, "Chairmen, Presidents, and Princesses: The Navajo Nation, Gender, and the Politics of Tradition," *Wičazo Ša Review* 21, no. 1 (2006): 9–28; Will Roscoe, "Gay American Indians Creating Identity from Past Traditions," *The Advocate*, October 29, 1985, 46, carton 1, folder 28, Roscoe Papers; and Charley Shiveley and Clover Chango, "Maurice Kenny: Gay Native American Poet," *Gay Community News* 7, no. 47 (June 21, 1980).

122. R. C. Gorman to Carl Gorman, n.d., private collection of Zonnie Gorman.

123. Martin Meeker, *Contacts Desired: Gay and Lesbian Communications and Community, 1940s–1970s* (Chicago: University of Chicago Press, 2006), 2–3.

FOUR "What to Do about Homosexuals?"

1. Agnes Martin identified as a woman and lesbian until 1967, then rejected the label "woman" and embraced an asexual existence. I use both she/her and they/them pronouns to identify Martin.

2. Katz, *Hide/Seek*, 45n95; Agnes Martin, *Nude*, 1947, oil on canvas, Harwood Museum of Art, University of New Mexico, Taos, https://harwood.emuseum.com /objects/3392/nude.

3. Nancy Princenthal, *Agnes Martin: Her Life and Art* (New York: Thames & Hudson, 2015), 55. Biographer Henry Martin agrees with Princenthal's assessment. Henry Martin, *Agnes Martin: Pioneer, Painter, Icon* (Tucson: Schaffner, 2018), 61. I also reached out to the Harwood Museum of Art, where the painting is housed. Curator Nichole Dial-Kay conveyed that the woman in the painting is unknown but "thought to be one of her [Agnes Martin's] fellow students at the time." Shemai Rodriquez, Marketing and Engagement Manager, Harwood Museum of Art, email message to author, January 10, 2022.

4. Jonathan D. Katz, "Agnes Martin and the Sexuality of Abstraction," in *Agnes Martin*, ed. Lynne Cooke, Karen J Kelly, and Barbara Schröder (New York: Dia Art Foundation, 2014), 97.

5. Martin quoted in Joan Simon, "Perfection Is in the Mind: An Interview with Agnes Martin," August 21, 1995, https://users.wfu.edu/~laugh/painting2/martin .pdf; "Agnes Martin Speaks about Emotion and Art," Solomon R. Guggenheim Museum, November 2016, https://soundcloud.com/guggenheimmuseum/agnes-martin -speaks-about-emotion-and-art.

6. Burke, *A Land Apart*, 269; Cooper, *Unbuttoned*, 96; Julie L. Belcove, "The Age of Agnes," *W* 32, no. 7 (July 2003), 99; Linda M. Grasso, *Equal under the Sky: Georgia O'Keeffe and Twentieth-Century Feminism* (Albuquerque: University of New Mexico Press, 2017), 1; "Janet Lippincott," Peyton Wright Gallery, Santa Fe, July 2007, https:// peytonwright.com/wp-content/uploads/2007/07/Bio-Lippincott-Janet-updated.pdf.

7. D. A. Miller, *The Novel and the Police* (Berkeley: University of California Press, 1988), 205–7.

8. There were exceptions. In the late 1950s and early 1960s, visibly queer pop artist Andy Warhol and poet Allen Ginsberg both succeeded in the arts as open homosexuals. However, their whiteness and residences in the queer mecca of New York City certainly played a role in their ability to be out. See Jonathan D. Katz, "Naked Politics: The Art of Eros 1955–1975," in *Queer Difficulty in Art and Poetry: Rethinking the Sexed Body in Verse and Visual Culture*, eds., Jongwoo Jeremy Kim and Christopher Reed (New York: Routledge, 2017), 74–86; and Kenneth Silver, "Modes of Disclosure: The Construction of Gay Identity and the Rise of Pop Art," in *Hand-Painted Pop: American Art in Transition, 1955–62*, ed. Paul Schimmel, David Deitcher, Donna M. De Salvo, and Russell Ferguson (Los Angeles: Museum of Contemporary Art), 179–204.

9. Concerns about gay people in the art world is sometimes referred to as *homoint-ern*—an international conspiracy about the alarming number of gay men in the arts. For the cultural evolution of the concept, see Butt, *Between You and Me*, 40–44, 46–49.

10. Butt, *Between You and Me*; Katz, *Hide/Seek*; Michael S. Sherry, *Gay Artists in Modern American Culture: An Imagined Conspiracy* (Chapel Hill: University of North Carolina Press, 2007), quote on 105; Silver, "Modes of Disclosure," 179–204.

11. Geneva Chávez professionally used the name Genoveva Chávez; I refer to her by her professional name. "Native Santa Fean Featured Vocalist with Mariachis at Santa Fe Fiesta," newspaper clipping, n.d., in Genoveva Chávez, vertical file, Fray Angélico Chávez History Library, New Mexico History Museum, Santa Fe (hereafter Chávez vertical file).

12. For a history of the Model Penal Code and sex laws, see William N. Eskridge, *Dishonorable Passions: Sodomy Laws in America, 1861–2003* (New York: Penguin, 2008), 118–27, 136–65, 176–84; and Wheeler, *How Sex Became a Civil Liberty*, 104–19.

13. *House Journal*, 25th sess., January 30, 1961, 5.

14. *New Mexico Laws of 1955*, ch. 78, §3, enacted March 4, 1955; *New Mexico Laws of 1963*, 303 § 29-3C, enacted March 25, 1963.

15. George Chauncey, "'What Gay Studies Taught the Court': The Historians' Amicus Brief in Lawrence v. Texas," *GLQ* 10, no. 3 (2004): 509–38.

16. Dale Carpenter, *Flagrant Conduct: The Story of Lawrence v. Texas* (New York: W. W. Norton, 2012), 6. Eskridge, *Dishonorable Passions*, 75, 86–87. For a longer history of sodomy in the state, see Brown, "'Abominable Sin' in Colonial New Mexico," 51–80; and George Painter, "New Mexico," History of Sodomy Laws in the United States, August 11, 2004, http://www.glapn.org/sodomylaws/sensibilities/new_mexico.htm. Case law on sodomy in New Mexico is scarce. Before the repeal of sodomy in New Mexico (1975), the state supreme court ruled on eight cases. I conducted a search on sodomy cases on the LexisNexis Legal Database, accessed August 2013.

17. The territorial legislature of New Mexico passed its first sodomy law in 1876, invoking the common-law definition of the crime. *The General Laws of New Mexico: Including All the Unrepealed General Laws from the Promulgation of the "Kearney Code" in 1846, to the End of the Legislative Session of 1880* (Albany: W.C. Little, 1880), 320.

18. *Bennett et al. v. Abram*, 57 N.M. 28; 253 P.2d 316 (1953), https://law.justia.com/cases/new-mexico/supreme-court/1953/5594-0.html; and US Army, *Manual for Courts-Martial* (Washington, DC: Government Printing Office, 1948), 244, https://www.loc.gov/rr/frd/Military_Law/pdf/manual-1949.pdf; *New Mexico Laws of 1955*, ch. 78, §3, enacted March 4, 1955.

19. For a critique of Kinsey's methodology, mainly his use of white and middle-class interviewees, see Janice M. Irvine, "Toward a 'Value-Free' Science of Sex," in *Sexualities in History*, ed. Kim M. Phillips and Barry Reay (New York: Routledge, 2001), 327–58.

20. Alfred C. Kinsey, Wardell B. Pomeroy, Martin E. Clyde, and Paul H. Gebhard, eds., *Sexual Behavior in the Human Female* (Philadelphia: Saunders, 1953), 20.

21. Jeffrey Escoffier, *American Homo: Community and Perversity* (Berkeley: University of California Press, 1998), 38–44.

22. Wheeler, *How Sex Became a Civil Liberty*, 108.

23. "American Law Institute Completes Ten-Year Study of Criminal Law in U.S.," *Mattachine Review*, June 1962, 9–10; and American Law Institute, *Model Penal Code: Proposed Official Draft Submitted by the Council to the Members for Discussion at the Thirty-Ninth Annual Meeting on May 23, 24, 25 and 26, 1962* (Philadelphia, 1962).

24. . Eskridge, *Dishonorable Passions*, 124, 144.

25. Henry Weihofen, "The Proposed New Mexico Criminal Code," *Natural Resources Journal* 1 (March 1961): 123.

26. New Mexico Criminal Law Study Committee, "Report of the Criminal Law Study Interim Committee," 1961–62, New Mexico Legislative Council Service Records 1971-005, box 724, folder 13, State Records Center and Archives, New Mexico Commission of Public Records (hereafter NMLCS Records).

27. Criminal Law Study Research Materials, New Mexico Legislative Council Service, August 23, 1957, box 724, folder 7, NMLCS Records.

28. Draft of Article 207—Sexual Offenses, January 7, 1955, quoted in Marie-Amelie George, "The Harmless Psychopath: Legal Debates Promoting the Decriminalization of Sodomy in the United States," *Journal of the History of Sexuality* 24, no. 2 (2015): 255.

29. Eskridge, *Dishonorable Passions*, 121–24.

30. For a list of states that decriminalized sodomy during what legal scholars have termed the Model Penal Code period, see Melinda D. Kane, "Timing Matters: Shifts in the Causal Determinants of Sodomy Law Decriminalization, 1961–1998," *Social Problems* 54 (May 2007): 214.

31. Eskridge, *Dishonorable Passions*, 124–27, 161–63.

32. McBride, *Out of the Neon Closet*, 243–44; Painter, "Arizona," History of Sodomy Laws in the United States, August 11, 2004, https://www.glapn.org/sodomylaws/sensibilities/arizona.htm.

33. Criminal Law Study Research Materials.

34. Alfred C. Kinsey, Wardell Baxter Pomeroy, and Clyde E Martin, *Sexual Behavior in the Human Male* (Philadelphia: W. B. Saunders, 1948), 264. Criminal Law Study Committee, Corresponding Sections, section 13.7, n.d., box 724, folder 11, NMLCS Records.

35. Brian Fehler, "'Sex Variants' Were Everywhere," *Gay & Lesbian Review Worldwide* 27, no. 6 (December 11, 2020): 20–22.

36. George W. Henry, ed., *Sex Variants: A Study of Homosexual Patterns* (New York: Paul B. Hoeber, 1948). See Henry L. Minton, "Community Empowerment and the

Medicalization of Homosexuality: Constructing Sexual Identities in the 1930s," *Journal of the History of Sexuality* 6, no. 3 (1996): 435–58.

37. Martin Meeker, "Behind the Mask of Respectability: Reconsidering the Mattachine Society and Male Homophile Practice, 1950s and 1960s," *Journal of the History of Sexuality* 10, no. 1 (2001): 91.

38. Jeannette H. Foster, *Sex Variant Women in Literature: A Historical and Quantitative Study* (New York: Vantage Press, 1956), 11.

39. "New Criminal Code Approved over Stiff Protests," *Albuquerque Journal*, January 31, 1961.

40. "Sodomy Bill Doomed," *New Mexican*, February 28, 1961.

41. *House Journal*, 25th sess., Jan 30, 1961, 5; "Drastic Revision of New Mexico Criminal Law Prepared," *Santa Fe New Mexican*, January 1, 1961, 31.

42. "Santa Fe Archdiocese Statistics Worked Out," *New Mexico Catholic Renewal*, May 14, 1967; "Prelate Hits Proposed Code," *Albuquerque Tribune*, February 3, 1961, A-18.

43. "Pornography Curb Sought," *Santa Fe New Mexican*, February 13, 1961. On Catholic opposition to decriminalizing sodomy in New York, see D'Emilio, *Sexual Politics, Sexual Communities*, 146.

44. Mrs. Vera Padilla, "Sodomy Proposal" (letter to the editor), *Albuquerque Journal*, February 4, 1961.

45. Boucher quoted in "Sodomy Clause to Be Dropped," *Albuquerque Journal*, March 1, 1961.

46. Nancy Mainville, "Legalized Sodomy Supported" (letter to the editor), *Santa Fe New Mexican*, February 28, 1961. For the association of "the city different" with queer people, see Betty E. Bauer, *My City Different* (Santa Fe: Sunstone, 2004); and Evans, "Gays in Santa Fe."

47. There are a few exceptions. The issue of censorship resurfaced in Judson Crews, review of *Book Selection and Censorship*, reprinted in Spud Johnson, *The Horse Fly*, Taos, June 9, 1960, in Spud Johnson vertical file 29, box 392. For a discussion of "The Horse Fly and The Gadfly," see Udall, *Spud Johnson and Laughing Horse*, 63–70.

48. Bauer, *My City Different*, 35.

49. David Baxter, "Sodom and the State Dept.," *Clovis News Journal*, August 6, 1950, 28.

50. Before the Cold War, homosexuality occasionally surfaced in the local press as a subject of ridicule directed at "fairies" of the art colonies. One editorial in the *Santa Fe New Mexican* stated: "Santa Fe has many eccentricities. . . . We fight over fairies . . . But they are the exception, and furnish some innocent amusements" (*Santa Fe New Mexican*, August 12, 1931, quoted in Gibson, *Santa Fe and Taos Colonies*, 79). Postwar, New Mexico newspapers used discriminatory language, such as "sexual perversion," and openly condemned homosexuality, spurred by reporting on the Lavender Scare. See, for example, "Press for Senate Probe of Perverts on Payroll," *Clovis News Jour-*

nal, May 21, 1950; and "Senate Speeds Inquiry of Perverts in Federal Government, 'Victims of Red,'" *Farmington Daily Times*, May 20, 1950.

51. Peter Boag, "Does Portland Need Homophile Society? Gay Culture and Activism in the Rose City Between World War II and Stonewall," *Oregon* 105, no. 1 (Spring 2004): 20. Some cities, such as Seattle, Washington, created their own gay civil rights organizations. Gary Atkins, *Gay Seattle* (Seattle: University of Washington Press, 2003), 107–11.

52. Bernstein, "Nothing Ventured, Nothing Gained," 361.

53. McBride, *Out of the Neon Closet*, viii; Faderman, *The Gay Revolution*, 72, 89; Davis and Kennedy, *Boots of Leather, Slippers of Gold*; and Noel, "Gay Bars," 59–74.

54. According to Craig Loftin, the circulation for ONE was in the low thousands (Loftin, *Letters to ONE*, 18). See Mr. P [New Mexico] and Mr. V.M. [New Mexico], letters to the editor, *Mattachine Review*, October 1961, 30; and W.C. [New Mexico] and J.M. [New Mexico], letters to the editor, *Mattachine Review*, May 1962.

55. "Daughters of Bilitis—Purpose," *Ladder*, October 1956, 4.

56. "A Report from the Legal Director, Mattachine Society," *San Francisco Mattachine Newsletter*, December 1955.

57. Editor's Note, *Mattachine Review*, March 1961, 26.

58. "Criminal Code Bill Forgotten," *Albuquerque Tribune*, March 10, 1961; "House Kills Bill on De-Earmarking," *Albuquerque Tribune*, March 6, 1961; "Sodomy Clause to Be Dropped."

59. "What to Do about Homosexuals?," *Mattachine Review*, May 1961, 4.

60. "Sodomy Bill Debated at Law School," *Albuquerque Journal*, July 15, 1961, A-7.

61. Alamilla Boyd, *Wide-Open Town*, 20–24, 57–61, 54–55; Horacio N. Roque Ramírez, "A Living Archive of Desire: Tereista la Campesina and the Embodiment of Queer Latino Community," in *Archive Stories: Facts, Fictions, and the Writing of History*, ed. Antoinette M. Burton (Durham, NC: Duke University Press, 2005).

62. J. D. Robb, Enrique R. Lamadrid, and Jack Loeffler, *Hispanic Folk Music of New Mexico and the Southwest: A Self-Portrait of a People* (Albuquerque: University of New Mexico Press, 2014); Jack Loeffler, Katherine Loeffler, and Enrique R. Lamadrid, *La Música de Los Viejitos: Hispano Folk Music of the Río Grande Del Norte* (Albuquerque: University of New Mexico Press, 1999); Jack Loeffler, email to author, July 1, 2020; Robert Martinez, email to author, June 16, 2020.

63. I implemented historian Emma Pérez's suggestion to look for a queer presence in *corridos*, narrative Mexican ballads. Pérez, "Queering the Borderlands," 125.

64. Stephanie Lewthwaite, *A Contested Art: Modernism and Mestizaje in New Mexico* (Norman: University of Oklahoma Press, 2015), 4.

65. For a general overview of gender and sexuality conceptions among US Latino populations, see Deena J. González and Ellie D. Hernandez, "Latina/o Gender and Sexuality," in Springate, *LGBTQ America*; and Mitchell, *West of Sex*, 104, 116–18.

66. Sembronio Gonzalez, "El hombre que fue pa Juarez," box 1, CD 103, Ruben Cobos Collection of Southwestern Folklore and Folk Music, MSS 892 BC, Center for Southwest Research, Zimmerman Library, University of New Mexico, Albuquerque (hereafter Cobos Collection).

67. Joe Davis, "El pirujo," box 1, CD 105, Cobos Collection.

68. Tomás Almaguer, "Chicano Men: Cartography of Homosexual Identity and Behavior," in *The Lesbian and Gay Studies Reader*, eds. Henry Abelove, Michèle Aina Barale, and David M. Halperin, 258–59 (New York: Routledge, 1993); Renato Rosaldo, "A List of Slang and Colloquial Expression of Mexico City," *Hispania* 31, no. 4 (1948): 437–45, https://doi.org/10.2307/332955.

69. Almaguer, "Chicano Men," 255.

70. Bennett Hammer, interview by author, July 14, 2013, transcript, box 1, folder 7, Hammer Collection.

71. Carla Mari Trujillo, ed., *Chicana Lesbians: The Girls Our Mothers Warned Us About* (Berkeley: Third Woman, 1991), x.

72. Videotape interview transcript, Nadine Armijo and Rosa Montoya, box 43, folder 6, Adair Papers.

73. Bruno J. Navarro, "Longtime Fiesta Singer Genoveva Chavez Dies at 55," *Santa Fe New Mexican*, December 6, 1997; Ana Pacheco, *Legendary Locals of Santa Fe* (Charleston, SC: Arcadia, 2013), 61; "Native Santa Fean Featured Vocalist."

74. Horton, *Santa Fe Fiesta*, 162–63. For an excellent discussion of expressing Mexican identity in the context of the United States, see Laura R. Barraclough, *Charros: How Mexican Cowboys Are Remapping Race and American Identity* (Oakland: University of California Press, 2019).

75. Daniel Sheehy, "Mexican Mariachi Music: Made in the U.S.A.," in *The Music of Multicultural America: Performance, Identity, and Community in the United States*, ed. Kip Lornell and Anne K. Rasmussen (Jackson: University Press of Mississippi, 2016), 138, 147, 151–53, 146.

76. Yolanda Broyles-González and Lydia Mendoza, *Lydia Mendoza's Life in Music: Norteño Tejano Legacies = La Historia de Lydia Mendoza* (New York: Oxford University Press, 2001).

77. "Miss Genoveva Chavez Rancheros Singer, Home to Sing with the Mariachi," newspaper clipping in Chávez vertical file; Navarro, "Longtime Fiesta Singer"; and Pacheco, *Legendary Locals of Santa Fe*, 61.

78. Denise Kusel, "Only in Santa Fe: Genoveva Chavez's Life Remembered" *Santa Fe New Mexican*, December 15, 1999.

79. Genoveva Chávez, Strachwitz Frontera Collection of Mexican and Mexican American Recordings, UCLA Digital Library, 2015, http://frontera.library.ucla.edu /artists/genoveva-ch%C3%A1vez; "Featuring Genoveva Chavez and the Mariachi

Alma Jaliciense," *New Mexican*, 1963, and "Ranchera singer Home from Coast," *New Mexican*, n.d. in Chávez vertical file.

80. The name of the bar has changed over the years from Readhead, to Reds, and finally Redz, which closed in 2010. Lillian Faderman and Stuart Timmons, *Gay L.A.: A History of Sexual Outlaws, Power Politics, and Lipstick Lesbians* (New York: Basic, 2006), 285; Stacy I. Macias, "Disappeared Spheres: Circling the Greater East Los Angeles Latina Lesbian Bar Orbit," *One Archives Foundation* (blog), accessed November 29, 2020, https://www.onearchives.org/disappeared-spheres/.

81. Barraclough, *Charros*, 41; Stacy I. Macias, "A Gay Bar, Some Familia, and Latina Butch-Femme: Rounding Out the Eastside Circle at El Monte's Sugar Shack," in *East of East: The Making of Greater El Monte*, eds. Romeo Guzmán, Carribean Fragoza, Alex Sayf Cummings, and Ryan Reft (New Brunswick, NJ: Rutgers University Press, 2020), 250–60.

82. Navarro, "Longtime Fiesta Singer." I wish I knew more about this transition and how Chavez's lesbianism operated in Santa Fe. I reached out to her partner for an interview but never heard back.

83. María Motez-Skolnik, "Shared Memories of Genoveva Chavez," *Voces de Santa Fe*, April 13, 2021, http://www.vocesdesantafe.org/explore-our-history/biographies people/217-shared-memories-of-genoveva-chavez; Linda Siegle, interview by author, December 9, 2013, transcript, box 1, folder 9, Hammer Collection.

84. Ana Castillo, "La Macha: Toward a Beautiful Whole Self," in Trujillo, *Chicana Lesbians*, 26, 37.

85. Teena Apeles, "The Rise of Female Mariachi: A Brief History," KCET, July 29, 2020, https://www.kcet.org/shows/southland-sessions/the-rise-of-the-female-mariachi-a-brief-history.

86. "Our View: 15 Years and Going Strong," *New Mexican*, March 11, 2015, https://www.santafenewmexican.com/opinion/editorials/our-view-15-years-and-going-strong/article_4beb7156-0474-52e0-9715-c4b6aab9c377.html; Navarro, "Longtime Fiesta Singer."

87. Lack of scholarly attention to Martin's gender and sexual nonconformity (which has been classified as lesbian, bisexual, asexual, and queer) is discussed in Katz, "Agnes Martin and the Sexuality of Abstraction," 97; Sarah Lowndes, *Contemporary Artists Working outside the City: Creative Retreat* (New York: Routledge, 2018), 21–22; Martin, *Agnes Martin*, 20–21; Princenthal, *Agnes Martin*, 11; and Ela Przybylo and Danielle Cooper, "Asexual Resonances: Tracing a Queerly Asexual Archive," *GLQ* 20, no. 3 (2014): 309–11.

88. Lowndes, *Contemporary Artists*, 35.

89. Martin, *Agnes Martin*, 48–52.

90. Princenthal, *Agnes Martin*, 46–47; Simon, "Perfection Is in the Mind."

91. After her relationship with Martin, Daphne Cowper was briefly married to John Vaughn. Martin, *Agnes Martin*, 59–63.

92. Rachel Ellison, "Pride: LGBTQ+ Artists and CAM," *Cincinnati Art Museum* (blog), June 18, 2019, https://www.cincinnatiartmuseum.org/about/blog/pride -blog-6182019/; Susan Fillin-Yeh, "Dandies, Marginality and Modernism: Georgia O'Keeffe, Marcel Duchamp and Other Cross-Dressers," *Oxford Art Journal* 18, no. 2 (1995): 33–44; Roxanna Robinson, *Georgia O'Keeffe: A Life* (New York: Harper & Row, 1989), 60, 510, 618; Benita Eisler, *O'Keeffe and Stieglitz: An American Romance* (New York: Penguin, 1992), 34n, 43n, 516–17; Barbara Buhler Lynes and Ann Paden, introduction, in *Maria Chabot—Georgia O'Keeffe: Correspondence, 1941–1949*, ed. Barbara Buhler Lynes, Ann Paden, and Sarah King, xi–xxv (Albuquerque: University of New Mexico Press, 2003).

93. Sarah Schulman, "Making Lesbian History Possible: A Proposal," *OutHistory* (blog), June 6, 2016, https://outhistory.org/blog/making-lesbian-history-possible -a-proposal/.

94. Vivien Green Fryd, *Art and the Crisis of Marriage: Edward Hopper and Georgia O'Keeffe* (Chicago: University of Chicago Press, 2003), 37–40.

95. Vivien Green Fryd points to the flirtatious correspondence of O'Keeffe and Harlem Renaissance participant Jean Toomer (Fryd, *Art and the Crisis of Marriage*, 41). Lynes et al., *Maria Chabot—Georgia O'Keeffe*. Maria Chabot's legal name was Mary Lea Chabot, but she went by Maria. Eisler, *O'Keeffe and Stieglitz*, 458.

96. Maria Chabot to Dorothy Stewart, July 27, 1939, quoted in Armstrong, *Mary Wheelwright*, 101; Linda M. Grasso, "Reading Published Letter Collections as Literary Texts: Maria Chabot—Georgia O'Keeffe Correspondence, 1941–1949 as a Case Study," *Legacy* 25, no. 2 (2008): 239–50.

97. Maria Chabot to Georgia O'Keeffe, May 8, 1942 (letter 120), in Lynes et al., *Maria Chabot—Georgia O'Keeffe*, 38.

98. Lynes and Paden, introduction, in Lynes et al., *Maria Chabot—Georgia O'Keeffe*, xxi; Cooper, *Unbuttoned*, 85.

99. Kristina Wilson, interview by Douglas Drieshpoon, June 25, 2001, Taos, New Mexico, 21–23, box 7, folder 41, Mandelman-Ribak Foundation Oral History Project, Beatrice Mandelman and Louis Ribak Papers, MSS 1002, Center for Southwest Research, Zimmerman Library, University of New Mexico, Albuquerque (hereafter Mandelman-Ribak Papers); Maria Chabot to Georgia O'Keeffe, May 8, 1942 (letter 12), Lynes et al., *Maria Chabot—Georgia O'Keeffe*, 38, 515.

100. *Georgia O'Keeffe*, produced and directed by Perry Miller Adato (Educational Broadcast Company, 1977).

101. Burke, "Spud Johnson and a Gay Man's Place," 86–90; Spud Johnson, entries for August 5, 6, and 7, [1935], Journal 3, box 12, folder 3, Johnson Collection.

102. Burke, *From Greenwich Village to Taos*, 179; Tom Collins, "Agnes Martin Re-

flects on Art & Life," *Geronimo* 2 (January 1999): 11, 13–15; Benita Eisler, "Life Lines," *New Yorker*, January 18, 1993, 73; Simon, "Perfection Is in the Mind."

103. Lowndes, *Contemporary Artists*, 27; Lisa Mintz Messinger, *Georgia O'Keeffe* (London: Thames and Hudson, 1989), 104.

104. Princenthal, *Agnes Martin*, 46; Simon, "Perfection Is in the Mind"; Martin quoted in Marja Bloem, "An Awareness of Perfection," in *Agnes Martin: Paintings and Drawings, 1974–1990*, exhibition catalog (Amsterdam: Stedelijk Museum, 1991) 33–34.

105. Lauren Jae Gutterman, *Her Neighbor's Wife: A History of Lesbian Desire within Marriage* (Philadelphia: University of Pennsylvania Press, 2019), 24. On the pressure to marry in the 1950s, see Stephanie Coontz, *Marriage, a History: From Obedience to Intimacy or How Love Conquered Marriage* (New York: Viking, 2005), ch. 14; Rebecca L. Davis, *More Perfect Unions: The American Search for Marital Bliss* (Cambridge, MA: Harvard University Press, 2010), ch. 3; and Elaine Tyler May, *Homeward Bound: American Families in the Cold War Era* (New York: Basic, 1988).

106. Kraft, *Who Is Witter Bynner?*, 102; and Burke, *A Land Apart*, 166.

107. Christopher Isherwood and Katherine Bucknell, *Diaries, Volume 1: 1939–1960* (New York: HarperCollins, 1997), 249–56; Goldberg, "Photographic Relations," 77–78.

108. Steven Watson, *Prepare for Saints: Gertrude Stein, Virgil Thomson, and the Mainstreaming of American Modernism* (New York: Random House, 1998), 195; Rudnick, *Cady Wells and Southwestern Modernism*, 39.

109. Lowndes, *Contemporary Artists*, 27–28. Martin and Parsons had met in New York City in the early 1950s. Parsons was intrigued by Martin's work but not enough to take Martin on as a client. Martin, *Agnes Martin*, 72.

110. Parsons gave solo shows to such queer artists as Forrest Bess, Sonja Sekula, Alfonso Ossorio, and Leon Polk Smith, to name a few. Justin Wolf, "Summary of the Betty Parsons Gallery," *The Art Story*, accessed April 25, 2021, https://www.theart story.org/gallery-betty-parsons.htm; and "Dealer Betty Parsons Pioneered Male Abstract Expressionists But Who Were the Unrecognized Women Artists She Exhibited?" *Artspace*, April 3, 2017, https://www.artspace.com/magazine/interviews _features/book_report/dealer-betty-parsons-pioneered-male-abstract-expression istsbut-who-were-the-unrecognized-women-54682. For a discussion of male dominance in postwar art, see Sherry, *Gay Artists in Modern American Culture*, 17.

111. Princenthal, *Agnes Martin*, 51; Henry *Agnes Martin*, 72, 82, 99, 110.

112. Betty Parsons and Agnes Martin, contract, October 2, 1958, box 11, folder 6, https://www.aaa.si.edu/collections/betty-parsons-gallery-records-and-personal -papers-7211/series-1/box-11-folder-6; "Betty Parsons Presents a First New York Showing of Oil Paintings by Agnes Martin," December 2–20, 1958, box 11, folder 10, https://www.aaa.si.edu/collections/betty-parsons-gallery-records-and-personal -papers-7211/series-1/box-11-folder-10; Betty Parsons, Agnes Martin Biographical

Materials, March 9, 1959, box 11, folder 5, https://www.aaa.si.edu/collections/betty
-parsons-gallery-records-and-personal-papers-7211/series-1/box-11-folder-5, all in
Betty Parsons Gallery records and personal papers, 1920–91, Archives of American
Art, Smithsonian Institution, Washington, DC.

113. "Paintings" by Agnes Martin, December 29–January 16, 1960, box 11, folder
10, Betty Parsons Gallery records and personal papers, 1920–91, https://www.aaa
.si.edu/collections/betty-parsons-gallery-records-and-personal-papers-7211/series
-1/box-11-folder-10.

114. Brendan Prendeville, "The Meanings of Acts: Agnes Martin and the Making
of Americans," *Oxford Art Journal* 31 no. 1 (2008), 72.

115. Lillian Faderman, *Odd Girls and Twilight Lovers: A History of Lesbian Life in
Twentieth-Century America* (New York: Penguin, 1992), 157.

116. Geneva M. Gano, *Little Art Colony and US Modernism: Carmel, Provincetown,
Taos* (Edinburgh: Edinburgh University Press, 2020); Brochure reprinted in Deborah
Boll, *Albuquerque '50s* (New Mexico: University of New Mexico Art Museum, 1989),
11; Catherine Lord and Richard Meyer, *Art and Queer Culture* (London: Phaidon,
2013), 88; Alida F. Sims, "The Provincetown of the Desert," *New York Times*, December 15, 1921.

117. Agnes Martin and Arnold B. Glimcher, *Agnes Martin: Paintings, Writings,
Remembrances* (New York: Phaidon, 2012), 8–9; Princenthal, *Agnes Martin*, 253.

118. Kristina Wilson interview by Douglas Drieshpoon, June 25, 2001, Taos, New
Mexico, 21–23, box 7, folder 41, Mandelman-Ribak Papers; Katz, *Hide/Seek*, 24,
44–45, 133, 144–45; Princenthal, *Agnes Martin*, 11.

119. Gianfranco Gorgoni, *Beyond the Canvas: Artists of the Seventies and Eighties*
(New York: Rizzoli, 1985), 177; Lowndes, *Contemporary Artists*, 39; Donald Wood-
man and Agnes Martin, *Agnes Martin and Me* (New York: Lyon Artbooks, 2016), 20;
Przybylo and Cooper, "Asexual Resonances," 297–318.

FIVE Land of Entwinement

1. Helene Vann, interview by author, October 1, 2014, Albuquerque, New Mexico,
audio file, in possession of author.

2. Rosanne Baca, film interview, 1991.1.34.28, VHS tape, box 58, Adair Papers.

3. I primarily learned about Cricket's through oral histories. See Baca film interview; Chavez interview; Havens Levitt, interview by author, July 14, 2014, audio
recording, box 1, folder 4, Hammer Collection; Ann Nihlen, interview by author,
May 21, 2014, audio recording, box 1, folder 7, Hammer Collection. Historian Trisha
Franzen mentions the bar in her article, "Differences and Identities: Feminism and
the Albuquerque Lesbian Community," *Signs: Journal of Women in Culture & Society*
18, no. 4 (Summer 1993): 895. Finally, I verified the location(s) of the bar using state

records: Ownership and Location First Quarter, List of Licensed Liquor Dealers and Registered Common Carriers, 1971, folder 84, box 7032, New Mexico Department of Alcoholic Beverage Control Records, Collection 1959-247, New Mexico State Records Center and Archives, Santa Fe.

4. Erna Pahe (Diné/Navajo), interview, July 17, 1985, transcript, box 1, folder 1, Roscoe Papers.

5. At UNM, women chose to call the program "Women Studies" instead of "Women's Studies." As of fall 2019, the program is called Women, Gender, and Sexuality Studies. For the birth of UNM's Women Studies Program, see Gail Baker, interview, 052199 tape 1, Women's Studies Oral History Collection, 1998–2013, UNMA 178, Center for Southwest Research, Zimmerman Library, University of New Mexico, Albuquerque (hereafter WMST Oral History Collection). GL-NM discusses its establishment in *Gay Liberation Newsletter*, February 1971, in vertical file, "New Mexico—1999 and Before," ONE National Gay and Lesbian Archives, Los Angeles (hereafter vertical file, "New Mexico"). The organization later changed its name to Gay Liberation Front to signal an alliance with political radicalism of the left.

6. "Juniper and Other Gay Organizations," *Seer's Catalogue*, September 1975, oversized file, Underground Newspaper Collection, MSS 514 BC, Center for Southwest Research, Zimmerman Library, University of New Mexico, Albuquerque (hereafter Underground Newspaper Collection).

7. The Women Studies Department and the Women's Resource Center, both established in 1972 on the UNM campus, served as spaces for the LGBTQ student population until August of 2010, when the LGBTQ Resource Center opened as a safe zone environment for people of all gender identities, gender expressions, sexual orientations, and other identities. "Mission and Vision," LGBTQ Resource Center, University of New Mexico, accessed March 1, 2017, http://lgbtqrc.unm.edu/.

8. Susan K. Freeman, "From the Lesbian Nation to the Cincinnati Lesbian Community: Moving toward a Politics of Location," *Journal of the History of Sexuality* 9, no. 1/2 (January 1, 2000): 137–74; Sally R. Munt, "Sisters in Exile: The Lesbian Nation," in *New Frontiers of Space, Bodies and Gender*, ed. Rosa Ainley, 3–19 (New York: Routledge, 2002); Becki Ross, *The House That Jill Built: A Lesbian Nation in Formation* (Buffalo: University of Toronto Press, 1995); Susan Sayer, "From Lesbian Nation to Queer Nation," *Hecate* 21, no. 2 (October 1, 1995): 29.

9. Catherine Kleiner, "Nature's Lovers: The Erotics of Lesbian Land Communities in Oregon, 1974–1984," in *Seeing Nature through Gender*, ed. Virginia J. Scharff, 242–26 (Lawrence: University Press of Kansas, 2003); Catriona Sandilands, "Lesbian Separatist Communities and the Experience of Nature: Toward a Queer Ecology," *Organization and Environment* 15 (June 2002): 131–63; and Nancy C. Unger, "From Jook Joints to Sisterspace: The Role of Nature in Lesbian Alternative Environment in the United States," in *Queer Ecologies: Sex, Nature, Politics, Desire*, ed. Catriona

Mortimer-Sandilands and Bruce Erickson, 173–98 (Bloomington: Indiana University Press, 2010).

10. Meeker, *Contacts Desired*, 200.

11. Zuni Mountain Sanctuary, accessed on September 24, 2013, http://www.zms .org/. On the formation of a permanent land community for gay men, an endeavor called Nomenus, see the Roscoe Papers. For the locations of sanctuaries, see Scott Lauria Morgensen, "Arrival at Home: Radical Faerie Configurations of Sexuality and Place," *GLQ* 15, no. 1 (January 1, 2009): n3, 92, https://doi.org/10.1215/10642684-2008-019.

12. Burke, *A Land Apart*, 141; Myla Vicenti Carpio, *Indigenous Albuquerque* (Lubbock: Texas Tech University Press), 52.

13. In defining the gay liberation movement, I have been most influenced by Emily K. Hobson, *Lavender and Red: Liberation and Solidarity in the Gay and Lesbian Left* (Oakland: University of California Press, 2016); and Whitney Strub, "Gay Liberation (1963–1980)," in Romesburg, *Routledge History of Queer America*.

14. Stein, *Rethinking the Gay and Lesbian Movement*, 89.

15. Anderson and Smith count two dozen communes in the vicinity of Taos. Terry H. Anderson, *The Movement and the Sixties* (New York: Oxford University Press, 1995), 271; Sherry L. Smith, *Hippies, Indians, and the Fight for Red Power* (New York: Oxford University Press, 2012), 109, 113, quote on 134.

16. On the "hippie invasion" of northern New Mexico, see Benjamin Klein and Tim Hodgdon, "From Innocence to Experience: Irwin B. Klein and 'The New Settlers of New Mexico, 1967–1971,'" *New Mexico Historical Review* 87, no. 1 (Winter 2012): 75–104; and Timothy Miller, "New Mexico's New Communal Settlers," *New Mexico Historical Review* 87, no. 1 (Winter 2012): 69–74.

17. Jill Johnston, *Lesbian Nation: The Feminist Solution* (New York: Simon and Schuster, 1973).

18. Chelsea Del Rio, "Voicing Gay Women's Liberation: Judy Grahn and the Shaping of Lesbian Feminism," *Journal of Lesbian Studies* 19, no. 3, (2015): 357–66; and Radicalesbians, "The Woman-Identified Woman," in *Radical Feminism: A Documentary Reader*, ed. Barbara A. Crow (New York: New York University Press, 2000), 236.

19. Johnston, *Lesbian Nation*, 58, 22, 181.

20. The University of Oregon holds the Southern Oregon Country Lesbian Archival Project and the Lesbian and Feminist Periodical Collection, which contains the richest collection of sources on the topic. Using UO holdings, sometimes supplemented by oral histories, scholars have analyzed the significance of rural separatist living in Oregon and along the Amazon Trail. Outside of these areas, Brock Thompson has a chapter on lesbian land in Arkansas's Ozarks in *The Un-natural State: Arkansas and the Queer South* (Fayetteville: University of Arkansas Press, 2010), ch. 13.

21. Kleiner, "Nature's Lovers," 243; Keridwen N. Luis, *Herlands: Exploring the Women's Land Movement in the United States* (Minneapolis: University of Minnesota Press, 2018), 3.

22. Gwynn quoted in Heather Burmeister, "Rural Revolution: Documenting the Lesbian Land Communities of Southern Oregon," (master's thesis, Portland State University, 2013), 89, https://doi.org/10.15760/etd.1080.

23. Juana María Paz, "Why I'm Not on Women's Land," *Maize*, Winter 1984–85, 8, Periodical, Newsletters, and Zines Collection, Lesbian Herstory Archives, Brooklyn, New York (hereafter LHA); "Country Connection," *Maize*, Winter 2009–10, 48, LHA.

24. Thyme Siegel, "Country Lesbians and Sisters on the Road," *Maize*, September 1996, 27–30, LHA. Thyme Siegel is not her given name. It was a common practice, especially among lesbian landers, to dispose of birth names and select a new identity, often one in homage to the natural world.

25. Pat Aspen, "Feminist Guide to Santa Fe," *Big Mama Rag*, August 1974, 9, geographic file "New Mexico," LHA; Linda Fowler, "Political, Spiritual Feminism Flourish in New Mexico," *Big Mama Rag*, June 1974, 3, https://www.jstor.org/stable/community.28033983; Shewolf, "Diversity in Women's Land," *Maize*, Spring 1993, 5, LHA.

26. Maize has also been published in Minneapolis, Minnesota, and Preston Hollow, New York. Elaine Mikels often published under the name Elana or Elana Freedom.

27. Elaine Mikels, "Adobe House," *Country Women*, January 1974; Elaine Mikels, *Just Lucky I Guess: From Closet Lesbian to Radical Dyke* (Santa Fe: Desert Crone Press, 1994), 189.

28. Rich Roberts, "Women's Show Scheduled for Sunday," *New Mexico Daily Lobo*, May 3, 1974, 12.

29. Mikels, *Just Lucky I Guess*, 203. A violent backlash against hippies occurred in the late 1960s, see Keith Green, "Hippie Problem Stirs More Local Groups to Investigate," *Taos News*, March 20, 1969, repr. in Iris Keltz, *Scrapbook of a Taos Hippie* (El Paso: Cinco Puntos, 2000), 31; Smith, *Hippies, Indians*, 133–35, 114; "Toaseno Dislikes Hippies," *Taos News*, May 23, 1969; and "Telling It Like It Isn't," *Fountain of Light*, October 1969, 5, Underground Newspaper Collection

30. Pelican Lee, "Nozama Tribe," in *Lesbian Land*, ed. Joyce Cheney, 152, 153 (Minneapolis: Word Weavers, 1985), 152, 153.

31. Mary L. Gray, *Out in the Country: Youth, Media, and Queer Visibility in Rural America* (New York: New York University Press, 2009), 3–4.

32. Arf in the sources is spelled inconsistently as "ARF," "Arf," and "A.R.F." The meaning behind the name is unclear. Pelican Lee speculated that it was due to the large number of roaming dogs on the property.

33. Sarah (pseudonym) quoted in Cheney, *Lesbian Land*, 13.

34. On collective lesbian feminist households and anticapitalism, see Hobson, *Lavender and Red*, 50–53.

35. Thyme Siegel's Journal, February 1980–May 1980, Oakland, San Francisco, Santa Fe, and Chimayo, Siegel Collection, LHA; Lee, "Nozama Tribe," 163.

36. See especially Sasha Archibald, "On Wimmin's Land," *Places Journal*, February 16, 2021, https://placesjournal.org/article/on-wimmins-land-the-heartland-of-lesbian -separatism/; and Hobson, *Lavender and Red*, 43–44. For example, Cherríe Moraga said, "no, thank you sisters," to the lesbian separatist utopia, finding it "exclusive and reactionary." See Cherríe Moraga and Gloria Anzaldúa, eds., *This Bridge Called My Back: Writings by Radical Women of Color* (Watertown, MA: Persephone Press, 1981), xiii–xix. Similarly, Audre Lorde visited two urban separatist communes in San Francisco in 1976. She critiqued them for not interrogating "assumptions based on privilege." See Alexis De Veaux, *Warrior Poet: A Biography of Audre Lorde* (New York: Norton, 2004), 170. There were short-lived lesbian land communities for women of color, such as Arco Iris in Arkansas and La Luz de la Lucha in California.

37. *Our Own Voices: A Directory of Lesbian and Gay Periodicals* estimates that 150 gay and lesbian publications circulated in 1972. For the number of lesbian publications, see Gina Covina quoted in Rodger Streitmatter, *Unspeakable: The Rise of the Gay and Lesbian Press in America*, 180 (Boston: Faber and Faber, 1995). For the history of lesbian print culture in the 1970s, see Meeker, *Contacts Desired*.

38. Strub, "Gay Liberation," 89.

39. Gloria, "Love Letters," *Amazon Quarterly*, 1972, 1; Gina Covina, "AQ the First Year: Changes," Special Double Issue, *Amazon Quarterly*, October 1973–January 1974, 50; Margo Hobbs Thompson, "'Dear Sisters': The Visible Lesbian in Community Arts Journals," *GLQ* 12, no. 3 (2006): 405–23; "From Us," *Amazon Quarterly*, July 1974, 5; "Resources," Special Double Issue, *Amazon Quarterly*, October 1973–January 1974, 60; Laurel Galana and Gina Covina, eds., *The New Lesbians: Interviews with Women across the U.S. and Canada* (Berkeley: Moon, 1977). *Amazon Quarterly* issues via Manuscripts and Archives Division, New York Public Library.

40. The first contact dyke directory was published in 1974. Terry McVannel Erwin, "For, by, and about Lesbians: A Qualitative Analysis of the *Lesbian Connection* Discussion Forum 1974–2004" (PhD diss., Ohio University, 2007), 104, 106; *Lesbian Connection*, July 1975; "Contact Dykes," *Lesbian Connection*, September 1982; Joan Nestle, "The Bathroom Line," *Lesbian Connection*, September 1981, 3; Richard Phillips, David Shuttleton, and Diane Watt, *De-Centering Sexualities Politics and Representations Beyond the Metropolis* (New York: Routledge, 2005), 204. *Lesbian Connection* issues via Manuscript and Archives Division, New York Public Library.

41. Letters to the Editor, *Lesbian Connection*, March 1976, 25, Manuscript and Archives Division, New York Public Library.

42. Calculations from US Census Bureau, 1970 *Census of Population: Characteristics of the Population, New Mexico* (Washington, DC: US Department of Commerce, 1973); Joseph P. Sánchez, Robert L. Spude, and Art Gómez, *New Mexico: A History* (Norman: University of Oklahoma Press, 2013), 312.

43. Streitmatter, *Unspeakable*, 161.

44. Heather Murray, "Free for All Lesbians: Lesbian Cultural Production and Consumption in the United States during the 1970s," *Journal of the History of Sexuality* 16, no. 2 (2007): 262, https://doi.org/10.1353/sex.2007.0046.

45. Streitmatter, *Unspeakable*, 173–75.

46. Juana María Rodríguez, *Queer Latinidad: Identity Practices, Discursive Spaces* (New York: New York University Press, 2003), 41; "Salsa Soul Sister: Honoring Lesbians of Color," Robert Blackburn Printmaking Workshop Program, May 9–June 29, 2018, http://www.rbpmw-efanyc.org/salsa-soul-sisters.

47. Letters to the Editor, *Lesbian Connection*, July 1976, 25; and Malflora Valverde, "Letters to the Editor," *Lesbian Connection*, September 1982, 13, both at Manuscript and Archives Division, New York Public Library. In 1982 Valverde took it upon herself to write "an article on third world lesbians," but sadly, her article never appeared in the newsletter.

48. For the history of *El Grito del Norte*, see Lorena Oropeza and Dionne Espinoza, eds., *Enriqueta Vasquez and the Chicano Movement: Writings from El Grito del Norte* (Houston: Arte Público, 2006). For a brief history of women writers published in *El Grito*, see Roberta Fernandez, "Abriendo Caminos in the Brotherland: Chicana Writers Respond to the Ideology of Literary Nationalism," *Frontiers* 14, no. 2 (1994): 23–51, esp. 31. Maylei Blackwell, *Chicana Power!: Contested Histories of Feminism in the Chicano Movement* (Austin: University of Texas Press, 2011), 32.

49. Estela Portillo Trambley, "The Day of the Swallows," *El Grito*, Spring 1971, 4–47 repr. in D. Soyini Madison, ed., *The Woman That I Am: The Literature and Culture of Contemporary Women of Color* (New York: St. Martin's, 1994), 358–90; See also Cherríe Moraga's argument that Portillo's writing set the stage for the development of Chicana lesbian literature, "The Obedient Daughter," in *The Sexuality of Latinas*, ed. Norma Alarcón, Ana Castillo, and Cherríe Moraga (Berkeley: Third Woman, 1993), 157–62.

50. Dionne Espinoza, introduction; Enriqueta Vasquez "¡Soy Chicana Primero!," April 26, 1971; and Vasquez, "¡Soy Chicana Primero!," repr. in *Enriqueta Vasquez and the Chicano Movement*, 111, 130, 131.

51. Blackwell, *Chicana Power!*, 40.

52. Juanita Sanchez, "Thoughts on a Chicana Lesbian Forum," *Sister Lode*, June/July 1984, 2, microfilm; "Feminist Newspaper Offers Forum," *Sister Lode*, November 1978, microfilm, both at Zimmerman Library, University of New Mexico.

53. Juanita M. Sanchez, "Sculpturing the Brown Woman," *Sister Lode*, December/January 1979/1980, 5, Gale Archives of Sexuality and Gender.

54. Yvonne Keller identifies two types of lesbian pulps: "pro-lesbian" and "virile adventures." The former are "women-centered, often told from a woman's point of view, dominated by a love story, without obviously extraneous sex scenes." Yvonne Keller, "'Was It Right to Love Her Brother's Wife So Passionately?': Lesbian Pulp Novels and US Lesbian Identity, 1950–1965," *American Quarterly* 57 (2005): 385–410.

55. Juanita Sanchez, "Kindling," *Sister Lode* 3, no. 5 (May–June 1982): 10, Gale Archives of Sexuality and Gender.

56. "Resources for Women," *Sister Lode*, August/September 1984, 7, microfilm, Zimmerman Library, University of New Mexico.

57. Trujillo, *Chicana Lesbians*.

58. Stuart Timmons, *The Trouble with Harry Hay: Founder of the Modern Gay Movement* (Boston: Alyson, 1990), 259.

59. D'Emilio, *Sexual Politics, Sexual Communities*; Faderman and Timmons, *Gay L.A.*; and Hurewitz, *Bohemian Los Angeles*.

60. Stuart Timmons, "The Making of a Tribe," in *The Fire in Moonlight: Stories from the Radical Faeries, 1975–2010*, ed. Mark Thompson (Maple Shade, NJ: White Crane, 2011), 32.

61. There is no singular Tewa worldview but multiple viewpoints that stem from the six Tewa-speaking Pueblos. Most histories of the Tewa draw on anthropological works that began with Adolph Francis Alphonse Bandelier, *Final Report of Investigations among the Indians of the Southwestern United States, Carried on Mainly in the Years from 1880 to 1885* (Cambridge, MA: Cambridge University Press, 1890). To the best of my ability I prioritize written accounts by Tewa people. Edward P. Dozier (Santa Clara Pueblo), "Factionalism at Santa Clara Pueblo," *Ethnology* 5, no. 2 (1966): 172–85; Alfonso Ortiz (Ohkay Owingeh Pueblo), *The Tewa World: Space, Time, Being, and Becoming in a Pueblo Society* (Chicago: University of Chicago Press, 1969). I also rely on the scholarship of Rina Swentzell (Pueblo of Santa Clara), Tito Naranjo (Pueblo of Santa Clara), and Tessie Naranjo (Pueblo of Santa Clara).

62. Morgensen, *Spaces between Us: Queer Settler Colonialism and Indigenous Decolonization* (Minneapolis: University of Minnesota Press, 2011), 128–29.

63. Those who identify with the movement author much of the literature on the Radical Faeries. For example, Thompson, *The Fire in Moonlight*; Don Kilhefner, "The Radical Faeries at Thirty (+ One)," *Gay & Lesbian Review Worldwide* 17, no. 5 (September/October 2010): 17–21; Douglas Sadownick, "The 'Secret' Story of the Radical Faeries," *Gay & Lesbian Review Worldwide* 18 (February 2011): 29–31. Others have actively participated in Faerie events through ethnographic research, Morgensen, "Arrival at Home"; Morgensen, *Spaces between Us*; Elizabeth A. Povinelli, *The Empire of Love: Toward a Theory of Intimacy, Genealogy, and Carnality* (Durham, NC: Duke University Press, 2006), ch. 2; and Rifkin, *When Did Indians Become Straight*, 233–35.

64. Morgensen mentions that Radical Faeries adapted "lesbian efforts to find a

home in opposition to modernity" but does not delve into specifics (Morgensen, "Arrival at Home," 77). Additionally, John Stover uses a feminist lens to address women within the movement in "When Pan Met Wendy: Gendered Membership Debates among the Radical Faeries," *Nova Religion* 11, no. 4 (2008): 31–55.

65. Thompson, *The Fire in Moonlight*, 16.

66. Povinelli, *The Empire of Love*, 112; Peter Hennen, *Faeries, Bears, and Leathermen: Men in Community Queering the Masculine* (Chicago: University of Chicago Press, 2008), ch. 3.

67. Harry Hay, "Towards the New Frontiers of Fairy Vision," 1975, 2, box 1, folder 18, Harry Hay Papers, 1867–2002, Co112011.003, ONE National Gay and Lesbian Archives, Los Angeles, California (hereafter Hay Papers, ONE); D'Emilio, *Sexual Politics, Sexual Communities*.

68. Hurewitz, *Bohemian Los Angeles*, 273–77; Timmons, *The Trouble with Harry Hay*, 216.

69. Notes on the Berdache, box 19 and 20, Harry Hay Papers, GLC 44, San Francisco History Center, San Francisco Public Library (hereafter Hay Papers, SFPL); Timmons, *The Trouble with Harry Hay*, 216.

70. Scholars posit that the French introduced the term *berdache* in reference to a social role, common among various tribes in North America, that crossed or mixed genders. The term circulated in the eighteenth century when Jesuit missionaries recorded their encounters with Native men and women who crossed gender lines. Other terms, including *hermaphrodite* and *sodomite*, spread in colonial accounts referencing nonbinary gender and sexual practices among Indigenous people. See John F. McDermott, *A Glossary of Mississippi Valley French, 1673–1850* (Saint Louis: Washington University, 1941), 22–23; and Jason Cromwell and Sue-Ellen Jacobs, "Visions and Revisions of Reality: Reflections on Sex, Sexuality, Gender, and Gender Variance," *Journal of Homosexuality* 23, no. 4 (1992): 43–69. V. F. Calverton, *The Making of Man: An Outline of Anthropology* (New York: Modern Library, 1931).

71. David S. Churchill, "Transnationalism and Homophile Political Culture in the Postwar Decades," *GLQ* 15, no. 1 (January 1, 2009): 31–66, https://doi.org/10.1215/10642684-2008-018. Not all biographers of Hay agree on this point. For example, Ben Miller argues that scholars have misinterpreted Hay as a universalist. Ben Miller, "Children of the Brain: The Life, Theory, and Activism of Harry Hay, 1953–1964" (honors thesis, New York University, 2014), 29–30.

72. Harry Hay, "The Homophile in Search of an Historical Context and Cultural Continuity," box 6, folder 1, Hay Papers, SFPL; Ruth Benedict, *Patterns of Culture*, 2nd ed. (Boston: Houghton Mifflin, 1959).

73. L. Bullough, *Before Stonewall: Activists for Gay and Lesbian Rights in Historical Context* (New York: Routledge, 2014), 81; Timmons, *The Trouble with Harry Hay*, 225; and Ben Miller, "What Are We For? Harry Hay and the Left," virtual exhibition,

outhistory, accessed February 6, 2021, http://outhistory.org/exhibits/show/what-are
-we-for/hay-harry.

74. I have been unable to find much information on "Enki." Timmons provides the most background information, explaining that "Enki" is a nickname derived from his baptismal name Encarnacion and that his Tewa name is Soh-kwa-wi or Soqueen. Timmons, *The Trouble with Harry Hay*, 224–25.

75. A friend of Harry Hay and an anthropologist and women's studies scholar named Sue-Ellen Jacobs claims to have met the last *kwidó* in the summer of 1972. After their death, Jacobs encountered resistance from Tewa-speaking people to acknowledge the role; instead Pueblo Indians argued that they "never had any people like that here." See Sue-Ellen Jacobs, "Is the 'North American Berdache' Merely a Phantom in the Imagination of Western Social Scientists?" in Jacobs et al., *Two-Spirit People*, 24–26.

76. Tito Naranjo and Rina Swentzell, "Healing Spaces in the Tewa Pueblo World," *American Indian Culture and Research Journal* 13, no. 3–4 (1989): 257–65; Wesley Thomas and Sue-Ellen Jacobs, "'And We Are Still Here': From Berdache to Two-Spirit People," *American Indian Culture and Research Journal* 23, no. 2 (1999): 91–107.

77. There is no definitive study of GAI. I relied primarily on GAI records as well as references in Jenny L. Davis, "More than Just 'Gay Indians': Intersecting Articulations of Two-Spirit Gender, Sexuality, and Indigenousness," in *Queer Excursions: Retheorizing Binaries in Language, Gender, and Sexuality*, ed. Lal Zimman, Jenny Davis, and Joshua Raclaw, 64 (New York: Oxford University Press, 2014); Sabine Lang, "Various Kinds of Two-Spirit People: Gender Variance and Homosexuality in Native Americans Communities," in Jacobs et al., *Two-Spirit People*, 110–11; Beatrice Medicine, "Changing Native American Roles in an Urban Context and Changing Native American Sex Roles in an Urban Context," in Jacobs et al., *Two-Spirit People*, 153–54; Morgensen, *Spaces between Us*, 4, 7–11, 78–83, 96–98, 118; and Scott Morgensen, "Unsettling Queer Politics," in Driskill, *Queer Indigenous Studies*, 135–43.

78. Randy Burns and Barbara Cameron, "Reclaiming the Old New World," *The Advocate*, 1975; Burns quoted in Jonathan Katz, *Gay American History: Lesbian and Gay Men in the U.S.A.* (New York: Thomas Crowell, 1976), 33.

79. Paul Gunn Allen, *The Sacred Hoop: Recovering the Feminine in American Indian Traditions* (Boston: Beacon, 1986), 255; GAI, "Chicago Resource Center Grant Proposal 1983 to 1985," box 1, folder 7, Roscoe Papers.

80. Erna Pahe, interview, July 17, 1985, transcript, box 1, folder 1, Roscoe Papers.

81. Henry Hay, "Letters," *Fag Rag/Gay Sunshine*, clipping, box 1, folder 60, Hay Papers, ONE.

82. Morgensen, *Spaces between Us*, 78.

83. Timmons, *The Trouble with Harry Hay*, 233–312, 263. On the El Llano Canal Project, see José A Rivera, *Acequia Culture: Water, Land, and Community in the*

Southwest (Albuquerque: University of New Mexico Press, 1998), 153–55; and Tom Sharpe, "El Llano Alternative Suggested," *New Mexican*, November 7, 1975.

84. "Gay People in Santa Fe Begin to Organize," *Seers Rio Grande Weekly*, March 25–April 1, 1977; Peter Katel, "Local GLF Plans First Activity," *New Mexico Daily Lobo*, April 1, 1971, 2.

85. J. K. Finer, "Out of the Closets and into the Streets," *Seer's Rio Grande Weekly* 6, no. 30 (July 1–8, 1997), clipping, Strong Papers.

86. Harry Hay, "Remarks on the Albuquerque Gay Pride Rally," 1977, Box 1, Folder 17, Hay Papers, ONE.

87. Lopez quoted in Timmons, *The Trouble with Harry Hay*, 274; PJ Sedillo, *Solidarity through Pride: 40 Years of GLBT Pride in Albuquerque, 1976–2016* (Albuquerque: ABQ Press, 2017), 20.

88. Timmons, *The Trouble with Harry Hay*, 272.

89. Richard Rodriguez, "Carnal Knowledge: Chicano Gay Men and the Dialectics of Being," in *Gay Latino Studies: A Critical Reader*, ed. Michael Hames-García and Ernesto Javier Martínez (Durham, NC: Duke University Press, 2011), 114.

90. Bobb Maestra, interview by Lester Q. Strong, n.d., transcript, box 5, folder 2, Strong Papers.

91. Timmons, *The Trouble with Harry Hay*, 265.

92. "Summer Solstice at A.R.F.," *Sister Lode*, June/July 1984, 19.

93. In addition to spending time with lesbian landers, Hay and Burnside visited Lama Foundation, a spiritual community near Taos. Jonathan Altaman (a founder of Lama), interview, November 12, 2005, transcript, box 1, folder 2, Oral History Interviews with the Lama Foundation, MSS 860 BC, Center for Southwest Research, Zimmerman Library, University of New Mexico, Albuquerque.

94. Ben Miller's online exhibition on Hay is the only scholarship that notes the importance of Richard Tapia to Hay's gay identity theory. Miller, "What Are We For." Harry Hay and Jørn Kamgren to Richard Tapia, 1961, box 13, folder 14, Hay Papers, SFPL.

95. Notes about Richard Tapia, circa 1962, box 13, folder 14, Hay Papers, SFPL.

96. Tito Naranjo, "Seeking Life," in Stephen Trimble, *Talking with Clay* (Santa Fe: School of American Research Press, 1987), 23, https://folklife-media.si.edu/docs/festival/program-book-articles/FESTBK1992_09.pdf; Naranjo and Swentzell, "Healing Spaces in the Tewa Pueblo World," 257–58.

97. Notes about Richard Tapia, circa 1962, box 13, folder 14, Hay Papers, SFPL.

98. Naranjo and Swentzell, "Healing Spaces in the Tewa Pueblo World," 258; Tessie Naranjo, "Life as Movement: A Tewa View of Community and Identity," in *The Social Construction of Communities: Agency, Structure, and Identity in the Prehispanic Southwest*, ed. Mark D. Varien and James M. Potter (Lanham, MD: Altamira, 2008), 251–62.

99. Carpio, *Indigenous Albuquerque*, 1. Not all urban Indigenous populations are transient. In Albuquerque, for example, Carpio cautions: "It is true that between 5,000 and 10,000 of the city's [Albuquerque] Indigenous residents are mobile," but "a significantly larger proportion of Albuquerque Indians, more than 30,000 are permanent residents" *Indigenous Albuquerque*, 56–57.

100. Rina Swentzell, "Mountain Form, Village Form: Unity in the Pueblo World," in Paul Logsdon, Stephen H. Lekson, and Rina Swentzell, *Ancient Land, Ancestral Places: Paul Logsdon in the Pueblo Southwest*, 45 (Santa Fe: Museum of New Mexico Press, 1993).

101. See Hay Harry, "The Hammond Report," *One Institute Quarterly*, winter/spring 1963; and Hay's keynote address at the West Coast Homophile Conference, February 14–15, 1971, repr. in *Speaking for Our Lives: Historic Speeches and Rhetoric for Gay and Lesbian Rights (1892–2000)*, ed. Robert B. Ridinger (New York: Harrington Park, 2004), 137–44.

102. Harry Hay, "Gay Liberation Chapter Two," box 1, folder 16, Hay Papers, ONE.

103. Hay quoted in Will Roscoe, "Prelude: Welcome to Planet Faerie," in Thompson, *The Fire in Moonlight*, 20.

104. Hay, "Gay Liberation Chapter Two."

105. Grahn, *Another Mother Tongue*, 105; Judy Grahn, "Strange Country This: Lesbianism and North American Indian Tribes," *Journal of Homosexuality* 12, nos. 3–4 (1986): 43–45. For an excellent analysis of Grahn's writings on queer history as "a colonial desire of non-Natives," see Morgensen, *Spaces between Us*, 4–12.

106. Hay met Mitch Walker in San Francisco at a lecture on gay male spirituality by writer Arthur Evans. The lectures were published as Arthur Evans, *Witchcraft and the Gay Counterculture: A Radical View of Western Civilization and Some of the People It Has Tried to Destroy* (Boston: Fag Rag, 1978). Hennen, *Faeries, Bears, and Leathermen*, 64, 68.

107. Carl Wittman, "A Gay Manifesto," repr. in *Out of the Closets: Voices of Gay Liberation*, ed. Karla Jay and Allen Young (New York: New York University Press, 1992), 330–42. Wittman's piece originally appeared as "Refugees from Amerika: A Gay Manifesto," *San Francisco Free Press*, December 22, 1969–January 7, 1970; Scott Herring, "Out of the Closets, into the Woods: RFD, Country Women, and the Post-Stonewall Emergence of Queer Anti-Urbanism," *American Quarterly* 59, no. 2 (2007): 341–47, https://doi.org/10.1353/aq.2007.0043; Stephen Vider, "'The Ultimate Extension of Gay Community': Communal Living and Gay Liberation in the 1970s," *Gender & History* 27, no. 3 (2015): 865–81, https://doi.org/10.1111/1468-0424.12167.

108. Kilhefner, "The Radical Faeries at Thirty (+ One)."

109. "A Call to Gay Brothers," *RFD*, June 20, 1979, 20; Harry Hay, *Radically Gay: Gay Liberation in the Words of Its Founder* (Boston: Beacon Press, 1996), 239–40.

110. Harry Hay, Circle of Loving Companions, Open Letter, March 26, 1979, box 1, folder 60, Hay Papers, ONE.

111. Morgensen, *Spaces between Us*, 135.

112. Gay American Indians History Project, 1985, folder 1, box 1, Roscoe Papers.

SIX Offending Moral Decency

1. There are two existing accounts of the "Love-Lust" controversy. The first was written by UNM law professor Leo Kanowitz, who served as academic counsel for Lionel Williams. Kanowitz investigates the incident through the lens of "emerging law of obscenity as developed by recent United States Supreme Court decisions." The second is an article I authored, from which this chapter is partially derived. I take a cultural approach to demonstrate how universities, faculty, and college students were conduits for spreading new sexual knowledge. Leo Kanowitz, "Love Lust in New Mexico and the Emerging Law of Obscenity," *Natural Resource Journal* 10 (April 1970): 339–52; Leo Kanowitz, *Poem Is a Four-Letter Word* (Lawrence, KS: Coronado Press, 1970); Jordan Biro Walters, "Offending Moral Decency: The Love-Lust Controversy of 1969 and the Sexual Revolution in New Mexico," *New Mexico Historical Review* 93, no. 4 (Fall 2018): 1–35.

2. The *New Mexico Daily Lobo*, the student paper at the University of New Mexico, also published as *New Mexico Lobo* until 1971. For clarity, I use the most contemporary name throughout the text.

3. *Screw* was a weekly tabloid newspaper devoted to sexually graphic articles and illustrations, pornography reviews, and advertisements for prostitutes. See "Al Goldstein, Screw Magazine Founder, Dies at 77," *NY Daily News*, accessed June 1, 2016, www.nydailynews.com/new-york/al-goldstein-screw-magazine-founder-dies-77-article-1.1552851; and Lambert, *Unclean Lips*, 15.

4. Katel, "Local GLF Plans First Activity," 2.

5. San Diego State University established the first women's studies program in 1970, followed by Cornell University. According to Florence Howe, by 1972 forty-six women's studies programs existed, and, of these, Howe chose fifteen well-established programs, including the University of New Mexico, to assess the progress of the field. See Florence Howe, *Seven Years Later: Women's Studies Programs in 1976: A Report of the National Advisory Council on Women's Educational Programs* (Washington, DC: National Advisory Council on Women's Educational Programs, 1977), 8, 23. For a discussion of the San Diego State and Cornell programs, see Carol Ahlum and Florence Howe, "Women's Studies and Social Change," in *Academic Women on the Move*, ed. Alice S. Rossi and Ann Calderwood (New York: Russell Sage Foundation, 1973), 393; and Christie Farnham, *The Impact of Feminist Research in the Academy* (Bloomington: Indiana University Press, 1987), 1.

6. Anthropologist John Bodine calls this the "tri-ethnic trap." See John Bodine, "A Tri-Ethnic Trap: The Spanish-Americans in Taos," in *Spanish-Speaking People in the United States*, ed. June Helm (Seattle: University of Washington Press, 1968), 145–53. Calculations from US Census Bureau, 1970 *Census of Population*.

7. Brittany C. Slatton and Kamesha Spates, *Hyper Sexual, Hyper Masculine? Gender, Race and Sexuality in the Identities of Contemporary Black Men* (Farnham, UK: Ashgate, 2014); Robert Staples, *Exploring Black Sexuality* (Lanham, MD: Rowman and Littlefield, 2006); and Cornel West, *Race Matters* (Boston: Beacon, 1993).

8. Judith Eaton, "The Evolution of Access Policy: 1965–1990," in *Public Policy and Higher Education*, ed. L. F. Goodchild, Cheryl D. Lovell, Edward R. Hines, and Judith I. Gill (Needham Heights, MA: Pearson, 1997), 237–46. Scholars are beginning to explore various forms of activism—cultural, electoral, coalitional, and consumer—in the evolution of gay liberation and its intersection with multiracial left politics. See, for example, Allyson Brantley, "'Hardhats May Be Misunderstood': The Boycott of Coors Beer and the Making of Gay-Labor-Chicana/o Alliances," *Pacific Historical Review* 89 (May 1, 2020): 264–96, https://doi.org/10.1525/phr.2020.89.2.264.

9. Patricia C. Gandara, *Over the Ivy Walls: The Educational Mobility of Low-Income Chicanos* (Albany: State University of New York Press, 1995), 10. For UNM's enrollment, see William E. Davis, *Miracle on the Mesa: A History of the University of New Mexico, 1889–2003* (Albuquerque: University of New Mexico Press, 2006), 385, appendix 2.

10. González and Hernández, "Latina/o Gender and Sexuality." A few short-form documentaries existed before *Word Is Out*. See Greg Youmans, *Word Is Out: A Queer Film Classic* (Vancouver: Arsenal Pulp, 2011), 36. Other queer life documentaries of the late 1970s include John Rechy's *The Sexual Outlaw* (1977), Arthur J. Bressan's *Gay USA* (1977), Iris Feminist Collective's *In the Best Interests of the Children* (1977), and Rosa von Praunheim's *Army of Lovers, or Revolt of the Perverts* (1979).

11. Coming out contributed to the development of a large-scale political movement for LGBTQ+ rights and remains an important component of the movement. For literature on the topic, see Donn Teal, *The Gay Militants* (New York: Stein and Day, 1971); and David Eisenbach, *Gay Power: An American Revolution* (New York: Carrol & Graf, 2006).

12. Lauren Berlant and Michael Warner, "Sex in Public," *Critical Inquiry* 24, no. 2 (1998): 558; Shah, "Queer of Color Estrangement and Belonging," 270. Some gay activists disagreed over the tactic of working though the legal and political systems, but during the late 1970s and 1980s advocates increasingly worked to ensure equal treatment under the law. See Button et al., "Politics of Gay Rights," 269–89.

13. Lenore Kandel, "Love-Lust Poem," in *Word Alchemy* (New York: Grove, 1967), 34–35.

14. Williams quoted in "Williams Hears No More about Obscenity Charge," *New Mexico Lobo*, March 25, 1969, 1, http://digitalrepository.unm.edu/cgi/viewcontent.cgi?article=1039&context=daily_lobo_1969.

15. Kanowitz, *Poem Is a Four-Letter Word*, 139. For a brief history of confessional poetry, see Steven K. Hoffman, "Impersonal Personalism: The Making of a Confessional Poetic," *ELH* 45 (December 1978): 687–709.

16. Kandel began to write as a member of the Beat generation when she moved to San Francisco, California, in 1960. The Beats wrote openly about sex, pleasure, and the body. See Ronna C. Johnson, "Lenore Kandel's *The Love Book*: Psychedelic Poetics, Cosmic Erotica, and Sexual Politics in the Mid-Sixties Counterculture," in *Reconstructing the Beats*, ed. Jennie Skerl (New York: Palgrave Macmillan, 2004); and Regina Marler, *Queer Beats: How the Beats Turned America on to Sex* (San Francisco: Cleis Press, 2004).

17. Jeffery M. Burns, "Lenore Kandel," *The Argonaut* 5, no. 1 (spring 1994), accessed July 16, 2016, http://foundsf.org/index.php?title=LENORE_KANDEL.

18. Kanowitz, *Poem Is a Four-Letter Word*, 125; Kanowitz, "Love Lust in New Mexico," 339–40.

19. Williams quoted in Kanowitz, *Poem Is a Four-Letter Word*, 126; Art Thomas, "Williams Explains Use of Poem," *New Mexico Lobo*, April 24, 1969, 1.

20. Special Advisory Committee Report, April 5, 1969, 21, box 10054, folder 909, Governor David F. Cargo Papers, col. no. 1969–001, New Mexico State Records Center and Archives, Santa Fe (hereafter Cargo Papers).

21. The legal definition of *obscenity* includes the term *pornography*. *Pornography*, a more limited term, refers only to erotic content. Maureen Harrison and Steve Gilbert, eds., *Obscenity and Pornography Decisions of the United States Supreme Court* (Carlsbad, CA: Excellent Books, 2000).

22. Calvin Horn, *The University in Turmoil and Transition: Crisis Decades at the University of New Mexico* (Albuquerque: Rocky Mountain Publishing, 1981), 23.

23. Prince quoted in Frankie McCarty, "Cargo Enters Poem Controversy," newspaper clipping, box 3, folder 8, Calvin Horn Papers, 1947–84, University Archives, UNMA 108, Center for Southwest Research, Zimmerman Library, University of New Mexico, Albuquerque.

24. House of Representatives Resolution, March 27, 1969, repr. in Horn, *University in Turmoil*, 22.

25. "Cargo Calls UNM Poem 'Filth,'" *Farmington Daily Times*, March 30, 1969, 5; David Francis Cargo, *Lonesome Dave: The Story of New Mexico Governor David Francis Cargo* (Santa Fe: Sunstone, 2010), 281–82.

26. Kanowitz, *Poem Is a Four-Letter Word*, 102; Chalmer R. Myer to Gov. David F. Cargo, May 19, 1969, box 10054, folder 909, Cargo Papers; Mesa Lodge No. 27, Resolution, June 9, 1969, box 10054, folder 909, Cargo Papers.

27. R. D. Thommarson and Mrs. P. J. Tyler to Gov. David F. Cargo, May 20, 1969, box 10054, folder 909, Cargo Papers.

28. Adron M. Brown to Gov. David F. Cargo, May 23, 1969, box 10054, folder 909, Cargo Papers.

29. Lenore Kandel, *The Love Book* (San Francisco: Stolen Paper, 1966); Kandel, *Word Alchemy*.

30. Barnett, "Corruption of Morals," 189–243; Lockhart and McClure, "Obscenity in the Courts," 587–607.

31. "Decency Group Slates Meeting," *Albuquerque Journal*, December 4, 1956, 17; and "Hathaway Will Hunt Pornography," *Santa Fe New Mexican*, December 7, 1956, 7.

32. *House Journal*, 25th sess., January 30, 1961, 5; New Mexico Criminal Law Study Committee, "Report of the Criminal Law Study Interim Committee"; Weihofen, "Proposed New Mexico Criminal Code," 139; "Anti-Obscenity Ordinance Due for 3rd Reading," *Albuquerque Journal*, December 1, 1963, 12; Barnett, "Corruption of Morals," 219; Martin Paskind, "Group Planning Action against Drive-In Theater," *Albuquerque Journal*, February 22, 1963, 2; "DA Investigates 'Obscene' Poetry," *Albuquerque Journal*, March 29, 1969, 6.

33. Layne Vickers, "City Man 'Guilty' in Pornography Case," *Albuquerque Journal*, May 15, 1968; "Obscenity Case Heard," *Albuquerque Tribune*, March 14, 1968, 4; "Poem Distribution Warning Is Issued," *Albuquerque Journal*, March 29, 1969, 6; Kanowitz, *Poem Is a Four-Letter Word*, 263.

34. For an excellent history of miscegenation in America, see Peggy Pascoe, *What Comes Naturally: Miscegenation Law and the Making of Race in America* (Oxford: Oxford University Press, 2009). The best example is McCarty, "Cargo Enters Poem Controversy." See also the letter postmarked March 29, 1969, repr. in Kanowitz, *Poem Is a Four-Letter Word*, 30.

35. Slatton and Spates, *Hyper Sexual, Hyper Masculine?*, 167; Sander Gilman, *Difference and Pathology: Stereotypes of Sexuality, Race, and Madness* (Ithaca: Cornell University Press, 1985); US Department of Labor, *The Negro Family: The Case for National Action* (Washington, DC: Government Printing Office, 1965).

36. "Businessman Tells Views on U. Poem," *Albuquerque Journal*, March 29, 1969, 6; Escoffier, "Pornography, Perversion and the Sexual Revolution," 211.

37. William Montgomery, "Poetry Rally Lures Big Attendance," *Albuquerque Journal*, March 29, 1969, 1; "BSU Gives Demands to Heady: Students Sit in at Ad Building," *New Mexico Lobo*, April 2, 1969, 1; Horn, *University in Turmoil*, 280–81.

38. Although protests occurred on numerous college campuses, UNM had been largely immune to these confrontations until the "Love-Lust" controversy. Enrollment at UNM was 14,4440. See Davis, *Miracle on the Mesa*, 229, 385.

39. Montgomery, "Poetry Rally Lures Big Attendance," 1; "Student Group Wants Boycott Set for April 1," *New Mexico Lobo*, March 31, 1969, 1.

40. "TA's Alleged Obscenities Bring University Action," *New Mexico Lobo*, March 24, 1969, 1. "To Find Consensus on Suspension Issue," *New Mexico Lobo*, March 31, 1969, 1. "Assistants Vote 'No Strike,'" *New Mexico Lobo*, April 2, 1969, 1; Wayne Ciddio, "200 Students Stage Protest at Heady's Home," *New Mexico Lobo*, April 11, 1969, 1.

41. Heady, "President Heady Issues Text on Suspensions," *Albuquerque Journal*, March 29, 1969, 6; Kanowitz, *Poem Is a Four-Letter Word*, 73; Special Advisory Committee Report, 14.

42. Unnamed student quoted in Kanowitz, *Poem Is a Four-Letter Word*, 139. Kanowitz quotes extensively from audio files of the hearing, but as I was unable to locate hearing transcripts, I rely on Kanowitz.

43. Special Advisory Committee Report, 1–2, 14, 25–27.

44. Heady also suspended English professor Roy Pickett from his directorship of freshman English. Heady rescinded Pickett's suspension along with Williams's, Pollack's, and Frank's. Davis, *Miracle on the Mesa*, 230.

45. Jon Bowman, "Longing for Lenore, Love Lust," *New Mexico Daily Lobo*, October 10, 1974, 4. The "Love-Lust" discussion did not decrease enrollment; enrollment grew by 1,252. See Davis, *Miracle on the Mesa*, 385. For a discussion of the Legislative University Investigating Committee, see Horn, *University in Turmoil*, 107–20.

46. "UNM 'Purification Day' Set," *New Mexico Lobo*, September 15, 1969, 1; Kanowitz, *Poem Is a Four-Letter Word*, 117; Michael Blake, "Ovation Greets Kandel," *New Mexico Lobo*, May 4, 1970, 1. Later in 1970 Kandel and her husband suffered injuries from a motorcycle accident. Kandel permanently injured her spine causing her chronic pain for the rest of her life. After her accident, she retreated from her writing career and never published again.

47. Sarah Laidlaw, "Gay Lib: Fighting the Stereotype," *New Mexico Daily Lobo*, October 7, 1970, 4; *Gay Liberation Newsletter*, February 1971, vertical file, "New Mexico"; Sandra McCraw, "Political Awareness Awakens in Gays," *New Mexico Daily Lobo*, July 6, 1972, 1; D'Emilio, *Making Trouble*, 130.

48. The New York Gay Liberation Front, founded in July 1969, led the way in establishing a militant coalition dedicated to a revolutionary struggle against the oppression of queer people. The Front inspired a wave of gay liberation organizations across the United States—many in places where gay political structures had never existed, such as Albuquerque. Terence Kissack, "Freaking Fag Revolutionaries: New York's Gay Liberation Front, 1969–1971," *Radical History Review*, no. 62 (March 1995): 105.

49. *Gay Liberation Newsletter*, February 1971, vertical file, "New Mexico." As an example, two gay liberation members made a presentation in a sociology class at Sandia High. See "Student Teachers React to Article on Gay Lib," *Albuquerque Tribune*, April 16, 1973, B-5.

50. GL-NM borrowed these tactics from another post-Stonewall organization,

the Gay Activist Alliance, which used street performance to garner media attention in San Francisco and bring gay issues to the forefront of public discussion. "Gay Liberation," *New Mexico Daily Lobo*, September 24, 1971, 8; Chuck Stewart, *Gay and Lesbian Issues: A Reference Handbook* (Santa Barbara: ABC-CLIO, 2003), 14.

51. "Minstrels Enact Guerrilla Theatre at Mall," *New Mexico Daily Lobo*, September 28, 1971, 3.

52. Carolyn Babb, "The Source," *New Mexico Daily Lobo*, October 4, 1971, 2; *Gay Liberation Newsletter*, August 1972, vertical file, "New Mexico"; Gay Liberation, "Sexism and War," handout, n.d., vertical file, "New Mexico"; "Gay Lib Asks Repeal of Sodomy Laws," *New Mexico Daily Lobo*, September 8, 1972.

53. Lisa Dawgert Waggoner, "New Mexico Joins the Twentieth Century: The Repeal of the Marital Rape Exemption," *New Mexico Law Review* 22 (Spring 1992): 551–69; Stein, *Rethinking the Gay and Lesbian Movement*, 81–91. The other eleven states included Illinois (1961), Connecticut (1969), Colorado (1971), Oregon (1971), Delaware (1972), Ohio (1972), Hawaii (1972), New Hampshire (1973), North Dakota (1973), California (1975), Maine (1975), and Washington (1975). Figures from Kane, "Timing Matters," 214.

54. To reconstruct this timeline, I relied on "Gay Calendar," *Seer's Catalogue*, August 8–22, 1975, 21; Evans, "All Is Not Dead Here," 15, 20; "Juniper and Other Gay Organizations"; and Kutz, *Grassroots New Mexico*, 112.

55. Ahlum and Howe, "Women's Studies and Social Change," 396–97; Alice E. Ginsberg, *The Evolution of American Women's Studies: Reflections on Triumphs, Controversies and Change* (New York: Palgrave Macmillan, 2008), 11.

56. Baker interview.

57. Baker interview.

58. Trisha Franzen, "Women Studies Evolves," *Sister Lode*, August/September 1984, 5. In the historiography of feminist studies thus far, gender has trumped sexuality in understanding the birth of women's studies programs, even though lesbians played a pivotal role in the formation and development of the discipline. Lesbians' lack of recognition in women's studies history is noted by feminist historian and former women's studies chair Marilyn Boxer in her well-documented book on the evolution of the field: Marilyn J. Boxer, *When Women Ask the Questions: Creating Women's Studies in America* (Baltimore, MD: Johns Hopkins University Press, 1998), 101.

59. Alesia Kunz, interview by Ann Nihlen 070913 tape 1, WMST Oral History Collection.

60. Erlinda Gonzales-Berry, "La Mujer Chicana," *Women's Studies Newsletter*, Winter 1974, 3, vertical file "Women's Center," University Archives, Center for Southwest Research, Zimmerman Library, University of New Mexico, Albuquerque.

61. I borrow the term *feminisms* from Benita Roth, *Separate Roads to Feminism: Black, Chicana, and White Feminist Movements in America's Second Wave* (Cambridge, MA:

Cambridge University Press, 2004), 3. The other three initial courses were Introduction to Women Studies, Women and the Law, and Women and Self Education. Beva Sanchez Padilla, interview by Ann Nihlen, 82213 tape 1, WMST Oral History Collection.

62. Gail Baker, "The Report of the Women Studies Program, July 1, 1973–June 30, 1974," in *Annual Report* (Albuquerque: University of New Mexico, 1973–74), 1537–44. I have found little research on Siren. It seems to have been a short-lived women's production organization headquartered at the Alternative Community Center on 106 Girard SE, Albuquerque. For the course offering Lesbian Feminism in America, see Gail Baker, "The Report of the Women Studies Program, July 1, 1974–June 30, 1975," in *Annual Report* (Albuquerque: University of New Mexico, 1974–75), 1600; "Innovative Courses to Be Offered This Fall," *New Mexico Lobo*, August 21, 1974, 35; and Pat Kailer, "Lesbians Find Shackles Breaking," *Albuquerque Journal*, February 17, 1977, 1.

63. Barbara J. Love, *Feminists Who Changed America, 1963–1975* (Urbana: University of Illinois Press, 2006), 500.

64. According to Ann Nihlen, prior to Lesbian Feminism in America twenty students was the high end of WMST course attendance. Thirty-six students enrolled in the class, and thirty-nine community members attended. Ann Nihlen, interview by author, May 21, 2014, transcript, box 1, folder 7, Hammer Collection.

65. Carol Ahlum and Florence Howe, *The New Guide to Current Female Studies* (Pittsburgh: Know, 1971). I suspect that some other courses also dealt with lesbian experiences. However, because the word *lesbian* was controversial, some programs used coded language. For example, at California State University–Sacramento, students approached teaching assistant and out lesbian Theresa Corrigan to teach a lesbian class in 1973. The course, Society of Women, had been taught once before, and the professor had used the benign title to mask the focus on lesbianism.

66. Gail Gottlieb, "Dean Wollman: American Studies 201 Was Never Approved," *New Mexico Daily Lobo*, September 19, 1974, 2, 4; John Rucker, "Wollman Versus Women Studies: Fight of the Century?," *New Mexico Daily Lobo*, October 1, 1974, 1; Stephen Beckerman, "Baker Is Evasive," *New Mexico Daily Lobo*, September 17, 1974, 4.

67. P. M. Duffy-Ingrassia, "Angered at Wollman," *New Mexico Daily Lobo*, September 16, 1974, 4; Kailer, "Lesbians Find Shackles Breaking," 1; "Lobo Offices Taken by Group," *New Mexico Daily Lobo*, September 23, 1974, 1, 5; "Opinions Wanted," *New Mexico Daily Lobo*, September 24, 1974, 1; Ann Doczi, "Lesbian Wants to Be Prom Queen," vertical file, "New Mexico"; "Gays Should Boycott Coors," *Seer's Catalogue*, September 1975, 5, 19; Dan Butler, "A Talk with P.M. Duffy Ingrassia," *Seer's Rio Grande Weekly*, March 1976, 12, 26.

68. John Bucker, "Ethnic Studies Directors React to Occupation," *New Mexico Daily Lobo*, September 24, 1974, 1.

69. "Las Chicanas," *New Mexico Daily Lobo*, April 27, 1974, repr. in *Joyous Struggle:*

The Women's Center Newsletter, June 1974, 1, box 32, Women Studies Collection, University Archives, University of New Mexico, Albuquerque (hereafter Women Studies Collection).

70. Lesbian baiting is discussed in Blackwell, *Chicana Power!*, 40.

71. Juanita Sanchez, "Thoughts on a Chicana Lesbian Forum," *Sister Lode*, June/July 1984, 2.

72. "Proposal for the University of New Mexico Ethnic and Women's Studies Coalition," 1981, box 32, Women Studies Collection.

73. Peter Adair, fundraising letter, June 1976, box 33, folder 10, Adair Papers; Peter Adair, speech presented to *Artlink*, October 2, 1993, in *Word Is Out* Press Kit (Milliarium Zero, 2010), https://wordisoutmovie.com/PressKit/WordIsOutPK.pdf; Lee Atwell, "Review of Word Is Out and Gay U.S.A.," *Film Quarterly* 32, no. 2 (1978): 57, https://doi.org/10.2307/1211942.

74. Youmans, *Word Is Out*, 33; Eric Brazil, "John Adair, Navajo Culture Anthropologist," *San Francisco Gate*, December 21, 1997, https://www.sfgate.com/bayarea/article/John-Adair-Navajo-culture-anthropologist-3084116.php; Eric Pace, "John Adair, 84, Anthropologist Who Studied Navajo Culture," *New York Times*, December 29, 1997, https://www.nytimes.com/1997/12/29/arts/john-adair-84-anthropologist-who-studied-navajo-culture.html.

75. Adair quoted in David W. Dunlap, "Peter Adair, 53, Director, Dies; Made Films with Gay Themes," *New York Times*, June 30, 1996, https://www.nytimes.com/1996/06/30/us/peter-adair-53-director-dies-made-films-with-gay-themes.html; Peter Adair to Robert Kotlowitz, December 17, 1975, box 33, folder 7, Adair Papers.

76. Adair received a fifty-thousand-dollar start-up grant from WNET, the New York City PBS affiliate. He also spearheaded a campaign to raise funds from the LGBTQ+ community. Nancy Adair and Casey Adair, *Word Is Out: Stories of Some of Our Lives* (San Francisco, CA: New Glide, 1978), 267.

77. Rob Epstein, "Word Is Out: Stories of Working Together," *Jump Cut: A Review of Contemporary Media* 24–25 (March 1981): 9–10, http://www.ejumpcut.org/archive/onlinessays/JC24-25folder/DoingWordIsOut.html.

78. Youmans, *Word Is Out*, 54–55.

79. Adair, speech presented to *Artlink*; radio spots script, n.d., box 33, folder 11, Adair Papers; Epstein, "Word Is Out."

80. "Primary Source Set: Briggs Initiative," GLBT Historical Society, accessed March 25, 2021, https://www.glbthistory.org/primary-source-set-briggs-initiative; Manuel Betancourt, "Cruising and Screening John: John Rechy's The Sexual Outlaw, Documentary Form, and Gay Politics," *GLQ* 23, no. 1 (January 1, 2017): 39, https://doi.org/10.1215/10642684-3672294; Youmans, *Word Is Out*, 23–24, 30, 85, 26; Peter Adair to Robert Kotlowitz, December 17, 1975, box 33, folder 7, Adair Papers.

81. Sadly, the bulk of the original letters are not in the Adair papers. I found a

smattering of letters in box 33, folder 5, and a form response letter in folder 4, box 33. Additionally, Adair discusses the fan mail and preserved six letters in folder 14, box 55. Letters were sent to an address that the filmmakers included at the end film.

82. Shirley R. Simeon to *The Word Is Out*, November 1980; Rex Wilkinson to *The Word Is Out*, n.d.; and Dana Bewer to *The Word Is Out*, November 15, 1980, all in box 33, folder 5, Adair Papers.

83. "Nadine Armijo," *Word Is Out*, DVD.

84. George Chauncey, *Why Marriage: The History Shaping Today's Debate over Gay Equality* (New York: Basic, 2009); Nathaniel Frank, *Awakening: How Gays and Lesbians Brought Marriage Equality to America* (Cambridge, MA: Belknap Press of Harvard University Press, 2017).

85. "Nadine Armijo," *Word Is Out*, DVD.

86. Nadine Armijo, pre-interview, 1991.1.34.23, VHS tape, box 58, Adair Papers.

87. Armijo and Montoya, film interview transcript.

88. "Nadine Armijo and Rosa Montoya," *Word Is Out*, DVD.

89. Armijo, pre-interview.

90. Gray, *Out in the Country*, 4, 168–9.

91. Cecilia and Marilyn, pre-interview, 1991.1.35.12y, VHS, box 59, Adair Papers.

92. Cecilia and Marilyn, pre-interview.

93. Cecilia and Marilyn, pre-interview.

94. Lourdes Torres, "Introduction," in Lourdes Torres and Inmaculada Perpetusa-Seva, *Tortilleras: Hispanic and U.S. Latina Lesbian Expression* (Philadelphia: Temple University Press, 2003), 5. The exception is Chicano filmmaker John Rechy. See Betancourt, "Cruising and Screening John," 31–49.

95. Gary J. Gates and Jason Ost, *The Gay & Lesbian Atlas* (Washington, DC: Urban Institute Press, 2004), 28, 52, 126–27.

CONCLUSION

Epigraph: Paula Gunn Allen, "Some Like Indians Endure," in Roscoe, *Living the Spirit*, 12.

1. Paula Gunn Allen, "Some Like Indians Endure," in Driskill et al., *Sovereign Erotics*, 21–24.

2. Scott Lauria Morgensen has interpreted Allen's poem as a decolonizing positionality of Native women and lesbians. Morgensen, *Spaces between Us*, 10.

3. M. Owlfeather, "Children of Grandmother Moon," in Roscoe, *Living the Spirit*, 104; Gay American Indians History Project, 1985, box 1, folder 1, Roscoe Papers; Will Roscoe, "Strange Country This: Images of Berdache Myths and Tales," in Roscoe, *Living the Spirit*, 61–3.

4. In the late 1990s, a growing number of curators and art historians developed

theories of queer feminism and gay male desire in relation to visual arts. See, for example, Helen Langa, "Seeing Queerly: Looking for Lesbian Presence and Absence in United States Visual Art, 1890 to 1950," *Journal of Lesbian Studies* 14, no. 2/3 (April 2010): 124–39, https://doi.org/10.1080/10894160903196509.

5. This trend continued in New Mexico. In 2001 an uproar ensued when Santa Fe's Museum of International Folk Art displayed Mexican-born queer Chicanx artist Alma López's provocative representation of the Virgin of Guadalupe. See Alicia Gaspar de Alba and Alma López, eds., *Our Lady of Controversy: Alma López's "Irreverent Apparition"*(Austin: University of Texas Press, 2011).

6. "Lucia Valeska," *Common Bond Ink*, May 1982. Copies of the Albuquerque-based gay newsletter are available at ONE National Gay and Lesbian Archives, University of Southern California; Rimmerman et al., *Politics of Gay Rights*, 62–65; Robert O. Self, *All in the Family: The Realignment of American Democracy since the 1960s* (New York: Hill and Wang, 2012), 239–40.

7. "NGTF Names Feminist—Lucia Valeska," *Lesbian Tide*, July–August 1979, 14; Ann Nihlen, interview by author, May 21, 2014, audio recording, box 1, folder 7, Hammer Collection; Atkins, *Gay Seattle*, 207.

8. Dudley Clendinen and Adam Nagourney, *Out for Good: The Struggle to Build a Gay Rights Movement in America* (New York: Simon and Schuster, 1999), 455–76; "Apuzzo New Director, NGTF Still Facing Flak," *Body Politics*, no. 89 (1982): 15–16.

9. Larry Bush, "Big Changes at NGTF: In with Apuzzo, Out with Valeska," *New York Native*, 1982, 17. To be fair, sometimes Valeska's focus on local groups, people of color, and women prevented a national gay agenda from moving forward. For example, Valeska refused to work in conjunction with the Gay Rights National Lobby on moderate California Republican representative Peter McCloskey's legislation that might have ended the military's ban on homosexuals. She feared that it would inflame the right, and I think her radical politics made her leery of working within mainstream institutions. Her stance jeopardized the reputation of NGTF within the national gay and lesbian population. However, I feel Valeska has received too much criticism in LGBT history. The reasons she was recruited to join the NGTF have been erased from the critiques of her performance as codirector.

10. Mark Thompson, "18 Years Ago," *The Advocate*, October 28, 1997, 10.

11. Common Bond, Statement of Purpose, August 1981, folder 18, Neil Isbin Papers AC 377, Fray Angélico Chávez History Library, Palace of the Governors, Santa Fe, New Mexico.

12. McBride, *Out of the Neon Closet*, 87–90, Loewy quote on 88.

13. For example, see Ray Jones, "Black Caucus Forms within Common Bond," *Common Bond Ink*, May 1987, 6.

14. UNM News Bureau, November 8, 1978, box 32, Women Studies Collection; Harmony Hammond, interview by Julia Bryan-Wilson, September 14, 2008, Galisteo,

New Mexico, transcript, Archives of American Art, Smithsonian Institution, Washington, DC, https://www.aaa.si.edu/collections/interviews/oral-history-interview -harmony-hammond-15635#transcript.

15. Hammond interview.

16. Harmony Hammond, *Lesbian Art in America: A Contemporary History* (New York: Rizzoli, 2000).

17. Hammond interview. In an interview with Jill Johnston, author of *The Lesbian Nation*, Martin stated: "I am not a woman." See Princenthal, *Agnes Martin*, 232; Martin told their neighbor Donald Woodman that they identified as "asexual." Woodman and Martin, *Agnes Martin and Me*, 41.

18. Hammond, *Lesbian Art in America*, 11, 40, 29, 45, 25.

19. Hammond, *Lesbian Art in America*, 49; Maya Valverde, "Caught between Two Worlds," *Sacramento Bee*, July 7, 1985. Tsinhnahjinnie is also a videographer. "For the 9 to 5 Side of Things," Hulleah J. Tsinhnahjinnie, accessed June 1, 2021, https:// www.hulleah.com/.

20. "Andrew Van Tsinhnahjinnie, Diné artist," Adobe Gallery Art of the Southwest Indian, accessed June 1, 2021, https://www.adobegallery.com/artist/Andrew_ Tsihnahjinnie_1916_200028922852; Hulleah Tsinhnahjinnie, résumé, circa 1987, box 3, folder 26, Roscoe Papers; Hulleah Tsinhnahjinnie quoted in Hammond, *Lesbian Art in America*, 64.

21. Hulleah J. Tsinhananhijinnie, November 17, 1992, box 3, folder 26, Roscoe Papers.

22. Anzaldúa, and Moraga, *This Bridge Called My Back*; Ramos, *Compañeras*; Kay Richter, "Words of Wisdom from Celebrated Author Carla Trujillo," *Out in SA*, January 14, 2016, https://outinsa.com/words-of-wisdom-from-celebrated-author-carla -trujillo/.

23. "4th Annual Lambda Literary Awards," *Lambda Literary*, July 13, 1992, https:// www.lambdaliterary.org/1992/07/lambda-literary-awards-1991/.

INDEX

Page numbers in *italics* refer to illustrations

Beckerley, J. G., 96
Beckerman, Stephen, 179
Bedell, Eleanor, 130
Beltrán, Lola, 122
Bennett, Fred, 109–10
Benson, AZ, 135, 161
Bewer, Dana, 184
bisexuals, 53, 55, 130, 146, 164, 196; discrimination and, 188; gay liberation and, 175; as terminology, 14. *See also* O'Keeffe, Georgia
Black, Hugo, 66–67
Blease, Coleman Livingston, 66
bohemian art colonies: cultural revivalists and, 27–30; European, 31; exploitation of Native and Latino peoples and, 34–35, 45–48; little magazines and, 54–55; as places of independence and belonging for women, 128; queer mobility and, 3, 8–11, 18–19, 38; significance of northern New Mexico, 12, 26, 30–35, 133, 135–36, 191. *See also* Albuquerque, NM; clothing; Lesbian Nation; New York City; Provincetown, MA; queer cultural production; San Francisco, CA; Santa Fe, NM; Taos, NM
Bond, Pat, 182
Boston, MA, 56, 116
Boucher, Mayo T., 113–14, 117
Boyer, Betty Kirk, 72
Brinig, Myron, 19, 37–38, 99
Briton, Earnest, 109–10
Brown, Andrew, 182, 183. *See also* Mariposa Film Group
Brown, Diane, 177
Brydon, Charles, 193
Burns, Randy, 8, 152, 191. *See also* Gay American Indians
Burnside, John, 153–54, 160, 182, 259n93. *See also* Circle of Loving Companions
Butler, Dan, 154, 156. *See also* Gay Co-Op
Bynner, Harold Witter "Hal," 43; Cutting

and, 51; *Eden Tree*, 40–41; Isherwood and, 129; Johnson and, 36, 39, 53, 56; *Laughing Horse* and, 57; Pasatiempo and, 45–46; The Rabble and, 38; Riggs and, 37, 72; role in establishing Santa Fe as a bohemian art colony, 19, 36–37, 40–42. *See also* Hunt, Robert; McCarthy, Clifford "Don"
Byrne, Edwin V., 114, 117

California: *Country Women* and, 140; *Laughing Horse* and, 56; lesbian artists and, 196–97; lesbian communes and, 134; mariachi music and, 122; Mattachine Society and, 116, 138; queer mobility and, 8, 36, 42, 79, 83, 90, 99–100, 102, 104, 118, 122–23, 140, 197; *Word Is Out* and, 182. *See also* Los Angeles, CA; San Francisco, CA; University of California, Berkeley
Cameron, Barbara, 8, 152. *See also* Gay American Indians
Campbell, Nancy, 44
Cargo, David, 168, 174
Catholicism, 10; De Vargas Pageant and, 46; Latinos and, 141; lesbian identity and, 2; opposition to decriminalizing sodomy laws, 108, 113–14, 117–18
censorship. *See* cultural censorship
Chabot, Maria, 27, 126–29, 132
Chanslor, Roy E., 49–50, 222n9. *See also* *Laughing Horse*
Chávez, Genoveva (Geneva), 108, 118–24, 119
Chavez, Vangie, 98
Cherokee Indians, 71, 101. *See also* Native Americans; Riggs, Rollie Lynn
Chicago, IL: Daughters of Bilitis and, 116; Klah and, 23; *Laughing Horse* and, 56; literary renaissance and, 64; *Little Review* and, 55; queer mobility and, 36, 84, 123; *Word Is Out* and, 183
Chicana lesbians: activism and, 147–49, 164, 177–78; bars and, 123, 134, 187;

Española, NM, 84, 147, 154, 155
ethnicity: cultural censorship and, 53–54; divisions within New Mexico and, 13, 46, 141, 163–64; ethnic studies, 180–81; methodology and, 4. *See also* African Americans; Asian Americans; Chicana lesbians; Chicanos/Chicanas; homophobia; intersectionality; Latina lesbians; Latinos/Latinas/Latinx; Native Americans
Executive Order 10450, 92–95, 238n95

Faerie Nation, 135–37, 149–53
Farmington, NM, 145, 213n37
Federal Bureau of Investigation (FBI), 89, 91–93, 235n54
feminism: Chicana feminism, 147, 163–64, 178, 180, 187–88, 198; consciousness-raising and, 161; cultural production and, 164; feminist anthropology, 34; feminist art movement, 195–97; feminist politics, 69, 163; as methodology, 8; Oquitadas Feminist Farm, 134, 140–42, 157; periodicals and, 133–34, 140, 144, 147–48, 198; racism and, 188; women's studies and, 176–81. *See also* lesbian feminism; O'Keeffe, Georgia; Parsons, Betty; Valeska, Lucia
Fermi, Enrico, 87
Fladden, Whitey, 182
Florida, 116, 138
Forster, Elizabeth W., 27, 129–30
Foster, Jeannette H., 113
Francis, Elías Lee, 1
Francis, Ethel Haines, 1
Francis, Paula Marie. *See* Allen, Paula Gunn
Frank, Joseph, 167, 173–74

Galana, Laurel, 144
Gay American Indians (GAI), 8, 152–53, 161, 191, 258n77

Gay Co-Op, 154, 176
Gay Liberation (GL-NM), 134, 175–76, 266n50
Gay Liberation Front, 99, 163, 175, 251n5
gay liberation movement: cultural activism and, 7–8, 12, 17, 100–101, 136, 148–49, 152–53, 161, 163–64, 181, 183, 188–89, 191–92, 195–99; expansion beyond urban queer meccas, 136; Hay and, 4, 135, 149–51, 153–54, 157–61, 185; origins of, 4–5, 160; political activism and, 99, 134, 163, 193–94, 270n9; queer cultural production and, 7, 11, 15–17, 192; queer mobility and, 8, 16, 136, 192–93; radical, 16, 135–36; sexual identities and, 164, 192; University of New Mexico and, 134, 175–76, 266n50. *See also* lesbian feminism; LGBTQ+ activism
gay men: Common Bond and, 194–95; employment discrimination and, 15, 77–78, 80–81, 84, 92–99; erotica and, 15, 51–52, 82, 88–90, 99, 235n54; long-term partnerships and, 38–39, 41–42, 43, 51, 56, 69, 73–75, 73, 75, 102, 129, 154, 155; misogyny and, 128, 135, 150, 159–60; Pueblo dances and, 33–35, 48; rurality and, 135–37, 149–53, 157; as terminology, 14; visibility of, 41–44, 81, 96–97, 163–64, 175–76, 189, 192. *See also* homosexuality, as terminology; sexual identities; sodomy
Gay People's Union, 176, 193
gender, 4–5, 13–14. *See also* intersectionality
gender identities: clothing and, 12, 41–42, 44–46, 69, 150, 161; creative expression and, 11, 70; gay men and, 103–4, 108–9, 161; genderfluid, 14; intersectionality and, 5, 13, 16, 19, 45, 144, 148, 163–64, 171–72, 195, 197; Native Americans and, 34, 102–3, 151–52, 190–91; open-secret strategy and, 16, 107–8, 123–24, 130–31; wide spectrum of, 4, 163, 182;

working-class African Americans and, 55. *See also* Allen, Paula Gunn; Chávez, Genoveva (Geneva); gender nonconformity; gender variance; Gorman, R. C.; Klah, Hastíín; Martin, Agnes; nonbinary people; queer mobility; Riggs, Rollie Lynn; transgender; two-spirit

gender nonconformity: as challenges to gender conformity, 7, 18, 188–89; dissolution of support for, among Native peoples, 2, 17, 20, 24, 34, 47, 71–72; nádleehí and, 14–15, 20, 22–24, 208n59, 211n20; widening of support for white artists and writers, 20, 27, 30, 48, 79. *See also* nonbinary people; transgender; two-spirit

gender variance: *berdache* and, 151; creative expression and, 5, 52, 76, 99–100, 106–7, 191–92; San Francisco and, 102, 104; second-class citizenship and, 118

Gidlow, Elsa, 182

Gilpin, Laura, 6, 27, 129–30

Gonzagowski, Gloria, 133

Gonzales-Berry, Erlinda, 178

Gorman, Carl N., 101

Gorman, R. C., 83, 99–104, 101, 103, 239n104, 240n19

Grahn, Judy, 160, 177

Gray, Russell, 98, 194

Greene, Carl "Carlo," 88

Gutiérrez, Pat, 154, 155

Gwynn, Bethroot, 138

Haggard, Jae, 138, 139

Hammer, Bennett, 121

Hammond, Harmony, 195–97. See also *Lesbian Art in America*

Harlem Renaissance, 52–53, 65

Hartley, Marsden, 19, 30–34, 31, 215n68, 216n83

Hathaway, A. H., 169

Hawley, Willis, 60. *See also* Smoot-Hawley Tariff Act

Hay, Calla, 42, 44

Hay, Harry, 156, 185; Circle of Loving Companions and, 153–54; Faerie Nation and, 135–37, 149–53; gay liberation politics and, 4, 153–54, 157–61, 259nn93–94; influence of lesbian feminism and, 135, 149–50, 157, 159–61; misappropriation of Native American traditions and, 135, 149–50, 158–59, 161; *Word Is Out* and, 182. *See also* Radical Faeries

Heady, Ferrel, 167–68, 171–73, 265n44

Heap, Jean, 55

Heflin, James Thomas, 66

Henderson, Alice Corbin, 34, 36, 38

heteronormativity: citizenship and, 10, 15, 79–80, 103–4; enforcement of, 96–98, 108–9; postwar era and, 121; resistance to, 81–82, 98–100, 116, 120–21, 137–38, 152, 162, 166, 188–89, 192–93, 196. *See also* homophobia; Kight, Morris

Hibbard, Margaret, 107

homophile movement, 78–79, 81–82, 102, 115–17. *See also* Hay, Harry; Mattachine Society

homophobia: Chicanos and Latinos and, 120–21, 163–64, 180 186, 188; Native Americans and, 2, 47, 213n37; pervasiveness of, 5, 10, 15, 79–80, 99, 104, 107–8; violence and, 154, 170, 213n37. *See also* heteronormativity

homosexuality, as terminology, 14, 232n17. *See also* sexual identities

Hull, John, 97

Hunt, Robert, 40–42, 43, 129

Illinois, 111–12. *See also* Chicago, IL

intersectionality, 5, 13, 16, 19, 45, 144, 148, 163–64, 171–72, 177, 188, 195, 197. *See also* Chicana lesbians; class; ethnicity; gender; gender identities: Latina lesbians; lesbian feminism; race

Isherwood, Christopher, 129

Jackson, Dolores, 146

Jackson, Pam, 182

Janon, Henry Somers, 59

Johnson, Walter Willard "Spud," 70, 73–74; anticensorship activism and, 54, 56–57, 59, 67–68; Bynner and, 36; fetishization of Pueblo dancers, 34; Harlem and, 53; *Horizontal Yellow*, 39–40; *Laughing Horse* and, 49–52, 56–57, 64–65, 115; O'Keeffe and, 128; queer mobility and, 19; The Rabble and, 38; Smoot-Hawley Tariff Act and, 60, 63, 65; Villagrá Book Shop and, 69

Johnston, Jill, 137

Johnston, Mercer G., 60–61

Juniper, 134, 157, 176

Kandel, Lenore, 162, 164–66, 169, 174, 263n16. *See also* "Love-Lust" controversy

Kight, Morris, 77–79, 82–83, 98–99. *See also* Gay Liberation Front

Kilhefner, Don, 160

Kinsey, Alfred, 108, 110–13

Klah, Hastíín, 25; as artist, 20, 22–24, 26–28; collaboration with Wheelwright, 28–30; early history of, 21–22; historical significance of, 47, 191; as nádleehí, 15, 20, 22–24, 47

Koltz, Clifton, 102, 104

Kunz, Alesia, 177

La Fonda (The Inn), 19, 42, 44, 87

Lambdas de Santa Fe, 154

Las Chicanas, 178, 180–81, 187

Las Cruces, NM, 145, 194

Latina lesbians: bar culture and, 123; cultural activism and, 148–49, 183; exclusion of, 142; feminism and, 11, 16, 163

Latinos/Latinas/Latinx: Catholicism and, 141; collegiate education and, 163–64; Cubero and, 2; exploitation of, 48; Hay's outreach to, 153, 157; homophobia and, 121, 163–64; queer cultural production and, 10–11, 17, 56, 120, 164, 198; queer mobility and, 136; Rowe, NM, and, 145; sexual identities and, 157, 188; as terminology, 13, 207n56; *Word Is Out* and, 3, 181–82, 187–88, 203n20. *See also* Chávez, Genoveva (Geneva); Latina lesbians

Laughing Horse, 49–51, 54–57, 63–65, 68, 72, 115

Lavender Scare, 80, 96

Law, Lisa, 140–41

Lawrence, D. H., 37, 50–51, 56, 172; *Lady Chatterley's Lover*, 57, 59–60, 62, 65–66, 226n53

Lee, Pelican, 141, 143

legal concerns: American Law Institute (ALI), 108, 110–12, 117; free speech and, 54, 67–68; Higher Education Act of 1965, 163–64, 187; House Bill 300, 167, 173–74; Model Penal Code (MPC), 108, 110–12; sodomy and, 108–10, 112–18, 169. *See also* Cutting, Bronson; sexual privacy; Smoot-Hawley Tariff Act; sodomy

Lesbian Art in America, 28, 195–96

lesbian feminism: Chicanas and, 164, 178, 180–81, 187–88; gay liberation politics and, 154, 171–72, 175–81, 193–94; influence on Radical Faeries, 135, 149–50, 157, 159–61; Latinas and, 163–64; Pueblo dances and, 34–35; queer cultural production and, 2, 16, 84, 123, 133–35, 137, 144–49, 164, 195–98, 206n41; Radicalesbians, 137; separatism and, 134–44, 157, 159–60; women's studies and, 176–81. *See also* Chicana lesbians; Davenport, Katherine; Grahn, Judy; Latina lesbians; Lesbian Nation

Lesbian Nation: Arf, 133–34, 138, 142–43, 157, 254n32; influence on Radical Faeries, 135, 149–50, 157, 159–61; Oquitadas Feminist Farm, 134, 140–42,

157; queer cultural production and, 144–49; racial diversity and, 135, 188; separatism and, 134–44, 157, 159–60

lesbians: challenges to patriarchy, 134, 137, 144, 176; classroom education and, 163, 176–81; conflicts over overt sexual expression and, 2, 123, 141–42, 186; employment discrimination and, 15, 80–81, 84, 86, 92–99; long-term partnerships and, 2–3, 121, 123–28, 184–88; open-secret strategy and, 107, 118, 123–24, 126, 130–32; rurality and, 134, 136–44, 157; as terminology, 14; visibility of, 41–44, 81, 96–97, 147, 149, 163–64, 175–77, 188–89, 191–92. *See also* Chicana lesbians; homosexuality, as terminology; Latina lesbians; lesbian feminism; sexual identities

Levine, David, 172

LGBTQ+ activism (post-1980), 98, 145, 148–49, 184, 188–89, 194–98. *See also* gay liberation movement

Lippincott, Janet, 107

little magazines: as challenges to censorship, 50, 53–56; *The Lark*, 49; *Little Review*, 55, 68, 131; *Morada*, 68. See also *Laughing Horse*; periodicals

Loewy, Michael, 194

Lopez, Alejandro, 154

Los Alamos, NM: lesbian subculture and, 85–86; Manhattan Project and, 15, 79, 82–84, 87, 90; post–World War II surveillance and, 90–97; queer resistance and, 81. *See also* Schwob, Claude R.; Stockly, Ed; Wells, Cady

Los Angeles, CA: Daughters of Bilitis and, 116; leftist milieu of, 14; Mattachine Society and, 81; queer mobility and, 79, 83, 99, 118, 122–23; as queer urban mecca, 9; Woman's Building and, 196

Love, Marion, 115

"Love-Lust" controversy: general public's and politicians' responses to, 166–70; origins of, 164–67, 166; outcome of, 172–74; race and, 163–64, 170–71; sexual politics and, 162–63; student activism and, 162, 171–74

Lujan, Joe, 35

Macleod, Norman, 68

Maestra, Bobb, 157

Manhattan Project, 79, 83–88, 90, 231n13. *See also* Atomic Energy Commission; security state

Mariposa Film Group, 3, 181–83, *183*, 186–87

Martin, Agnes, 125; *Nude* (1947), 106; O'Keeffe and, 128–29; open-secret strategy and, 124, 126, 130–32; Parsons and, 130; queer mobility and, 105–7, 129, 131; Kristina Wilson and, 127, 132

Mathews, Tede, 18

Mattachine Society (previously Mattachine Foundation), 81, 113, 116–17, 149–50

Matthews, Washington, 28

Maxine, Mary, 177

Mayne, Philip, 169–70

McCarthy, Clifford "Don," 40, 42, 69, 130

McKibbin, Dorothy Scarritt, 87

Medina, Ada, 197

Mellon, Andrew W., 59, 62, 65

Mendenhall, George, 182

Mendoza, Lydia, 122

Mesilla, NM, 145

methodology, 4–5, 8–10

Mikels, Elaine, 140–42, 253n26

Millington, Rusty, 182

Minnesota, 111, 138, 253n26

Monroe, Harriet, 65

Montoya, Rosa, 2–4, 8, 182, 184, 186–87

Morgenthau, Hans, 95

Museum of Navajo Religion. *See* Wheelwright Museum of the American Indian music: changing sexual standards in 1920s and, 36; Harlem and, 53; musicals, 37; Nuevomexicanos and, 120; postwar sexual permissiveness and, 55; queer mobility and, 1, 18. *See also* Chávez, Genoveva (Geneva)

Myer, Chalmer R., 168

nádleehí, 14–15, 20, 22–24, 208n59, 211n20. *See also* Klah, Hastíín; two-spirit

National Gay Task Force (NGTF), 193–94, 270n9

Native Americans: activism and, 8, 100–101, 152–53, 161, 164, 191; ceremonial knowledge and, 26; declining cultural support for sexual variance, 2, 19–20, 24, 28–29, 35, 71, 74, 103, 190–91; gender identities and, 34, 102–3, 151–52, 190–91; misappropriation of traditions of, 135, 149–50, 158–59, 161; nádleehí and, 14–15, 20, 22–24; Native American studies, 180; objectification of, 33–35, 48; queer cultural production and, 71, 74, 76, 151, 190–91, 197; queer mobility and, 2, 7–8, 47, 99–100, 102, 104, 135–36, 152–53, 158–59; Santa Fe Fiesta and, 46–47; sexual politics and, 158–61, 197–98; sexual variance and, 14–15, 20, 22–24, 151–52; as terminology, 13. *See also* Allen, Paula Gunn; Cherokee Indians; Navajo/Diné Indians; Pueblo Indians; Tewa Pueblos; two-spirit; Zuni Pueblos

Navajo/Diné Indians: Cubero and, 2; declining cultural support for sexual variance, 17, 20, 24, 103; flexible sex/gender system and, 14, 22–23, 102; forced removal and internment of, 20–21; Manhattan Project and, 84; preservation of language and culture of, 28–30; queer mobility and, 7, 47,

99–100, 102, 152–53; textile arts and, 10–11, 23–24, 26–27. *See also* Gorman, R. C.; Klah, Hastíín; Native Americans; Tsinhnahjinnie, Hulleah J.

Naya, Ramón, 72–74, 73, 75, 229n107

Nevada, 5, 7, 116, 194

Newcomb, Arthur, 23, 27

Newcomb, Frances "Franc" Johnson, 23, 27–29, 30, 210n15, 211n22

New York (state), 111, 114

New York City: arts community and networks, 30, 56, 63, 102, 129–30, 195–96; *The Cherokee Night* and, 74; Daughters of Bilitis and, 116; gay drag balls and, 46, 70; Greenwich Village, 32, 70, 72, 131; Harlem, 46, 53, 55, 70, 223n27; Mattachine Society and, 116; obscenity laws, 60; queer mobility and, 32, 53, 64, 72, 83, 99, 129–31, 138, 174, 204n30; as queer urban mecca, 9; Salsa Soul Sisters and, 146

Nihlen, Ann, 178, 181

nonbinary people, 13–15, 17, 20, 26–27, 195–96, 257n70

Nuevomexicanos/Nuevomexicanas/Nuevomexicanx: assimilation and, 48; cultural censorship and, 53–54; culture of privacy and, 44, 120, 142, 157, 161; *Laughing Horse* and, 56; Manhattan Project and, 84–85; narrowing of attitudes toward nonbinary gender and homoeroticism, 17, 20, 121; open-secret strategy and, 118; queer cultural production and, 120–22, 147–48, 188, 198; Santa Fe Fiesta and, 46–47, 220n134; as terminology, 13

Nugent, Richard Bruce, 52–53

Ohkay Owingeh Pueblo. *See* Tewa Pueblos

Ojo Caliente, NM, 145

O'Keeffe, Georgia, 27, 107, 124, 126–29, 132, 197

queer cultural production (*continued*)
190–91, 197; New Mexico as key site
of, 7, 9, 11–12, 129; Nuevomexicanos/
Nuevomexicanas/Nuevomexicanx and,
120–22, 147–48, 188, 198; as obscene,
50–52, 54, 57, 59–63, 66–69, 89, 165–
70; paintings and, 19, 105–7, 129–30;
periodicals, 5, 16, 134–35, 140, 144–49;
plays and, 71, 74, 76; poetry and, 7, 19,
33–34, 36–40, 141, 148; queer resistance
and, 7, 20, 47, 76, 82, 116, 191, 196, 198;
resurgence of, 11, 192, 195–99; security
state and, 10, 15–16, 78, 107–9, 118, 131,
192; settler colonialism and, 46–48; as
terminology, 11–12; textile arts and,
20, 22–24, 26–29. *See also* Allen, Paula
Gunn; bohemian art colonies; Brinig,
Myron; Bynner, Harold Witter "Hal";
Chabot, Maria; cultural censorship;
Dodge, Mabel; Gilpin, Laura; Gorman,
R. C.; Grahn, Judy; Hartley, Marsden;
Hay, Harry; Henderson, Alice Corbin;
Isherwood, Christopher; Johnson, Walter Willard "Spud"; Latinos/Latinas/
Latinx; "Love-Lust" controversy; Martin, Agnes; O'Keeffe, Georgia; queer
mobility; Rabble, The; Riggs, Rollie
Lynn; Schwob, Claude R.; Sims, Agnes
"Agi"; Siren; Wells, Cady; Winnek,
Marian; *Word Is Out*
queer mobility: belonging and, 7, 30, 32,
47–48, 71, 72, 82, 100, 128, 135, 188,
190–91, 215n68; bohemian art colonies
and, 3, 8–11, 18–19, 38; California and,
8, 36, 42, 79, 83, 90, 99–100, 102, 104,
118, 122–23, 140, 197; Chicago and,
36, 84, 123; Chicana lesbians and, 3–4,
8–9; communes and, 9, 16, 134–44,
149–53; gay liberation movement and,
8, 16, 136, 192–93; Latinos/Latinas/
Latinx and, 16, 136; lesbian feminists
and, 134–44, 157, 159–60; as method-

ology, 8–9, 12; music and, 1, 18; Native
Americans and, 2, 7–8, 99–100, 102,
104, 135–36, 152–53, 158–59; New York
City and, 32, 53, 64, 72, 83, 99, 129–31,
138, 174, 204n30; queer resistance and,
7, 137, 153, 192; rural to urban, 2, 9,
99–100, 135, 158–59; sexual identities
and, 11, 104, 152–53; as terminology, 9;
urban to rural, 9, 16, 104, 133, 135, 138,
140, 143–44, 152–53, 160, 191; urban
to urban, 7, 9. *See also* Allen, Paula
Gunn; Gorman, R. C.; Johnson, Walter
Willard "Spud"; Martin, Agnes; Riggs,
Rollie Lynn; Sims, Agnes "Agi"
queer people of color, 52–53, 135, 146,
153, 163, 188, 195. *See also* African
Americans; Asian Americans;
Chicanos/Chicanas; Latinos/Latinas/
Latinx; Native Americans; race
queer resistance: Los Alamos and, 81;
queer cultural production and, 7, 20, 47,
76, 82, 116, 191, 196, 198; queer mobility
and, 7, 137, 153, 192; "rural turn" and,
5. *See also* gay liberation movement;
LGBTQ+ activism

Rabble, The, 19, 36, 38, 39
race: identity and, 2, 13, 53–54, 71, 74, 76,
146; lesbian bars and, 123; lesbian communes and, 143; as methodology, 4–5;
New Mexico's racial system, 13, 128,
141, 163, 187; San Francisco art scene
and, 100; *Word Is Out* and, 182, 186,
187. *See also* African Americans; Chica-
nos/Chicanas; intersectionality; Lati-
nos/Latinas/Latinx; Native Americans;
queer people of color; racism; whites
racism: academia and, 164; cross-racial
dressing and, 45–46; "Love-Lust" controversy and, 163, 170–71; misappropriation of Native traditions and, 135,
149–50, 158–49, 161; Pueblo dances

Sego, William A., 167

Selver, Veronica, 182, *183*, 184, 186. *See also* Mariposa Film Group

settler colonialism: Cherokee society and, 71; cross-racial dressing and, 45–46; disintegration of Indigenous cultural networks and, 2, 19, 24, 28, 191; Pueblo society and, 35; queer white artists and, 16–17, 48, 135; resistance to, 24–25, 135, 190–91

sexology: accessibility and, 52, 62, 66, 112; gender and sexual variation and, 55, 112, 222n18, 224n38; Hartley and, 30; Johnson and, 69, 70. *See also* Kinsey, Alfred

sexual identities: Catholicism and, 2; Chicanas and, 2, 180, 186 198; concealment of, 5, 15, 44, 84, 86, 99, 104, 114, 118, 121; gay liberation movement and, 164, 192; Latinos/Latinas/Latinx and, 157, 188; as perceived security risk, 95–97; political identity and, 137, 144; queer mobility and, 11, 104, 152–53; terminology and, 232n17. *See also* Chávez, Genoveva (Geneva); gay men; Gorman, R. C.; homosexuality, as terminology; Klah, Hastíín; lesbians; Maestra, Bobb; Martin, Agnes; queer, as terminology; Tsinhnahjinnie, Hulleah J.; two-spirit; Valverde, Malflora

sexuality: as methodology, 4–5, 12; terminology and, 14. *See also* asexuals; bisexuals; gay men; intersectionality; lesbians

sexual nonconformity: bohemian art colonies and, 11, 17, 48; Chávez and, 124; Martin and, 105, 107, 124, 196; Native Americans and, 2, 76, 151–52; 191; queer cultural production and, 5; San Francisco Renaissance and, 80; security state and, 80–81; silencing of, 16–17, 34, 118, 161. *See also* gender

nonconformity; Schwob, Claude R.; sexual identities; sexuality

sexual politics: creative expression and, 12, 16, 164–74, 192; feminist publications as form of, 5, 16, 134–35, 140, 144–49; homophile movement, 78–79, 81–82, 102, 115–17; identity politics, 7, 9, 14, 192; little magazines and, 54–56; queer mobility and, 3, 135; resistance to heteronormativity, 81–82, 98–100, 116, 120–21, 137–38, 152, 162, *166*, 188–89, 192–93, 196; security state and, 10, 90–98, 118. *See also* cultural censorship; gay liberation movement; heteronormativity; legal concerns; lesbian feminism; LGBTQ+ activism; sodomy; students

sexual privacy: cultural censorship and, 67, 169; definition of, 61; origins of, 15, 52, 226–27n61; vs. sexual secrecy, 79–80; sodomy and, 108, 112–13

sexual revolution, 222n17; of 1910s–1930s, 4, 15, 52; of 1960s–1970s, 175

sexual secrecy: definition of, 80; implications for queer community and activism, 109, 114, 116, 131; Nuevomexicano society and, 44, 120, 142, 157, 161; security state and, 77–79, 84, 85–87, 90–91, 97–98, 104, 118; vs. sexual privacy, 79–80. *See also* opensecret strategy

sexual subjectivities, 3, 5, 19, 149

"sex variant," 113

Siegel, Thyme, 138, 143, 253n24

Siegle, Linda, 123

Simeon, Shirley R., 183

Simmons, Barbara Brown, 171

Simms, John F., 169

Sims, Agnes "Agi," 6; clothing and, 45; queer cultural production and, 11; queer mobility and, 1, 3–4, 7–8, 19, 127; White and, 129

Siren, 178, 267n62

Valeska, Lucia, 177, 193–94, 270n9
Valverde, Malflora, 145–46, 255n47
Van Rensselaer, James T., 49
Van Vechten, Carl, 53, 223n25
Vigil, Bernadette, 197
Vigil, Martin, 35
Villagrá Book Shop, 19, 42, 69
violence, 154, 170, 213n37. *See also* settler colonialism
von Freyburg, Karl, 31–32

Walker, Mitch, 160–61, 260n106
Washington, DC, 96, 116, 178, 182
Watts, Joan, 197
Wechsler, Herbert, 111
Well of Loneliness, The, 61–62, 68, 70
Wells, Cady, 19, 37, 99
Wheelwright, Mary Cabot: collaboration with Klah, 23, 27–30; Los Luceros and, 27, 126–27, 129; open-secret era and, 132
Wheelwright Museum of the American Indian, 27–30
White, Mary Louise, 129
whites: bohemian art colonies and, 30–33, 36–38, 41–47; as cultural norm and, 71, 86, 94, 162, 193–95; as early art colonists, 18–19, 37–38, 44; influence of LGBT literature and, 52, 70; lesbian feminism and, 134–35, 146, 178, 181, 188; sexualization of nonwhite

bodies, 33–35, 48, 53; as terminology, 13. *See also* Austin, Mary; Beckerley, J. G.; Bynner, Harold Witter "Hal"; Chabot, Maria; Dodge, Mabel; Grahn, Judy; Hammond, Harmony; Hartley, Marsden; Hay, Harry; Henderson, Alice Corbin; Johnson, Walter Willard "Spud"; Martin, Agnes; racism; settler colonialism; Sims, Agnes "Agi"; Wells, Cady; Wheelwright, Mary Cabot
Wilkinson, Rex, 183–84
Williams, Lionel, 162–63, 165–68, 166, 170–74
Wilson, Jane, 86–87
Wilson, Kristina, 127, 132
Winnek, Marian, 19, 37, 44
Winter, Kate, 178
Wisconsin, 111–12, 138
Wollman, Nathaniel, 179–80
Women's Army Corps (WAC), 86, 94, 107
Woodul, Jennifer, 178
Word Is Out, 3, 164, 181–89. *See also* Adair, Peter
World War I, 32, 54, 61, 222n17
Wyoming, 194

Yale Street Grasshopper Bookstore, 169
Youtzy, Mark, 176

Zuni Mountain Sanctuary, 135, 252n11
Zuni Pueblos, 14, 151, 181